Motivating Students to Learn

Motivating Students to Learn

Jere Brophy
Michigan State University

Boston, Massachusetts   Burr Ridge, Illinois   Dubuque Iowa
Madison, Wisconsin   New York, New York   San Francisco, California   St. Louis, Missouri

McGraw-Hill

A Division of The **McGraw·Hill** *Companies*

MOTIVATING STUDENTS TO LEARN

2 3 4 5 6 7 8 9 0 QF/QF 9 0 9 8

ISBN 0-07-008198-0

Editorial director: *Jane Vaicunas*
Sponsoring editor: *Beth Kaufman*
Developmental editor: *Selena Luftig*
Marketing manager: *Dan Loch*
Senior project manager: *Gladys True*
Production supervisor: *Heather D. Burbridge*
Senior designer: *Crispin Prebys*
Compositor: *Shepherd, Inc.*
Typeface: *10/12 Palatino*
Printer: *Quebecor Printing Book Group/Fairfield*

Library of Congress Cataloging-in-Publication Data

Brophy, Jere E.
    Motivating students to learn / Jere Brophy.
      p.   cm.
    Includes bibliographical references and index.
    ISBN 0-07-008198-0 (alk. paper)
    1. Motivation in education.   I. Title.
LB1065.B776   1998
370.15'4—dc21   97–1283

http://www.mhcollege.com

For Christian Thomas Speier

About the Author

JERE BROPHY is University Distinguished Professor of Teacher Education and formerly co-director of the Institute for Research on Teaching at Michigan State University, East Lansing. He earned a Ph.D. in Human Development and Clinical Psychology from the University of Chicago and since has become known for his research on the interpersonal dynamics of teacher-student relationships, teacher expectation effects, classroom management, student motivation, and other topics in educational psychology and research on teaching. He is the author of *Teaching Problem Students* (1996) and co-author with Thomas L. Good of *Contemporary Educational Psychology* (5th edition, 1995), and *Looking in Classrooms* (7th edition, 1997), as well as author or co-author of numerous articles on student motivation and related topics.

Brief Contents

Contents

4   Rebuilding Discouraged Students' Confidence and Willingness to Learn

7   Stimulating Students' Motivation to Learn   162

Preface

This book offers teachers principles and strategies to use in motivating their students to learn. It is written explicitly for teachers: addressing them directly, focusing on concepts and principles that are the most feasible for use in the classroom, and presenting these with a minimum of jargon and an emphasis on applications. It is not a "bag of tricks" developed from my own personal philosophy or culled randomly from everywhere. Instead, it is the product of a systematic review of the motivational literature followed by synthesizing efforts that involved: (1) identifying those portions of this vast literature that are most relevant to teachers, (2) summarizing this relevant material using a basic vocabulary to counteract the proliferation of multiple terms for the same basic concept, and (3) organizing the material within a few categories that are rooted in motivational theory and research but also supportive of teachers' efforts to incorporate motivational principles into their instructional planning.

My treatment of relatively obvious principles (e.g., warm, caring teachers are more likely to be successful motivators than indifferent or rejecting teachers) emphasizes their fundamental importance but does not go on to include unnecessarily detailed explanation or documentation. More detail is provided for less obvious and familiar principles, although even here I have focused on what teachers need to know rather than providing broad coverage of the history and development of related theory and research. Similar concepts are treated together with emphasis on their common implications, avoiding "distinctions without difference."

Much of the scholarly literature on motivation is not relevant to teachers because it deals with animals rather than humans. Furthermore, much of the human motivation literature is only tangentially relevant to teachers because it focuses on individual differences in motivational systems as predictors of differences in behavior (e.g., students who value success and do not fear failure are more likely to prefer challenging tasks than students with the opposite motivational pattern).

Concepts such as success seeking or failure avoidance can help teachers to understand their students' current motivational orientations and related behavior. However, teachers mostly need to learn strategies for socializing their students' motivational orientations toward optimal patterns (in this example, strategies for helping students to reduce their fear of failure and become more persistent in their efforts to achieve success). Consequently, although the book explains concepts needed to understand students' motivational orientations, it focuses on teachers' strategies for optimizing those orientations.

Furthermore, it does so with an eye toward the realities of classroom teaching. First, it recognizes that schools are not day camps or recreational centers; they feature an instructional agenda that teachers and students are expected to accomplish. Consequently, teachers' motivational strategies need to focus on motivating their students to learn—to achieve the intended curricular outcomes—not merely to enjoy their time in school. Learning should be experienced as meaningful and worthwhile, but it requires sustained goal-oriented efforts to construct understandings.

Second, the classroom setting complicates the motivational challenges facing teachers. Instruction can be individualized only to an extent, so some students may often be bored and others may often be confused or frustrated. Also, students' concentration on learning may be impaired by worries about getting bad grades or embarrassing themselves in front of their classmates.

These and other constraints on teachers' options underscore the need for an emphasis on motivational goals and strategies that are realistic and feasible for use in the classroom. Consequently, although I draw on the intrinsic motivation literature to describe the ideal forms of motivation that may be observed when people are engaged in activities of their own choosing without any felt pressure to respond to external constraints, I emphasize that such conditions of self-determination can only be achieved partially and occasionally in classrooms. Thus, the motivational challenge facing teachers is to find ways to encourage their students to accept the goals of classroom activities and seek to develop the intended knowledge and skills that these activities were designed to develop, regardless of whether or not the students enjoy the activities or would choose to engage in them if other alternatives were available. This is what I mean by motivating students to learn, and much of the book is devoted to presentation of strategies for doing so.

The book also presents strategies for capitalizing on students' existing intrinsic motivation and for reinforcing their learning efforts using rewards and other extrinsic incentives. In the process, I review and critique the often-contentious literature on these topics and develop principles for using intrinsic and extrinsic motivational strategies compatibly. An eclectic approach to motivation that incorporates both sets of strategies (as well as strategies for motivating students to learn) is likely to be much more powerful than a more limited approach.

Finally, the book offers guidelines for adapting motivational principles to group and individual differences in students and for doing "repair work" with students who have become discouraged or disaffected learners. These adaptation and problem-solving suggestions are embedded within the overall approach developed throughout the book. They are extensions of it, compatible with its basic principles.

To reduce the verbiage and passive-voice sentence constructions that accompany third-person language, I have written much of the book in second-person language addressed directly to the reader, who is construed as a teacher. Readers who currently work as inservice teachers or student teachers can respond to this directly; preservice teacher education majors or other readers who are not currently teaching can respond by projecting themselves into the teacher role.

I have eliminated most gender-specific language by pluralizing. Where this was not feasible (most notably in many of the examples involving individual students), I have standardized the format by routinely referring to the teacher as female and the student as male. Finally, in sections on gender differences, I have referred to teachers as male or female and to students as boys or girls.

Acknowledgments

This book was completed in part while I was on sabbatical leave from Michigan State University and in residence as a Fellow at the Center for Advanced Study in the Behavioral Sciences. I wish to thank both of these institutions for their financial support during that sabbatical year. In addition I wish to thank the Spencer Foundation, which provided part of the funds for the support I received through the Center for Advanced Study in the Behavioral Sciences (Spencer Foundation Grant No. B-1074).

I thank Lane Akers for helping me to develop my ideas into book form, as well as Phyllis Blumenfeld, Lyn Corno, and Allan Wigfield, who provided detailed feedback on an earlier draft.

I thank the many colleagues and students who contributed to my thinking through discussions about motivation over the years, particularly Carole Ames, Tom Good, Neelam Kher, Okhee Lee, Mary McCaslin, and Eva Sivan.

Finally, I wish to thank June Benson, who has been providing me with outstanding manuscript preparation assistance for 18 years now, and who did so once again in working on this book.

CHAPTER 1

Student Motivation: The Teacher's Perspective

Learning is fun and exciting, at least when the curriculum is well matched to students' interests and abilities and the teacher emphasizes hands-on activities. When you teach the right things the right way, motivation takes care of itself. If students aren't enjoying learning, something is wrong with your curriculum and instruction—you have somehow turned an inherently enjoyable activity into drudgery.

School is inherently boring and frustrating. We require students to come, then try to teach them stuff that they don't see a need for and don't find meaningful. There is little support for academic achievement in the peer culture, and frequently in the home as well. A few students may be enthusiastic about learning, but most of them require the grading system and the carrots and sticks that we connect to it to pressure them to do at least enough to get by.

These italicized paragraphs express the core ideas behind much of the advice traditionally offered to teachers about motivating students. The two views are contradictory, even though both are frequently expressed. Neither is valid, but each contains elements of truth.

The first view incorporates overly romantic views of human nature and unrealistic expectations about students' learning of school subjects in classroom settings. We can and should expect students to experience academic activities as meaningful and worthwhile. However, we cannot expect them to view these activities as "fun" in the same sense that they experience recreational games and pastimes as fun. Even when they find the content interesting and the activity enjoyable, learning requires sustained concentration and effort.

The second view incorporates overly cynical or hedonistic views of human nature and negative expectations about teachers' potential for enticing their students to engage in classroom activities with motivation to learn. Besides seeking to maximize pleasure and minimize pain, children learn to experience satisfaction in setting and working toward goals, acquiring new knowledge, developing their skills, satisfying their curiosity—in a word, learning. Teachers can shape students' behavior by manipulating reinforcement contingencies, but they also can help students to appreciate their learning opportunities and to find academic activities meaningful and worthwhile for reasons that include intrinsic motivation and self-actualization.

If the two extreme views are not valid, what might be a more balanced and fruitful way to think about student motivation? I will develop my answer to this question in this book, based on the notion of socializing students' motivation to learn. Before you begin to read my views, however, you might wish to take stock of your own. Think about the following questions and write down your answers to them.

1. What activities do you engage in frequently because you enjoy them? Why? (What makes these activities so enjoyable? What do you get out of them?)

2. What activities do you engage in frequently even though you don't enjoy them (because they are responsibilities that you can't evade or because you view them as necessary steps toward some important goal)? How do you motivate yourself to engage in these unenjoyed activities and to do them well or at least well enough?

3. Most people prefer certain kinds of books, movies, sports, and hobbies over others. For example, they may prefer realistic fiction over fantasy, comedy over drama, golf over tennis, or collecting historical memorabilia over collecting stamps. What might account for these contrasting preferences? Why do you prefer certain types of books, movies, sports, or hobbies over others, especially others that appear similar but don't quite "do it" for you?

4. As a student, which subjects or learning activities have you found most enjoyable or rewarding? Which are boring or merely OK rather than stimulating or worthwhile? Are some anxiety-provoking, irritating, or in some other way aversive for you, so that you try to avoid them? What is it about these school subjects or activities that explains your contrasting motivational responses?

5. What self-motivational and coping strategies do you call on to help you do what you need to do when you find a school activity boring or aversive?

6. In what ways have your teachers and professors affected your motivation positively or negatively (not just your liking for the subject matter and learning activities featured in their classes, but also your motivation to learn with understanding and to do your best work on assignments)?

7. How have your answers to these questions evolved as you progressed from childhood through adolescence into adulthood?

8. What do your answers suggest about strategies to emphasize or avoid in your attempts to motivate students to learn (given the ages of your students)?

Save your responses to these questions. As you read through the book, revisit them to compare your own experience-based ideas about motivation with the ideas I have drawn from the scholarly literature on the subject. If you note any contradictions, try to identify the reasons for them and any implications they may have for your practice as a teacher.

The remainder of Chapter 1 provides a general introduction to motivation and to the perspective I have taken on the topic. First, the chapter offers definitions of some basic concepts and a brief summary of ways in which theorizing about motivation has evolved over the past century, culminating in notions of intrinsic motivation or flow as the ideal state. Next, it argues that it is unrealistic to expect to routinely produce this ideal motivational state in the classroom and proposes the goal of producing motivation to learn as a more feasible alternative. A preview of what is involved in stimulating and socializing students' motivation to learn follows. Finally, the chapter concludes with an overview of the rest of the book.

EVOLVING VIEWS OF MOTIVATION

Motivation is a theoretical construct used to explain the initiation, direction, intensity, and persistence of behavior, especially goal-directed behavior. In the classroom context, the concept of *student motivation* is used to explain the degree to which students invest attention and effort in various pursuits, which may or may not be the ones desired by their teachers. Motivation refers to students' subjective experiences, especially their willingness to engage in lessons and learning activities and their reasons for doing so. This book develops the argument that your primary motivational goals and strategies should focus on encouraging your students to engage in classroom activities with *motivation to learn,* that is, with the intention of acquiring the knowledge or skills that the activities are intended to develop.

Behavior Reinforcement Theories

Most contemporary views on student motivation emphasize its cognitive and goal-oriented features. These conceptions represent considerable evolution from earlier views, which were influenced heavily by behavioral theory and research (much of it done on animals rather than humans). Early behavioral views depicted humans as responsive to basic drives or needs, but otherwise relatively passive. As one observer put it, "The behaviorist view was that of a creature quietly metabolizing in the shade, occasionally goaded into action by the hot sun or the lure of a cold glass of beer" (Murray, 1964, p. 119).

Behaviorists stress reinforcement as the primary mechanism for establishing and maintaining behavior. They define a reinforcer as anything that increases or maintains the frequency of a behavior when it is made contingent on performance of that behavior. For example, careful work on assignments leading to successful task completion might be reinforced by giving verbal or written praise, awarding high grades, affixing stars or other symbols of excellence, allowing access to some privilege, awarding points that can be exchanged for prizes or applied to a competition, or in some other way compensating students for their efforts or recognizing them for their accomplishments by providing rewards that they value.

In explaining how to establish and maintain desired behavior patterns, behaviorists usually talk about control rather than motivation. They speak of using reinforcement to "bring behavior under stimulus control." The stimulus is a cue that tells learners that certain forms of behavior are desired in the situation and that performing these behaviors will gain them access to reinforcement. If the learners are not able to perform the desired behaviors immediately, gradual improvement toward target performance levels is shaped through successive approximations. Once the desired performance level is established, it is maintained by reinforcing it often enough to ensure its continuation. Any behaviors that are incompatible with the desired pattern are extinguished through nonreinforcement or suppressed through punishment.

Much of the culture of schooling reflects the behavioral view, especially grading and report card systems, conduct codes, and honor rolls and awards ceremonies. With respect to everyday motivation in the classroom, behavioral views lead to carrot-and-stick approaches: Teachers are advised to reinforce students when they display desired learning efforts and withhold reinforcement when they do not—and if necessary, punish them for persistently engaging in incompatible behaviors (O'Leary & O'Leary, 1977; Schloss & Smith, 1994).

Behavioral models of motivation that emphasize manipulation of learners through reinforcement are still around, although most have evolved into more complicated forms that include at least some consideration of learners' thoughts and intentions. Meanwhile, cognitive models have developed that place more emphasis on learners' subjective experiences such as their needs, goals, or motivation-related thinking. These cognitive models of motivation include the concept of reinforcement but portray its effects as mediated through learners' cognitions. In other words, the degree to which task engagement can be motivated by reinforcer availability depends on the degree to which learners value the reinforcer, expect its delivery upon completion of the task, believe that they are capable of completing the task successfully, and believe that doing so in order to gain access to the reinforcer will be worth the costs in time, effort, and foregone opportunities to pursue alternative courses of action.

Need Theories

Need theories were among the first motivational theories to emerge as alternatives to behavior reinforcement theories. These theories explain behaviors as responses to felt needs. The needs may be either inborn and universal (e.g., self-preservation, hunger, thirst) or learned through cultural experience and developed to different degrees in different people (e.g., achievement, affiliation, power).

Many scientific psychologists do not accept need theories because of circular logic and other theoretical problems with the concept of need, and because of difficulties in generating convincing research support for the lists of supposed needs that have been compiled (e.g., Murray, 1938). Nevertheless, one motivation model based in need theory has remained popular and influential: *Abraham Maslow's hierarchy of human needs.*

Maslow (1962) suggested that needs function within a hierarchy arranged in the following order of priority:

1. Physiological needs (sleep, thirst).
2. Safety needs (freedom from danger, anxiety, or psychological threat).
3. Love needs (acceptance from parents, teachers, peers).
4. Esteem needs (mastery experiences, confidence in one's ability).
5. Needs for self-actualization (creative self-expression, satisfaction of curiosity).

The hierarchy model implies that needs must be satisfied in the order given. Unless lower needs are satisfied, higher needs may not even be recognized, let alone motivate behavior. Physiological needs are basic to survival, but once they are met, attention can be directed to higher needs. If both physiological and safety needs are satisfied, people can appreciate warm, interpersonal relationships, and love needs may begin to motivate their behavior. If love needs are reasonably satisfied, people may begin to seek to satisfy their esteem needs and perhaps ultimately their self-actualization needs.

In the classroom, Maslow's hierarchy implies that students who come to school tired or hungry are unlikely to become engrossed in lessons. Similarly, students who feel anxious or rejected are unlikely to take the intellectual risks involved in seeking to overcome confusion and construct clear understandings, and even less likely to try to be creative when working on assignments.

Students do not always act in accord with Maslow's hierarchy. They may deprive themselves of sleep in order to study for a test, for example, or become so engrossed in an activity that they forget about their fatigue, hunger, or personal problems (Neher, 1991; Wahba & Bridwell, 1976). On the whole, however, Maslow's hierarchy is a helpful motivational model. It is a useful reminder that, in order to motivate our students successfully, we may need to address their lower needs along with their higher needs that are associated more closely with school learning.

Goal Theories

Behavior reinforcement theories and need theories both pictured people's motivated actions as reactive to pressures, either from extrinsic incentives or from internally felt needs. Gradually, motivation theories began to acknowledge that in addition to being pushed and pulled in this manner, we are sometimes more proactive in deciding what we want to do and why we want to do it.

Reflecting this evolution, most motivational theorists have shifted from talking about our needs to talking about our goals. For example, Martin Ford (1992) has developed a theory of human motivation that includes a taxonomy of 24 goals arranged within six categories:

1. Affective goals: entertainment, tranquility, happiness, pleasurable bodily sensations, and physical well-being.

2. Cognitive goals: exploration to satisfy one's curiosity, attaining understanding, engaging in intellectual creativity, and maintaining positive
   self-evaluations.
3. Subjective organization goals: unity (experiencing a spiritual sense of
   harmony or oneness with people, nature, or a greater power) and
   transcendence (experiencing optimal or extraordinary states of functioning that go beyond ordinary experience).
4. Self-assertive social relationship goals: experiencing a sense of individuality, self-determination, superiority (in comparisons with others), and resource acquisition (obtaining material and social support
   from others).
5. Integrative social relationship goals: belongingness, social responsibility (meeting one's ethical and social obligations), equity (promoting
   fairness and justice), and resource provision (giving material and social support to others).
6. Task goals: mastery, task creativity, management (handling everyday
   tasks with organization and efficiency), material gain, and safety.

Ford's list is unusually lengthy. Goal theorists usually work with sim-
pler taxonomies that contain just a few categories of goals. These are more
convenient and flexible to apply, and they avoid the theoretical problems
that come with postulating long lists of human needs or goals. Even so,
longer lists such as Ford's are useful as reminders of the many competing
agendas facing teachers who seek to motivate their students to focus on
learning goals. Doing so successfully involves making it possible for students to coordinate their goals so that many different goals are being satisfied, and few if any are being frustrated, as they engage in classroom activities with motivation to learn.

Most of the concepts and motivational strategies discussed in Chapters 2–4
were developed within *goal theory* frameworks that focus on the goals that people adopt in achievement situations. When students adopt *learning goals* (also
called mastery goals or task-involvement goals), they focus on trying to learn
whatever they need to know in order to complete the task successfully. In contrast, when students adopt *performance goals* (also called ego-involvement
goals), they focus more on themselves than on the task, at least if they encounter failure. They are more concerned about preserving their self-
perceptions and public reputations as capable individuals than they are
about learning what the task is designed to teach. Finally, when students adopt
work-avoidant goals, they refuse to accept the achievement challenges inherent in
the task and instead seek to minimize the time and effort they devote to it.

Goal theorists have developed a great deal of information about personal
dispositions and situational characteristics that predict people's tendencies to
adopt these different goals in achievement situations. Other motivational researchers have explored related cognitive and affective experiences (success or
failure expectations, self-efficacy perceptions, attributions of performance outcomes to causes), and the ways in which these motivational factors influence

the quality of people's engagement in tasks and the ultimate levels of success that they achieve. Classroom applications of goal theories emphasize (1) establishing supportive relationships and collaborative learning arrangements that encourage students to adopt learning goals and (2) avoiding creating the sorts of pressures that dispose students toward performance goals or work-avoidant goals. In other words, when conditions emphasized by goal theorists are established in classrooms, students are able to focus their energies on learning without becoming distracted by fear of embarrassment or failure, or by resentment of tasks that they view as pointless or inappropriate.

Intrinsic Motivation Theories

The shift in emphasis from motivation as response to felt pressures to motivation as self-determination of goals and self-regulation of actions is most obvious in theories of intrinsic motivation. Even if they include concepts such as needs or drives, theories of intrinsic motivation picture people as pursuing their own agendas—doing what they do because they want to rather than because they need to.

Self-Determination Theory

A prominent recent example is the self-determination theory of Edward Deci and Richard Ryan (1985, 1991). When people are motivated, they intend to accomplish something and undertake goal-oriented action to do so. Motivated action may be either self-determined or controlled. To the extent that it is self-determined, it is experienced as freely chosen and emanating from one's self, not done under pressure from some internal need or external force.

The prototype of self-determined behavior is *intrinsically motivated action* that entails curiosity, exploration, spontaneity, and interest in one's surroundings. We engage in intrinsically motivated actions because we want to. They require no separate motivating consequences; the only necessary "reward" for them is the spontaneous interest and enjoyment that we experience as we do them.

Self-determination theory specifies that social settings promote intrinsic motivation when they satisfy three innate psychological needs: *competence* (developing and exercising skills for manipulating and controlling the environment), *autonomy* (self-determination in deciding what to do and how to do it), and *relatedness* (affiliation with others through prosocial relationships). In other words, people are inherently motivated to feel connected to others within a social milieu, to function effectively in that milieu, and to feel a sense of personal initiative while doing so. Students are likely to experience intrinsic motivation in classrooms that support satisfaction of these competence, autonomy, and relatedness needs. Where such support is lacking, students will feel controlled rather than self-determined and their motivation will be primarily extrinsic rather than intrinsic.

Flow

Mihaly Csikszentmihalyi (1993) has captured what peak experiences of intrinsic motivation feel like in his concept of flow. He developed the concept after interviewing people about their subjective experiences during times when they were absorbed in activities they enjoyed. He had expected to find that most flow experiences occur during relaxing moments of leisure and entertainment. Instead, he found that they usually occur when we are actively involved in challenging tasks that stretch our physical or mental abilities. He listed *eight characteristic dimensions of the flow experience:*

1. The activity has clear goals and provides immediate feedback about the effectiveness of our responses to it.
2. There are frequent opportunities for acting decisively, and they are matched by our perceived ability to act. In other words, our personal skills are well suited to the activity's challenges.
3. Action and awareness merge; we experience one-pointedness of mind.
4. Concentration on the task at hand; irrelevant stimuli disappear from consciousness; worries and concerns are temporarily suspended.
5. A sense of potential control.
6. Loss of self-consciousness, transcendence of ego boundaries, a sense of growth and of being part of some greater entity.
7. Altered sense of time, which usually seems to pass faster.
8. Experience becomes autotelic: the activity becomes worth doing for its own sake.

In summary, we tend to experience flow when we become absorbed in doing something challenging. We remain aware of the goals of the task and of the feedback generated by our responses to it, but we concentrate on the task itself without thinking about success or failure, reward or punishment, or other personal or social agendas. At least for awhile, we focus completely on meeting the challenges that the task offers, refining our response strategies, developing our skills, and enjoying a sense of control and accomplishment. We are most likely to experience flow when engaged in hobbies or recreational activities (e.g., artistic endeavors, sports, arcade or computer games), but we may also experience them on the job, in the classroom, or in any other activity setting.

Flow potential differs across both persons and situations. Some people develop a "flow personality." They seek out challenges and relish stretching their limits. When required to engage in a more routine activity (e.g., mowing a lawn or working on a practice assignment at school), they tend to "complexify" it by trying to do it artistically, seeking to increase their efficiency, or in other ways setting goals that will make the activity more challenging and interesting for them. Other people rarely experience flow because they fear failure and therefore try to avoid challenging situations.

People report flow experiences most frequently during activities that offer high degrees of challenge in areas in which they perceive themselves as possessing high degrees of skill. Other situations produce different experiences.

TABLE 1.1. Subjective Experiences During Goal-Oriented Activity as Related to Perceived Levels of Challenge and Skill*

| | | Perceived Level of Skill | |
		Low	High
Perceived Level of Challenge	Low	Apathy	Boredom
	High	Anxiety	Flow

*Based on Csikszentmihalyi (1993).

When skill is high but the task offers low challenge, we experience boredom; when both challenge and skill levels are low, we experience apathy; and when we face a challenging task for which we think we possess low levels of skill, we experience anxiety (see Table 1.1).

In school, anxiety is the chief threat to flow potential. If students routinely are faced with overly challenging situations that are beyond their abilities to handle effectively, they may come to prefer the boredom of "safe" routines to the flow opportunities of challenging activities. Eventually, their potential for experiencing flow in the classroom will erode away. Csikszentmihalyi, Rathunde, & Whalen (1993) suggested that teachers can encourage flow experiences in three ways: (1) by being knowledgeable about their subjects, enthusiastic in teaching them, and acting as models pursuing the intrinsic rewards of learning; (2) by maintaining an optimal match between what is demanded and what students are prepared to accomplish (urging but also helping students to achieve challenging but reasonable goals); and (3) by providing a combination of instructional and emotional support that enables students to approach learning tasks confidently and without anxiety.

Key ideas relating to the four general types of motivational theories featured in this historical overview are given in Table 1.2.

MOTIVATION IN THE CLASSROOM

Like most people, I find the concepts of intrinsic motivation and flow to be very appealing. I also find them useful for interpreting a range of motivational situations. However, I do not believe that they are feasible to serve as the primary concepts underlying models of motivation in education. These concepts apply best when people are freely engaging in self-chosen activities. Usually these are play or recreational activities rather than work or learning activities. Even when people are intrinsically motivated to learn, their learning usually features leisurely exploration to satisfy curiosity rather than sustained efforts to accomplish knowledge- or skill-development goals. Moreover, even when intrinsically motivated learning is more goal oriented, it tends to occur under

TABLE 1.2. Views of the Human Condition and Implications for Motivating Students Embedded in Four Types of Motivational Theories

Theories	Views of the Human Condition	Implications for Motivating Students to Learn
Behavior reinforcement	Reactive to external reinforcement and associated situational cues	Cue and reinforce desired learning behavior (attention to lessons, careful work on assignments, etc.)
Needs	Reactive to felt pressures from internal needs	Make sure that competing needs are satisfied or at least muted so that students can focus on mastery- and achievement-related needs; design curriculum and instruction to help them meet the latter needs without undue difficulties
Goals	Both reactive and proactive in formulating and coordinating goals so as to satisfy needs and desires	Coordinate classroom climate, curriculum, instruction, and assessment practices so as to encourage students to adopt learning goals rather than performance goals or work-avoidant goals
Intrinsic motivation	Autonomously determining goals and regulating actions to pursue interests, gain satisfactions	Emphasize curriculum content and learning activities that connect with students' interests; provide opportunities for them to make choices in deciding what to do and to exercise autonomy in doing it

autonomous and self-determined conditions. Unfortunately, these conditions are difficult to establish in classrooms, for several reasons.

First, school attendance is compulsory, and curriculum content and learning activities are selected primarily on the basis of what society believes students need to learn, not on the basis of what students would choose if given the opportunity to do so. Schools are established for the benefit of students, but from the students' point of view their time in the classroom is devoted to enforced attempts to meet externally imposed demands. Second, teachers usually must work with classes of 20 or more students and therefore cannot always meet each individual student's needs. As a result, certain students sometimes are bored and certain others sometimes are confused or frustrated. Third, classrooms are social settings, so that failures often produce not only personal disappointment but public embarrassment. Finally, students' work on assignments and performance on tests are graded, and periodic reports are sent home to their parents. In combination, these factors tend to focus students' attention on concerns about meeting demands successfully rather than on any personal benefits that they might derive from learning experiences. In short, it's hard to just enjoy an activity and "go with the flow" when the activity is compulsory and your performance will be evaluated, especially if you fear that your efforts will not be successful.

Even in classrooms where fear of failure is minimized, both teachers and students can easily settle into familiar routines as the school year progresses. To the point that these routines become the "daily grind," classroom activities that were designed as means toward curricular ends tend to become ends in themselves. That is, attention becomes focused on what must be done to complete the activities rather than on the knowledge or skills that the activities were designed to develop.

You can make curricular and instructional adjustments that will increase the frequencies with which your students experience intrinsic motivation and flow in your classroom. Strategies for doing so are discussed in Chapter 6. For now, however, I ask you to face up to some important constraints on your options for motivating students: As a teacher, you are not a camp counselor or recreational worker who provides experiences that are enjoyable but not necessarily educational. Nor are you a private tutor who can individualize the curriculum to a single learner's needs and interests. Instead, you must work with classes of 20 or more students and concentrate on helping them to accomplish curricular goals.

These constraints make it unrealistic to adopt intrinsic motivation or flow as the model of student motivation that you will seek to maintain on an all-day, everyday basis. You can provide frequent opportunities for choice and autonomy and you can phrase instructions and feedback in ways that downplay your control over students, but it will remain true that students are required to come to your class to try to master a largely externally imposed curriculum, and that their efforts will be evaluated and graded. Under these conditions, intrinsic motivation will be the exception rather than the rule.

The same will be true of flow experiences, especially for students who are underchallenged and thus bored much of the time or overchallenged and thus anxious much of the time. Even students who enjoy a consistently good match between your demands on them and their current readiness to meet those demands will vary in their desire for flow experiences. Some will prefer the boredom of safety over the risk of challenge. Others will be more disposed toward flow experiences, but even these students cannot be in (or seeking) flow all of the time because it would be too exhausting.

STUDENT MOTIVATION TO LEARN AS YOUR GOAL

If intrinsic motivation is ideal but unattainable as an all-day, everyday motivational state for you to seek to develop in your students, what might be a more feasible goal? I believe that it is realistic for you to seek to develop and sustain your students' motivation to learn from academic activities—their tendency to find academic activities meaningful and worthwhile and to try to get the intended learning benefits from them.

Motivation to learn differs both from extrinsic, reinforcement-driven motivation and from intrinsic, enjoyment-driven motivation, although it may overlap with either of them. The difference between motivation to learn and extrinsic motivation is closely related to the difference between learning and performance. *Learning* refers to the information processing, sensemaking, and advances in comprehension or mastery that occur when one is acquiring knowledge or skill; *performance* refers to the demonstration of that knowledge or skill after it has been acquired. Strategies for stimulating students' motivation to learn apply not only to performance (work on assignments or tests) but also to the information processing that is involved in learning content or skills in the first place (attending to lessons, reading for understanding, comprehending instructions, putting things into one's own words). Thus, stimulating students' motivation to learn includes encouraging them to use thoughtful information-processing and skill-building strategies when they are learning. This is quite different from merely offering them incentives for good performance later.

The difference between intrinsic motivation and motivation to learn is closely related to the difference between affective and cognitive task engagement experiences. Intrinsic motivation refers primarily to *affective* experience—enjoyment of the processes involved in engaging in an activity. In contrast, motivation to learn is primarily a *cognitive* response involving attempts to make sense of the information that an activity conveys, to relate this information to prior knowledge, and to master the skills that the activity develops. *Students may be motivated to learn from a lesson or activity whether or not they find its content interesting or its processes enjoyable.*

Student motivation to learn can be viewed either as a general disposition or as a situation-specific state. As a *disposition,* it is an enduring tendency to value learning—to approach the process of learning with effort and thought and to seek to acquire knowledge and skill. In specific situations, a *state* of motivation to learn exists when a student engages purposefully in an activity by adopting its goal and trying to learn the concepts or master the skills it develops. Students who are high in motivation to learn (as a disposition) tend to do these things routinely, as if they possess a motivated learning schema that is triggered whenever they enter a learning situation. Even students who do not have much motivation to learn as a general disposition may display such motivation in specific situations because the teacher has sparked their interest or made them see the importance of the content or skill (Deci et al., 1991). Students who are motivated to learn will not necessarily find classroom activities intensely pleasurable or exciting, but they will take them seriously, find them meaningful and worthwhile, and try to get the intended benefits from them.

Motivation to learn refers primarily to the quality of students' cognitive engagement in a learning activity, not the intensity of the physical effort they devote to it or the time they spend on it. For most tasks, there is a curvilinear relationship between motivational intensity and degree of success achieved. That is, performance is highest when motivation is at an optimal level rather than either below or above this optimal level. Furthermore, the optimal level varies with task complexity: High levels of arousal maximize performance on simple tasks, but lower levels of arousal maximize performance on more complex tasks. It helps to be "psyched up" if your task is to break open a door or win a 50-meter dash, but such high arousal is counterproductive if your task is to solve some problem that requires sustained mental concentration and thought.

The latter description characterizes most academic tasks facing students in classrooms. Students are likely to handle these tasks most successfully when their motivation is positive (they are engaged in the task and free from distractions, anxieties, and fear of failure) but not necessarily high in an absolute sense. They are alert and oriented toward learning, but not psyched up or focused on winning a competition or obtaining a reward.

In other words, we always want to maximize students' motivation to learn, but not necessarily to maximize their total motivation. Similarly, we want to maximize successful achievement outcomes, but only insofar as this can be done by maximizing motivation to learn and supplying supportive incentives and rewards. Attempts to increase motivation still further are likely to be counterproductive, especially if they involve pressuring students or making them unnecessarily anxious or dependent. We want to develop life-enhancing dispositions in students, not neurotic needs.

STIMULATING AND SOCIALIZING MOTIVATION TO LEARN

Much of the motivational advice typically offered to teachers boils down to the following general principle: Find out what topics your students want to learn about and what activities they enjoy doing, then build these into your curriculum as much as possible. This is a useful principle as far as it goes; many of the suggestions offered in later chapters in this book are based on the notion of capitalizing on students' existing motivation. This is only part of what needs to be done, however. *If you confine yourself to responding to the motivational orientations that your students bring into your classroom with them, you will limit your options* and fail to capitalize on opportunities to guide your students' motivational development in desirable directions.

People are born with the potential to develop a great range of motivational dispositions. A few such dispositions appear to be inborn as part of the human condition and observable in everyone. Most, however, especially higher level dispositions such as motivation to learn, are developed gradually through exposure to learning opportunities and socialization influences. The degree to which a particular motivational disposition develops, as well as the qualitative nuances it takes on in the individual person, are influenced by the modeling and socialization (communication of expectations, direct instruction, corrective feedback, reward and punishment) provided by "significant others" in the person's social environment. Along with family members and close friends, teachers are significant others in the lives of their students, and thus in a position to influence the students' motivational development.

In this regard, it is helpful to view motivation to learn as a *schema*—a network of connected insights, skills, values, and dispositions that enable students to understand what it means to engage in academic activities with the intention of accomplishing their learning goals and with awareness of the strategies they use in attempting to do so. The total schema cannot be taught directly, although some of its conceptual and skills components can. In addition, its value and dispositional components can be stimulated and supported through modeling, communication of expectations, and socialization of students into a cohesive learning community.

The development of motivation to learn and related self-actualization motives is especially dependent on modeling and socialization by adults. These motivational dispositions include key cognitive insights and strategies that are learned primarily as a result of sophisticated socialization at home and instruction at school. Many students have not had much exposure to these higher level and cognitive aspects of motivation. These students view school tasks as imposed demands rather than as learning opportunities, and thus engage in them (if at all) with work-avoidant goals and perhaps performance goals, but not learning goals. They will have to be helped to understand and appreciate what motivation to learn means before such motivation can begin to influence their decisions and actions. Strategies for motivating such students will be discussed in Chapter 8.

Therefore, in addition to capitalizing on students' existing motivation, make the best of your opportunities to stimulate and socialize their motivation to learn. In each particular teaching situation, try to stimulate motivation to learn the knowledge or skills that the activity is designed to develop. Bring this motive to the forefront relative to any other motives that may be operating at the time. Over the long run, these everyday motivational efforts should have cumulative effects encouraging your students to develop motivation to learn as an enduring disposition. In addition, you can socialize this disposition more directly, using the strategies described in Chapter 7.

MOTIVATION AS EXPECTANCY X VALUE

Much of what researchers have learned about motivation, including implications for teachers, can be organized within an expectancy x value model (Feather, 1982; Pekrun, 1993). The *expectancy x value model of motivation* holds that the effort that people are willing to expend on a task is the product of (1) the degree to which they *expect* to be able to perform the task successfully if they apply themselves (and thus the degree to which they expect to get whatever rewards that successful task performance will bring), and (2) the degree to which they *value* those rewards as well as the opportunity to engage in the processes involved in performing the task itself.

Effort investment is viewed as the product rather than the sum of the expectancy and value factors because it is assumed that no effort at all will be invested in a task if one factor is missing entirely. People do not willingly invest effort in tasks that they do not enjoy and that do not lead to valued outcomes even if they know that they can perform the tasks successfully. Nor do they willingly invest effort in even highly valued tasks if they believe that they cannot succeed on those tasks no matter how hard they try. If required to engage in such tasks unwillingly, they are likely to experience negative affective and cognitive reactions (see Tables 1.3 and 1.4). Thus, *the expectancy x value model of motivation implies that teachers need to (1) help students appreciate the value of school activities and (2) make sure that students can achieve success in these activities if they apply reasonable effort.*

Hansen (1989) suggested that students tend to adopt one of four general approaches to coping with classroom tasks, depending on their success expectations and task values. *Engaging* is likely when students see value in the task and are reasonably confident of their ability to meet its demands. When engaged, they seek to make sense of the task by discovering meanings, grasping

TABLE 1.3. Students' Subjective Experiences Relating to the Expectancy Aspects of Task Engagement

	Reaction to the Processes Involved in the Task Itself	Anticipated Implications of Task Engagement
When Fearing or Expecting Failure	*Affect:* Anxiety, embarrassment, fear of failure.	*Affect:* Apathy, resignation, resentment.
	Cognition: Task focus is "invaded" by perception of confusion, failure, helplessness. Attribution of (poor) performance to insufficient ability.	*Cognition:* Perception that one cannot "win," that one has no realistic chance to earn desired rewards, satisfactory grades, etc.
When Expecting to Succeed	*Affect:* Satisfaction (perhaps occasional excitement) as skills or insights develop. Pride in craftsmanship, successful performance.	*Affect:* Excitement, happy anticipation of reward.
	Cognition: Perception of progress toward goals, achieved with relative ease. Attribution of (successful) performance to (sufficient) ability plus (reasonable) effort. Focus on one's developing knowledge and skills.	*Cognition:* Recognition that one can attain desired rewards with relative ease. Focus on meeting stated performance criteria.

TABLE 1.4. Students' Subjective Experiences Relating to the Value Aspects of Task Engagement

	Reactions to the Processes Involved in the Task Itself	Anticipated Implications of Task Engagement
When Engaged in a Negatively Valued Task	*Affect:* Anger or dread. Student dislikes the task, which is in effect a punishment.	*Affect:* Alienation, resistance. Student doesn't want to acquire this knowledge or skill.
	Cognition: Task focus is "invaded" by resentment, awareness of being coerced into unpleasant or pointless activity.	*Cognition:* Perceptions of conflict between what this task represents and one's self-concept, gender role identification, etc. Anticipation of undesirable consequences to involvement in such tasks.
When Engaged in a Positively Valued Task	*Affect:* Enjoyment, pleasure. Engagement in this task is a reward in its own right.	*Affect:* Energized, eager to learn this knowledge or skill (for its instrumental value).
	Cognition: Relaxed concentration on the processes involved in doing this task. Flow. Metacognitive awareness of what the task requires and how one is responding to it. Focus on the academic content when learning, and on the quality of the product when performing.	*Cognition:* Recognition that the task is a sub-goal related to attainment of important future goals (often as a "ticket" to social advancement). Focus on the "relevant" aspects of the learning.

new insights, and generating integrative interpretations. The task's unfamiliar aspects are viewed as challenging but are valued because they provide a basis for extending one's understandings.

Dissembling is likely when students recognize value in the task but do not feel capable of meeting its demands. They would like to complete the task successfully, but are uncertain of what to do, how to do it, or whether they can do it. These uncertainties threaten their identity and self-esteem, so they pretend to understand, make excuses, deny their difficulties, or engage in other behavior focused more on protecting their ego than on developing task-related knowledge and skill.

Evading is likely when success expectancies are high but task value perceptions are low. The students feel confident of their ability to meet task demands but don't see a reason to do so. In response to the grading system and other pressures, they may go through the motions by focusing sufficiently on

TABLE 1.5. Students' Strategies for Responding to Classroom Activities as Related to Their Expectancy and Value Perceptions*

	Has Low Success Expectations	Has High Success Expectations
Does Not Value the Activity	*Rejection:* Refuses to participate	*Evading:* Does the minimum
Values the Activity	*Dissembling:* Protects image of competence	*Engagement:* Seeks to learn

*Based on Hansen (1989).

the task to avoid teacher interventions and perhaps even to accomplish the task goal. However, their attention is scattered, frequently drifting to competing interests such as daydreaming, interacting with classmates, or thinking about their personal lives.

Finally, *rejecting* is likely when both success expectations and task value perceptions are low. Lacking both reasons to care about succeeding on the task and confidence that they could do so if they tried, students in this situation withdraw from the task. Some become passive and psychologically numbed. Others smolder with anger or alienation. Rejecting the task completely, they not only don't engage in it but don't even feel the need to dissemble by pretending to themselves or others that they are capable of meeting its demands. Hansen's model is depicted graphically in Table 1.5.

ORGANIZATION OF THE BOOK

This first chapter has introduced the concept of motivation, described how motivational theories have evolved, argued for student motivation to learn as the primary focus of your motivational efforts, and introduced the expectancy x value model. Introduction of general concepts and principles continues in Chapter 2, which emphasizes the importance of establishing your classroom as a learning community in which the participants collaborate in pursuing worthwhile learning goals. That chapter describes general classroom management and student socialization strategies that produce a positive classroom climate and set the stage for use of the more specific motivational strategies presented in Chapters 3–8. It also summarizes key curricular and instructional features that complement the motivational features of powerful learning programs.

Chapters 3–8 are organized within the expectancy x value model.[1] Chapters 3 and 4 focus on expectancy issues: protecting students' confidence as learners and providing extra support to those who have become discouraged. Chapters 5–8 focus on strategies for helping students to appreciate the value of engaging in academic activities (because successful engagement will earn them extrinsic rewards, will bring them intrinsic satisfactions, or will allow them to develop meaningful and worthwhile knowledge). All of these chapters assume that the guidelines in Chapter 2 have been followed so that a learning community has been established in your classroom to support your more direct motivational efforts.

For the most part, the material in Chapters 1–8 reflects research-based principles that are known or at least believed to apply to all students, regardless of age, gender, social class, race, culture, or other personal characteristics. Certain principles might be more applicable with certain students (e.g., younger ones rather than older ones) or in certain situations (e.g., a whole-class lesson versus a follow-up assignment). Wherever the principle is applicable, however, it should have the same implications for practice (i.e., that motivational strategies consistent with the principle are advisable and contradictory strategies are not).

This focus on universally applicable principles in Chapters 1–8 reflects my belief that, at least with respect to motivation, people are much more similar than different. I acknowledge the need to adapt motivational strategies to students' individual needs and experiences. However, I believe that this individualization mostly involves adaptations of a single set of basic principles. I do not see a scientific basis for proceeding on the assumption that separate sets of motivational principles (and separate psychologies generally) are needed in order to understand and work effectively with students who differ in age, gender, or cultural background. However, researchers have identified some group and individual differences that seem worth bringing to your attention, and these are discussed in Chapter 9. Most of what I have to say about adapting motivational strategies to different students or situations is found in that chapter, although suggestions made in other chapters are sometimes qualified with reference to students' ages or grade levels.

Chapter 10 concludes the book. First it offers suggestions about ways to incorporate the ideas developed in Chapters 1–9 into your instructional planning. Then it shifts attention from the motivation of students to the motivation of teachers. It points out that the same principles that we use to understand the motivation of students facing academic challenges can be used to understand the motivation of teachers facing professional challenges, including difficulties in motivating certain students. It calls attention to some of the pitfalls you may encounter in your efforts to become a successful classroom motivator and suggests ways to avoid or overcome them.

SUMMARY

Theories of human motivation have evolved from an emphasis on reactive responses to pressures (external reinforcement contingencies or internally felt needs) to an emphasis on intrinsically motivated, self-determined actions. Flow experiences and other manifestations of intrinsic motivation are usually considered ideal and thus held up to teachers as goals to achieve with their students. These ideal motivational states should be developed in the classroom when it is feasible to do so. However, the goal of achieving sustained intrinsic motivation is not realistic as a basis for planning your all-day, everyday motivational strategies, because classroom learning requires students to try to master a largely imposed curriculum while often being observed by peers and evaluated by teachers.

It is realistic, however, to expect (and help) your students to experience classroom activities as meaningful and worthwhile, and to try to get the intended learning benefits from them. You can encourage this by stimulating students to engage in classroom activities with motivation to learn, which they can do whether or not they find the activities intrinsically enjoyable. Developing your students' motivation to learn involves socializing it as a general disposition as well as stimulating it situationally in the process of implementing lessons and learning activities.

The conception of motivation as expectancy x value is useful as a general model for thinking not only about students' existing motivation but also about potential intervention strategies. This model has been used to organize the book: Chapters 3 and 4 address expectancy aspects of motivation, whereas Chapters 5–8 address value aspects. Individual and group differences that may provide a basis for adapting motivational strategies to students' personal characteristics are addressed in Chapter 9. Finally, Chapter 10 concludes the book by offering suggestions about ways to address motivational issues in your instructional planning and to apply the ideas presented here to your attempts to optimize your own motivation as a teacher.

NOTE

1. As introduced in this chapter and as used to organize Chapters 3–8, the notion of motivation as expectancy x value is used as a relatively informal general model. It is *not* meant to refer to the more formal and specific expectancy x value theory of achievement motivation, or to convey the precise definitions, assumptions, or connotations associated with that theory. For example, applications of the more specific theory usually are limited to achievement situations that call for meeting clear standards of excellence. In contrast, I also apply the more general model to informal and exploratory learning situations that do not involve striving to accomplish well-articulated goals. As another example, the meaning of the value term is usually restricted to the value that the person places on the rewards that he or she expects to earn by completing the task successfully. In contrast, I also include within the value term any intrinsic enjoyment or satisfaction that the person may anticipate or derive from engaging in the processes involved in carrying out the task.

   I have used the expectancy x value model rather than possible alternatives (e.g., goals, attributions, self-perceptions) as an organizer for the book because I find it most useful for synthesizing the motivational literature to focus on the strategies that teachers might use with their students. This alternative complements the organizing and synthesizing schemes used by psychologists (which focus on students' motivational characteristics) and facilitates a shift in primary attention from descriptive information to intervention principles. Consequently, it better meets teachers' needs for information about ways to establish and maintain desired motivational patterns in their students.

   My treatment of related theoretical concepts emphasizes their commonalities and complementary implications for teachers, not their differences. Thus, for the most part I have omitted arguments about issues such as whether adaptive achievement goals are best construed as learning goals, task goals, or mastery goals, or whether adaptive expectancy-related perceptions are best construed as success expectations, confidence, efficacy perceptions, attributions of success to internal and controllable causes, internal locus of control, etc. Instead, I have focused on the common implications of theory and research relating to all these concepts, namely that teachers should seek to foster learning goals rather than performance or work-avoidant goals and success expectations rather than failure expectations.

REFERENCES

Csikszentmihalyi, M. (1993). *The evolving self: A psychology for the third millennium.* New York: HarperCollins.

Csikszentmihalyi, M., Rathunde, K., & Whalen, S. (1993). *Talented teenagers: The roots of success and failure.* Cambridge: Cambridge University Press.

Deci, E., & Ryan, R. (1985). *Intrinsic motivation and self-determination in human behavior.* New York: Plenum.

Deci, E., & Ryan, R. (1991). A motivational approach to self: Integration in personality. In R. Dienstbier (Ed.), *Nebraska Symposium on Motivation, Vol. 38, Perspectives on motivation* (pp. 237–288). Lincoln: University of Nebraska Press.

Deci, E., Vallerand, R., Pelletier, L., & Ryan, R. (1991). Motivation and education: The self-determination perspective. *Educational Psychologist, 26,* 325–346.

Feather, N. (Ed.). (1982). *Expectations and actions.* Hillsdale, NJ: Erlbaum.

Ford, M. (1992). *Motivating humans: Goals, emotions, and personal agency beliefs.* Newbury Park, CA: Sage.

Hansen, D. (1989). Lesson evading and lesson dissembling: Ego strategies in the classroom. *American Journal of Education, 97,* 184–208.

Maslow, A. (1962). *Toward a psychology of being.* Princeton, NJ: VanNostrand.

Murray, E. (1964). *Motivation and emotion.* New York: Prentice-Hall.

Murray, H. (1938). *Explorations in personality.* New York: Oxford University Press.

Neher, A. (1991). Maslow's theory of motivation: A critique. *Journal of Humanistic Psychology, 31,* 89–112.

O'Leary, K., & O'Leary, S. (Eds.). (1977). *Classroom management: The successful use of behavior modification.* (2nd ed.). New York: Pergamon.

Pekrun, R. (1993). Facets of adolescents' academic motivation: A longitudinal expectancy-value approach. In P. Pintrich & M. Maehr (Eds.), *Advances in motivation and achievement* (Vol. 8, pp. 139–189). Greenwich, CT: JAI.

Schloss, P., & Smith, M. (1994). *Applied behavior analysis in the classroom.* Boston: Allyn & Bacon.

Wahba, M., & Bridwell, L. (1976). Maslow reconsidered: A review of research on the need hierarchy theory. *Organizational Behavior and Human Performance, 15,* 212–240.

Establishing Your Classroom as a Learning Community

Introduction of basic motivational concepts and principles began in Chapter 1 and continues here in Chapter 2. This chapter describes key features of classroom management, curriculum, and instruction that prepare the way for successful use of the motivational strategies discussed in subsequent chapters. Those strategies are meant to be used systematically as part of an overall pattern of effective teaching that includes compatible approaches to managing the classroom and teaching the curriculum. Students will not respond to your motivational attempts if they are fearful, resentful, or otherwise focused on negative emotions. To create conditions that favor your motivational efforts, you will need to establish and maintain your classroom as a learning community— a place where students come primarily to learn, and succeed in doing so through collaboration with you and their classmates. You will also need to focus your curriculum on things that are worth learning and to develop this content in ways that help students to appreciate its significance and application potential.

It is commonly observed that *certain preconditions must be in place before motivational strategies can be effective.* Maslow's hierarchy of needs, for example, implies that lower level needs must be satisfied before higher level needs can become operative. Other examples have been developed by industrial psychologists studying factors that affect workers' satisfaction and productivity. Their studies indicate that workers' motivation is affected not only by the nature of their work and the rewards they expect to earn, but also by their job environment and other working conditions, their social relationships with coworkers, and especially, their feelings about the boss. Even workers who do not derive much intrinsic satisfaction from their work will put forth reasonable effort if they like their boss; however, they may develop apathy or resistance if they view their boss as oppressive.

Citing studies of management practices that have been used successfully in business and industry, William Glasser (1990) urged teachers to act as lead managers rather than boss managers. *Lead managers* motivate by reinforcing rather than punishing, showing rather than telling, empowering rather than overpowering, and emphasizing cooperative work toward shared goals rather than rule enforcement. Lead managers are more likely than boss managers to elicit students' cooperation and empower them to assume responsibility for controlling their lives at school.

Similar ideas about establishing caring and collaborative relationships with students and their families have been advanced by James Comer (1980) in his book *School Power,* by William Purkey and John Novak (1996) in their book *Inviting School Success,* and by Carl Rogers and H. Jerome Freiberg (1994) in their book *Freedom to Learn.* These sources advocate creating a school environment in which students feel comfortable, valued, and secure. This encourages them to form positive emotional bonds with teachers and a positive attitude toward school, which in turn facilitates their academic motivation and learning.

Various lines of theory and research point to three important agendas for you to accomplish in setting the stage for effective motivation of students: (1) make yourself and your classroom attractive to students; (2) focus their attention on individual and collaborative learning goals and help them to achieve these goals; and (3) teach things that are worth learning, in ways that help students to appreciate their value.

MAKE YOURSELF AND YOUR CLASSROOM ATTRACTIVE TO STUDENTS

You—your own personality and everyday behavior in the classroom—can become your most powerful motivational tool. To do so, you will need to cultivate and display the attributes of individuals who are effective as models and socializers. These begin with the characteristics that make people well liked: a cheerful disposition, friendliness, emotional maturity, sincerity, and other qualities that indicate good mental health and personal adjustment. Your attempts to socialize students will have positive effects to the extent that the students admire you, value your opinions, and believe that you are sincere in what you say and have their best interests in mind when saying it. Engagement in classroom activities tends to be high when students perceive their teachers as involved with them (liking them, responsive to their needs), but students tend to become disaffected when they do not perceive such involvement (Skinner & Belmont, 1993).

Therefore, get to know and enjoy your students. Learn their names quickly and use these names frequently as you interact with them. Greet them warmly each day and spend some time getting to know them as individuals. In the process, you will learn a lot about their backgrounds and interests that you can incorporate into your teaching in ways that are compatible with curricular goals. Also, help your students get to know and appreciate you as a person by sharing some of your background, life experiences, interests, and opinions. If you do this appropriately, it will help your students to become more open and genuine in their interactions with you, even while retaining their respect for your authority as the teacher.

Create an inviting physical environment in your classroom. To the extent possible, see that it is furnished comfortably and arranged in a way that is both aesthetically pleasing and compatible with your instructional methods. Include attractive displays and decorations that relate to the curriculum. As photos of your students and products from their completed assignments become available, incorporate these into your displays in ways that encourage the students to take pride in their accomplishments and appreciate those of their classmates.

Authoritative Management and Socialization of Students

In managing your classroom and socializing students, emphasize the strategies that have emerged repeatedly in studies of the most effective teachers: Teachers who approach management as a process of establishing a productive learning environment tend to be more successful than teachers who emphasize their roles as disciplinarians. That is, successful managers focus on helping their students learn what is expected and how to meet those expectations, not on threatening or punishing them for failing to do so. These teachers are clear and consistent in articulating their expectations. If necessary, they model and instruct students in desired procedures and remind students when these procedures are needed. They keep students engaged in worthwhile lessons and activities; they monitor their classrooms continually and respond to emerging problems before they become disruptive; and when possible they intervene in ways that do not disrupt lesson momentum or distract students who are working on assignments (Brophy, 1983, 1988; Doyle, 1986; Evertson & Harris, 1992; Jones, 1996).

Why I am discussing management strategies in a section on making yourself and your classroom attractive to students? Because students want and expect teachers to act as authority figures and create predictable structures in their classrooms (Brantlinger, 1993; Metz, 1978; Nash, 1976; Schmuck & Schmuck, 1991). When asked about their favorite teachers, students unsurprisingly mention such qualities as caring about them as individuals and seeking to help them succeed as students; teaching interesting things and explaining them clearly; being pleasant and friendly; being fair and not playing favorites, humiliating them, appearing to look down on them when they make mistakes or ask for help, yelling at them, or overreacting to their minor misbehavior. However, students also say that they want teachers to articulate and enforce clear standards of behavior. They view this not just as part of the teacher's job but as evidence that the teacher cares about them (Cabello & Terrell, 1994; Hayes, Ryan & Zseller, 1994).

A dependable classroom structure provides students with the information and assistance they need to enable them to learn successfully. You can provide structure by communicating your expectations clearly; by responding consistently, predictably, and contingently to students' behavior; by offering help and support to those who are struggling; and by adjusting your teaching strategies to individual differences. Students who experience optimal levels of this kind of structure are likely to be the most effortful, persistent, and highly engaged in classroom activities (Skinner & Belmont, 1993).

In managing your classroom and socializing your students, seek to maintain a classroom structure that is optimal not only in the degree of direction that you provide but also in the manner in which you exercise your leadership. *Use authoritative strategies that help students to become active, self-regulated learners;* avoid both (1) authoritarian strategies that produce passive obedience rather than thoughtful self-regulation and (2) laissez-faire strategies that offer students autonomy but fail to provide them with needed guidance (McCaslin & Good, 1992).

Parents who are the most successful in getting their children to adopt their ideals and internalize their standards for behavior are those who use authoritative rather than authoritarian strategies (Baumrind, 1991). Authoritarian parents make little attempt to explain their demands, which they expect to be obeyed without questioning or discussion. In contrast, authoritative parents explain the rationales for their demands and help their children to understand that the demands are made for the children's own good. The authoritative pattern that promotes optimal personal and social development in children includes the following socialization practices:

- Accepting the child as an individual.
- Communicating this acceptance through warm, affectionate interactions.
- Socializing by teaching the child prosocial values and behavioral guidelines, not just imposing "discipline."
- Clarifying rules and limits, but with input from the child and with flexibility in adapting to developmental advances (e.g., allowing more opportunities for autonomy and choice as children develop greater ability to handle these opportunities responsibly).
- Presenting expectations in ways that communicate respect for and concern about the child, as opposed to "laying down the law."
- Explaining the rationales underlying demands and expectations.
- Justifying prohibitions by citing the effects of children's actions on themselves and others rather than by appealing to fear of punishment or essentially empty logic such as "good children don't do that."
- Modeling as well as teaching well-articulated value systems.
- Continually projecting positive expectations and attitudes; treating children as if they already are, or at least are in the process of becoming, prosocial and responsible people.

Authoritative socialization practices are optimal in the classroom as well as in the home. Besides supporting your management system, they set the stage for successful motivation efforts by creating a positive classroom atmosphere and encouraging students to view you as a caring teacher whom they trust and want to please.

Appealing Communication Practices

The linkage between authoritative classroom management and successful student motivation was demonstrated in a series of studies done in college classrooms by communication theorists. Some of these studies focused on instructors' *compliance-gaining strategies.* They indicated that coercive, authoritarian approaches to gaining compliance had very negative effects on students' liking of instructors and on the degree to which they achieved the classes' learning goals. In contrast, the use of authoritative techniques helped pave the way for the instructors' motivational efforts by developing positive relationships between them and their students.

Other studies in the series showed the importance of teacher *immediacy,* a term for actions that enhance physical and psychological closeness with students. Nonverbal immediacy includes eye contact, smiling, positive gestures, vocal variety, forward body lean, and a relaxed body position. Verbal immediacy includes use of humor, personal examples, "we" and "our" language, and students' first names. Immediacy behaviors increase students' liking for the instructor, their interest in the course, and their desire to study thoughtfully and do good work on assignments. Working together, the compliance-gaining and immediacy aspects of instructors' communication styles reinforce each other to produce positive effects on motivation and learning, especially in students who are not highly motivated at the beginning of the term (Christophel, 1990; Frymier, 1993; Gorham, 1988; Richmond & McCroskey, 1992).

This book is about motivating students rather than managing classrooms, so I will not pursue the latter topic further. For more research-based information about classroom management and detailed suggestions about applications, see Brophy (1996), Evertson et al. (1994), Good and Brophy (1995, 1997), Jones and Jones (1995), or Weinstein and Mignano (1993). For now, bear in mind that an important part of making your students feel comfortable in your classroom is providing them with a reliably safe and humane learning environment. If you interact with them in an authoritative rather than authoritarian manner, you will be viewed as meeting their needs and helping them to accomplish shared goals rather than as "bossing them around."

FOCUS STUDENTS' ATTENTION ON INDIVIDUAL AND COLLABORATIVE LEARNING GOALS

At any given time, you will want your students to focus on certain goals but may find that some of them pursue other goals in addition or instead. Many of these goals will be social rather than academic. Social goals sometimes complement academic goals (as when students seek to achieve at a high level in order to please you, their parents, or peers who value such achievement). However, social goals also can undermine academic goals (as when students minimize their attention and work output in an attempt to please peers who have rejected the school's agenda, or more typically, when their attention is distracted from lessons and assignments to social interactions with class-mates). You can increase the power of your motivational efforts by attending to your students' social goals as well as their academic goals (Urdan & Maehr, 1995; Wentzel, 1992). In particular, create a social environment in which every-one feels welcome and learning is accomplished through the collaborative ef-forts of yourself and your students.

During lessons and times when students are working on assignments, you will need to keep attention focused on learning goals rather than on social goals or other competing agendas. You are likely to get the best results if you help students to frame their learning goals in terms of acquiring the knowl-edge or skills that you intend to teach (e.g., learning to find the lowest com-mon denominator), not just in terms of completing tasks or obtaining particu-lar grades (e.g., getting all the answers right or doing an "A" paper). This will encourage students to take more responsibility for managing their own learn-ing by actively setting goals, seeking to construct understandings, persisting in their efforts to overcome confusions, and assessing and reflecting on what they have learned.

Fostering a Learning Orientation

Hermine Marshall (1988) illustrated ways to highlight learning goals by contrasting classrooms that featured a learning orientation with a classroom that featured a work orientation. The teachers who promoted a *learning ori-entation* introduced activities with emphasis on what students would learn from them, encouraged students to work collaboratively and help one an-other, and treated errors as natural parts of the learning process and stimu-lants for follow-up instruction. In contrast, the teacher who promoted a *work orientation* spoke primarily in terms of task completion rather than learning. She stressed completing the work within stated time limits when introducing activities, emphasized competition rather than cooperation among students, and gave the correct answers following errors but did not use the errors as occasions for helping students to overcome their difficul-ties in learning. As a result, the work-oriented teacher inadvertently created a threatening environment in which students were forced to try to cope with (often vaguely understood) task demands, without much help from her or from their classmates but with the knowledge that mistakes could trigger low grades and perhaps public embarrassment. In contrast, the teachers who fostered a learning orientation created supportive learning en-vironments that encouraged students to engage in academic activities re-flectively and often collaboratively.

Emphasizing Learning Goals

The consequences of creating these contrasting environments have been studied by motivational researchers interested in what has become known as achievement goal theory or simply *goal theory* (Ames, 1992; Blumenfeld, 1992; Meece, 1994). *Achievement goals* refer to students' beliefs about the purposes of engaging in achievement-related behavior. Students who approach the same lesson or activity with different achievement goals may engage in it quite differently and emerge with different outcomes.

Research has concentrated on two sets of contrasting achievement goals, variously called *learning versus performance goals* (Dweck & Leggett, 1988), mastery versus performance goals (Ames & Archer, 1988), or task-involvement versus ego-involvement goals (Nicholls, 1984). Students who approach academic activities with *learning goals* (also called mastery or task-involvement goals) focus on acquiring the knowledge or skills that the activities are designed to develop. They seek to construct accurate understandings by paraphrasing the material into their own words and connecting it to prior knowledge. When they encounter difficulties they are likely to seek help or if necessary to persist in their own self-regulated learning efforts, buoyed by the belief that these efforts are worthwhile and by the confidence that the efforts will pay off eventually.

In contrast, when *performance goals* (also called ego-involvement goals) predominate, students treat the task more as a test of their ability to perform rather than as an opportunity to learn. Their primary concern is preserving their self-perceptions and public reputations as capable individuals who possess the ability needed to succeed on the task. In striving to meet task demands and avoid failure, they may rely on rereading, memorizing, guessing, and other surface-level learning strategies instead of deeper-level knowledge construction strategies, and their learning efforts may be impaired by fear of failure or other negative affect. They seek to avoid challenging tasks and tend to give up easily when frustrated because they believe that their abilities are limited, so they lack confidence that persistent efforts will eventually pay off. Rather than ask for help when they need it, they prefer to conceal their difficulties by leaving items blank, taking wild guesses, or perhaps copying from neighbors.

Some of the most alienated or discouraged students may not show much evidence of either learning goals or performance goals. These students are not cognitively engaged in learning activities and instead have adopted *work-avoidant goals;* they seek to meet minimal requirements with minimal effort investment (Meece & Holt, 1993).

Applying Goal Theory: The TARGET Program

Goal theorists have consolidated their research findings to develop guidelines for managing classrooms in ways that encourage students to adopt learning goals rather than performance or work-avoidant goals. An example is the TARGET program, developed by Carole Ames (1990). Ames began with Joyce Epstein's (1989) synthesis of research on family structures that influence children's developing motivational systems at home (see Chapter 9). Epstein organized her findings within six categories that are represented in the TARGET acronym: *t*ask, *a*uthority, *r*ecognition, *g*rouping, *e*valuation, and *t*ime. Noting that these home structures have parallels at school, Ames blended in additional principles from goal theory research to develop TARGET into a program for managing these six facets of classrooms in ways that encourage students to engage in activities with a focus on learning rather than on their public performance and how it reflects on their abilities.

Tasks are selected so as to provide an optimal level of challenge and to emphasize activities that students find interesting and intrinsically engaging. *Authority* is shared with students and exercised with consideration of their needs and feelings. *Recognition* is provided to all students who make noteworthy progress, not just the highest achievers. *Grouping* is managed in ways that promote cooperative learning and minimize interpersonal competition and social comparison. *Evaluation* is accomplished using multiple criteria and methods, focusing on individualized assessment of progress rather than comparisons of individuals or groups. Finally, *time* is used in creative ways that ease the constraints of rigid scheduling and allow for more use of valuable learning activities that are hard to fit into 30–60 minute class periods.

TARGET is best viewed not as a fixed program but rather as a framework that is adaptable to different teaching situations and useful for building motivational considerations into your instructional plans. Table 2.1 summarizes ways in which the TARGET recommendations contrast with traditional ways of addressing the facets of classroom structure encompassed within the six TARGET categories.

Maehr and Midgley (1991) extended Ames's TARGET model from the classroom level to the school level, reasoning that the motivational efforts of individual teachers will have more powerful cumulative effects on students if the school as a whole supports students' motivation to learn. Consequently, the schoolwide TARGET model calls for adjustments such as reinforcing the intrinsic value of learning by extending it through field experiences and other extracurricular participation, arranging for public recognition of students' accomplishments, creating opportunities for students to learn study skills and strategies for managing their own learning, and revising time schedules to allow for more flexible curricular planning.

In summary, focusing students' attention on individual and collaborative learning goals means much more than merely keeping them on task. It means creating a supportive, collaborative learning environment that enables students to feel comfortable in accepting the challenges implied in learning goals, persisting with self-regulated learning efforts when they encounter failure or frustration, and asking for help when they need it. It also means seeing that they get the help they need, building confidence that persistent efforts will eventually pay off, and treating mistakes as expected parts of an ongoing

TABLE 2.1. TARGET Recommendations Contrasted With Traditional Classroom Structures

TARGET Structure	Traditional Practices	TARGET Recommendations
Task	Textbook-based curriculum emphasizing textbook reading, recitation lessons, workbook tasks, and tests. All students are exposed to the same input and engaged in the same activities, with emphasis on content coverage and memorization. Motivation is addressed primarily through the grading system, perhaps augmented by various forms of extrinsic rewards.	There is a greater variety of learning activities, selected to emphasize tasks that students find interesting and intrinsically engaging and to connect with students' backgrounds and experiences. Activities are introduced with emphasis on their purposes and are developed in ways designed to maximize their intrinsic appeal and help students to appreciate the value of what they are learning (rather than with emphasis on tests, grades, or extrinsic rewards). To help ensure that activities are optimally challenging for all students, students are taught goal-setting and self-regulation skills, and if necessary, are assigned to information sources and learning tasks of varying difficulty.
Authority	The teacher dictates classroom rules and makes unilateral decisions regarding curriculum and instruction. Students' general behavior is tightly regimented within school and classroom rules and their exposure to learning opportunities is heavily determined by the teacher and their textbooks.	Authority is shared with students and exercised with consideration of their needs and feelings. Their content-related interests and questions are solicited and addressed. They frequently have opportunities to make choices in deciding what to do, to exercise autonomy in deciding how to do it, and to participate in decision making about classroom rules, procedures, or learning opportunities.

(Continued)

TABLE 2.1. TARGET Recommendations Contrasted With Traditional Classroom Structures—*Continued*

TARGET Structure	Traditional Practices	TARGET Recommendations
Recognition	At least implicitly, students are always in competition for recognition and rewards. Certain students consistently receive high grades, have their work praised and publicly displayed, and win whatever competitions, prizes, or awards are made available. Other students rarely if ever enjoy these recognitions and rewards, which are based primarily if not solely on absolute levels of accomplishment, without regard to individual differences in the levels of effort that went into the accomplishments.	Recognition is provided to all students who make noteworthy progress, not just to the highest achievers. Students are recognized for a broad range of achievements (not just high scores on tests); recognition is based on levels of progress made toward individually established goals; and most recognition takes the form of privately communicated appreciations of effort and progress rather than public celebration of the accomplishments of the highest achievers.
Grouping	The class is an aggregate of individuals rather than a coherent learning community. Students interact frequently with the teacher but rarely with one another, and they work mostly alone on assignments. If used at all, grouping is used to set up competitions or to differentiate students by ability or achievement level.	The class functions as a learning community that features collaborative norms and expectations. Students frequently work in pairs or small groups to engage in the social construction of knowledge. Group assignments are varied and based on friendships, common interests, or other considerations in addition to or instead of achievement level, and students are encouraged to cooperate rather than compete as learners.

TABLE 2.1. TARGET Recommendations Contrasted With Traditional Classroom Structures—*Concluded*

TARGET Structure	Traditional Practices	TARGET Recommendations
Evaluation	All students are evaluated using the same assessment instruments (typically conventional tests). Feedback is often public and emphasizes absolute levels of performance (number or percentage of items answered correctly) or normative comparisons (a students' relative standing within the class or some larger sample). It often is delivered in ways that encourage students to view it as assessment of fixed levels of performance capacity rather than of increments in ability development.	Evaluation features a variety of assessment instruments and an emphasis on helping students to recognize and appreciate the progress they have made toward individually suitable goals. The system for converting assessment results into report card grades includes provisions for allowing students to take alternate tests, revise their work on assignments, and in other ways improve on initially disappointing performance levels.
Time	Teacher and students are locked into a rigid schedule in which each day is divided into 30–60 minute periods. Activities that require more time than this schedule allows are not included in the curriculum, and even scheduled activities frequently must be cut short or interrupted and resumed on another day because a time period is ending.	Time is scheduled more flexibly so that a greater range of activities can be included. In addition, instead of always being told what to do and when to do it, students frequently work on major projects that allow them to exercise autonomy in managing time and other learning resources (e.g., interactions with information sources or collaborating classmates). Students who need it are given extra time to complete their assignments.

learning process rather than as evidence of limited ability. Finally, it means avoiding practices that tend to make students feel psychologically isolated or threatened in their efforts to meet your academic expectations.

Goal theory applications are explored in more detail in Chapters 3 and 4. For now, let us consider two teachers who are good at managing their classrooms and relating to their students, and committed to supporting their students' progress as learners, but who approach motivation quite differently.

TWO TEACHERS WITH CONTRASTING MOTIVATIONAL ORIENTATIONS

Laura Hirsch and Rachel Dewey both teach language arts and social studies at a large middle school. The school assigns students to classes randomly, so their classes are similar in size and average achievement level. Both teachers are authoritative in managing their classes and interacting with students, so that their classes generally run smoothly, with high rates of student engagement in activities and low rates of disruption. Both Laura and Rachel are warm, friendly, and optimistic people who are devoted to their profession and well liked by their students. Each devotes considerable attention to student motivation in planning her classroom routines, lessons, and learning activities. However, the motivational principles that they emphasize are quite different. As you read about these two teachers, think about the motivational strategies they use and consider the probable effects of these strategies on their students' motivation and learning.

Laura Hirsch

Laura knows that grades are important to students, so she strives to make sure that her students can achieve success if they invest reasonable effort. In her class, grades are determined by performance on daily assignments (one-third) and on weekly quizzes and unit tests (two-thirds). Laura prepares her students well for these assignments and tests.

First, she leads the class through a reading of the story in the reader or the chapter section in the social studies textbook. She works her way methodically through the rows, allowing each student an opportunity to read a paragraph or two, then moving on to the next student. She suspends the reading periodically in order to provide explanations or ask questions designed to underscore key ideas that were developed in the section just read or will be developed in the upcoming section. Laura's students know that they should pay careful attention to and take notes on these explanations and questions, because they are likely to appear again in some form on the assignments, quizzes, and tests. As the reading progresses, Laura also invites and responds to students' questions and comments about the material, but she makes sure that the discourse doesn't stray too far from the key ideas she wants to emphasize.

Following these text-based lessons, students work individually on seat-work assignments. Laura insists on quiet during these work times, so that everyone can concentrate. The worksheets feature comprehension questions, mostly calling for matching, true/false, or fill-in-the-blank responses. Most questions have been supplied by the textbook publishers, although Laura has eliminated a few ambiguous or controversial items and added some items of her own on points that had been neglected in the publisher-supplied exercises and tests. As students work on the assignments, Laura circulates to help those who need it. A few students may finish these assignments during class time, but most will have some items left to complete as homework.

Prior to major quizzes and tests, Laura leads the class through review exercises designed to prepare them for the assessment. She usually structures these reviews as elimination bees or games, especially the popular "Jeopardy!" television show format. Occasionally she announces that prizes (small treats such as candy bars) will be awarded to winning individuals or team members. She reminds everyone, though, that the main purpose of these contests and games is to review the material for the upcoming test.

The major quizzes and tests include some short-answer essay questions in addition to the more familiar matching, true/false, and fill-in-the-blank questions. Unit tests also include questions that call for integrating across chapter sections or relating material from the chapter to big ideas being developed across the school year. However, none of these questions strays too far from the text or contains elements that students who have studied carefully would find surprising or unfair. As Laura frequently reminds her students, if they pay attention to lessons and work conscientiously on assignments, they should be successful on her tests.

Even so, Laura includes "safety nets" for students who struggle. First, everyone is allowed to have one bad day: When Laura calculates total scores to use for grading, she disregards each students' worst daily assignment score. Second, students can partially regain lost credit on quizzes (although not on unit tests): If they return the quizzes to her with correction of each mistake accompanied by a statement about why the original answer was incorrect, they will receive half credit for these items. Third, students can earn a few extra credit points during each unit by selecting from a menu of extra credit assignments and completing a maximum of three of these successfully.

During English classes, Laura's questions focus on the details of the stories and how these exemplify the genre (e.g., mystery stories) and techniques (e.g., foreshadowing) under study. Daily assignment and weekly quiz questions focus on defining and recognizing examples of these genres and techniques. Unit tests call for more integrated responses through series of questions such as the following: (1) define foreshadowing; (2) give three examples of foreshadowing in stories read during the unit; and (3) give at least two reasons why an author might choose to use the foreshadowing technique (for extra credit, give additional valid reasons).

In social studies, Laura's daily assignments and weekly quizzes focus on basic facts about the topics under study, for example, South American Nations: the nations' geographical location, climate, major cities and places of interest, historical highlights, primary imports and exports, etc. Unit tests also include short-answer essay questions calling for students to demonstrate understanding of connections among these facts, such as by showing awareness that much of the economy and cultures of Chile can be explained by the fact that it is a mountainous country in which internal travel is difficult and access to the sea is limited.

Rachel Dewey

Rachel also realizes that grades are important to students, but her motivational strategies emphasize personalizing the curriculum and engaging students in collaborative learning rather than preparing students for tests. She does give a short test early in each unit as a way to make sure that all of her students can define and give examples of key terms, and sometimes she includes a major unit test as a way to assess students' accomplishment of unit goals. For the most part, however, her students' grades are determined by their work on a variety of learning activities and assignments, and her feedback to them emphasizes qualitative critiques and suggestions for improvement rather than letter grades or numerical scores.

In English, she covers fewer stories than Laura does but spends more time on the stories that she does cover. Instead of beginning by leading her students through a reading of the story in class, she has the students read and discuss each new story with a partner. Rachel prepares them for this by introducing the class to the genre and to some of its key techniques, and by providing the students with questions to guide their analyses. First, the students read the story individually to enjoy the aesthetic experience. Next, they discuss the story with their partner, focusing on what they liked and didn't like about it and why, and noting questions or comments about this to bring up in class. Then the partners work through Rachel's questions, designed to help them analyze the stories with respect to genre techniques. They record their answers and again make notes about questions and comments to raise in class.

During the whole-class discussion that follows, Rachel first focuses on the students' aesthetic reactions and related questions and comments. She tosses in a few of her own as food for thought (e.g., Would the story have been better if it had been set in the present instead of the past or if it had a happier ending? What might have happened if the hero had kept his secret instead of telling it to his friend?). When discussion of the aesthetic appreciation aspects of the story has run its course (or if necessary, when time constraints loom), Rachel shifts to the topic of genre techniques, starting by eliciting students' answers to her questions and listing these on the board. She then leads a discussion of these issues, making sure to highlight ways that the author used key techniques to construct the story and ways in which the use of these techniques enhanced the story. Her goal here is not just to help students to understand the key features of the genre and recognize the authors' use of characteristic genre techniques, but also to enable them to appreciate what the genre has to offer them as readers and the ways that good applications of genre techniques enhance the power and enjoyment of the stories they read.

Following these class discussions are quiet times during which students work individually to write in their journals about their reactions to the story and its moral and about what they learned from the story about the genre and its characteristic techniques. Rachel supplies a list of questions that the students can use to guide their journal writing if they wish. However, she encourages students to write in depth about aspects that they found especially interesting or meaningful, rather than to try to answer each question on the list or to confine themselves to the issues raised on the list. At minimum, she wants them to address two main areas of response to the story (their personal aesthetic response and what they have learned about the genre from reading it). Her goal here is to engage students in using writing as a way to formulate and record both their aesthetic responses to literature as readers and the key insights that they have constructed as students of the genre under study.

As a culmination activity for genre-based units, students compose an original example of the genre (e.g., a mystery story). These are published in a class anthology and some of the best ones are read (or acted out in drama form) in class or at performances staged in other classrooms or at school assemblies.

In social studies, rather than give equal time to each of the South American nations studied, Rachel introduces the continent as a whole and its major regions and characteristics but then focuses on a few nations in more depth. These countries are selected because they exemplify key ideas or social studies themes that she wants to emphasize in her teaching (e.g., Brazil for studying its rain forest and the cultural and ecological preservation issues it raises, Venezuela for studying the effects of the discovery of oil and the development of a modern oil industry on a traditional agrarian economy, and Chile as an example of life in a mountain region).

For most of the countries studied, and in particular for those addressed in depth, Rachel supplements the text with nonfiction tradebooks, children's literature, videos, and classroom visits by people who come from or have visited the country. She selects these supplementary sources with an eye toward personalizing what the students learn about the country, and especially about the everyday lives and activities of families that include children their age.

Rachel assigns her students to work in four- or five-member teams to develop illustrated booklets about these key countries. One member of each team focuses on the country's geography, climate, and natural resources; another on its history, language, and culture; another on its economy; and so on. Rachel meets with these "specialists" as groups to suggest other data sources they might consult, such as encyclopedias, books, and CD-ROMs, and to encourage them to help one another to develop expertise in their specialization area. In addition to acquiring this specialized knowledge and collaborating with group mates in producing the illustrated booklets, each student writes an individual report summarizing what he or she has learned about the country.

These reports call for information about all aspects studied, not just about the area in which the student has specialized, so the student will be required to learn from the textbook and from the supplementary information accumulated by group mates.

The students also are required to write in their journals about what they are learning in social studies. All students are asked to record their thinking on two questions: (1) What would I like and not like about living in the country? and (2) What have I learned about why things in that country are as they are and why they are similar to or different from the way they are in our country? In addition, students are encouraged to elaborate about whatever aspects of the country they have found particularly interesting or meaningful to learn about.

In grading, Rachel emphasizes students' performance on individual and group assignments as much as their performance on tests. For tests she assigns credit points for each item and notes the total score, provides qualitative feedback, and invites students to revise their responses to earn partial credit for items on which they failed to receive credit. She responds similarly to group and individual reports. Finally, she holds biweekly meetings with each student, during which she reads and comments on the students' journal entries and reviews and makes suggestions about the students' general progress in the subject.

Comparison

Concerning principles already introduced in this chapter, Laura Hirsch and Rachel Dewey could be described as similar in their emphasis on authoritative classroom management strategies but different in their orientation toward learning goals. The classroom task and reward structures emphasized by Laura are primarily individual but also somewhat competitive and not at all collaborative. In contrast, those emphasized by Rachel are primarily collaborative and secondarily individual, with very little emphasis on competition.

Despite the competitive elements in her approach to motivation, Laura tries to emphasize learning goals over performance goals. She minimizes ambiguity and risk, practically guaranteeing her students good grades in exchange for paying attention to class, working conscientiously on assignments, and studying for tests. Rachel offers no such guarantees, but her emphasis on collaborating with peers and exploring the personal implications of learning tends to focus her students on learning goals without causing them to worry much about performance goals. Also, she allows her students more choice and autonomy in working on her assignments, so they are more likely to experience intrinsic motivation. Even so, students who fear ambiguity and risk may be anxious in her class unless she is sufficiently specific in answering their questions about what she expects from them and sufficiently reassuring in giving them feedback about how well they are doing.

Along with these differences in motivational strategies, there are associated differences between these two teachers in their general approaches to curriculum and instruction—differences likely to affect their students' motivation and learning. By sticking so closely to the text in her curriculum, instruction, and assessment practices, Laura is virtually ensuring that her students will achieve success if they invest reasonable effort, but she also is restricting her curriculum to broad but shallow coverage of mostly disconnected content. This encourages students to focus on memorizing material for tests rather than constructing more elaborate and better connected representations of learning that are likely to be more permanent and more available for use in relevant application situations.

In contrast, Rachel covers more limited content but focuses on developing key ideas in depth, seeks to personalize the learning to her students' backgrounds and experiences, and provides her students with opportunities to elaborate and connect their learning, both through communication with peers and through individual report and journal writing. Rachel's teaching incorporates several of the principles in the TARGET model (more varied and interesting tasks, grouping to allow cooperative learning, evaluation using multiple criteria and methods). It also exemplifies many of the principles involved in teaching school subjects for understanding, appreciation, and application to life outside of school, whereas Laura's approach is more confined to content coverage via transmission of information. These approaches to curriculum and instruction and their implications for student motivation and learning are discussed in the following sections.

TEACH THINGS THAT ARE WORTH LEARNING, IN WAYS THAT HELP STUDENTS TO APPRECIATE THEIR VALUE

Even if you have set the stage by making yourself and your classroom attractive to students and by focusing their attention on individual and collaborative learning goals, you cannot expect students to sustain much motivation to learn unless they view the learning as meaningful and worthwhile. Students are not likely to be motivated to learn when engaged in pointless or meaningless activities such as continued practice on skills that have already been mastered thoroughly; memorizing lists for no good reason; looking up and copying definitions of terms that are never used in activities or assignments; reading material that is written in such sketchy, technical, or abstract language as to make it essentially meaningless; or working on tasks assigned merely to fill time rather than to accomplish worthwhile learning goals.

Goal-Oriented Planning

The key to making your students' learning experiences worthwhile is to *focus your planning on major instructional goals, phrased in terms of desired student outcomes.* These major goals are the knowledge, skills, attitudes, values, and dispositions that you want to develop in your students. Goals, not content coverage or learning processes, provide the rationale for curriculum and instruction. All of the elements of your instructional program—content sources, discussion questions, activities, assignments, and assessment methods—should be included because you consider them useful as means to accomplish important instructional goals.

It may seem obvious to you that curriculum planning should be guided by major instructional goals, but research on instructional materials and on teachers' planning and teaching suggest that this principle is not often realized in classrooms. Teachers typically plan by concentrating on the content they will teach and the activities their students will do, without giving much thought to the goals that provide the rationale for the content and activities in the first place (Clark & Peterson, 1986).

In effect, most teachers leave crucially important decisions about goals to the publishing companies who supply them with instructional materials. This would work out well if sustained focus on important goals guided the development of these materials. However, analyses indicate that popularly used textbook series typically treat content coverage as an end in itself. As a result, too many topics are covered in not enough depth; content exposition often lacks coherence and is cluttered with insertions and illustrations that have little to do with the key ideas that should be developed; skills are taught separately from knowledge content rather than integrated with it; and in general, neither the students' texts nor the questions and activities suggested in the teachers' manuals are structured around powerful ideas connected to important goals (Beck & McKeown, 1988; Brophy, 1992b; Dreher & Singer, 1989; Elliott & Woodward, 1990; Tyson-Bernstein, 1988).

Adapting Instructional Materials

You will not be able to achieve a coherent program of curriculum and instruction simply by following the teaching suggestions that come with your textbooks. Instead, you will need to elaborate on, or even substitute for, much of the content in the texts and many of the activities suggested in the accompanying manuals.

To do so, examine your instructional materials and unit plans in light of your major instructional goals. Identify what content to ignore or downplay and what content to emphasize. You may need to augment the latter content if major ideas or themes are not well developed in the texts. Identify pointless questions and activities to skip, and develop other questions and activities that will support progress toward major goals. Treat the textbook as just one among many potential resources to draw upon in planning and implementing curricula. There is no need to view the textbook as "the" curriculum and thus limit yourself and your students to its contents.

Developing Powerful Ideas in Depth

You won't have time to teach everything worth learning. Only so many topics can be included in the curriculum, and not all of these can be developed in sufficient depth to promote deep understanding of key ideas, appreciation of their significance, and exploration of their applications to life outside of school. This tension between breadth of coverage and depth of topic development is an enduring dilemma that teachers have to manage as best they can; it is not a problem that you can solve in any permanent or completely satisfactory manner.

In recent years, curricula have drifted into an overemphasis on breadth at the expense of depth. Critics routinely complain that textbooks offer parades of disconnected facts instead of coherent networks of connected content structured around powerful ideas. Reports of teaching in classrooms suggest a similar picture. Although there are exceptions, most of these descriptions portray teachers as hurriedly attempting to cover too much content and students as frequently memorizing but not often reflecting and discussing. Students spend too much time reading, reciting, filling out worksheets, and taking memory tests, and not enough time engaging in sustained discourse about powerful ideas or applying these ideas in authentic activities (Goodlad, 1984; Stodolsky, 1988).

Disconnected factual information is not very meaningful or memorable. When students lack contexts within which to situate such information and richly connected networks of ideas to enhance its meaningfulness, they are forced to rely on rote memorizing instead of using more sophisticated learning and application strategies. They remember as much as they can until the test, but then forget most of it afterwards. Furthermore, most of what they do remember is inert knowledge that they are not able to use in relevant application situations (Prawat, 1989; Resnick, 1989).

There is general agreement about what needs to be done to enable students to construct meaningful knowledge that they can access and use in their lives outside of school. First, there needs to be a retreat from breadth of coverage in order to allow time to develop the most important content in greater depth. Second, this important content needs to be represented as networks of connected information structured around powerful ideas. Third, the content needs to be developed with a focus on explaining these important ideas and the connections among them (see Box 2.1).

Planning and Implementing Powerful Activities and Assignments

The best learning activities and assignments are built around powerful ideas. Students will not necessarily learn anything important from merely carrying out the processes of an activity (i.e., spending "time on task"). The key to the effectiveness of good activities is their *cognitive engagement potential*—the degree to which they get students actively thinking about and applying key ideas, preferably with conscious awareness of their learning goals and control of their learning strategies. The most valuable activities are not merely hands-on, but minds-on.

The success of an activity in producing thoughtful student engagement with key ideas depends not only on the activity itself but on the teacher structuring

Box 2.1.   Teaching with Emphasis on Powerful Ideas

As an example of the value of structuring content around powerful ideas, consider the topic of shelter. Elementary social studies textbook series typically emphasize that shelter is a basic human need and then go on to identify and illustrate a great variety of shelter forms (tepees, igloos, stilt homes, etc.). However, the texts typically say very little about the reasons why people live in these different kinds of homes and nothing at all about advances in construction materials and techniques that have made possible the features of modern housing that most children in the United States take for granted. Students often emerge from these units thinking that people from the past or from other societies have inexplicably chosen to live in strange or exotic forms of housing, without appreciating that local responses to shelter needs usually are quite inventive given the available construction knowledge, technology, and materials.

Units on shelter and other cultural universals (food, clothing, transportation, communication, occupations, government, etc.) will be much more powerful if taught with emphasis on how practices relating to the cultural universal have evolved over time, how and why they vary across societies today, and what all of this might mean for personal, social, and civic decision making. This will expand students' purviews on the human condition and help them to put the familiar into historical, geographical, and cultural perspective.

Rather than teach only that shelter is a basic human need and that different forms of shelter exist, instruction might help students to understand and appreciate the reasons for these different forms of shelter. Students could learn that shelter needs are determined in large part by local climate and geographical features, and that most housing is constructed using materials adapted from natural resources that are plentiful in the local area. They could learn that certain forms of housing reflect cultural, economic, or geographic conditions (tepees and tents as easily portable shelters used by nomadic societies, stilt homes as adaptation to periodic flooding, highrises as adaptation to land scarcity in urban areas). They also could acquire a better appreciation of the fact that inventions, discoveries, and improvements in construction knowledge and materials have enabled many modern people to live in housing that offers better durability, weatherproofing, insulation, and temperature control, with fewer requirements for maintenance and labor (e.g., cutting wood for a fireplace or shoveling coal for a furnace) than what was available to even the richest of their ancestors.

These and related ideas would be taught with appeal to students' sense of imagination and wonder. There might also be emphasis on values and dispositions (e.g., consciousness-raising through age-suitable activities relating to the energy efficiency of homes or the plight of the homeless). Development and application activities might include a tour of the neighborhood (in which different types of housing are identified and discussed) or an assignment calling for students to take home an energy-efficiency inventory to fill out and

---

Box 2.1. Teaching with Emphasis on Powerful Ideas—*Concluded*

---

discuss with their parents. There might also be reading and discussion of children's literature selections on life in the past (e.g., in log cabins on the frontier) or in other societies or about the homeless in our society today, as well as activities calling for students to plan their ideal homes or simulate the thinking involved in making decisions about where to live given certain location and budgetary constrictions.

Similarly, units on history need not be seemingly random parades of facts. If planned with focus on instructional goals, they can be structured around powerful ideas that students can appreciate and apply. For example, units on the American Revolution might be planned to develop understanding and appreciation of the origins of American political values and policies. Treatment of the Revolution and its aftermath would emphasize the historical events and political philosophies that shaped the thinking of the writers of the Declaration of Independence and the Constitution. Content coverage would focus on the issues that developed between England and the colonies and the ways that these impacted on various types of people, as well as on the ideals, principles, and compromises that went into the construction of the Constitution (especially the Bill of Rights). Assignments calling for research, critical thinking, or decision making would focus on topics such as the various forms of oppression that different colonial groups had experienced (and the influence of this on their thinking about government), as

well as the ideas of Jefferson and other key framers of the Constitution. There would be less emphasis on Paul Revere or other revolutionary figures who were not known primarily for their contributions to American political values and policies, and no emphasis at all on the details of particular battles. Students might role-play journalists or pamphleteers writing about the Boston Massacre or Boston Tea Party, simulate a town meeting or Continental Congress session discussing possible responses to the Intolerable Acts, hold a debate on whether the Revolution was justified, or pretend to be citizens of Boston writing to friends elsewhere about their experiences.

These examples are not meant to imply that the suggested approaches are the only or even necessarily the best ones to take in addressing these two topics. Instead, they illustrate how clarity of primary goals encourages development of units and lessons likely to cohere and function as tools for accomplishing those goals, and in the process, to produce instruction that students find meaningful, relevant, and applicable to their lives outside of school. The particular goals to emphasize will vary with one's educational philosophy, the ages and needs of the students, and the purposes of the course. Teachers of military history in a service academy, for example, would have very different goals and would approach the unit on the American Revolution with very different content emphases than those in the example.

and the teacher–student discourse that occur before, during, and after the time period in which students respond to the activity's demands. Activities are likely to have maximum impact when you (1) introduce them in ways that clarify their purposes and engage students in seeking to accomplish those purposes; (2) scaffold[1] students' work on the activity, monitor their progress, and provide appropriate feedback; and (3) lead the students through appropriate post-activity sharing of and reflection on the insights that have been developed.

In planning activities and assignments, begin with a focus on the unit's major goals and consider the kinds of activities that would promote progress toward those goals. This will help you to make good decisions about whether to use activities suggested in the manual that accompanies your textbook and about what other activities might need to be included. A synthesis of principles for designing and implementing learning activities (Brophy & Alleman, 1991) concluded that all of the activities in a unit of instruction should meet four *primary criteria:*

1. *Goal relevance:* Each activity is believed to be essential, or at least directly relevant and useful, as a means enabling students to achieve the unit's learning goals.
2. *Difficulty level:* Each activity is pitched within the optimal range of difficulty—challenging enough to extend learning, but not so difficult as to leave many students confused or frustrated.
3. *Feasibility:* Each activity is feasible for implementation within the constraints under which you must work (space and equipment, time, types of students, etc.).
4. *Cost effectiveness:* The educational benefits expected to be derived from each activity justify its anticipated costs in time and trouble (both for you and for your students).

In selecting from among activities that meet all four of these primary criteria, you might consider applying several *secondary criteria:*

1. Students are likely to find the activity interesting or enjoyable.
2. The activity provides opportunities for interaction and reflective discourse, not just solitary seatwork.
3. If the activity involves writing, students will compose prose, not just fill in blanks.
4. If the activity involves discourse, students will engage in critical or creative thinking, problem solving, or decision making, not just regurgitate facts and definitions.
5. The activity focuses on application of important ideas, not incidental details or interesting but ultimately trivial information.
6. As a set, the activities offer variety and in other ways appeal to student motivation to the extent that this is consistent with curriculum goals.
7. As a set, the activities include many ties to current events or local and family examples or applications.

Emphasizing Authentic Activities

Be conscious of potential applications when selecting and implementing learning activities. As much as possible, allow your students to learn through engagement in authentic activities. *Authentic activities* require using what is being learned for accomplishing the very sorts of life applications that justify inclusion of this learning in the curriculum in the first place. If it is not possible to engage students in the actual life applications that the learning experiences are designed to prepare them for, then at least engage them in realistic simulations of these applications.

Where skills must be practiced until they become smooth and automatic, most of this practice should occur within whole-task application activities rather than be confined to isolated practice of subskills. Elementary students should have opportunities to read for information or pleasure in addition to practicing word attack skills, to solve problems and apply mathematics in addition to practicing number facts and computations, and to write prose or poetry compositions or actual correspondence in addition to practicing spelling and penmanship. Secondary students should learn how and why knowledge was developed in addition to acquiring the knowledge itself and should have opportunities to apply what they are learning to their own lives or to current social, civic, or scientific issues.

Teaching for Understanding

In recent years, both the findings of research on effective teaching and the instructional guidelines issued by organizations serving subject-matter specialists have emphasized the importance of teaching school subjects for understanding. Students who learn content with understanding not only learn the content itself but appreciate the reasons for learning it and retain it in a form that makes it usable when needed. When the new learning is complex, the construction of meaning required to develop clear understanding of it takes time and is facilitated by the interactive discourse that occurs during lessons and activities. Clear explanations and modeling from the teacher are important, but so are opportunities to answer questions about the content, discuss or debate its meanings and implications, and apply it in problem-solving or decision-making contexts.

These activities allow students to process the content actively and make it their own by paraphrasing it into their own words, exploring its relationships to other knowledge and to past experience, appreciating the insights it provides, and identifying its implications for personal decision making or action. The teacher provides whatever structuring and scaffolding students need in order to accomplish the goals, but gradually fades this assistance as students develop expertise. Ultimately, the students engage in independent and self-regulated learning.

Analysis of programs that have been developed to teach school subjects for understanding have identified a set of principles that are common to most

**TABLE 2.2. Teaching for Understanding
10 Key Features**

1. The curriculum is designed to equip students with knowledge, skills, values, and dispositions that they will find useful both inside and outside of school.
2. Instructional goals emphasize developing student expertise within an application context and with emphasis on conceptual understanding of knowledge and self-regulated application of skills.
3. The curriculum balances breadth with depth by addressing limited content but developing this content sufficiently to foster conceptual understanding.
4. The content is organized around a limited set of powerful ideas (basic understandings and principles).
5. The teacher's role is not just to present information but also to scaffold and respond to students' learning efforts.
6. The students' role is not just to absorb or copy input but also to actively make sense and construct meaning.
7. Students' prior knowledge about the topic is elicited and used as a starting place for instruction, which builds on accurate prior knowledge and stimulates conceptual change if necessary.
8. Activities and assignments feature tasks that call for critical thinking or problem solving, not just memory or reproduction.
9. Higher order thinking skills are not taught as a separate skills curriculum. Instead, they are developed in the process of teaching subject-matter knowledge within application contexts that call for students to relate what they are learning to their lives outside of school by thinking critically or creatively about it or by using it to solve problems or make decisions.
10. The teacher creates a social environment in the classroom that could be described as a learning community featuring discourse or dialogue designed to promote understanding.

if not all of them (Brophy, 1992a). These common elements are shown in Table 2.2. Although these principles emerged from research focused primarily on learning rather than motivation, note how well they complement the principles emerging from motivational research. They fit especially well with the principles for establishing a learning orientation rather than a work orientation in the classroom and for encouraging students to adopt learning goals rather than performance or work-avoidant goals when engaging in activities. The case examples described by Judith Meece further illustrate this complementarity (see Box 2.2). For more information about teaching for understanding, see Good and Brophy (1995, 1997).

SUMMARY

Certain preconditions must be in place before motivational strategies can be effective. To create conditions that favor your motivational efforts, establish and maintain your classroom as an attractive and psychologically supportive learning community by accomplishing three important agendas: (1) make yourself and your classroom attractive

Box 2.2.   Contrasting Mastery Orientations

Meece (1994) reported case studies of fifth- and sixth-grade science teachers whose students showed contrasting degrees of orientation toward learning (mastery) goals. Lesson transcripts and other case material from their classrooms were analyzed not only for motivational strategies but for lesson presentations, questioning patterns, feedback patterns, grouping arrangements, and evaluation practices. Analyses indicated that differences in students' goal orientations and related achievement behaviors were associated with differences in their teachers' approaches to motivation and instruction.

In the low mastery classes, learning activities emphasized memorization and recall of isolated bits of information. Students had limited opportunities to actively construct meaning, to view themselves as sources of knowledge, or to apply what they were learning to new situations. Their teachers made little effort to adapt lessons to the students' ability levels and interests, and provided them with few opportunities for peer collaboration and self-directed learning. The teachers' motivational attempts were focused on the grading system (via reminders to students that their work would be evaluated or that they needed to prepare for an upcoming test). These instructional practices that emphasized simple transmission and recall of facts did not encourage the development of mastery goals and self-regulated learning.

In contrast, the high mastery teachers used instructional approaches that promoted meaningful learning. They expected their students to understand, apply, and make sense of what they

were learning. To encourage active involvement in lessons, they modified material to increase its personal relevance to their students, provided opportunities for peer collaboration, and emphasized the intrinsic value of the material. They did not place much emphasis on grades or other extrinsic incentives for learning.

Students in one of the two high mastery classes reported more active engagement in learning activities than did the students in the other high mastery class. The teacher in the first class presented coherent lessons that proceeded in small steps and allowed students to see the connections between ideas. She also regularly monitored her students' lesson comprehension and held them individually accountable for what they were learning. The other high mastery teacher summarized and connected ideas for his students but did not follow up by monitoring their understanding closely and helping them to construct understandings. When his students were confused, he was more likely to simply provide the correct answer than to help the students figure it out for themselves.

Although both of the high mastery teachers used motivational strategies that helped generate interest in the content, one was less successful than the other because he did not provide adequate instructional support or consistently hold his students accountable for understanding the material. He was good at conveying the inherent value of learning the content he taught, but less skilled at involving all of his students in learning activities and supporting their independent problem-solving efforts.

to students; (2) focus their attention on individual and collaborative learning goals and help them to achieve these goals; and (3) teach things that are worth learning, in ways that help students to appreciate their value.

In one sense, these considerations enlarge and complicate the challenge of motivating your students to learn, because they extend it to include aspects of your classroom management and your instructional program. In another sense, however, they simplify your motivational efforts by emphasizing that optimal instruction implies classroom management and motivational strategies and curriculum and instructional features that all function as mutually supportive components of a coherent program of effective teaching. The remainder of this book will focus on the motivational components, but bear in mind the need to incorporate these components within a larger program that includes compatible approaches to classroom management and to curriculum and instruction.

Successful use of the motivational strategies discussed in the remainder of the book implies that the prerequisites discussed in this chapter are already in place. To the extent that this assumption does not hold true in your classroom, your efforts to improve your students' motivation to learn will require adjustments in your approach to classroom management, your curriculum, or your instructional practices, in addition to implementation of appropriate motivational strategies.

NOTE

1. Instructional *scaffolding* is a general term for the task-assistance or simplification strategies that teachers use to bridge the gap between what students are capable of doing on their own and what they are capable of doing with help. Scaffolds help students progress from their current abilities toward the intended goal. As with the scaffolds used by house painters, the support provided by instructional scaffolds is temporary, adjustable, and removed when it is no longer needed. Examples of scaffolds include cognitive modeling (in which the teacher demonstrates task performance while articulating the thinking that guides it), prompts or cues that help students move on to the next step when they are temporarily stuck, and questions that help them to diagnose the reasons for errors and develop repair strategies.

REFERENCES

Ames, C. (1990). Motivation: What teachers need to know. *Teachers College Record, 91,* 409–421.

Ames, C. (1992). Classrooms: Goals, structures, and student motivation. *Journal of Educational Psychology, 84,* 261–271.

Ames, C., & Archer, J. (1988). Achievement goals in the classroom: Students' learning strategies and motivation processes. *Journal of Educational Psychology, 80,* 260–267.

Baumrind, D. (1991). The influence of parenting style on adolescent competence and substance abuse. *Journal of Early Adolescence, 11,* 56–94.

Beck, I., & McKeown, M. (1988). Toward meaningful accounts in history texts for young learners. *Educational Researcher, 17*(6), 31–39.

Blumenfeld, P. (1992). Classroom learning and motivation: Clarifying and expanding goal theory. *Journal of Educational Psychology, 84,* 272–281.

Brantlinger, E. (1993). *The politics of social class in secondary school: Views of affluent and impoverished youth.* New York: Teachers College Press.

Brophy, J. (1983). Classroom organization and management. *Elementary School Journal, 83,* 265–285.

Brophy, J. (1988). Educating teachers about managing classrooms and students. *Teaching and Teacher Education, 4,* 1–18.

Brophy, J. (1992a). Probing the subtleties of subject-matter teaching. *Educational Leadership, 49*(7), 4–8.

Brophy, J. (1992b). The *de facto* national curriculum in U.S. elementary social studies: Critique of a representative example. *Journal of Curriculum Studies, 24,* 401–447.

Brophy, J. (1996). *Teaching problem students.* New York: Guilford.

Brophy, J., & Alleman, J. (1991). Activities as instructional tools: A framework for analysis and evaluation. *Educational Researcher, 20*(4), 9–23.

Cabello, B., & Terrell, R. (1994). Making students feel like family: How teachers create warm and caring classroom climates. *Journal of Classroom Interaction, 29,* 17–23.

Christophel, D. (1990). The relationships among teacher immediacy behaviors, student motivation, and learning. *Communication Education, 39,* 323–340.

Clark, C., & Peterson, P. (1986). Teachers' thought processes. In M.C. Wittrock (Ed.), *Handbook of research on teaching* (3rd ed., pp. 255–296). New York: Macmillan.

Comer, J. (1980). *School power: Implications of an intervention project.* New York: The Free Press.

Doyle, W. (1986). Classroom organization and management. In M.C. Wittrock (Ed.), *Handbook of research on teaching* (3rd ed., pp. 392–431). New York: Macmillan.

Dreher, M., & Singer, H. (1989). Friendly texts and text-friendly teachers. *Theory Into Practice, 28,* 98–104.

Dweck, C., & Leggett, E. (1988). A social-cognitive approach to motivation and personality. *Psychological Review, 95,* 256–273.

Elliott, D., & Woodward, A. (Eds.). (1990). *Textbooks and schooling in the United States. 89th Yearbook of the National Society for the Study of Education, Part I.* Chicago: University of Chicago Press.

Epstein, J. (1989). Family structures and student motivation: A developmental perspective. In C. Ames & R. Ames (Eds.), *Research on motivation in education. Volume 3. Goals and cognitions* (pp. 259–295). San Diego: Academic Press.

Evertson, C., Emmer, E., Clements, B., & Worsham, M. (1994). *Classroom management for elementary teachers* (3rd ed.). Boston: Allyn & Bacon.

Evertson, C., & Harris, A. (1992). What we know about managing classrooms. *Educational Leadership, 49,* 74–78.

Frymier, A. (1993). The impact of teacher immediacy on students' motivation: Is it the same for all students? *Communication Education, 41,* 454–464.

Glasser, W. (1990). *The quality school: Managing students without coercion.* New York: Harper & Row.

Good, T., & Brophy, J. (1995). *Contemporary educational psychology* (5th ed.). White Plains, NY: Longman.

Good, T., & Brophy, J. (1997). *Looking in classrooms* (7th ed.). New York: Longman.

Goodlad, J. (1984). *A place called school.* New York: McGraw-Hill.

Gorham, J. (1988). The relationship between verbal teacher immediacy behaviors and student learning. *Communication Education, 37,* 40–53.

Hayes, C., Ryan, A., & Zseller, E. (1994). The middle-school child's perceptions of caring teachers. *American Journal of Education, 103,* 1–19.

Jones, V. (1996). Classroom management. In J. Sikula, T. Buttery, & E. Guyton (Eds.), *Handbook of research on teacher education* (Volume 2, pp. 503–521). New York: Macmillan.

Jones, V., & Jones, L. (1995). *Comprehensive classroom management* (4th ed.). Boston: Allyn & Bacon.

Maehr, M., & Midgley, C. (1991). Enhancing student motivation: A schoolwide approach. *Educational Psychologist, 26,* 399–427.

Marshall, H. (1988). In pursuit of learning-oriented classrooms. *Teaching and Teacher Education, 4,* 85–98.

McCaslin, M., & Good, T. (1992). Compliant cognition: The misalliance of management and instructional goals in current school reform. *Educational Researcher, 21*(3), 4–17.

Meece, J. (1994). The role of motivation in self-regulated learning. In D. Schunk & B. Zimmerman (Eds.), *Self-regulation of learning and performance: Issues and educational applications* (pp. 25–44). Hillsdale, NJ: Erlbaum.

Meece, J., & Holt, K. (1993). A pattern analysis of students' achievement goals. *Journal of Educational Psychology, 85,* 582–590.

Metz, M. (1978). *Classrooms and corridors: The crisis of authority in desegregated secondary schools.* Berkeley: University of California Press.

Nash, R. (1976). Pupils' expectations of their teachers. In M. Stubbs & S. Delamont (Eds.), *Explorations in classroom observation* (pp. 83–100). New York: Wiley.

Nicholls, J. (1984). Achievement motivation: Conceptions of ability, subjective experience, task choice, and performance. *Psychological Review, 91,* 328–346.

Prawat, R. (1989). Promoting access to knowledge, strategy, and disposition in students: A research synthesis. *Review of Educational Research, 59,* 1–41.

Purkey, W., & Novak, J. (1996). *Inviting school success: A self-concept approach to teaching, learning, and democratic practice* (3rd ed.). Belmont, CA: Wadsworth.

Resnick, L. (Ed.). (1989). *Knowing, learning, and instruction.* Hillsdale, NJ: Erlbaum.

Richmond, V., & McCroskey, J. (Eds.). (1992). *Power in the classroom: Communication, control, and concern.* Hillsdale, NJ: Erlbaum.

Rogers, C., & Freiberg, H.J. (1994). *Freedom to learn* (3rd ed.). New York: Merrill.

Schmuck, R., & Schmuck, P. (1991). The attitudes of adolescents in small-town America. *NASSP Bulletin, 75,* 85–90.

Skinner, E., & Belmont, M. (1993). Motivation in the classroom: Reciprocal effects of teacher behavior and student engagement across the school year. *Journal of Educational Psychology, 85,* 571–581.

Stodolsky, S. (1988). *The subject matters.* Chicago: University of Chicago Press.

Tyson-Bernstein, H. (1988). *A conspiracy of good intentions: America's textbook fiasco.* Washington, DC: Council for Basic Education.

Urdan, T., & Maehr, M. (1995). Beyond a two-goal theory of motivation and achievement: A case for social goals. *Review of Educational Research, 65,* 213–243.

Weinstein, C., & Mignano, A., Jr. (1993). *Elementary classroom management: Lessons from research and practice.* McGraw-Hill.

Wentzel, K. (1992). Motivation and achievement in adolescence: A multiple goals perspective. In D. Schunk & J. Meece (Eds.), *Student perceptions in the classroom* (pp. 287–306). Hillsdale, NJ: Erlbaum.

Supporting Students' Confidence as Learners

Chapter 1 focused on helping you to think about motivation and identify realistic motivational goals for your students. Chapter 2 focused on establishing your classroom as a learning community that both reflects and supports your efforts to motivate your students to learn. Beginning here in Chapter 3, I address these motivational efforts directly, working within the expectancy x value model. Chapters 3 and 4 focus on expectancy issues: protecting students' confidence as learners and providing extra support to those who have become discouraged.

Information about the expectancy aspects of motivation has been developed by studying people's reactions to achievement situations. *Achievement situations* require people to perform some goal-oriented task knowing that their performance will be evaluated. Some achievement situations pit people in direct competition with one another and produce winners and losers. Other achievement situations may not involve such personal competition, but do involve characterizing performance with reference to standards of excellence. If there is a single clear-cut goal, people either succeed or fail in their efforts to meet it. If the task allows for more graduated or varied assessment, the quality of people's performance may be characterized more comprehensively than by simply stating that they succeeded or failed.

The common element of achievement situations is that they require goal-oriented task performance that can be evaluated with reference to absolute standards of excellence or to performance norms established by some reference group (e.g., one's classmates). Subjective experiences of relative success or failure flow from these evaluations, viewed in the light of performance expectations (e.g., among students who earn a grade of B, any who expected a lower grade will feel successful but any who expected an A will feel that they failed to accomplish what they should have).

EARLY WORK ON TASK CHOICE AND GOAL SETTING IN ACHIEVEMENT SITUATIONS

Early work on achievement situations indicated that people approach these situations differently depending on the makeup of their achievement motivation. Atkinson (1964) noted that two key components of *achievement motivation* are motivation to succeed and motivation to avoid failure. In any given achievement situation, *motivation to succeed* is determined by the strength of one's overall need for achievement, one's estimate of the probability of succeeding on the task at hand, and the degree to which one values the rewards that such success would bring. Counterbalancing these components of motivation to succeed are the parallel components of *motivation to avoid failure*: the strength of one's overall need to avoid failure, one's estimate of the probability of failing the task, and the degree to which one fears the negative outcomes that such failure would bring (e.g., private disappointment, public embarrassment).

Individual differences in approach to achievement situations are predictable from the relative strengths of people's motivation to succeed and their motivation to avoid failure. When our motivation to succeed is stronger, we engage in the task willingly. When our motivation to avoid failure is stronger, we seek to avoid the task, or if that is not possible, to engage in it in such a way as to minimize the likelihood of failure.

Atkinson and Litwin (1960) showed that when task avoidance was not possible, people who focused on avoiding failure engaged in tasks in ways that helped them to achieve this goal, at least subjectively. People in this experiment played a ring-toss game. They were free to stand anywhere from 1 to 15 feet from the target peg. Those whose motivational patterns emphasized seeking success tended to toss their rings from 9–11 feet away. This was a moderate-difficulty, optimal-challenge distance: far enough away to challenge them (they would be successful only about half the time), but not so far away that success depended more on luck than skill.

In contrast, people whose achievement motivation profiles emphasized avoiding failure tended to respond in either of two contrasting ways. Some stood very close to the peg, so that most if not all of their tosses would be successful. These people ensured a high probability of success but their frequent "successes" didn't mean much because they were not significant accomplishments. Other people who sought to avoid failure were less obvious about it. In fact, they tossed the rings from the maximum distances of 12–15 feet away. This enabled them to give the appearance of taking risks and accepting challenges without really doing so. By standing so far away, they converted a skill task into a luck task. Any successes they achieved were causes for celebration but their frequent misses were not considered embarrassing failures because most tosses from 12–15 feet away were expected to be misses.

Other work by achievement motivation theorists confirmed these early findings. People who focus on achieving success tend to approach achievement situations willingly, to prefer tasks that are moderately difficult for them, and to engage in those tasks with emphasis on developing their skills. In contrast, people who focus on avoiding failure tend to fear achievement situations and thus to avoid them when possible. When required to engage in them, they do so in ways that minimize their risk of failure. One way is to stick with easy tasks and avoid risks. Another is to set goals so high that failure is virtually certain but does not carry the stigma that would be attached to failure to accomplish more realistic goals.

Attempts to draw teaching implications from early studies on achievement motivation are hampered by contrasts between the situations facing the people in those studies and the situations facing students in classrooms. The experiments often involved informal or play settings and engagement in physical activities such as ring toss games. Under these conditions, achievement motivation was maximized when the probability of success on the task was 50 percent. This does not mean that students' motivation will be maximized when classroom tasks produce a 50 percent success rate, however, for several reasons. First, later work clarified that the 50 percent figure refers to the person's subjective estimate of the probability of attaining his or her own goal and not to a score of 50 percent on some absolute scale. Thus, theoretically, teachers could maximize students' achievement motivation by inducing them to set performance goals at levels that the students believed they had 50 percent chances to attain. The absolute levels of performance corresponding to these subjective estimates of 50 percent chance of attainment would vary with individual students.

However, even this idea only takes into account success seeking; it does not consider fear of failure. Individuals who are driven more by fear of failure than by a desire to achieve success try to avoid achievement situations in which their chances of success hover around 50 percent. Instead, they seek situations in which the probability of success is either much higher, near 100 percent, or much lower, near zero (so that failure is not "real," because success is not really expected anyway). In the classroom, where activities are compulsory, performance is often public and failure has a variety of negative consequences, few if any students are likely to be maximally motivated in situations in which they believe they have only a 50 percent chance of succeeding. Most students prefer a much higher success probability.

Furthermore, given that most classroom tasks involve cognitive rather than physical work, a higher success rate is not merely preferable but necessary. Research indicates that learning proceeds most smoothly when it involves continuous progress achieved through small, easy steps with consistent success all along the way. Novelty and challenge are important, but overly difficult tasks produce confusion and discouragement. The degree of cognitive strain that would be produced by tasks that allowed students only a 50 percent success rate would be so great as to discourage most students and make learning unduly difficult for the rest.

RECENT WORK ON GOAL ORIENTATIONS AND RELATED CONCEPTS

Research on people's thinking and behavior in achievement situations has continued, but its emphasis has shifted from achievement needs to achievement goals. Also, it has broadened from recreational tasks and settings to include learning tasks in classrooms. Finally, it has broadened from only measuring the difficulty levels of goals to describing larger motivational patterns that include goal setting and related task engagement strategies.

Achievement motivation research initially established that effort and persistence on achievement tasks are greater in people who set goals of moderate difficulty (neither too hard nor too easy for their current abilities), who seriously commit themselves to pursuing these goals rather than treat them as mere "pie-in-the-sky" hopes, and who concentrate on trying to achieve success rather than on trying to avoid failure (Dweck & Elliott, 1983). As this work extended to include more cognitive factors, information was developed about the role of the following perceptions and concepts:

- *Effort-outcome covariation:* Effort and persistence are greater when people perceive a continuing connection between the level of effort they invest in a task and the level of mastery that they achieve (Cooper, 1979).
- *Internal locus of control:* Effort and persistence are greater when people believe that the potential to control outcomes (e.g., achieve success on the task) lies within themselves rather than in external factors that they cannot control (Stipek & Weisz, 1981; Thomas, 1980).
- *Concept of self as origin rather than pawn:* Effort and persistence are greater when people believe that they can bring about desired outcomes through their own actions (act as origins) rather than feeling that they are pawns whose fate is determined by factors beyond their control (deCharms, 1976).

Recent work on the expectancy aspects of motivation includes these and many other cognitive features. Three lines of work have been especially productive: research on implicit theories of ability, causal attributions, and self-efficacy perceptions.

Implicit Theories of Ability

Carol Dweck and her colleagues have explored the connections between people's goal setting and behavior in achievement situations and their implicit theories of ability. The researchers' work began with a description of the contrasting ways in which two groups of children responded to an experimental concept-formation task that allowed them to succeed on the first eight problems but then encounter four problems that were too difficult for them. The children were asked to think out loud as they worked on the problems. Soon after the onset of the more difficult problems, *helpless* children began to define themselves as having failed and to give reasons for their failure, typically attributing it to limited ability. Besides denigrating their abilities, they began to express negative affect toward the task, to make pessimistic predictions about their future performance, and to show declines in the sophistication of their strategies. In summary, helpless children quickly perceived themselves to be failing, construed these failures as indicators of limited ability, and "became mired in them as past and future successes seemed to recede from their grasp" (Dweck, 1991, p. 203).

Mastery-oriented children responded to this task much more productively. When they encountered the more difficult problems, they did not become upset or talk about how they were failing. Instead, they redoubled their concentration on the task and began issuing more self-instructions—planning and instructing themselves in strategies designed to overcome their difficulties. Also, instead of losing confidence and beginning to predict continued failure, they maintained positive affect and spoke of meeting the challenge of mastering the more difficult problems. Most maintained or even increased the sophistication of their strategies. In summary, "the mastery-oriented children appeared to see failure as an interlude between past and future successes and as an opportunity for new learning and mastery" (Dweck, 1991, p. 203).

The next stage in the research was aimed at understanding why helpless children react to failure as though their ability is being assessed and discredited, whereas mastery-oriented children react to it as an opportunity for learning. Elliott and Dweck (1988) showed that these contrasting response patterns were linked to contrasting goals. Children who established *learning goals* focused on learning something new or mastering the task. Consequently, they processed information in terms of its relevance for problem solving and responded to errors as indications that they needed to adjust their strategies. In contrast, children who set *performance goals* were more concerned about gaining favorable judgments of their competence than about learning something new. Consequently, they processed information primarily in terms of its relevance for assessing their ability. This made them vulnerable to the helpless pattern because when they encountered failure, they tended to view it as calling their ability into question. Once this occurred they were prone to lose confidence, become upset, and begin to use less sophisticated strategies.

At this point, Dweck and her colleagues had shown that children with comparable ability levels may respond very differently in achievement situations. Those who set learning goals tend to adopt a mastery orientation and focus on improving their ability, whereas those who set performance goals tend to focus on displaying their ability and are prone to adopt a helpless orientation if they perceive that they have failed to do so. To explain why children might follow such contrasting patterns, Dweck (1991) suggested that children with different goals have different conceptions of ability—that is to say, they have different implicit theories about the nature of their intelligence. Two contrasting theories are the entity theory and the incremental theory.

Children who subscribe to the *entity theory* think of intelligence as a fixed entity over which they have no control. In contrast, children who hold an *incremental theory* believe that intelligence can be increased incrementally through effort. Entity theorists of ability are more likely to set performance goals in achievement situations, whereas incremental theorists are more likely to set learning goals.

Implications for the Classroom

The classroom implications of Dweck's work are straightforward. As a teacher, encourage your students to adopt incremental theories rather than entity theories of ability, to set learning goals rather than performance goals, and to adopt a mastery orientation rather than a helpless orientation to achievement situations.

Encouraging learning goals rather than performance goals is accomplished primarily by establishing your class as the kind of learning community described in Chapter 2. This will focus your students' attention on self-improvement rather than comparisons with classmates. It also will lend credibility to your efforts to counter whatever ego-protective behavior that does occur by reminding students that mistakes are part of learning, that ordinarily we move toward mastery through successive approximations rather than attain it quickly in one or two giant steps, and that the idea in your classroom is to learn, not to compete.

You can encourage the incremental theory of ability and a mastery orientation toward learning activities by portraying these activities as opportunities to acquire (not just to display) knowledge or skill and by giving feedback to students in ways that reinforce this idea. Where relevant, help students to see how an activity fits into a larger learning unit or strand (e.g., "We've been learning how to compose well-structured paragraphs. Starting today, we're going to extend this by learning how to combine a sequence of paragraphs into a well-structured composition that starts with a clear statement of purpose and then builds toward a conclusion.").

When giving feedback to the class as a whole or to individuals, phrase your comments so as to stimulate appreciation of accomplishments to date and imply confidence that ultimate goals will be attained (e.g., "You've done a good job of establishing your purpose in the first paragraph and structuring each paragraph around a main idea. However, the idea flow across paragraphs was a little choppy. As you revise [or in your next composition], take time to outline the flow of ideas so that your argument builds step-by-step from start to finish, and use this outline to sequence your paragraphs. Then you'll have a nicely constructed argument!"). [Notice that nothing in this example says anything directly about the students' abilities or the teacher's confidence that they will be successful. Yet, both by what it does and what it does not say, the statement implies that the teacher is pleased (or at least satisfied) with the students' progress, unbothered (or at least unsurprised) by the need for improvements in some aspects of performance, and fully expecting to see those improvements emerge as students continue to develop their expertise.]

Causal Attributions

Bernard Weiner (1992) and other attribution theorists have focused on the *causal attributions* that people make in achievement situations—the explanations they generate to explain their behavior. Some causal attributions address task value aspects of motivation (e.g., What benefits do I expect to derive from engaging in this task?). However, attribution theorists have focused on people's causal attributions for the level of performance they achieved on a task (e.g., Why did I fail that math test?), and the implications of these attributions concerning expectations about future performance (e.g., I must not be very smart in math, so I'm never going to do very well on math tests). People are most likely to engage in attributional thinking when what actually occurs is much different from what they expected to occur, and especially when their performance falls below their expectations (Clifford, 1986; Whitley & Frieze, 1985).

Causal attributions generated during or after a performance are likely to affect subsequent motivation in that situation and others like it. The effects will depend on the nature of the causes to which the performance is attributed. Causal attributions have been distinguished according to whether they are used to explain perceived success or perceived failure. Furthermore, both success attributions and failure attributions have been classified according to whether the attributed causes are internal or external to the person, controllable or uncontrollable by the person, and stable or unstable across situations.

Research on causal attributions for performance has shown that effort and persistence are greater when we attribute our performance to internal and controllable causes rather than to external or uncontrollable causes. *Concerning explanations for successful performance, optimal patterns of motivation are associated with attributions of successes to the combination of sufficient ability and reasonable effort.* Sufficient ability implies that we entered the achievement situation already possessing whatever abilities were needed or that we were able to develop those abilities in the process of responding to the task. Reasonable effort implies that we had to apply ourselves in order to succeed, but we did not have to extend ourselves to the limits of our capacities. That is, we were able to succeed through relatively normal levels of effort that we would expect to apply in any achievement situation, rather than only through heroic efforts that we would not be able to sustain on a daily basis.

Attributing a successful performance to internal and mostly stable and controllable causes gives us reason to believe that we will continue to succeed on this and similar tasks in the future. We would have less reason for confidence if we attributed our success to more external, less stable and controllable causes (e.g., we were successful because this task happened to be an easy one; we lucked into the solution; we got unexpected help that we probably would not get the next time).

Concerning explanations for unsuccessful performance, effort and persistence are greater when we attribute our failures to internal but controllable causes such as insufficient knowledge (of task-relevant information or response strategies) *or insufficient effort* (if we did not prepare or concentrate as much as we should have). These failure attributions provide a basis for believing that we can improve performance and ultimately achieve success (by acquiring the needed information or response strategies or by increasing our level of effort). We would have less basis for confidence in improved performance if we attributed our failure to external causes (e.g., poor textbook or teacher). Worse yet, we would establish a basis for continued failure expectations if we attributed our failure to the internal cause of low ability, especially if we viewed this cause as stable and uncontrollable (i.e., if we held an entity theory of ability).

Implications for the Classroom

Again, implications for the classroom seem straightforward. As a teacher, help your students learn to attribute their successes to the combination of sufficient ability and reasonable effort, and to attribute their failures to (temporary) lack of task-relevant information or response strategies (or to lack of effort, where this has been the case). At the same time, avoid leading students to infer that their failures are due to fixed ability limitations that are beyond their control.

Success attributions ordinarily should be implied rather than stated directly, so as to avoid calling students' attention to self-worth issues. However, at least occasionally you might wish to give feedback that expresses appreciation for effort and reinforces confidence in abilities (e.g., "I appreciate the careful work that you put into your compositions. It's really paid off—that's a set of compositions you can be proud of! Your writing is very clear and interesting to read."). Failure attributions ordinarily should be expressed only privately with individuals rather than publicly with the class, unless the class as a whole has performed poorly on an assignment or test (in which case, unless you have good reason to chide students for poor effort, you might tell them that their poor performance was surprising given your experience with previous classes, that it tells you that you didn't teach key ideas or skills effectively this time, and that therefore you'll reteach and make sure that they attain your learning goals).

Individual students may verbalize attributions to low ability (e.g., "I can't do math.") either spontaneously or in response to your questions about why they "blew" an assignment. When this occurs, gently but firmly refuse to accept this explanation. Instead, suggest that the student has the ability to succeed but failed to do so because he lacked key knowledge or addressed the task using an ineffective strategy (or if relevant, because he failed to put forth serious efforts to attain the task's goal). If possible, cite direct evidence that the student possesses the needed ability (e.g., successful performance on similar tasks in the past). Otherwise, construct a successful scenario that includes this implication (e.g., based on your general experience at the grade level and your personal observations of this student, you know that he will soon be successful if he trusts you and makes an honest effort to do what you ask him to do). If you are unable to "turn around" such a student immediately, at least make it clear that you have confidence in his abilities and do not accept his low estimation of them.

Self-Efficacy Perceptions

Research has shown that effort and persistence in achievement situations are greater when people possess a sense of efficacy or competence—that is, confidence that they have the ability (including the specific strategies needed) to succeed on the task if they choose to invest the necessary effort (Bandura, 1989; Bandura & Schunk, 1981; Schunk, 1991; Schunk & Hanson, 1985).

Self-efficacy perceptions are judgments of one's performance capabilities in given achievement situations. These judgments can influence task choice and the quality of task engagement. They are especially important in situations that contain novel, unpredictable, or possibly stressful features. People with a high sense of self-efficacy are likely to approach achievement situations with confidence and engage in tasks willingly and persistently. However, people who doubt their capabilities for acquiring the needed skills are likely to avoid achievement situations, or if this is not possible, to give up easily when they encounter frustration or failure. In these and other respects, the implications of high versus low self-efficacy perceptions are similar to those for mastery versus helpless orientations and for attributing performance outcomes to internal and controllable causes versus external or uncontrollable causes.

Self-efficacy theorists have been especially active in identifying ways that teachers can support their students' self-efficacy perceptions and in the process optimize their motivation and task engagement patterns. Studies by Albert Bandura, Dale Schunk, and others have shown that increases in self-efficacy perceptions, in task effort and persistence, and in ultimate performance levels can be achieved by (1) encouraging students to set specific and difficult but attainable goals; (2) modeling and cueing effective task response strategies; (3) providing feedback that helps students to achieve success; and (4) making attributional statements that help them to appreciate that they are developing their abilities by accepting challenges and applying consistent effort. These findings provide the basis for many of the suggestions about protecting your students' success expectations that are given in the remainder of this chapter and in Chapter 4.

INTEGRATION OF EXPECTANCY-RELATED CONCEPTS AND PRINCIPLES

The motivational concepts and principles introduced in this chapter were derived from different theoretical traditions. Some refer to general dispositions, while others refer to thinking or behavior in specific situations. Some refer to perceptions, some to cognitive inferences, some to affective experiences, and some to strategies for accomplishing goals or solving problems. All of them, however, refer to the expectancy (versus value) aspects of motivation in situations that call for striving to accomplish goals. Taken together, they compose a rich portrait of adaptive versus maladaptive patterns of response to these achievement situations (see Table 3.1).

TABLE 3.1. General Dispositions, Situational Goals, Subjective Experiences, and Response Strategies Relating to the Expectancy Aspects of Motivation in Achievement Situations

Productive/Adaptive Alternatives	Unproductive/Maladaptive Alternatives
GENERAL DISPOSITIONS	
• Perceived effort-outcome covariation	• Perceived lack of covariation
• Internal locus of control	• External locus of control
• Concept of self as origin	• Concept of self as pawn
• Incremental theory of ability	• Entity theory of ability
• Outcomes attributed to internal and controllable causes	• Outcomes attributed to external or uncontrollable causes
• Perceived self-efficacy	• Perceived lack of efficacy
SITUATIONAL GOALS/FOCUS	
• Learning, Mastery Goals	• Performance goals
• Focus on Task	• Focus on ego, self-worth protection
• Seek to acquire knowledge, skill	• Seek to meet "sufficient success" criteria
• Seek optimal challenges, flow experiences	• Minimize risk of failure
SUBJECTIVE EXPERIENCES AND COPING RESPONSES	
If success is achieved easily:	
• Complete task, integrate learning	• Complete task, feel relieved/reinforced
• Attribute success to sufficient ability plus reasonable effort	• Attribute success to ability alone or to ability plus external, uncontrollable causes
If difficulties are encountered:	
• Continued focus on task	• Task focus invaded by self/ego concerns
• Continued emphasis on deep-processing strategies	• Increased reliance on surface-level strategies
• Calm, analytic problem solving	• Increasingly anxious, frustrated
• Sustained confidence	• Fear of failure, plunging confidence, eventual learned helplessness
If success is not achieved:	
• Attribute failure to remediable deficits in knowledge, strategy selection, or effort	• Attribute failure to fixed limitations in ability
• Seek to acquire needed knowledge and skill, eventually reach mastery	• Seek to avoid such tasks if possible; otherwise, defend against perception of incompetence or at least hide one's incompetence from others

Experiments involving motivational treatments have begun to combine elements drawn from different theoretical traditions into more complete and powerful packages that simultaneously address several of the expectancy-related aspects of motivation summarized in Table 3.1. For example, Bell and Kanevsky (1996) blended motivational instruction into a series of mathematics lessons taught to second graders. The motivational instruction incorporated three components: (1) learning goal, (2) nature of learning, and (3) attribution training. Instruction relating to the learning goal emphasized the importance of persistence in putting forth effort (i.e., "that you don't give up and that you practice until you learn"). Instruction relating to the nature of learning was designed to develop appropriate expectations about time and effort and inoculate students against becoming overly frustrated by initial failures (i.e., "It often takes lots of hard work and lots of tries and lots of time and lots of mistakes before something is learned."). Attribution training sought to develop students' awareness that learning results from their own efforts. It was supported by a poster summarizing the four parts in a self-attribution strategy developed to help students sustain their learning efforts: (1) I can learn, (2) Where to start?, (3) What do I already know?, and (4) Help? This support encouraged students to first look to their own resources when faced with difficulties and then if necessary get help, but not give up.

Shawaker and Dembo (1996) incorporated a five-element motivational component into reading comprehension instruction for middle-school students. The five elements were as follows:

1. *Task analysis:* Students were taught a four-step procedure that involved first reading the entire paragraph reflectively, then identifying its main idea, then deciding what type of paragraph it was (concept, generalization, sequence, process, or comparison), and finally marking evidence within the paragraph that supported the students' decisions.
2. *Proximal goal-setting:* Students were taught to work through the task analysis sequence one step at a time, using the steps as proximal goals to guide their information processing.
3. *Reciprocal teaching:* Students took turns with the teacher or with other students in modeling task processes, thinking aloud while doing so.
4. *Attribution training:* Attributional statements were incorporated into the feedback given to students, frequently reinforcing the notion that they had the ability to succeed on the task if they applied themselves toward doing so.
5. *Self-talk reminders:* Students occasionally were reminded to use their own self-talk to guide their behavior (e.g., "Talk yourself through the steps and be sure to compliment yourself when you work hard.").

SUPPORTING STUDENTS' CONFIDENCE AS LEARNERS

To encourage your students to adopt the more adaptive of the alternatives shown in Table 3.1, help them to maintain their confidence as learners and approach learning activities with productive goals and strategies. In this section I suggest ways for you to take these motivational concerns into account when planning the three major features of your teaching: curriculum, instruction, and assessment.

Curriculum: Program for Success

The simplest way to ensure that students expect success is to make sure that they achieve it consistently so that they can adjust to each new step without much confusion or frustration. However, two points need to be made about this strategy to clarify that it does not mean assigning mostly under-challenging busy work.

First, success here means gradual mastery of appropriately challenging objectives, not quick, easy successes achieved through automatic application of overlearned skills to overly familiar tasks. You should pace your students through the curriculum as briskly as they can progress without undue frustration. Programming for success is a means toward the end of maximizing your students' ultimate achievement, not an end in itself.

Second, keep in mind your role as the teacher. Potential levels of success depend not only on the difficulty of the task itself, but also on the degree to which you prepare students through advance instruction and scaffold their learning efforts through guidance and feedback. A task that would be too difficult for students left to their own devices might be just right when learned with your help. In fact, learning theorists believe that instruction should focus on the *zone of proximal development,* which refers to the range of knowledge and skills that students are not yet ready to learn on their own but can learn with help from their teachers (Tharp & Gallimore, 1988).

Programming for success involves continually challenging students within their zones of proximal development, yet making it possible for them to meet these challenges by providing sufficient instruction, guidance, and feedback. You may need to provide extra instruction to slower students, monitor their progress more closely, and give them briefer or easier assignments if they cannot handle the regular ones even with extra help. Even so, continue to expect these students to put forth reasonable effort and progress as far as their abilities will allow. Don't give up on them or allow them to give up on themselves. Instead, continue to encourage them and convey positive expectations concerning their ability to achieve success with your help. I will discuss this further in Chapter 4.

One paradoxical feature of the success expectancy aspects of student motivation is that *self-efficacy perceptions are optimized when they are not at issue at all. That is, learning tends to proceed most smoothly when students are concentrating on the task rather than on evaluating their performance, even successful performance.* In effect, then, student motivation is optimized not only by teacher techniques traditionally recognized as promoting such motivation, but also by techniques traditionally considered instructional rather than motivational: clarity and specificity of explanation and demonstration, modeling of task performance strategies, and provision of specific corrective feedback. Of these, modeling of task-related thinking and problem-solving strategies is especially important, because so many school tasks are primarily cognitive rather than physical (so that the processes used to accomplish them cannot be observed directly).

Theoretically, any task that lies within the zone of proximal development is appropriate for a given student. In practice, however, the difficulty level of tasks is determined not only by the task itself but by your success in providing clear and complete instruction. If you present instruction that students can understand and follow with ease, successful performance and perceptions of efficacy are likely to follow. However, low efficacy perceptions and feelings of anxiety and frustration would emerge if you explained the same task so poorly so that your students experienced difficulty with it. This would be true even if you kept reassuring the students that the task was well within their abilities. This is just one example of how instructional and motivational strategies are intimately linked and need to be mutually supportive in order to be effective.

Instruction: Help Students to Set Goals, Evaluate Their Progress, and Recognize Effort-Outcome Linkages

Teach Goal Setting, Performance Appraisal, and Self-Reinforcement

Students' reactions to their own performance depend not just on the absolute levels of success they achieve but also on their perceptions of what this means. Some students may not fully appreciate their accomplishments unless you help them to identify and use appropriate evaluation standards. You can provide such help in your everyday teaching, especially when introducing assignments and when providing students with feedback about their performance.

The process begins with *goal setting*. Research indicates that setting goals and making a commitment to trying to reach these goals increase performance levels (Bandura & Schunk, 1981; Locke & Latham, 1990). Goal setting is especially effective when goals are (1) *proximal* rather than distal, that is, they refer to a task to be attempted here and now rather than to some ultimate goal for the distant future, (2) *specific* (e.g., complete a page of math problems with no more than one mistake) rather than global (e.g., do a good job), and (3) *challenging* (difficult but reachable) rather than too easy or too hard.

For example, suppose you have given a mathematics assignment that involves 20 problems of varying difficulty. If some of your students have been struggling in mathematics, it may not be realistic to expect them to solve all of the problems correctly on their own. Therefore, you might ask them to adopt the goals of making a serious attempt to solve each problem and persisting until confident that at least 15 of the problems have been solved correctly. This is likely to lead to more persistent and higher quality problem-solving efforts than asking them to "do the best you can" or "do as many as you can." These suggestions are too vague to function as specific challenges toward which students can work as goals.

For a brief assignment, meeting the instructional objective is the appropriate goal. However, perfect performance on more comprehensive assignments or tests is not a realistic goal for many students, and these students may need help in formulating challenging but reachable goals. In the case of a long series of activities that ultimately leads to some distal goal, establish proximal goals for each successive activity and, as students accomplish these goals, make them aware of the linkages between these advances and achievement of the ultimate goal (Bandura & Schunk, 1981; Morgan, 1985). Proximal goals usually seem attainable with reasonable effort even to students who doubt their capacities for attaining ultimate goals. Thus, if you keep these students moving forward (acquiring more knowledge and skill in a domain) as they pursue proximal goals, eventually they will attain ultimate goals as well. For additional information about goal setting, see Box 3.1.

Goal setting is not enough by itself; students must show *goal commitment* by taking goals seriously and committing themselves to trying to reach them. You may need to negotiate goal setting with some students, or at least provide them with guidance and stimulate them to think about their performance potential. One way is to list potential goals and ask students to commit themselves to a particular subset (and to associated levels of effort). Another is performance *contracting,* in which students formally contract for a certain level of effort or performance in exchange for specified grades or rewards (Tollefson et al., 1984). This method is time consuming and may call more attention to rewards than is desirable, but it does ensure active teacher–student negotiation about goal setting and it formalizes students' commitments to goals. Students are more likely to follow through on these commitments when they have had a voice in establishing them.

In giving feedback, help students to use *appropriate standards for judging levels of success.* In particular, teach them to compare their work with absolute standards or with their own previous performance rather than with the performance of classmates. Provide accurate feedback about specific responses (i.e., errors will need to be labeled as such if they are to be recognized and corrected), but also provide encouragement in your more general evaluative comments (e.g., "You've shown good understanding of the events that led up to the Revolutionary War, but not the reasons why the colonies were able to win it. Go over those reasons again and discuss them with your study partner until you're sure that you know them."). You might note levels of success achieved in meeting established goals or describe accomplishments with reference to what is reasonable to expect rather than with reference to absolute perfection (e.g., "You know how to do the basic steps in multiplying and reducing fractions. The errors you're still making are mostly computation errors. I think you can eliminate most of them if you double check your answers before you turn in your assignment.").

Box 3.1.   Things to Keep in Mind When Helping Students Set Goals

Goal setting can be a powerful motivational technique if implemented effectively, but it also can be used counterproductively. Therefore, keep in mind the following qualifications on its use (Bandura & Wood, 1989; Deci, 1992; Reeve, 1996).

First, make sure that your suggested goals are realistic for the student. Difficult goals are likely to yield better performance than easier goals, but beyond some optimal level, goals become too difficult. If you consistently urge students to perform beyond their capacities, you will lose your credibility. Students will begin to find your urgings irritating or depressing rather than encouraging and energizing. Especially for tasks that must be confronted day after day, establish goals that call for reasonable effort rather than extraordinary effort. Most students will find it exhilarating to push themselves to their limits on occasion, but few will want to be required to do so on a daily basis.

Second, setting highly specific goals is most appropriate when the task is relatively uninteresting, repetitive, or amenable to quantitative performance assessment (e.g., arithmetic computation, spelling, typing, free-throw shooting). Imposition of highly specific goals may undermine intrinsic motivation and lead to a lower quality of performance on complex tasks that require creativity or cognitive flexibility. In giving instructions for a composition or research assignment, for example, it is better to focus on qualitative goals (e.g., build a coherent argument that leads to and supports your conclusions; identify information relevant to your research question and then synthesize it so as to answer the question or indicate what additional information will be needed in order to develop an answer), rather than to be overly specific about the formal aspects of the product to be developed (e.g., the composition will consist of at least 300 words and will include at least five paragraphs, each beginning with a topic sentence; the research report will include reference to at least 10 sources). Students should see the goals as helpful guides to their learning efforts, not as externally imposed hoops that they must jump through.

Finally, attempts to influence students' notions of reasonable effort are most likely to be successful if goals are established before the students have gained experience with the task and begun to set their own goals informally. A difficult but reasonable teacher-suggested goal might be viewed as a worthwhile challenge initially, but students might reject the same goal if it were imposed later after they had established expectations for themselves. Goal-setting programs that rely on externally imposed goals tend to lose their effectiveness over time, so it will be important for you to help your students learn to evaluate their own work and reset goals in response to their growing expertise.

Some students need *specific, detailed feedback* concerning both the strengths and weaknesses of their performance (Butler, 1987; Elawar & Corno, 1985; Krampen, 1987). Those who have only a vague appreciation of when and why they have done well or poorly will need not only general evaluative feedback but also concepts and language that they can use to describe their performance with precision. This is especially true for compositions, research projects, laboratory experiments, and other complex activities that are evaluated qualitatively.

Concerning compositions, for example, you might comment on the relevance, accuracy, and completeness of the content; the organization and sequencing of the content into a coherent beginning, middle, and end; the structuring of paragraphs to feature main ideas; the appropriateness of the style and vocabulary; and the mechanics of grammar, spelling, and punctuation. To the extent that performance is unsatisfactory, provide additional instruction and opportunities for improvement, along with continued encouragement that realistic goals will be achieved if the student continues to put forth reasonable effort.

Students who have been working toward specific proximal goals and who have the concepts and language needed to evaluate their performance accurately are in a position to *reinforce themselves* for their successes. Many do this habitually, but others will need encouragement to check their work and to take credit for their successes—that is, to attribute these successes to the fact that they had the ability and were willing to make the required effort. If necessary, compare the students' current accomplishments with performance samples from earlier in the year or have them keep portfolios, graphs, or other records to document their progress. Schunk (1996) found that arranging for students to periodically assess their progressively improving performance capabilities had positive effects on their motivation and learning.

Help Students to Recognize Effort–Outcome Linkages

Blend motivational elements into your everyday teaching that will help your students to appreciate the connections between learning efforts and learning outcomes. The following strategies are useful for developing an internal locus of control and a sense of efficacy in students and helping them to recognize that they can achieve success if they put forth reasonable effort.

First, *model* beliefs about effort–outcome linkages when talking to students about your own learning and when demonstrating tasks by thinking out loud as you work through them. When you encounter frustration or temporary failure in performing everyday classroom activities, model confidence that you will succeed if you persist and search for a better strategy or for some error in your application of strategies already tried.

Also, stress effort–outcome linkages when *socializing your students or giving them feedback.* Explain that your curriculum goals and instructional practices have been established to make it possible for them to succeed if they apply themselves. If necessary, reassure certain students that persistence (perhaps augmented by extra help) eventually pays off. Some students may need repeated statements of your confidence in their abilities to do the work or your willingness to accept slow progress so long as they consistently put forth reasonable effort.

Extra socialization will be needed with low achievers when grades must be assigned according to fixed common standards or comparisons with peers or norms rather than according to the degree of effort expended or the degree of success achieved in meeting individually negotiated goals. You may need to socialize low achievers to take satisfaction in receiving Bs or Cs when such grades represent, for them, significant accomplishments. When this is the case, express to these students (and their parents) recognition of their accomplishments and appreciation of the progress they are making.

Acknowledge that learning takes effort, but *portray effort as investment rather than risk.* Make your students aware that learning may take time and involve confusion or mistakes, but that persistence and careful work eventually yield knowledge or skill mastery. Furthermore, help them to appreciate that such mastery not only represents success on the immediate task but also provides them with knowledge or skills that will make them more prepared to handle higher-level tasks in the future. If they give up on a task because of frustration or fear of failure, they cheat themselves out of this growth potential.

In characterizing students' achievement progress, *portray skill development as incremental and domain-specific.* Help your students to appreciate that their intellectual abilities are open to improvement rather than fixed and that they possess a great many such abilities rather than just a few. Difficulties in learning usually occur not because students lack ability or do not make an effort but because they lack experience with the type of task involved. With patience, persistence, and help from you, your students can acquire knowledge and skills specific to the domain that the task represents. Development of such domain-specific knowledge and skills will enable them to succeed on this task and others like it. Difficulty in learning mathematics need not imply difficulty in learning other subjects, and within mathematics, difficulty in learning to graph coordinates need not mean difficulty in learning to solve differential equations or to understand geometric relationships. Even within a particular problem area, students can expect to build up knowledge and skills gradually if they persistently apply themselves, accept your help, and do not lose patience or give up whenever success is not achieved easily.

In monitoring performance and giving feedback, *focus on mastery.* Stress the quality of your students' task engagement and the degree to which they are making continuous progress toward mastery rather than comparisons with how their classmates are doing. Treat failures as indicators of a need for additional instruction and learning opportunities, not as evidence of lack of ability in the domain. For additional information about giving feedback to students, see Box 3.2.

Box 3.2.   Attributional Aspects of Feedback

Research done or influenced by attribution theorists offers clear guidelines for feedback following student failures (i.e., attribute the failures to lack of information, strategy knowledge, or effort, but not to lack of ability). Implications are less clear, however, concerning feedback following successful performance. Opinions vary on the degree to which feedback should emphasize attributions of success to ability or effort.

In one study that addressed the matter directly, Schunk (1983) found that attributing students' success to (high) ability was more effective than attributing their success to effort or even to ability plus effort. Apparently, even mentioning effort can cause some students to doubt their abilities. Also, effort attributions tend to remind students that their performance is being evaluated by an authority figure, whereas ability attributions tend to be experienced simply as praise. Findings by Hau and Salili (1996) and by Koestner, Zuckerman, and Koestner (1987) suggest similar conclusions.

Nicholls (1989) questioned the wisdom of attributions that stress ability, noting that you can't make all of your students feel smart. As alternatives, he suggested allowing students to evaluate their own work as much as possible so that they are less likely to see it as teacher imposed, and also giving feedback that stresses intrinsic or "motivation to learn" reasons for successful engagement.

Covington (1992) questioned the wisdom of attributing success to effort, and in particular, cautioned against stating that students achieved success because they worked very hard. To the extent that the students are aware that other students achieved similar success without working so hard, they may appreciate your praise of their hard work but at the same time infer that you believe their ability is limited.

These cautions are well taken. Ordinarily, the notions that students have the ability to succeed, are making good progress, and are putting forth sufficient effort should be implied rather than stated directly in your feedback. Students who are clearly achieving well below their capabilities need to be informed of this and motivated to commit themselves to higher goals. However, effort probably should not be mentioned at all if it is satisfactory. If you want to express appreciation to students whose efforts are more than satisfactory, do so in ways that do not imply limited ability (e.g., note their careful work or their willingness to stick with a problem until they solve it, but don't tell them that they succeeded because they worked hard).

With struggling students, feedback usually should not emphasize praise of hard work so much as encouragement of persistence and patience to allow time for the relevant skills to develop. Focus struggling students' attention on their accomplishments (e.g., "Yes, it's hard, but look at what you are doing!"). Portray difficult work not so much as hard and therefore requiring strenuous effort but as challenging them to stay goal oriented and persist in using adaptive learning strategies (e.g., "Don't work hard, work smart!").

When giving help, emphasize instrumental help (probing and prompting) rather than gratuitous help (giving answers). The latter, especially when

---

Box 3.2.   Attributional Aspects of Feedback—*Concluded*

unsolicited by the student, is likely to be perceived as evidence that you believe that the student lacks the ability needed to succeed on the task. The same message may be communicated through gratuitous praise of minor accomplishments or gratuitous expressions of sympathy to students who are struggling, especially if these affective supports are not accompanied by forms of assistance designed to help the student master the task (Graham, 1984; Graham & Barker, 1990; Horn, 1985; Meyer, 1982).

Assessment: Emphasize Informative Feedback, Not Grading or Comparing Students

Even if it were not required for report card purposes, testing and other assessment of students' progress would be necessary to provide needed feedback, both to you as the teacher and to your students as learners. Therefore, help your students to understand that getting and following up productively on informative feedback is an integral part of the learning process. Include this idea in molding your classroom into the kind of learning community described in Chapter 2.

If assessment methods are goal-oriented and integrated within a larger program of curriculum and instruction, they can provide valuable information to students. When students are clear about what they are expected to learn and how this learning will be evaluated, they can guide their learning efforts accordingly. After they engage in an evaluation activity and get the feedback it generates, both you and they will have a clearer picture of areas of strength in which they have progressed nicely as well as areas of weakness in which they need follow-up instruction and learning activities. Certain mistakes may require only brief correction (e.g., minor factual or computational errors), but others that suggest misunderstanding of basic concepts or principles may require more sustained follow-up.

Unfortunately, classroom evaluation and grading systems also have the potential to undermine students' motivation and learning strategies: To the extent that they are perceived as controlling students by placing extrinsic pressures on them to study or do homework, evaluation and grading systems are likely to erode the students' intrinsic motivation. To the extent that test content is confined to matching or fill-in-the-blank items, students are likely to emphasize surface-level memorizing strategies rather than deeper-level information processing strategies as they study the material. To the extent that you have been overly specific in specifying the nature and content of test items, students may narrow their focus to preparing to answer the kinds of questions they expect on the test, rather than engaging in more integrative learning.

Finally, to the extent that the demands of tests are not well matched to the knowledge and skill levels of some of your students, the desired covariation between effort and outcome (grades) will be missing. Some students will learn that they can get high grades without exerting much effort, and others will learn that they cannot get high grades no matter how hard they try. These undesirable effects of classroom assessment and grading systems are always lurking as potential problems to teachers, for reasons explained in Chapter 1. However, motivational theorists and researchers have developed suggestions to help you to maximize desirable effects and minimize undesirable effects of your evaluation and grading strategies (Ames, 1992; Baron & Wolf, 1996; Butler, 1987; Butler & Nisan, 1986; Covington & Omelich, 1984; Crooks, 1988; Natriello, 1987; Thomas, 1993; Wlodkowski & Jaynes, 1990).

Uses and Forms of Assessment

Think of assessment as part of your larger program of curriculum and instruction—a set of tools to help your students reach your instructional goals. Viewed in this light, assessment is important as a way for you to keep track of the progress of the class as a whole and alert you to the need for adjustments in your instructional plans, not just to provide a basis for grading individual students.

Closed-ended, "one right answer" questions may be needed to test mastery of certain basic knowledge and skills (e.g., spelling, multiplication tables). Also, some use of matching or fill-in-the-blank items may be appropriate for testing basic vocabulary knowledge in English, foreign languages, science, or social studies. Unfortunately, however, studies of teacher-made tests and the tests supplied with publishers' instructional materials indicate widespread overreliance on these low-level recognition or memory reproduction items. Assessment information will be most useful to you and to your students if it reflects progress made toward major instructional goals. Ordinarily, this will mean emphasizing authentic tasks that require students to integrate and apply what they are learning, not just to recognize or retrieve miscellaneous items of information.

Tests also ought to sample from the full range of content taught and include enough items to allow reliable measurement. Sampling from all content taught helps to ensure that you recognize areas of weakness and that your students are accountable for learning all of the material. It also helps to ensure that your students will view the test as fair. They may not view it as fair if it emphasizes only a small portion of what was taught in a unit, especially if they viewed this material as relatively unimportant and concentrated their study efforts on other material.

Grant Wiggins (1993) offered detailed suggestions on ways for teachers to make assessment both more fair and more authentic. He recommended that: (1) assessments feature worthwhile tasks that are educative and engaging; (2) instead of being secretive about grading standards, teachers clarify to students what constitutes exemplary performance and provide models for them to emulate; (3) assessment methods allow students the time to produce thoughtful and complete work; and (4) assessment is followed up with opportunities to improve on areas of weakness and ultimately produce products in which the students can take pride.

Assessment and *evaluation* are much broader terms than *testing*, and should not be equated with it. *Ordinarily, daily lesson participation and work on assignments, especially work on significant projects, should be used at least as much as tests to provide a basis for assessing progress and grading students.* This is especially the case in the elementary grades, where limitations in the students' cognitive developmental levels and academic skill repertoires limit the kinds of tests that can be used productively. Even in the secondary grades, overreliance on tests is likely to lead to memorizing and forgetting instead of integrated learning.

Increasingly, *portfolio assessment* is being recommended as an alternative that is better suited than testing as a way to meet students' informational and motivational needs. Portfolios are organized sets of student work that illustrate their progress over time. Students have opportunities to exercise a degree of choice in deciding what to include in their portfolios, and to revise and improve the items in response to feedback from the teacher or their peers. The portfolio approach reflects several motivational principles by focusing attention on quality standards rather than just grades or scores, by incorporating the use of assessment data as informative feedback, by encouraging students to become more reflective about their work and more oriented toward self-improvement over time, and by allowing them to assemble a collection of their best work that they can share with parents and other family members.

Helping Students Prepare for Assessment

In talking about assessment generally, and in preparing students for any particular assessment experience, *emphasize the role of assessment in providing informative feedback about progress, not its role in providing a basis for grading or a means to pressure students to keep up with study assignments.* Portray tests as opportunities to find out how "we" are doing and portray projects as opportunities to apply what "we" are learning. Express confidence that students will succeed if they apply themselves to lessons and learning activities.

Also, portray yourself as a helper and resource person who assists your students in learning and preparing for assessment, not as a remote evaluator. Encourage students to see you as allied with them in preparing for tests, not as allied with the tests in pressuring or threatening them.

Clarify your goals and assessment criteria in ways that will help students to understand what they need to learn and what strategies are likely to be most useful for enabling them to do so. At least in general terms, let them know how their learning will be assessed. However, avoid overspecificity that might tempt certain students to focus only on what is needed to pass the test and thus fail to develop more integrated learning.

Follow-Up Feedback and Grading

In addition to (or instead of) letter, number, or percentage grades, provide students with informative feedback designed to help them appreciate their accomplishments but also recognize areas of weakness and commit themselves to making needed improvements. Deliver such feedback privately and emphasize students' progress relative to their own prior accomplishments rather than comparisons with other students. Some of your best opportunities for encouraging incremental theories of ability and desirable performance attributions and efficacy perceptions occur when you are giving feedback to students following tests or other assessment experiences. The feedback should imply continuous progress in learning with your assistance (e.g., "Here is where you are progressing nicely and here is where we need to improve"), not a closing of the book on that domain of learning (e.g., "You got a B").

Although Thomas (1993) questions the practice, most motivational researchers advise teachers to include "safety nets" for failing students as part of their assessment follow-up and grading system. That is, students who have failed to earn satisfactory grades are given the opportunity to do so by taking an alternative test following a period of review and relearning. Or, they are allowed to earn extra credit by engaging in learning activities and producing some kind of product to indicate that they have overcome the deficiencies identified in their test performance. By making the extra effort to provide such safety nets, you can encourage struggling students to make the extra effort needed to accomplish your instructional goals.

If the cumulative level of performance that would earn a report card grade of A is not a realistic goal, help students to identify and commit themselves to realistic goals that, if reached, would yield grades of B or C. In doing so, you might use a strategy emphasized in Mastery Learning programs: Provide a list of potential goals (graduated in terms of the effort required to meet them and the grades earned if success is achieved) and ask the students to commit themselves to particular goals and associated levels of effort. Whatever you do, be sure to arrange conditions so that every student who consistently puts forth reasonable effort can earn report card grades of C or better. If you fail to do this, your struggling low achievers will have little incentive to keep trying and your efforts to motivate them will not have much chance to succeed.

The principle of emphasizing informative feedback over student comparisons applies to report card grades as well as to feedback on individual tests and assignments. Wlodkowski and Jaynes (1990) suggested that a well-designed report card informs students about their progress in learning and encourages their continuing motivation to learn. This is accomplished more through qualitative comments than letter or number grades. Separate sets of comments can be made for the students' achievement progress, effort and persistence in learning, noteworthy academic strengths and talents, areas needing improvement, and social development (i.e., cooperation, maturity, classroom participation). Where weaknesses are identified, the comments should emphasize the kinds of improvements needed rather than criticism of the student.

Reducing Test Anxiety

To the extent that you use tests or other formal evaluation methods, you may find that certain students show symptoms of test anxiety. They may learn effectively in informal, pressure-free situations but become highly anxious and perform considerably below their potential on tests or during any testlike situation in which they are aware of being monitored and evaluated. Test anxiety problems are most likely to be observed among low achieving students, but they occur in average- or high-achieving students as well. Several strategies have been developed for minimizing test anxiety problems (Hembree, 1988; Hill & Wigfield, 1984; Naveh-Benjamin, 1991; Wigfield & Eccles, 1989; Zeidner, 1995).

The most widely recommended of these strategies are the following:

- Avoid time pressures unless they are truly central to the skill being taught.
- Stress the feedback functions rather than the evaluation or grading functions of tests when discussing tests with your students.
- Portray tests as opportunities to assess progress rather than as measures of ability.
- Where appropriate, tell your students that some problems are beyond their present achievement level (so that they will not become upset if they fail to solve these problems).
- Give pretests to accustom students to "failure" and provide base rates for comparison when you administer posttests later.
- Teach your students stress management skills and effective test-taking skills and attitudes.
- Help your students to understand that the best way for them to prepare for tests is to concentrate their energies on learning what they need to know, without spending much time worrying about what will be on the test or how they will cope with anxiety in the test situation.

SUMMARY

Much of this book is organized according to the expectancy x value model of motivation, which holds that the effort that people are willing to expend on a task is the product of (1) the degree to which they expect to be able to perform the task successfully and garner whatever rewards successful task performance will bring, and (2) the degree to which they value those rewards. This chapter and the next focus on expectancy aspects of motivation.

Expectancy concepts are especially relevant to achievement situations that require people to perform some goal-oriented task knowing that their performance will be evaluated. Early work on achievement motivation indicated that people focused on motivation to succeed tend to approach achievement situations willingly, to prefer tasks that are moderately difficult for them, and to engage in these tasks with emphasis on developing their skills. In contrast, people focused on avoiding failure tend to fear and seek to avoid achievement situations. When required to engage in them, they seek to minimize risk of failure by setting goals either very low or impossibly high.

More recent work on people's thinking and behavior in achievement situations has shown that effort and persistence are greater when people perceive effort–outcome covariation, believe that the potential to control outcomes lies within themselves rather than in external factors that they cannot control, view themselves as origins rather than pawns, possess an incremental rather than an entity theory of intelligence, attribute their performance to internal and controllable causes, and possess a sense of efficacy or competence. In addition, people who possess these desirable dispositions are likely to engage in achievement situations with an emphasis on learning goals rather than performance goals and to process information using deeper-level strategies rather than surface-level memorizing (these and other contrasts are summarized in Table 3.1).

Research findings on the expectancy aspects of motivation underscore the importance of supporting your students' confidence as learners, and thus encouraging them to adopt learning goals rather than performance goals. You can do this through your curriculum (teaching students in their zones of proximal development and helping them to achieve success), your instruction (including instruction in goal setting, performance appraisal, and self-reinforcement along with instruction in the formal curriculum and helping your students to recognize effort–outcome linkages), and your assessment (using sources of assessment that promote accomplishment of your instructional goals, emphasizing informative feedback over categorizing or comparing students, and taking steps to minimize test anxiety).

In combination with the principles outlined in Chapter 2, consistent application of the principles outlined in this chapter will enable you to support your students' confidence as learners and thus encourage them to adopt learning rather than performance goals, to focus on processing information and developing skills rather than on worrying about failing or being embarrassed as they engage in tasks, and to persist and stay focused on the task when they encounter difficulties. This combination of preventive and supportive strategies will be sufficient for many if not most of your students. However, some students will require more individualized and intensive attention to the expectancy aspects of their motivation. Strategies for assisting these students are discussed in Chapter 4.

REFERENCES

Ames, C. (1992). Classrooms: Goals, structures, and student motivation. *Journal of Educational Psychology, 84,* 261–271.

Atkinson, J. (1964). *An introduction to motivation.* Princeton, NJ: VanNostrand.

Atkinson, J., & Litwin, G. (1960). Achievement motive and test anxiety as motives to approach success and avoid failure. *Journal of Abnormal and Social Psychology, 60,* 52–63.

Bandura, A. (1989). Human agency in social cognitive theory. *American Psychologist, 44,* 1175–1184.

Bandura, A., & Schunk, D. (1981). Cultivating competence, self-efficacy, and intrinsic interest through proximal self-motivation. *Journal of Personality and Social Psychology, 41,* 586–598.

Bandura, A., & Wood, R. (1989). Effect of perceived controllability and performance standards on self-regulation of complex decision making. *Journal of Personality and Social Psychology, 56,* 805–814.

Baron, J., & Wolf, D. (Eds.). (1996). *Performance-based student assessment: Challenges and possibilities. Ninety-fifth yearbook of the National Society for the Study of Education, Part I.* Chicago: University of Chicago Press.

Bell, C., & Kanevsky, L. (1996, April). Promoting positive achievement motivation in a regular Grade 2 classroom. Paper presented at the annual meeting of the American Educational Research Association, New York.

Butler, R. (1987). Task-involving and ego-involving properties of evaluation: Effects of different feedback conditions on motivational perceptions, interest, and performance. *Journal of Educational Psychology, 79,* 474–482.

Butler, R., & Nisan, M. (1986). Effects of no feedback, task-related comments, and grades on intrinsic motivation and performance. *Journal of Educational Psychology, 78,* 210–216.

Clifford, M. (1986). The effects of ability, strategy, and effort attributions for educational, business, and athletic failure. *British Journal of Educational Psychology, 56,* 169–179.

Cooper, H. (1979). Pygmalion grows up: A model for teacher expectation communication and performance influence. *Review of Educational Research, 49,* 389–410.

Covington, M. (1992). *Making the grade: A self-worth perspective on motivation and school reform.* Cambridge, UK: Cambridge University Press.

Covington, M., & Omelich, C. (1984). Task-oriented versus competitive learning structures: Motivational and performance consequences. *Journal of Educational Psychology, 76,* 1038–1050.

Crooks, T. (1988). The impact of classroom evaluation practices on students. *Review of Educational Research, 58,* 438–481.

deCharms, R. (1976). *Enhancing motivation: Change in the classroom.* New York: Irvington.

Deci, E. (1992). On the nature and functions of motivation theories. *Psychological Science, 3,* 167–171.

Dweck, C. (1991). Self-theories and goals: Their role in motivation, personality, and development. In R. Dienstbier (Ed.), *Perspectives on motivation: Nebraska Symposium on Motivation 1990* (Vol. 38, pp. 199–235). Lincoln: University of Nebraska Press.

Dweck, C., & Elliott, E. (1983). Achievement motivation. In P. Mussen (Ed.), *Handbook of child psychology* (4th ed.), Vol. IV: *Socialization, personality, and social development* (pp. 643–691). New York: Wiley.

Elawar, M.C., & Corno, L. (1985). A factorial experiment in teachers' written feedback on student homework: Changing teacher behavior a little rather than a lot. *Journal of Educational Psychology, 77,* 162–173.

Elliott, E., & Dweck, C. (1988). Goals: An approach to motivation and achievement. *Journal of Personality and Social Psychology, 79,* 474–482.

Graham, S. (1984). Teacher feelings and student thoughts: An attributional approach to affect in the classroom. *Elementary School Journal, 85,* 91–104.

Graham, S., & Barker, G. (1990). The down side of help: An attributional-developmental analysis of helping behavior as a low-ability cue. *Journal of Educational Psychology, 82,* 7–14.

Hau, K., & Salili, F. (1996). Motivational effects of teachers' ability versus effort feedback on Chinese students' learning. *Social Psychology of Education, 1,* 69–85.

Hembree, R. (1988). Correlates, causes, effects, and treatment of test anxiety. *Review of Educational Research, 58,* 47–77.

Hill, K., & Wigfield, A. (1984). Test anxiety: A major educational problem and what can be done about it. *Elementary School Journal, 85,* 105–126.

Horn, T. (1985). Coaches' feedback and changes in children's perceptions of their physical competence. *Journal of Educational Psychology, 77,* 174–186.

Koestner, R., Zuckerman, M., & Koestner, J. (1987). Praise, involvement, and intrinsic motivation. *Journal of Personality and Social Psychology, 53,* 383–390.

Krampen, G. (1987). Differential effects of teacher comments. *Journal of Educational Psychology, 79,* 137–146.

Locke, E., & Latham, G. (1990). *A theory of goal setting and task performance.* Englewood Cliffs, NJ: Prentice-Hall.

Meyer, W. (1982). Indirect communications about perceived ability estimates. *Journal of Educational Psychology, 74,* 888–897.

Morgan, M. (1985). Self-monitoring and attained subgoals in private study. *Journal of Educational Psychology, 77,* 623–630.

Natriello, G. (1987). The impact of evaluation processes on students. *Educational Psychologist, 22,* 155–175.

Neveh-Benjamin, M. (1991). A comparison of training programs intended for different types of test-anxious students: Further support for an information-processing model. *Journal of Educational Psychology, 83,* 134–139.

Nicholls, J. (1989). *The competitive ethos and democratic education.* Cambridge, MA: Harvard University Press.

Raffini, J. (1988). *Student apathy: The protection of self-worth.* Washington, DC: National Education Association.

Reeve, J. (1996). *Motivating others: Nurturing inner motivational resources.* Boston: Allyn & Bacon.

Schunk, D. (1983). Ability versus effort attributional feedback: Differential effects on self-efficacy and achievement. *Journal of Educational Psychology, 75,* 848–856.

Schunk, D. (1991). Self-efficacy and academic motivation. *Educational Psychologist, 26,* 207–231.

Schunk, D. (1996). Goal and self-evaluative influences during children's cognitive skill learning. *American Educational Research Journal, 33,* 359–382.

Schunk, D., & Hanson, A. (1985). Peer models: Influence on children's self-efficacy and achievement. *Journal of Educational Psychology, 77,* 313–322.

Shawaker, T., & Dembo, M. (1996). The effects of efficacy building instruction on the use of learning strategies. Paper presented at the annual meeting of the American Educational Research Association, New York.

Stipek, D., & Weisz, J. (1981). Perceived personal control and academic achievement. *Review of Educational Research, 51,* 101–137.

Tharp, R., & Gallimore, R. (1988). *Rousing minds to life: Teaching, learning, and schooling in social context.* Cambridge: Cambridge University Press.

Thomas, J. (1993). Expectations and effort: Course demands, students' study practices, and academic achievement. In T. Tomlinson (Ed.), *Motivating students to learn: Overcoming barriers to high achievement* (pp. 139–176). Berkeley: McCutchan.

Thomas, J. (1980). Agency and achievement: Self-management and self-reward. *Review of Educational Research, 30,* 213–240.

Tollefson, N., Tracy, D., Johnsen, E., Farmer, W., & Buenning, M. (1984). Goal setting and personal responsibility for LD adolescents. *Psychology in the Schools, 21,* 224–233.

Weiner, B. (1992). *Human motivation: Metaphors, theories and research.* Newbury Park, CA: Sage.

Whitley, B., & Frieze, I. (1985). Children's causal attributions for success and failure in achievement settings: A meta-analysis. *Journal of Educational Psychology, 77,* 608–616.

Wigfield, A., & Eccles, J. (1989). Test anxiety in elementary and secondary school students. *Educational Psychologist, 24,* 159–183.

Wiggins, G. (1993). Assessment: Authenticity, context, and validity. *Phi Delta Kappan, 75,* 200–214.

Wlodkowski, R., & Jaynes, J. (1990). *Eager to learn: Helping children become motivated and love learning.* San Francisco: Jossey-Bass.

Zeidner, M. (1995). Adaptive coping with test situations: A review of the literature. *Educational Psychologist, 30,* 123–133.

CHAPTER 4

Rebuilding Discouraged Students' Confidence and Willingness to Learn

Certainly, it is unfair to force tortoises to race against hares. Hares will become lazy and fall asleep while tortoises will become discouraged at the impossibility of winning. Both, however, can benefit from a system that helps all participants become better runners.

If the goal is maximum performance from all students, the schools must provide hope to all students that increased effort can result in success.

—RAFFINI (1988, pp. 13–14) (original italics)

Some of your students will achieve less than most of their classmates, even if you meet their individual needs effectively and they progress as rapidly as it is reasonable to expect. You can help protect their confidence as learners by establishing the kind of learning community described in Chapter 2 and by consistently implementing the curriculum, instruction, and assessment principles put forth in Chapter 3. Even so, these students may need additional motivational support. Also, many of them will bring into your classroom expectancy-related motivational problems that they have developed through prior experiences with failure and its consequences. These problems may continue unless you address them effectively.

This chapter considers four types of students with expectancy-related motivational problems: (1) students with limited ability who have difficulty keeping up and develop chronically low expectations and numbed acceptance of failure; (2) students whose failure attributions or ability beliefs make them susceptible to learned helplessness in failure situations; (3) students who are obsessed with self-worth protection and thus focus on performance goals rather than learning goals; and (4) students who underachieve due to a desire to avoid responsibilities. Students who do not put forth much effort because they do not find school very meaningful or worthwhile also require special motivational attention. However, their problems lie in the value aspects rather than the expectancy aspects of motivation, so they will be addressed in Chapter 8.

SUPPORTING THE MOTIVATION OF LOW ACHIEVERS

Some students continuously struggle to keep up with their classmates due to limitations in academic ability or learning disabilities that impede their progress. For example, they may be able to decode text, yet not understand and remember what they read well enough to learn efficiently through independent study. Or, they may know basic number facts but have difficulty understanding and generating solutions to application problems. To the extent that these students fall behind, it becomes more difficult to teach them using instructional materials and methods developed for their grade level. Some of them may be able to keep up with the class if provided with tutoring or other forms of special help, but others may begin to require individualized materials and instruction.

If you are able to provide them with sufficient instructional support, slow learners can make steady progress and achieve enough to satisfy both you and themselves, even though they may remain at or near the bottom of the class in overall achievement. However, if they often become frustrated because they cannot handle tasks or get help when they need it, or if they frequently feel humiliated because they are not keeping up with their classmates, they may begin to show *"failure syndrome" symptoms.* That is, they may lose their motivation to persist with learning efforts and instead begin to give up quickly at the first sign of frustration. Or, they may become more concerned with covering up their confusion than with learning what the activity is intended to teach. Some may begin to withdraw into passivity rather than participate in lessons, to leave items blank or simply guess at answers instead of seeking help, or to become behavior problems. At this point, low achievement due to limited academic ability would be compounded by underachievement due to motivational problems..

Strategies for Helping Low Achievers

Theorists and researchers who discuss strategies for teaching low achievers tend to disagree about what can be expected from these students and how much effort should be devoted to their needs relative to the needs of the rest of the class. However, reviews of this literature do converge on certain strategies, especially the strategies of providing tutorial help to low achievers and individualizing their assignments.

For example, McIntyre (1989) culled four sets of suggestions from a variety of sources. The first set focused on *individualizing activities and assignments:* reduce the difficulty levels of the tasks that you assign to struggling students; use multisensory input sources to reduce their need to learn by studying texts; build assignments around their interests; tailor your instruction to take advantage of their strongest learning modality; make sure that assignments are well structured and within the range of their ability level; keep assignments short; and make sure that the first part of the assignment is easy or familiar enough to provide initial success experiences.

The second group of suggestions focused on *providing directions to structure tasks* for low achievers. These included the following: have them repeat the instructions to you to make sure that they know what is supposed to be done; model task performance for them by thinking out loud as you perform demonstrations; train them in methods of self-instructional guidance; outline exactly what must be done to achieve the desired level of accomplishment; and set time limits within which the work should be done, preferably longer limits than necessary to allow these students to "beat the clock."

A third set of suggestions focused on *providing task assistance or tutoring.* This might be done either by yourself or by an aide, adult volunteer, older student, or classmate. Specific suggestions included the following: rephrase questions or provide hints when these students are unable to respond; praise them when they respond acceptably; have them revise work that is unacceptable; reassure them that help is available if needed; sit them among average (not superior) classmates with whom they enjoy friendly relationships, and ask these classmates to help keep the low achievers "on track" by providing task assistance and reminders of assignments and due dates; and set up a "study buddy" system to encourage low achievers to collaborate with a neighborhood friend during study sessions at their homes.

The fourth set of strategies focused on *maintaining motivation.* These included: provide encouragement and positive comments on papers; help low achievers to establish realistic goals and evaluate their accomplishments; call attention to their successes and send positive notes home; encourage them to focus on trying to surpass their previous day's or week's performance rather than to compete with classmates; use performance contracting methods; and give marks and report card grades on the basis of effort and production rather than in relation to the rest of the class.

Abbott (1978) published a similar collection of strategies. Along with many of those mentioned by McIntyre, she included the following: keep directions simple, if necessary by dividing the task into parts rather than providing lengthy directions that the student may not be able to remember; seat the student toward the front of the class and maintain frequent eye contact; provide extra assignments that address learning needs and allow the student to earn extra credit toward grades; and keep in close communication with anyone who tutors the student, to make sure that the tutoring focuses on his or her primary needs and that you keep abreast of progress and problems.

Low achievers also may benefit from strategies used in *Mastery Learning* approaches: make success likely by giving them tasks that they should be able to handle, provide them with individualized tutoring as needed, and allow them to contract for a particular level of performance and to continue to study, practice, and take tests until that level is achieved. By virtually guaranteeing success, this approach builds confidence and increases discouraged students' willingness to take the risks involved in seriously committing themselves to challenging goals (Grabe, 1985). For more information about mastery learning, see Box 4.1.

Box 4.1. Mastery Learning

Mastery Learning adjusts whole-class pacing by allowing slower students more time, and usually providing them with tutoring or other special assistance, to enable them to learn material that classmates have mastered more quickly. Originally Mastery Learning emphasized individualized tutoring, but the approach has since been adapted for use in tandem with whole-class or group-based instruction (Anderson, 1985; Bloom, 1980; Levine, 1985).

Mastery Learning principles often are used with curricula that feature clearly specified learning objectives, preset mastery performance standards, and frequent assessment using criterion-referenced tests. The heart of Mastery Learning is the cycle of teaching, testing, reteaching, and retesting. Students are informed of the unit's objectives and then receive instruction designed to enable them to master those objectives. Upon completion of instruction and related practice activities, the students take tests designed to assess their mastery. Those who achieve preset performance standards (usually, passing at least 80 percent of the items) are certified as having mastered the unit and are not required to do further work on it. These students then move on to the next unit, or more typically, work on enrichment activities or activities of their own choosing until the entire class is ready to move on. Meanwhile, students who do not meet mastery criteria receive corrective instruction and additional practice before their mastery levels are assessed again. Theoretically, cycles of assessment and reteaching

would go on indefinitely until all students reached mastery, but in practice, attempts to bring students to mastery usually cease after the second test, and the class then moves on to the next unit.

Mastery Learning methods increase, often dramatically, the percentage of students who master basic objectives. They benefit low achievers by providing extra time and instruction to enable them to master more content than they would otherwise. This additional mastery is likely to bring motivational benefits as well. However, the approach is time consuming and often viewed as impractical by teachers (Kurita & Zarbatany, 1991).

Also, Mastery Learning's potential benefits for slower learners may be counterbalanced by deficits to faster learners, unless the needs of all students in the classroom are taken into account in designing the system. Activities planned for faster learners should be selected for sound pedagogical reasons and not as mere time fillers to give them something to do while they wait for slower students to catch up. A feasible adaptation of the Mastery Learning approach may be to identify those learning objectives that seem most essential and see that all of your students master them, while tolerating more variable performance on objectives that are less essential. You then can supplement the basic curriculum with enrichment opportunities that classmates work on individually or in groups during times when you are busy teaching a remedial or enrichment lesson to a small group of students.

Good and Brophy (1997) reviewed research indicating that low achievers need frequent monitoring and supplementary tutoring from their teacher (or an adequate substitute), not just exposure to so-called individualized instructional materials. Too many of these materials are restricted to low-level repetitive tasks that amount to busy work rather than truly remedial instruction. Also, low achievers often need to be retaught using varied and enriched forms of instruction, not just to be recycled through the original instruction followed by additional drill and practice.

Other strategies identified in their review included the following: collect books and instructional materials that address content taught at your grade but are written at easier reading levels; tutor slow learners in independent reading and study skills, not just in subject-matter content; identify the most basic and necessary learnings embedded in each curriculum unit and make sure that the low achievers master those, even if they do not learn some of the less necessary things that their classmates may be learning; provide them with study guides and related learning supports; and combine empathy for these students with determination to see that they meet established learning goals, not just that they are happy in school.

Findings from the Classroom Strategy Study

I collected advice on teaching low achievers as part of the Classroom Strategy Study. For this study, 98 experienced teachers working in Grades K–6 were interviewed in depth concerning their strategies for working with 12 categories of students who present chronic achievement, motivation, or behavior problems (Brophy, 1996). Half of these teachers had been rated as outstanding in their ability to teach such students effectively, whereas the other half had been rated as average or typical. Analyses focused on common themes in the teachers' responses, especially those of the higher-rated teachers.

Concerning low achievers, most of these teachers' responses centered around the following set of principles: focus on providing academic help; supplement this with counseling or motivational support if needed; provide extra monitoring, feedback, and tutoring; enlist help from peers, parents, or other students or adults; and view low achievers as challenges to your professionalism as a teacher rather than as candidates for retention in grade or transfer into special education.

At first, I was surprised to find that the higher-rated teachers placed more emphasis on providing low achievers with academic help than with motivational support. However, follow-up analyses indicated that much of the intended motivational support reported by lower-rated teachers amounted to ineffectual attempts at encouragement. The difference is illustrated in the following examples of two teachers' handling of a situation in which a student is stuck on a math problem.

Here is how the situation might be handled effectively:

STUDENT: I can't do Number 4.
TEACHER: What part don't you understand?

STUDENT: I just can't do it, it's too hard!

TEACHER: I know you can do part of it because you've done the first three problems correctly. The fourth one is similar, but just a little more complicated. You start out the same way, but there's one extra step. Review the first three; then see if you can figure out Number 4. I'll come back in a few minutes to see how you are doing.

Compare this with the following less effective scenario:

STUDENT: I can't do Number 4.

TEACHER: You can't! Why not?

STUDENT: I just can't do it, it's too hard!

TEACHER: Don't say you can't do it—we never say we can't do it. Did you try hard?

STUDENT: Yes, but I can't do it.

TEACHER: You did the first three; maybe if you worked a little longer you could do the fourth. Why don't you do that and see what happens?

The first teacher communicated positive expectations and provided a specific suggestion about how to proceed, yet did not give the answer or do the work. In giving feedback about performance on the first three problems, she was more specific in noting that the answers were correct and in attributing this success to the student's knowledge and abilities, thus supporting the student's self-efficacy beliefs. She also provided some instructional assistance, and in the process, embedded some desirable socialization of the student's expectancy-related beliefs. The second teacher provided neither useful instructional guidance nor a credible basis for encouragement. Instead, she communicated half-hearted and somewhat contradictory expectations, leaving the student with no reason to believe that further effort would succeed.

Concluding Comments About Low Achievers

In elaborating on principles culled from the research literature and from interviewing experienced teachers, I would stress the following suggestions for teaching low achievers. First, accept the situation and make the best of it. Identify essential (although not necessarily low-level or easily attained) objectives and make sure that low achievers master these, even if this means skipping other things. Also, help them to view their situation realistically, yet still try to progress as best they can. Let them know that their work is acceptable to you so long as they apply themselves, even if they are unable to keep up with most of their classmates. Elicit their commitment to establishing and working on feasible goals. Explain that extra practice may be necessary for them, even if it is not enjoyable. Empathize with them, but stress that you want to see them learn, too.

Low achievers need extra help, especially individualized help provided during tutoring interactions. However, their helpers will need to be patient and caring. If you use peer or cross-age tutors, make sure that the tutors understand this. Also, arrange for low achievers to tutor peers or younger students. This will help them to master material more thoroughly and also avoid making them always the receivers but never the givers of help.

As soon as possible after settling your class into assignments, give personal attention to low achievers to make sure that they understand what to do and get off to a good start. Don't let them "practice errors" or end up turning in completed papers that are "all wrong." If they are not ready for independent pencil-and-paper work, build toward it through successive approximations. If they don't read well, help them learn to do so. At other times, engage them in worthwhile learning activities that do not require significant reading skills or that can be explained to them orally. In mathematics, use concrete manipulables and other specialized instructional materials designed to help them grasp basic concepts. In language arts and the content subjects, ask them questions that focus on key ideas and require them to compose thoughtful oral or written responses. In providing feedback, focus on their grasp of the key ideas rather than on the formal correctness of their language or writing.

In effect, strike a deal with low achievers: It's OK if they can't keep up with the rest of the class, because you have special goals and activities for them. You will be pleased if they accomplish these goals and are prepared to help them do so, but they will have to work hard and hold up their end, too. You are demanding effort and progress, but not necessarily the attainment of grade-level norms or the performance of the class as a whole.

RESOCIALIZING STUDENTS WITH FAILURE SYNDROME PROBLEMS

Failure syndrome is one of several terms that teachers commonly use to describe students who approach assignments with very low expectations of succeeding and who tend to give up at the first sign of difficulty. Other such terms include "low self-concept," "defeated," and "frustrated." Unlike low achievers, who often fail despite their best efforts, failure syndrome students often fail needlessly because they do not invest their best efforts. Instead, they begin tasks half-heartedly and simply give up when they encounter difficulty. Psychologists use more technical terms to describe these students, such as "low self-efficacy," "entity theorist," or "attributes failure to internal, stable, and uncontrollable causes" (i.e., low ability).

Psychologists also refer to *learned helplessness,* giving it a somewhat more restrictive and technical definition. Compared to students who develop more generalized failure syndrome patterns, students who develop learned helplessness reactions can be found at all levels of academic ability, and these reactions may appear only in particular achievement situations. Galloway and his colleagues (1996), for example, found that many students showed learned helplessness symptoms in mathematics but not in English, or vice versa.

Students who are prone to learned helplessness reactions may not routinely develop high anxiety in response to evaluation cues or begin all tasks with failure expectations. As long as they do not question their ability to succeed, they may be able to handle even challenging activities smoothly and successfully. However, they are prone to develop "catastrophic" reactions when they encounter serious frustration, followed by progressive deterioration in the quality of their coping once they have *begun* to fail (Dweck & Elliott, 1983).

Butkowsky and Willows (1980) noted the following tendencies in learned helplessness students confronted with challenging academic tasks: (1) they had low initial expectancies for success on the tasks, (2) they gave up quickly when they encountered difficulty, (3) they attributed their failures to lack of ability rather than to controllable causes such as insufficient effort or reliance on an inappropriate strategy, (4) they attributed their successes to external and uncontrollable causes (e.g., luck, easy task) rather than to their own abilities and efforts, and (5) following failure, they made unusually severe reductions in their estimates of future success probabilities.

Some students, especially in the early grades, show failure syndrome tendencies as part of a larger pattern of emotional immaturity that includes low frustration tolerance and avoidance, inhibition, or overdependency on adults as reactions to stress. These students may focus more on their dependency-related desires for attention from their teacher than on trying to learn what an academic activity is designed to teach.

Other students acquire failure expectations from their parents or teachers. Parents sometimes lead their children to believe that school will be difficult for them or that they have only limited academic potential, especially if the children's first few report cards contain low grades (Entwisle & Hayduk, 1982). Teachers sometimes communicate low expectations through a variety of direct and indirect means, especially to students who have been assigned labels such as "learning impaired" (see Box 4.2).

However, most failure syndrome problems develop through social learning mechanisms centered around experiences with failure. Most children begin school with enthusiasm, but many begin to find it anxiety provoking and psychologically threatening. They are accountable for responding to their teachers' questions, completing assignments, and taking tests. Their performances are monitored, graded, and reported to their parents. These accountability pressures might be tolerable under conditions of privacy and consistent success, but they become threatening in classrooms where failure carries the danger of public humiliation. Learned helplessness reactions are especially likely to appear in classrooms where the teacher uses controlling (versus autonomy-supporting) strategies and the students have developed extrinsic (versus intrinsic) motivational orientations (Boggiano et al., 1992).

Given these conditions, it is not surprising that some students, especially those who have experienced a continuing history of failure or a recent progressive cycle of failure, begin to believe that they lack the ability to succeed. Once this belief takes root, failure expectations and other self-conscious thoughts begin to disrupt their concentration and limit their coping abilities. Eventually, they abandon serious attempts to master tasks and begin to

Box 4.2.   How Some Teachers Communicate Low Expectations to Their Low Achievers

Like some students who have become discouraged by repeated academic failures, some teachers become discouraged by repeated instructional failures and begin to show the same kinds of symptoms: lowered self-efficacy perceptions, reduced expectations for future success, attribution of failure to external or uncontrollable causes, and a shift from persistent and adaptive problem-solving strategies to half-hearted and maladaptive ones. In extreme cases, teachers burn out and display such behavior most of the time with most of their students. More typically, however, teachers develop learned helplessness in teaching certain students, particularly low achievers who continue to struggle to keep up with the rest of the class. Some teachers redouble their efforts and make the best of the situation, but others gradually give up and begin just going through the motions with these students, communicating their low expectations in the process.

For example, most teachers know that low achievers need patience and encouragement. However, Brophy and Good (1970) observed teachers who were not practicing these seemingly obvious strategies, at least not toward the end of the school year when the observations were made. Consider these teachers' behavior when they called on a student to answer a question and the student made no response, said "I don't know," or answered incorrectly. At these times, the teachers could either stay with the student by repeating the question, giving a clue, or asking a new question, or else give up on the student by giving the answer or calling on someone else. Observations indicated that these teachers were twice as likely to stay with high-achieving students as with low-achieving students.

There also were differences in the teachers' rates of praise and criticism of students' responses. Good answers from high achievers were praised 12 percent of the time, but good answers from low achievers were praised only 6 percent of the time. Meanwhile, 6 percent of the high achievers' response failures yielded teacher criticism, whereas this occurred 18 percent of the time with low achievers. Thus, the students who most needed patience and encouragement often were treated with impatience when they struggled to respond. They also were less likely to be praised when they responded correctly (even though this happened less often), and more likely to be criticized when they were unable to respond correctly (even though this happened more often). Clearly, these teachers had drifted into counterproductive patterns of interacting with their low achievers.

Subsequent research has shown that some teachers do provide their low achievers with patience, encouragement, and other supportive treatment that helps these students to work up to their potential. Other teachers, however, drift into maladaptive patterns that feature low expectations and counterproductive modes of interacting with their low achievers. Examples that

(Continued)

Box 4.2.   How Some Teachers Communicate Low Expectations to Their Low Achievers—*Continued*

have been documented in various studies (reviewed by Good and Brophy, 1995, 1997) include the following:

1. Waiting less time for low achievers to answer a question (before giving the answer or calling on someone else).
2. Giving answers to low achievers or calling on someone else rather than trying to improve their responses by giving clues or repeating or rephrasing questions.
3. Inappropriate reinforcement: rewarding inappropriate behavior or incorrect answers by low achievers.
4. Criticizing low achievers more often for failure.
5. Praising low achievers less often for success.
6. Failing to give feedback following the public responses of low achievers.
7. Generally paying less attention to low achievers or interacting with them less frequently.
8. Calling on low achievers less often to respond to questions, or asking them only easier, nonanalytic questions.
9. Seating low achievers farther away from the teacher.
10. Generally demanding less from low achievers (attempting to teach them less than they are capable of learning, accepting low-quality or even incorrect responses from them and treating them as if they were correct responses, substituting misplaced sympathy or gratuitous praise for sustained teaching that ultimately leads to mastery).
11. Interacting with low achievers more privately than publicly, and monitoring and structuring their activities more closely.
12. Giving high achievers but not low achievers the benefit of the doubt in grading tests or assignments.
13. Being less friendly in interactions with low achievers, including less smiling and fewer other nonverbal indicators of support.
14. Providing briefer and less informative answers to their questions.
15. Interacting with them in ways that involve less eye contact and other nonverbal communication of attention and responsiveness (e.g., forward lean, positive head nodding).
16. Using fewer effective but time-consuming instructional methods with low achievers when time is limited.
17. Showing less acceptance and use of low achievers' ideas.
18. Limiting low achievers to an impoverished curriculum (low-level and repetitive content, emphasis on factual recitation rather than lesson-extending discussion, emphasis on drill and practice tasks rather than application and higher-level thinking tasks).

Some of these differences are due, at least in part, to the behavior of the students. For example, if low achievers seldom raise their hands, it is difficult for the teacher to ensure that they get as many response opportunities as high achievers. Similarly, if their contributions to lessons are of lower quality, the teacher cannot accept and use their ideas as frequently. Also, some forms of differential treatment are appropriate at times and may even represent appropriate

---

Box 4.2.   How Some Teachers Communicate Low Expectations to Their Low Achievers—*Concluded*

individualizing of instruction. Low achievers may require more structuring of their activities and closer monitoring of their work, for example, and under some circumstances it may make sense to interact with them more privately than publicly or to ask them easier questions. However, these differential patterns are danger signals, especially if the differences are large and occur on many dimensions rather than just one or two. Such differences suggest that a teacher is merely going through the motions of instructing low achievers, without seriously working to help them achieve their potential.

---

concentrate instead on preserving their self-esteem in their own eyes and their reputations in the eyes of others.

Strategies for Helping Students with Failure Syndrome Problems

Students with failure syndrome problems need assistance in regaining self-confidence in their academic abilities and in developing strategies for coping with failure and persisting with problem-solving efforts when they experience difficulty. Over the years, reviewers of the literature in education and psychology have identified quite a collection of strategies for accomplishing these goals.

Wlodkowski (1978) suggested that teachers:

1. Guarantee that failure syndrome students experience success regularly (by seeing that they know what to do before asking them to do it independently, providing immediate feedback to their responses, and making sure that they know the criteria by which their learning will be evaluated).
2. Encourage their learning efforts by giving them recognition for real effort, showing appreciation for their progress, and projecting positive expectations.
3. Emphasize personal causation in their learning by allowing them to plan and set goals, make choices, and use self-evaluation procedures to check their progress.
4. Use group process methods to enhance positive self-concepts (activities that orient these students toward appreciating their positive qualities and getting recognition for them from their peers).

Swift and Spivack (1975) suggested most of these same strategies. In addition, they recommended exploring with these students which classroom situations they find comfortable and which they find anxiety-provoking, and why;

helping them to gain better insight into and sense of control over their anxieties; and reassuring them of your willingness to help. Forms of help might include minimizing evaluation and competition, marking and grading with emphasis on noting successes rather than failures, using individualized instructional materials, and calling on these students only when they volunteer (or alternatively, only when you have prepared them through advance warning and study suggestions).

McIntyre (1989) suggested reading and discussing with these students *The little engine that could;* praising them for attempting difficult tasks as well as for whatever successes they achieve; requiring them to complete (or at least to make a serious attempt to complete) a certain portion of an assignment before asking you for help; pointing out the similarities between the present task and work completed successfully earlier; and allowing them extra time if necessary but insisting that their work be completed.

More specific and elaborated suggestions have emerged from research on particular theoretical concepts or treatment approaches. Many of these involve what Ames (1987) called "cognition retraining." Three prominent approaches to cognition retraining are attribution retraining, efficacy training, and strategy training (See Table 4.1).

Attribution Retraining

Attribution retraining involves inducing changes in students' tendencies to attribute their failures to lack of ability rather than to remediable causes such as insufficient effort or use of inappropriate strategies. Typically, attribution retraining treatments expose students to a planned series of experiences, couched within an achievement context, in which modeling, socialization, practice, and feedback are used to teach them to (1) concentrate on the task at hand rather than worry about failing, (2) cope with failures by retracing their steps to find their mistake or by analyzing the problem to find another approach, and (3) attribute their failures to insufficient effort, lack of information, or use of ineffective strategies rather than to lack of ability (Craske, 1988; Dweck & Elliott, 1983). Failure syndrome students are especially likely to benefit from exposure to programs that combine attribution retraining with training in strategies for accomplishing tasks (VanOverwalle, Sagebarth, & Goldschstein, 1989).

Research on attribution retraining has led to significant advances over the commonsense idea of programming students for success. This work has shown that *success alone is not enough*—even a steady diet of success will not change an established pattern of learned helplessness. In fact, *a key to successful attribution retraining is controlled exposure to failure.* Rather than being exposed only to "success models" who handle tasks with ease, students are exposed to "coping models" who struggle to overcome mistakes before finally succeeding. In the process, they model constructive responses to mistakes as they occur (e.g., by verbalizing continued confidence, attributing failures to remediable causes, and coping by first diagnosing the source of the problem and then correcting the mistake or approaching the problem in a different way). Following exposure to such modeling, students begin to work on the tasks

TABLE 4.1. Cognition Retraining Methods

Cognition retraining methods use combinations of direct instruction, modeling with verbalized self-instruction (thinking aloud), coaching, and scaffolded practice under controlled task conditions to teach students productive strategies for responding to achievement situations and help them learn to self-regulate their application of these strategies. Different cognitive retraining methods have been developed to pursue different goals by focusing on different aspects of students' coping strategies.

Training Method	Primary Focus	Major Goals
Attribution retraining	Performance attributions (especially explanations for and strategies for recovering from failures)	Teach students to attribute failures to remediable causes (insufficient knowledge or effort, reliance on an inappropriate strategy) and thus to persist with problem-solving efforts instead of giving up
Efficacy training	Self-efficacy perceptions	Teach students to set and strive to attain reasonable proximate goals and approach ultimate goals through successive approximations, and in the process, to appreciate their developing expertise in the domain
Strategy training	Domain- and task-specific skills and strategies	Help students to acquire and self-regulate their use of effective learning and problem-solving strategies, through comprehensive instruction that includes attention to propositional knowledge (what to do), procedural knowledge (how to do it) and conditional knowledge (when and why to do it)

themselves. Conditions are arranged so that they sometimes experience difficulty or failure, but accompanied by coaching that encourages them to respond constructively rather than becoming frustrated and giving up.

These treatments reflect a growing recognition that successful socialization of students' motivational attitudes and beliefs includes attention to frustration tolerance, persistence in the face of difficulties, and related aspects of constructive response to failure. This is quite different from programming for success, especially if this idea is translated into attempts to enable students to avoid experiencing failure altogether (Clifford, 1984; Rohrkemper & Corno, 1988).

Early attribution retraining programs stressed attribution of failures to insufficient effort ("I didn't try hard enough or concentrate carefully enough"). More recently developed programs stress attributing failure to using an ineffective strategy ("I went about the problem in the wrong way"; "I misunderstood the directions"; "I made a mistake at a certain point that negated my efforts thereafter"). This shift recognizes the fact that most students at least subjectively put forth their best efforts, so that failure results not so much from lack of effort as from a limited repertoire of relevant knowledge and coping strategies. That is, they do everything they know how to do but still don't succeed, and they don't know how to diagnose and overcome the problem on their own.

Efficacy Training

Efficacy training programs also involve exposing students to a planned set of experiences within an achievement context and providing them with modeling, instruction, and feedback. However, whereas attribution retraining programs were developed specifically for learned helplessness students and thus focus on teaching constructive response to failure, efficacy training programs were developed primarily for low achievers who have become accustomed to failure and have developed generalized low self-concepts of ability. Consequently, efficacy training helps students to set realistic goals and pursue them with the recognition that they have the ability (efficacy) needed to reach these goals if they apply reasonable effort.

Schunk (1985) identified the following practices as effective for increasing students' self-efficacy perceptions:

- Cognitive modeling that includes verbalization of task strategies, the intention to persist despite problems, and confidence in achieving eventual success.
- Explicit training in strategies for accomplishing the task.
- Performance feedback that points out correct operations, remedies errors, and reassures students that they are developing mastery.
- Attributional feedback that emphasizes the successes being achieved and attributes these to the combination of sufficient ability and reasonable effort.
- Encouraging students to set goals prior to working on tasks (goals that are challenging but attainable, phrased in terms of specific performance standards and oriented toward immediate short-term outcomes).
- Focusing feedback on how students' present performance surpasses their prior attainments rather than on how they compare with other students.
- Supplying rewards contingent on actual accomplishment (not just task participation).

Strategy Training

In strategy training, modeling and instruction are used to teach problem-solving strategies and related self-talk that students will need to handle tasks successfully. Strategy training is a component of good cognitive skills instruction to all students; it is not primarily a remedial technique. However, it is especially important to use with discouraged students who have not developed effective learning and problem-solving strategies on their own but who can learn them through modeling and explicit instruction.

Poor readers, for example, can be taught reading comprehension strategies such as identifying the purpose of the assignment and keeping it in mind when reading, activating relevant background knowledge, identifying major points and attending to the outline and flow of content, monitoring their understanding by generating and trying to answer questions about the content, and drawing and testing inferences by making interpretations, predictions, and conclusions (Duffy & Roehler, 1989; Palincsar & Brown, 1984; Raphael, 1984). Two keys to effective strategy instruction are that (1) it includes attention not just to propositional knowledge (what to do) but also to procedural knowledge (how to do it) and conditional knowledge (when and why to do it), and (2) it includes cognitive modeling (thinking out loud that makes visible the covert thought processes that guide problem solving).

Programs also have been developed for training students in general study skills (Devine, 1987) and learning strategies (Weinstein & Mayer, 1986). Cognitive elements of these programs include instruction in strategies such as: rehearsal (repeating material to remember it more effectively), elaboration (putting material into one's own words and relating it to prior knowledge), organization (outlining material to highlight its structure and remember it), comprehension monitoring (keeping track of the strategies used and the degree of success achieved with them, and adjusting strategies accordingly), and affect monitoring (maintaining concentration and task focus, minimizing performance anxiety and fear of failure). The programs also contain affective management components similar to those used in attribution retraining and efficacy training programs (McCombs & Pope, 1994; Rohrkemper & Corno, 1988). A comprehensive cognition retraining program for failure syndrome students will include attention to both the cognitive and the affective aspects of task engagement and persistence.

Dweck & Elliott (1983) recommended that strategy training programs encourage incremental rather than entity views of ability. This involves: acting more as a resource person than a judge, focusing students more on learning processes than on outcomes, reacting to errors as natural and useful parts of the learning process rather than as evidence of failure, stressing effort over ability and individualized standards over normative standards when giving feedback, and attempting to stimulate achievement efforts through primarily intrinsic rather than extrinsic motivational strategies.

Findings from the Classroom Strategy Study

Teachers interviewed for the Classroom Strategy Study (Brophy, 1996) also were asked about strategies for teaching failure syndrome students. Findings indicated that the higher-rated teachers suggested a combination of support, encouragement, and task assistance to help shape gradual improvement in work habits. They would make it clear that these students were expected to work conscientiously and persistently so as to turn in assignments done completely and correctly. However, they also would reassure the students that they would not be given work that they could not do, monitor their progress and provide any needed help, and reinforce them by praising their successes, calling attention to their progress, and providing them with opportunities to display their accomplishments publicly. Such special treatment would be faded gradually as the students gained confidence and began to work more persistently and independently.

None of these teachers were familiar with the term "efficacy training," but most of them intuitively favored strategies stressed in efficacy training programs (negotiating agreement to strive to meet specific proximal goals, giving feedback that stresses that the student has the ability to succeed). However, their responses appeared less satisfactory from the standpoint of attribution retraining and remediation of learned helplessness. Most of them mentioned support, encouragement, and instructional assistance but did not say much about learned helplessness symptoms (catastrophic reactions to frustration, giving up quickly, attributing failure to lack of ability). Nor was there much mention of modeling to teach better coping strategies or of teaching the student how to persist in the face of difficulty. Thus, it bears repeating that failure syndrome students, especially those with learned helplessness symptoms, do not so much need a steady diet of success as they need to learn how to cope with frustration and failure productively.

Concluding Comments About Failure Syndrome Students

Failure syndrome students require patience and persistence, especially if their problems have been developing for years. You cannot quickly cure those who have become convinced that they lack ability by providing a few success experiences and words of encouragement. However, you can begin to undermine their certainty of failure and get them moving toward confidence by making sure that they are prepared to handle the challenges you present, teaching them needed task skills and more general learning and study strategies, and applying the principles involved in attribution retraining, efficacy training, and related treatment approaches.

Whether or not you undertake such treatments formally, you can include relevant socialization messages in your everyday interactions with failure syndrome students. Much of this socialization can be subtle and informal, as in the earlier example of effective handling of a student who was stuck on a math problem (pp. 79–80). Students treated in this manner every day should slowly but surely begin to gain confidence and become less prone to catastrophic reactions to failure.

Also, help these students learn to understand when they do or do not need help and to become willing to get help when they need it. Give them a set of procedures to follow when they encounter difficulties, starting with strategies for diagnosing possible causes of their problem and perhaps solving it on their own. If they cannot solve the problem on their own, they then should seek help. You may need to encourage them to do so, because most students are not willing to seek help overtly (Good et al., 1987; Newman & Goldin, 1990; van der Meij, 1988).

Therefore, give these students one or more options to use to signal their need for help unobtrusively. Then, get to them as quickly as you can and provide the help that they need. In this regard, teach them to distinguish when they do and do not need help. If they have failed to engage the strategies you have taught them and thus have not yet determined whether they can handle the problem on their own, require them to engage these strategies before getting help. If they really do need help, provide it, but emphasize "instrumental" help (i.e., explanations, questions, or hints that will stimulate the students' thinking about the problem and encourage them to work out the rest of it on their own) rather than "executive" help (i.e., giving them answers). Instrumental help scaffolds students' problem solving just enough to enable them to make needed connections and construct the knowledge or skill that the task was intended to teach, whereas executive help eliminates the need for further thinking and leaves them possessing correct answers but lacking key understandings (Butler & Neuman, 1995; Nelson-LeGall, 1987).

WEANING STUDENTS AWAY FROM PERFORMANCE GOALS AND OVEREMPHASIS ON SELF-WORTH PROTECTION

Struggling low achievers or students beset with failure syndrome problems are especially likely to focus on performance goals instead of learning goals. However, certain capable or even confident students also may emphasize performance goals over learning goals, especially as they approach adolescence and become more concerned about social comparison and reputation issues. Some may become predisposed toward learned helplessness in a steadily growing range of achievement situations. In other cases, the problem may be less extreme but still worrisome because self-worth preoccupations distract the students' attention from learning goals and cause them to engage in activities using less-than-ideal strategies (Covington, 1992; Hansen, 1989; Nicholls, 1989).

Such students may attempt to escape being called on by scrunching down in their seats and avoiding eye contact with you (or by conspicuously waving their hands and projecting a confident demeanor, if they have discovered that this will make you less likely to call on them). If you do call on them and they are not sure how to answer, they may hesitate in the hope that you will help them. Or, they may offer a vague and rambling response in the hope that you will accept it and move on. During work times they may appear to be thinking when they are actually daydreaming or may appear to be working thoughtfully when they are actually just guessing at answers or perhaps copying from a neighbor. They may procrastinate in getting started and then hurry to finish as time runs out. They may skip items, do the minimum required, or in other ways perform marginally rather than accept the challenge of working up to their capabilities. Or, they may display unrealistic perfectionism by constantly rejecting their partially completed efforts and starting over (thus giving the appearance of commitment to high goals while actually not accomplishing much). These and related stratagems allow students who are obsessed with self-worth protection to go through the motions of achievement striving while actually avoiding acceptance of genuine challenges and arming themselves with excuses for potential failures.

Lehtinen et al. (1995) described the development of several of these mechanisms in a student named Heli, whom they studied between third and sixth grade. Heli was a fluent reader and viewed herself as one of the top students. However, she had great difficulties with text comprehension, restlessness, and lack of concentration, so her teacher rated her much lower. Fear of failure and symptoms of learned helplessness emerged whenever Heli encountered difficulty in her work or even picked up a cue from the teacher that the task was going to be difficult. She often complained that a new task was too long, too hard, or that she didn't like it. She would attempt to wheedle help through social dependence strategies (e.g., appealing for help, babyish chatting, or smooth-tongued questioning aimed at eliciting teacher guidance). If this did not succeed, she would escalate to passive avoidance strategies (e.g., absent-minded staring, averting her gaze from the task, or "silent treatment" of the teacher). At other times, she proceeded to more active or manipulative forms of avoidance (e.g., attempting to leave the classroom, engaging in stereotyped rituals or mannerisms, signaling tiredness, or resorting to intensive whining or tantrums).

Heli's symptomatic behaviors typically escalated as long as the stress continued, and sometimes carried over to the next activity. However, they typically disappeared and were replaced by a smiling, cooperative demeanor if the teacher gave up attempts to get more out of her. Over time, Heli perfected her techniques to the point that they were quite successful in limiting her teachers' (and her parents') willingness to persist in seeking to get her to work up to her abilities.

Some students do not usually fear failure and thus are not obsessed with protecting their self-worth, but they are frequently distracted from learning goals by social goals such as trying to please you as the teacher or trying to impress their peers (sometimes by displaying intelligence or task skills, but sometimes by showing off or acting cool). To the extent that students are distracted from learning goals by these social concerns, they are less likely to use optimal learning strategies that focus on constructing meaningful understandings and remembering them for later use in appropriate application situations (Lehtinen et al., 1995; Meece & Holt, 1993).

Strategies for Reducing Preoccupation with Self-Worth Protection

The most powerful strategies for dealing with such problems focus on prevention rather than cure. You can minimize your students' needs for self-worth protection by establishing your classroom as a learning community (Chapter 2) and consistently modeling, socializing, and instructing students in ways that orient them toward learning goals rather than performance goals (Chapter 3).

Martin Covington (1992) has written at length about self-worth protection problems and experimented with methods for minimizing them. He recommended the following six general strategies:

1. Provide students with inherently engaging assignments that appeal to their curiosity and personal interests and that offer challenging yet manageable goals. To the extent feasible, allow them some choice of tasks and control over the level of challenge they face (but encourage them to increase levels of challenge in response to increases in their levels of expertise).

2. Provide sufficient rewards. Arrange the reward system so that all students (not just the brighter ones) can earn desired rewards. Also, dispense rewards in ways that reinforce students for setting meaningful goals, posing challenging questions, and working to satisfy their curiosity. Seek to make the act of learning itself a sought-after goal.

3. Enhance effort–outcome covariation beliefs. Help students learn to set realistic goals and develop confidence that they can be successful and earn rewards through reasonable (not superhuman) effort.

4. Strengthen the linkage between achievement efforts and self-worth. Help students learn to take pride in their accomplishments and their developing expertise, and to minimize attention to competition and social comparison.

5. Promote positive beliefs about ability. Help students to adopt multidimensional definitions of their abilities and to take an incremental rather than an entity view towards them.

6. Improve teacher–student relations. Emphasize your role as a resource person who assists these students' learning efforts, not your role as an authority figure who controls their behavior.

Other sources offer similar advice about minimizing or coping with self-worth protection problems (Adelman & Taylor, 1983; Lehtinen et al., 1995; Nicholls, 1989; Raffini, 1988). In addition to the suggestions advanced by Covington, these sources suggest the following strategies: attempt to socialize the students' values and learning goals by helping them see the need for what they are learning in their present and future lives outside of school; teach them cognitive and metacognitive strategies for regulating their learning more effectively so that they will have less need for self-worth protection; encourage them to ask for help when they need it and make it possible for them to get such help without suffering public embarrassment; emphasize cooperative learning and avoid competition; and use individual criterion-referenced grading standards rather than absolute standards or grading on a curve.

Concluding Comments About Students Obsessed with Self-Worth Protection

I would add the following suggestions about socializing the attitudes and beliefs of students who are obsessed with self-worth protection. First, help these students to understand how this focus ironically limits their current performance and future development (in effect, explain Table 3.1 to them). Help them to appreciate that they develop their abilities only when they extend them by accepting new challenges; sticking to what is easy and familiar minimizes risk but keeps them standing still while their classmates are moving forward.

Similarly, help them to understand that a focus on competing with peers is ultimately a losing game, even if they win most of the time. It distracts attention from learning efforts and is likely to create problems with peers (who usually do not appreciate overcompetitiveness). It also diverts energies that should be devoted to synthesizing their learning, appreciating its value, and remembering it with an eye toward using it in their lives outside of school. Portfolio assessment and related approaches for focusing students on progress over time can be helpful here.

Finally, take seriously these students' needs to look good in public situations. Don't dismiss their fears or suggest that they are groundless. Instead, ask if there are things that you can do to help them feel more comfortable in your classroom and become more willing to accept genuine challenges. Follow through on any requests that are feasible. Make sure that your everyday interactions with these students are consistent with the notions that you care about them personally as well as about their achievement progress, that you would not want to embarrass them, and that you will try to provide any form of help that they may need.

RESOCIALIZING COMMITTED UNDERACHIEVERS

Most students with problems in the expectancy-related aspects of motivation would like to achieve more than they do but are hampered by one or more of the problems described in earlier sections of this chapter. However, you also may encounter a few *committed underachievers* who set low goals and resist accepting responsibility for their successes because they do not want to be expected to maintain a high level of performance. These students need reassurance that they can attain consistent success with reasonable effort (i.e., not superhuman effort). They also may benefit from counseling designed to help them see that their deliberate underachievement is contrary to their own long-run best interests.

McCall, Evahn, and Kratzer (1992) completed the largest study of underachievers done to date, beginning when they were still in school but following them into adulthood. As students, these underachievers displayed such characteristics as low self-concept, low perception of abilities, unrealistic goal setting, lack of persistence, responding impulsively rather than thoughtfully to assignments, social immaturity and poor peer relationships, oppositional and aggressive response to authority, and a tendency to make excuses for continued underachievement rather than accept responsibility and make a serious commitment to change.

This underachievement in school was part of a larger syndrome of underachievement characterized by failure to persist in the face of challenge, whether the challenge was educational, occupational, or marital. The underachievers followed in this study were less likely to complete college and to display job and marital stability than comparison groups, including a group that earned similar grades but had lower aptitude scores. Thus, there is no reason to believe that underachievement problems will take care of themselves once underachievers "find what interests them" or "leave school and enter the work world." This type of underachievement syndrome tends to persist if left untreated.

Strategies for Helping Committed Underachievers

McCall and his colleagues also reviewed the treatment literature and concluded that most treatment programs have shown at least some success in remediating targeted symptoms. However, many programs failed to improve achievement because they targeted peripheral symptoms such as self-esteem or social relationships but not the core symptoms of low achievement motivation and the desire to avoid increased expectations and responsibilities. The best results have been obtained with comprehensive programs that address the full range of observed symptoms and include treatment elements aimed at parents and teachers as well as students. The most common approach is teacher–parent collaboration in using behavior modification strategies. That is, the teacher sends home a daily or weekly report of the students' achievement efforts and accomplishments, and the parents withhold or dispense privileges or other rewards contingent on their child's achievement of previously negotiated academic and behavioral goals.

A Confrontational Strategy

Mandel and Marcus (1988) described a strategy designed to pressure committed underachievers to stop generating excuses for their continued failure to apply themselves and instead begin to take responsibility for doing so. These authors argued that less confrontive strategies, such as providing a lot of encouragement or making the work easier or more interesting, will not lead to any fundamental change because these students are motivated to continue their underachievement pattern so as to avoid increased expectations and responsibilities. They claimed that their approach has been successful but warned that it requires resisting the temptation to try to take over by telling the student how to solve problems. It also requires recognizing that the student will not necessarily follow through on seemingly sincere commitments, and thus being prepared to patiently work through the student's excuses and resistance strategies.

The first step is to ask whether the underachiever wants to get better grades in school (as opposed to announcing that you are going to help the student do so). For the overwhelming majority of students who respond positively to this initial question, the relationship has now been structured such that it is the responsibility of the student to set goals, whereas your role is to help the student achieve them. Step 2 involves taking detailed stock of current progress and problems in each subject, along with any plans that the student may have for addressing the problems. At this point, your role is to elicit information nonjudgmentally, without giving any interpretations or recommendations.

Step 3 involves focusing on specific problems and isolating the student's excuses for them. You ask what problems are getting in the way of better grades, probe for specifics when the student offers only vague generalizations, and if necessary, challenge questionable claims. For example, the student might claim to spend an hour every day studying, but specific questions about how much he or she has studied in the last few days might establish that the real average study time is more like 10 or 20 minutes per day. Step 4 involves linking each excuse to its natural consequence by describing (or better yet, eliciting from the student) what will happen if the student does not address this problem effectively. Step 5 involves asking the student to suggest solutions for each identified hindrance to success, then engaging the student in a detailed discussion of these suggestions in order to clarify their practicality, anticipate snags, and refine plans. Here, you need to be careful to elicit plans from the student rather than tell the student what to do. Once the student "owns" the goal of better grades, has recognized the connection between current study habits and future consequences, and has identified a specific and workable solution, there is no way to "unrecognize" these connections again. The student must accept personal responsibility for improving the grades.

The sixth step is a call for action (saying OK, now what do you propose to do? followed by questions about specifics). The seventh step is follow-up to assess whether the student has implemented the plan and eliminated the problem. Given the student's motivation to continue to underachieve, it is likely that the assessment will indicate either that the student continued to underachieve but simply dropped this one excuse and substituted another one, or else began to achieve in just the one area but not in others. This leads to a possibly lengthy Step 8, which involves repeating Steps 3–7 with one different excuse each time. Eventually, the student will run out of excuses and be forced to accept personal responsibility for academic performance.

When this occurs, there may be accompanying reactions such as panic, depression, anxiety, anger, regret, energy toward achievement, confusion, changes in social relationships, or intense introspection. At this point, your role shifts from taking away excuses and pressing for acceptance of responsibility to becoming a supportive, nonjudgmental listener and resource person who helps the student begin to express and struggle with questions such as,

Why did I allow myself to get such poor grades? and What do I want my future to be?

Other Strategies

Other sources of advice about coping with underachievers describe a great many strategies that range between the primarily confrontive approach represented by Mandel and Marcus and the primarily supportive approach that they rejected as ineffective. For example, Blanco and Bogacki (1988) culled the following recommendations from school psychologists: peer and cross-age tutoring; contracts that feature collaboration with the student in setting goals and with the parents in withholding or providing performance-contingent rewards; counseling sessions designed to allow underachievers to ventilate their concerns but also to pressure them to accept responsibility for their performance and commit themselves to realistic goals; and requiring the students to make up missed homework assignments during recess or after school.

McIntyre (1989) emphasized many of the same strategies, especially contracts and reward systems, collaborative learning with peers, improving performance gradually through successive approximations, and requiring the student to redo shoddy work and complete unfinished work. Other suggestions included:

- Small-group cooperative learning methods in which each individual has a unique function to perform (thus creating peer pressure on underachievers to do their part).
- Monitoring these students closely and checking back with them frequently to make sure that they stay on task during work times.
- Teaching them study habits and self-regulation skills.
- Making their work as interesting as possible and helping them to see its current or future application potential, but at the same time making it clear that they have the responsibility to apply themselves to accomplishing all curricular goals (i.e., boredom is not a valid excuse).
- Letting them do extra credit work in areas of interest.
- Discussing their occupational plans and then helping them to see that academic skills are required in those occupations.
- Soliciting their suggestions about how you might be helpful to them and following through on those that are feasible.

Thompson and Rudolph (1992) developed a similar list and included the following strategies:

- Increase work production gradually through escalating contracts.
- Avoid lecturing, nagging, or threatening.
- Where feasible, have underachievers study or at least talk about study habits with a friend who models motivation to learn and conscientious work on assignments.
- Reinforce and build on current accomplishments rather than emphasizing past faults and failures.

- Structure the students' work by providing clear instructions and identifying specific goals.

Findings from the Classroom Strategy Study

Findings from the Classroom Strategy Study (Brophy, 1996) indicated that the higher-rated teachers would be more demanding and less willing to make allowances with students who underachieved because they were unmotivated, compared to students who believed that the work was too difficult for them. Most of these teachers recommended performance contracting and related approaches that call for rewarding unmotivated students if they meet imposed or negotiated performance expectations but punishing them if they do not. However, the higher-rated teachers also spoke of building positive relationships with these students and resocializing their attitudes by helping them to appreciate the connections between school work and their current or future needs or by stressing the work's potential for enriching their lives. Additional suggestions were linked to the teachers' views on the nature and causes of the underachievement syndrome. For example, teachers who believed that devaluing of school work reflects attitudes modeled at home tended to speak of working with the parents, whereas teachers who thought the problem was lack of interest tended to speak of making changes in the curriculum.

Several teachers noted that underachievement problems do not so much indicate alienation from school work as lack of a positive value on it, which leads to a "do as little as you can get away with" attitude. Reward and punishment systems can control work output but socialization is needed to change students' attitudes. The goal is not just to get underachievers to perform more acceptably, but to teach them to see benefit in school work and take pride in their efforts and successes. A variation on this idea, expressed frequently by teachers working in the early grades, was that underachievers aren't so much alienated or unsocialized as they are lacking in direction. They need imposition of responsibilities and expectations, at home as well as at school.

Concluding Comments About Underachievers

Themes noted both in the scholarly literature and in the teachers' interview responses suggest that, until they reach age 10 or so, most underachievers do not settle into the pattern of systematic avoidance of responsibility described by Mandel and Marcus (1988) or the failure to persist in the face of challenge described by McCall, Evahn, and Kratzer (1992). Even when younger underachievers are drifting toward this pattern, it usually hasn't hardened yet. They may be adult dependent, attention seeking, unprepared to assume responsibilities, or otherwise immature, but they have not yet become committed underachievers who systematically work below their potential because they are consciously or unconsciously motivated to do so.

This implies that encouraging and instructional strategies might be more effective with younger underachievers, but confrontive and persuasive strategies might be more effective with older ones. This implication has not been tested directly, but it is consistent with the fact that research findings that favor supportive strategies tend to come from the elementary grades, whereas findings supporting confrontive strategies tend to come from junior high and high schools. Thus, in the elementary grades, and especially the primary grades, it may be best to avoid treating underachievers as hardened cases unless there is clear evidence that they have become so. Instead, it is probably better to give them the benefit of the doubt and treat them as well meaning but in need of socialization and instruction concerning what they will need to do in order to get the most out of lessons and assignments. In short, you will need to teach these students about motivation to learn (see Chapter 7).

CONCLUSION

The expectancy aspects of student motivation depend less on the degree of objective success that students achieve than on how they view their performance: what they see as possible for them to achieve with reasonable effort, whether or not they define this achievement as success, and whether they attribute their performance to controllable causes or uncontrollable causes. The motivation of all students, even the most extreme cases of learned helplessness, is open to reshaping. Empty reassurances or a few words of encouragement will not do the job, but a combination of appropriately challenging demands, socialization designed to make the students see that success can be achieved with reasonable effort, and coaching them in strategies for self-regulating their learning should be effective.

Students need to learn to view academic frustrations and failures realistically and to respond to them adaptively. As Rohrkemper and Corno (1988) pointed out, not only is some student failure inevitable, but a manageable degree of student failure is desirable. When students are challenged at optimal levels of difficulty, they make mistakes. The important thing about these mistakes is not that they occur but that they trigger informative feedback and students use this feedback to respond to the mistakes with renewed motivation rather than discouragement.

SUMMARY

This chapter suggested strategies for working with four types of students whose expectancy-related motivational problems require additional attention beyond the preventive strategies discussed in Chapters 2 and 3. Low achievers who have difficulty keeping up and have developed chronically low expectations and numbed acceptance of failure will require continuous reassurance that they can meet the demands that you make on them, that you will provide them with whatever help they may need, and that you appreciate their efforts and are accepting of their progress so long as they continue to put forth reasonable effort. These students will need considerable instructional assistance along with motivational encouragement, and they may need individualized instructional materials or activities as well. If they are not able to keep up with their classmates despite their best efforts, at least make sure that they master the most important learning objectives.

Students with failure syndrome problems need attribution retraining, efficacy training, strategy training, and related techniques for helping them learn to cope productively rather than give up when faced with frustration or failure. Bear in mind that even a steady diet of success experiences will not eliminate these students' potential for catastrophic reactions to failure; they need information and strategy training designed to help them realize that they can remain focused on the task and rely on a repertoire of strategies for working through such problems, and in the process, increase their levels of knowledge and skill in the domain.

Students obsessed with self-worth protection need help in realizing that their emphasis on performance goals over learning goals is contrary to their own best interests (and is unnecessary in any case, if you have established your classroom as the kind of learning community described in Chapter 2). At the same time, however, communicate empathy with their self-worth protection concerns and a willingness to take steps to help them feel more comfortable in the classroom. With less serious cases of students who do not have genuine self-worth protection concerns so much as a focus on social goals rather than learning goals, help them to realize that their preoccupation with short-term social goals is keeping them from engaging in the strategies they need to use in order to develop integrated understandings that will provide a basis for applying what they are learning in their lives outside of school.

Finally, committed underachievers also need help in realizing that their behavior is contrary to their long-run self-interests. They also need reassurance and perhaps a degree of task assistance in coming to understand that they can expect to enjoy continuous success if they continuously put forth reasonable effort—that you do not expect them to extend themselves to their limits every day. In hardened cases that feature work avoidance and excuses, you may need to supplement encouragement and motivational resocialization attempts with pressuring strategies such as home–school collaboration on behavior contracts or the confrontational approach recommended by Mandel and Marcus (1988).

Like people in general in any setting, students in classrooms pursue multiple goals and experience shifting priorities. Your goal as the teacher is to focus them as much as possible on learning goals that reflect the instructional objectives of the task at hand, while at the same time minimizing their attention to other goals. Regarding the expectancy aspects of motivation, this means minimizing threats to students' egos or self-worth perceptions. Systematic implementation of the principles outlined in Chapters 2 and 3 will minimize the need for students to focus on performance goals rather than learning goals. Those students who do so anyway will need additional treatment using strategies described in Chapter 4.

Chapters 3 and 4 have addressed the expectancy aspects of motivation, which flow from the question, Can I expect to complete this task successfully if I put forth reasonable effort? Chapters 5–8 now turn to the value aspects of motivation, as expressed in the question, Why should I care about completing this task successfully in the first place?

REFERENCES

Abbott, J. (1978). *Classroom strategies to aid the disabled learner.* Cambridge, MA: Educators Publishing Service.

Adelman, H., & Taylor, L. (1983). Enhancing motivation for overcoming learning and behavior problems. *Journal of Learning Disabilities, 16,* 384–392.

Ames, C. (1987). The enhancement of student motivation. In M. Maehr & D. Kleiber (Eds.), *Advances in motivation and achievement, Vol. 5: Enhancing motivation* (pp. 123–148). Greenwich, CT: JAI Press.

Anderson, L. (1985). A retrospective and prospective view of Bloom's "learning for mastery." In M. Wang and H. Walberg (Eds.), *Adapting instruction to individual differences* (pp. 254–268). Berkeley, CA: McCutchan.

Blanco, R., & Bogacki, D. (1988). *Prescriptions for children with learning and adjustment problems: A consultant's desk reference* (3rd Ed.). Springfield, IL: Charles C. Thomas.

Bloom, B. (1980). *All our children learning.* Hightstown, NJ: McGraw-Hill.

Boggiano, A., Shields, A., Barrett, M., Kellam, T., Thompson, E., Simons, J., & Katz, P. (1992) Helplessness deficits in students: The role of motivational orientation. *Motivation and Emotion, 16,* 271–296.

Brophy, J. (1996). *Teaching problem students.* New York: Guilford.

Brophy, J., & Good, T. (1970). Teachers' communication of differential expectations for children's classroom performance: Some behavioral data. *Journal of Educational Psychology, 61,* 365–374.

Butler, R., & Neuman, O. (1995). Effects of task and ego achievement goals on help-seeking behaviors and attitudes. *Journal of Educational Psychology, 87,* 261–271.

Butkowsky, I.S., & Willows, D.M. (1980). Cognitive motivational characteristics of children varying in reading ability: Evidence for learned helplessness in poor readers. *Journal of Educational Psychology, 72,* 408–422.

Clifford, M. (1984). Thoughts on a theory of constructive failure. *Educational Psychologist, 19,* 108–120.

Covington, M. (1992). *Making the grade: A self-worth perspective on motivation and school reform.* Cambridge: Cambridge University Press.

Craske, M. (1985). Improving persistence through observational learning and attribution retraining. *British Journal of Educational Psychology, 55,* 138–147.

Devine, T. (1987). *Teaching study skills: A guide for teachers* (2nd ed.) Boston: Allyn & Bacon.

Duffy, G., & Roehler, L. (1989). The tension between information-giving and mediation: Perspectives on instructional explanation and teacher change. In J. Brophy (Ed.) *Advances in research on teaching: Vol. 1. Teaching for meaningful understanding and self-regulated learning* (pp. 1–33). Greenwich, CT: JAI Press.

Dweck, C., & Elliott, E. (1983). Achievement motivation. In P. Mussen (Ed.), *Handbook of child psychology: Vol. 4. Socialization, personality, and social development* (pp. 643–691). New York: Wiley.

Entwisle, D., & Hayduk, L. (1982). *Early schooling: Cognitive and affective outcomes.* Baltimore: Johns Hopkins University Press.

Galloway, D., Leo, E., Rogers, C., & Armstrong, D. (1996). Maladaptive motivational style: The role of domain specific task demand in English and mathematics. *British Journal of Educational Psychology, 66,* 197–207.

Good, T., & Brophy, J. (1995). *Contemporary educational psychology* (5th ed). White Plains, NY: Longman.

Good, T., & Brophy, J. (1997). *Looking in classrooms* (7th ed.). New York: Longman.

Good, T., Slavings, R., Harel, K., & Emerson, H. (1987). Student passivity: A study of question-asking in K–12 classrooms. *Sociology of Education, 60,* 181–199.

Grabe, M. (1985). Attributions in a mastery instructional system: Is an emphasis on effort harmful? *Contemporary Educational Psychology, 10,* 113–126.

Hansen, D. (1989). Lesson evading and lesson dissembling: Ego strategies in the classroom. *American Journal of Education, 97,* 184–208.

Kurita, J., & Zarbatany, L. (1991). Teachers' acceptance of strategies for increasing students' achievement motivation. *Contemporary Educational Psychology, 16,* 241–253.

Lehtinen, E., Vauras, M., Salonen, P., Olkinuora, E., & Kinnunen, R. (1995). Long-term development of learning activity: Motivational, cognitive, and social interaction. *Educational Psychologist, 30,* 21–35.

Levine, D. (1985). *Improving student achievement through mastery learning programs.* San Francisco: Jossey-Bass.

Mandel, H., & Marcus, S. (1988). *The psychology of underachievement: Differential diagnosis and differential treatment.* New York: Wiley.

McCall, R., Evahn, C., & Kratzer, L. (1992). *High school underachievers.* Newbury Park, CA: Sage.

McCombs, B., & Pope, J. (1994). *Motivating hard to reach students.* Washington, DC: American Psychological Association.

McIntyre, T. (1989). *A resource book for remediating common behavior and learning problems.* Boston: Allyn & Bacon.

Meece, J., & Holt, K. (1993). A pattern analysis of students' achievement goals. *Journal of Educational Psychology, 85,* 582–590.

Nelson-LeGall, S. (1987). Necessary and unnecessary help seeking in children. *Journal of Genetic Psychology, 148,* 53–62.

Newman, R., & Goldin, L. (1990). Children's reluctance to seek help with homework. *Journal of Educational Psychology, 82,* 92–100.

Nicholls, J. (1989). *The competitive ethos and democratic education.* Cambridge, MA: Harvard University Press.

Palincsar, A., & Brown, A. (1984). Reciprocal teaching of comprehension-fostering and comprehension-monitoring activities. *Cognition and Instruction, 1,* 117–175.

Raffini, J. (1988). *Student apathy: The protection of self-worth.* Washington, DC: National Education Association.

Raphael, T. (1984). Teaching learners about sources of information for answering comprehension questions. *Journal of Reading, 27,* 303–311.

Rohrkemper, M., & Corno, L. (1988). Success and failure on classroom tasks: Adaptive learning and classroom teaching. *Elementary School Journal, 88,* 299–312.

Schunk, D. (1985). Self-efficacy and classroom learning. *Psychology in the Schools, 22,* 208–223.

Swift, M., & Spivack, G. (1975). *Alternative teaching strategies: Helping behaviorally troubled children achieve.* Champaign, IL: Research Press.

Thompson, C., & Rudolph, L. (1992). *Counseling children* (3rd ed.). Pacific Grove, CA: Brooks/Cole.

van der Meij, H. (1988). Constraints on question-asking in classrooms. *Journal of Educational Psychology, 80,* 401–405.

VanOverwalle, F., Segebarth, K., & Goldschstein, M. (1989). Improving performance of freshmen through attributional testimonies from fellow students. *British Journal of Educational Psychology, 59,* 79–85.

Weinstein, C., & Mayer, R. (1986). The teaching of learning strategies. In M. Wittrock (Ed.), *Handbook of research on teaching* (3rd ed., pp. 315–327). New York: Macmillan.

Wlodkowski, R. (1978). *Motivation and teaching: A practical guide.* Washington, DC: National Education Association.

CHAPTER 5

Providing Extrinsic Incentives

THE VALUE ASPECTS OF STUDENTS' MOTIVATION

The expectancy x value model implies the need to attend to the value aspects of students' motivation, not just the expectancy aspects. Without a sense of value, your students may be asking themselves, I know I can do this, but where is my motivation? To be motivated to do something, we need good reasons for doing it, not just confidence that we can do it if we try.

Eccles and Wigfield (1985) suggested that subjective task value has three major components: (1) *attainment value* (the importance of attaining success on the task in order to affirm our self-concept or fulfill our needs for achievement, power, or prestige); (2) *intrinsic value, or interest value* (the enjoyment that we get from engaging in the task); and (3) *utility value* (the role that engaging in the task may play in advancing our career or helping us to reach other larger goals).

This is a useful classification scheme, but for applications to the classroom I would expand it to place more emphasis on the cognitive aspects of student motivation to learn academic content. A broadened version would include ex-periencing *the satisfaction of achieving understanding or skill mastery* under attainment value, *aesthetic appreciation of the content or skill* under intrinsic value, and *awareness of the role of learning in improving the quality of one's life or making one a better person* under utility value.

Until recently, research on motivation in education concentrated on its ex-pectancy aspects (Berndt & Miller, 1990). Attention to value aspects was needed not only to balance the expectancy x value equation but also to broaden the purview from a focus on achievement situations that feature rela-tively specific goals to consideration of the complete range of learning situa-tions. Principles drawn from attribution theory, self-efficacy theory, and even goal theory apply most clearly to achievement situations that call for some

particular performance that will be evaluated with reference to relatively specific success criteria. In contrast, theories dealing with the value aspects of motivation apply not only to these achievement situations but also to self-guided
exploration and discovery learning, curricular enrichment activities, interest-
driven reading done in or out of school, and other activities that offer opportunities for learning but do not involve striving to accomplish a particular goal.

The expectancy aspects of motivation feature attributions about performance (e.g., Can I succeed on this task? Why did I achieve the level of success
that I did?). In contrast, the value aspects feature attributions concerning the
reasons for engaging in the task in the first place (e.g., What am I trying to accomplish here? What benefits will I obtain from engaging in this task?). Traditionally, teachers have been advised to supply answers to the latter questions
either by offering incentives for good performance (extrinsic motivation approach) or by teaching content and designing activities that students find enjoyable (intrinsic motivation approach).

Strategies reflecting these two general approaches are described here in
Chapter 5 (extrinsic strategies) and in Chapter 6 (intrinsic strategies). Then,
Chapter 7 presents strategies for implementing a third approach: stimulating
students' motivation to learn. Finally, coverage of the value aspects of motivation concludes in Chapter 8 with discussion of strategies for working with
alienated or unmotivated students who do not value schooling.

The ordering of these four chapters (and of the chapters in the book as a
whole) has been established to facilitate the coherent flow of ideas. Nothing
should be inferred from this order concerning the relative importance of the
content addressed in the various chapters. Each chapter contributes to a network of ideas that together constitute a comprehensive approach to motivating students. A complete system that incorporates the whole network will be
more powerful than a partial system that omits parts of it.

COMMON BELIEFS ABOUT REWARDS

To begin thinking about the effects of extrinsic incentives, consider Students A
and B:

> A and B are both fourth graders who enjoy and do well in school, although
> they approach school and relate to their teachers in different ways. For exam-
> ple, B did all this week's reading on the solar system knowing that completing
> assignments pleases the teacher. B made a couple of points during class dis-
> cussion so the teacher would know B had done the reading. A also finished
> the reading because A got really interested in knowing all about the solar sys-
> tem. A continued to ask questions during the discussion, even after some of
> the other kids seemed tired of the topic. Since A knows grades don't always
> reflect work quality, A isn't that interested in grades and doesn't pay much at-
> tention to them, but B pays close attention to grades and uses them as a gauge
> by which to judge how B has been doing on recent work (Flink et al., 1992,
> p. 208).

Given this information, how would you rate Students A and B in basic ability, degree of responsibility as students, or overall effort in school work? Which student would exert greater effort following failure? Which would show enhanced performance following success?

Barrett and Boggiano (1988) put these questions to groups of parents and of college students. They found that the majority of both groups believed that extrinsically motivated Student B would exert more effort after failure, show enhanced performance following success, exert more overall effort in school work, and take more responsibility for completing work than intrinsically motivated Student A. However, they believed that B would have lower self-esteem than A. Only the last belief is supported by research comparing extrinsically and intrinsically motivated students.

This was one of a series of studies by Ann Boggiano and her colleagues on adults' beliefs about factors that motivate children. In other studies, they presented descriptions of students displaying either high or low intrinsic interest in various academic activities, then asked parents or college students to rate how effective they thought each of four social control techniques (rewards, reasoning, punishment, or noninterference) would be for maximizing the student's enjoyment or interest in the depicted activity. Both groups of adults rated rewards as more effective than the other three strategies, both short-term and long-term, regardless of the student's depicted level of interest in the activity. They also believed that larger rewards would be more effective than smaller rewards. Studies in this series repeatedly confirmed that most adults believe that rewards are effective, not only as incentives for motivating students to put forth effort on academic activities, but also for stimulating their development of intrinsic interest in these activities (Boggiano et al., 1987; Flink et al., 1992).

Given these and related research findings, it is likely that *you* share these beliefs in the effectiveness of rewards as motivators, at least in part. Do you? Before reading on in the chapter, pause to take stock. Is using rewards an effective way to motivate students? A desirable way? Are rewards helpful for certain students or situations but not for others? Why?

STRATEGIES FOR SUPPLYING EXTRINSIC MOTIVATION

In some respects, extrinsic motivation strategies are the simplest, most direct, and most adaptable of the methods for addressing the value aspects of motivation. These strategies do not attempt to increase the value that students place on the task itself. Instead, they link successful completion of the task to delivery of consequences that students already do value. By reminding students that successful completion is instrumental to accomplishment of some valued goal (where this contingency exists naturally) or by establishing an incentive system that offers extrinsic rewards contingent on successful completion, you can spur students to invest more effort in the task than they might invest otherwise.

However, from the standpoint of most motivational theorists, this is *control of behavior*, not *motivation of learning* (see Box 5.1). Some educators always

Box 5.1.   A Note on Reinforcement and Behavior Modification

Chapter 5 includes a section on using rewards as incentives but does not include sections on contingency contracting, behavior modification, token economy programs, or related applications of applied behavior analysis used to bring selected behaviors under stimulus control. This is because these methods are conceived and implemented as behavioral control strategies rather than as motivation strategies. They work by making desired behavior (e.g., careful and persistent work on assignments) instrumental to attainment of contingent extrinsic rewards, usually by making this contingency explicit to students in advance. Heavy emphasis on these behavioral control techniques, and in particular the use of a token economy or some other earned-credits incentive system as one's basic approach to classroom management, is in many respects incompatible with the strategies that have emerged from research on motivation in education. As Reeve (1996) noted, motivation is not about principles of operant conditioning or behavior management; it is about how students' inner resources energize and direct their behavior.

You will need to make a fundamental choice between emphasizing a behavioral control system or a student motivational system as your basic approach to classroom management and motivational issues. The two general approaches are not completely incompatible, so if you choose one as your basic approach you can still supplement it with selected strategies drawn from the other. You cannot implement each approach fully, however, because there are too many contradictions.

This book is for teachers who opt for the motivational approach, which I recommend for two primary reasons. First, although it is more difficult than it may seem to learn to implement consistently, the motivational approach is nevertheless more feasible for most teachers. In order to use reinforcement to shape students' behavior in ways that reflect consistent application of behavior modification principles, teachers have to be in position to supply reinforcement when and where it is needed. This is not possible in regular classrooms where teachers work with 20 or more students, although it may be possible in special classrooms with very low student-to-teacher ratios. Even here, though, it will require heavy reliance on programmed instructional materials, rather than tutoring or small-group instruction from the teacher, as the primary approach to curriculum and instruction (thus leaving the teacher free to circulate, monitor progress, and dispense reinforcements). A great deal of classroom research suggests that students need active instruction from their teachers, not solitary work with instructional materials, in order to make good achievement progress (Brophy & Good, 1986).

Second, the motivational approach seems clearly preferable to the behavioral control approach when students' long-run best interests are taken into account. Even when behavioral control methods work effectively, they accomplish only temporary, situational, and external control over students' behavior. Their behavior can and often does change drastically when the incentive system is terminated or when the

(Continued)

> ## Box 5.1.   A Note on Reinforcement and Behavior Modification—*Concluded*
>
> students are in situations in which the system is not operative. In contrast, motivational approaches are designed not just to induce situational compliance in students but to develop attitudes, values, beliefs, and self-regulated learning strategies that they will use in appropriate learning situations in and out of school throughout their lives. To the extent that the motivational approach is successful in developing these self-regulation orientations and capacities in students, it yields desirable outcomes that generalize far beyond the immediate classroom situation.
>
> Although this book clearly focuses on motivational strategies, it does ad-vocate limited use of what appear to be behavioral control strategies, especially in discussing the use of contracts in Chapter 4 and the use of rewards as incentives in Chapter 5. Note, however, that it advocates using these strategies in ways that deemphasize their behavioral control aspects to make them compatible with more purely motivational strategies. In particular, the suggestions call for encouraging students to commit themselves to difficult yet realistic goals and helping students to appreciate their progress and accomplishments, while avoiding placing too much emphasis on reinforcement contingencies or salient rewards.

have opposed extrinsic motivational methods on principle, viewing them as bribing students for doing what they should be doing anyway because it is the right thing to do or because it is in the best interests of themselves or of society. This position was reaffirmed recently by Kohn (1993) in a popular book claiming that the effectiveness of rewards has been exaggerated and that rewarding students for learning undermines their intrinsic interest in the material. The subtitle of Kohn's book refers to "gold stars, incentive plans, A's, praise, and other bribes."

Research findings that emerged during the 1970s and 1980s provided what at first appeared to be strong support for opponents of extrinsic rewards. These findings indicated that if you begin to reward people for doing what they already were doing for their own reasons, you may decrease their intrinsic motivation to continue that behavior in the future (Deci & Ryan, 1985; Heckhausen, 1991; Lepper & Greene, 1978). Furthermore, to the extent that you focus their attention on the reward rather than on the task, their performance tends to deteriorate (Condry & Chambers, 1978). They develop a piecework mentality, doing whatever will garner them the most rewards with the least effort, rather than trying to do the job as well as they can in order to create a high-quality product. If allowed to choose, they select tasks that will maximize their access to rewards over tasks that offer more challenge or opportunities for them to develop their knowledge or skills.

For a time, it was thought that these undesirable outcomes were inherent in the use of rewards (or other extrinsic pressures, as discussed in Box 5.2).

Box 5.2.   Undermining Intrinsic Motivation

Research on ways in which extrinsic considerations can undermine intrinsic motivation initially focused on rewards offered as incentives, and explanations for the undermining effect focused on people's attributional inferences. In fact, an early term for this undermining was the *overjustification* effect: To the extent that people become aware that they are being "bribed" to engage in a particular behavior, they are likely to infer that such bribing is considered necessary because people do not tend to engage in the behavior voluntarily. That is, the opportunity to engage in the behavior is not sufficient justification for doing so, and therefore extra incentives must be added. This line of reasoning leads to the conclusion that the overjustified behavior is aversive, or at least not worth performing in the absence of an extrinsic incentive for doing so. This inference would undermine any intrinsic motivation for performing the behavior that might have been present originally.

As research findings accumulated, it became clear that this undermining effect can occur not only when people are offered rewards for engaging in a behavior, but whenever they became aware of any extrinsic factor that leads them to attribute their engaging in the behavior to external pressures rather than to their own intrinsic motivation. Other examples include awareness that the behavior is required (with ex-

pressed or at least implied threat of punishment if it is not performed), that one's performance is being monitored closely, that one's performance will be evaluated or compared to that of others, or that one is under pressure to meet a time deadline (Kohn, 1993; Lepper, 1983). Therefore, what undermines intrinsic motivation is not the use of rewards as such but offering rewards in advance as incentives and following through in ways that lead students to believe that they engaged in the rewarded behaviors only because they had to do so in order to earn the rewards, not because these behaviors have value in their own right or produce other outcomes that are in the students' best interests.

Pintrich, Marx, and Boyle (1993) noted that students often are in situations where multiple incentives or goals are operating. For example, students may have intrinsic interest in a topic or activity, may also value learning about it because such learning is important to their future career plans, and furthermore may be aware of the need to display their learning by meeting certain performance standards that will enable them to get acceptable grades. The important thing is that these and any other motivational influences that might be operating work in such a way as to encourage students to "think it through" rather than just to "get it done."

More recently, it has become clear that the effects of rewards depend on what rewards are used and especially on how they are presented. Decreases in performance quality and in intrinsic motivation are most likely when rewards have the following characteristics:

High salience: The rewards are very attractive or are presented in ways that call attention to them.

Noncontingency: The rewards are given for mere participation in the activity, rather than being contingent on achieving specific goals.

Unnatural/unusual: The rewards are artificially tied to behaviors as control devices, rather than being natural outcomes of the behaviors.

Unfortunately, misguided attempts to use rewards to motivate students' learning are not uncommon, in or out of schools. For example, a well-known program that supplies free pizzas to students who read a certain number of books has all three of the characteristics listed above. Pizzas are very attractive rewards to most children, the program artificially makes reading a certain number of books instrumental to receiving free pizzas, and the pizzas are awarded merely for certifying that the required number of books have been read (not for reading them carefully, responding to them thoughtfully, or taking something meaningful away from the experience). This contingency is likely to undermine students' intrinsic motivation to read because it implies that their behavior is controlled externally—that they are reading the books only because they must do so in order to earn pizzas. In effect, they are encouraged to select short, simple books, zip through them quickly, and move on to the next one. As John Nicholls (quoted by Kohn, 1993, p. 73) once noted, this approach is more likely to produce "a lot of fat kids who don't like to read" than a nation of thoughtful and intrinsically motivated readers.

Fortunately, research has shown that extrinsic rewards do not necessarily undermine intrinsic motivation and even can be used in ways that support its development. One way is to provide unannounced rewards *following* task completion, so that the rewards are seen as expressions of appreciation rather than as delivery of promised incentives. Other ways involve using rewards as informative feedback rather than as control mechanisms. Even if announced in advance as performance incentives, rewards are likely to have desirable effects if they are offered not merely for participating in activities but for accomplishing specified goals (Cameron & Pierce, 1994, 1996; Chance, 1993). It also helps to emphasize social rewards over material rewards and to deliver rewards in ways that encourage students to value the accomplishments being rewarded. These principles are illustrated in the following section.

REWARD STUDENTS FOR GOOD PERFORMANCE

Most teachers want to reward their students' praiseworthy efforts and accomplishments. They find it natural to do so in the process of building good relationships with students and encouraging and supporting their learning efforts. Types of rewards commonly used by teachers include: (1) material rewards (money, prizes, trinkets, consumables); (2) activity rewards and special privileges (opportunities to play games, use special equipment, or engage in self-selected activities); (3) grades, awards, and recognitions (honor rolls, displaying good papers); (4) praise and social rewards; and (5) teacher rewards (special attention, personalized interaction, opportunities to go places or do things with the teacher).

If you enjoy rewarding your students in one or more of these ways, you do not need to stop doing so for fear of undermining their intrinsic motivation. It is now clear that intrinsic motivation and extrinsic motivation are relatively independent, so that students in a given situation can be high in both or low in both, not just high in one and low in the other. It also is clear that rewards can be used in ways that support or at least do not undermine intrinsic motivation. However, it is important that you learn when and how to dispense rewards effectively, to ensure that your rewards have only positive and not mixed or even negative effects.

When to Reward

Rewards are more effective for increasing the intensity of effort than for improving the quality of performance. They guide learning more effectively when there is a clear goal and a clear strategy to follow than when goals are more ambiguous or when students must discover or invent new strategies rather than merely activate familiar ones. Therefore, rewards are better used with routine tasks than with novel ones, better with specific intentional learning tasks than with incidental learning or discovery tasks, and better with tasks where steady performance or quantity of output is of more concern than creativity, artistry, or craftsmanship.

It is better to offer rewards as incentives for meeting performance standards (or performance *improvement* standards) on skills that require a great deal of drill and practice (e.g., arithmetic computation, musical scales, typing, spelling, free-throw shooting) than it is for work on a major research or demonstration project. With low-level tasks that demand rote learning, no other source of motivation may be operating, so rewards may be needed to motivate sustained effort (although a more important strategy would be to minimize students' encounters with such boring or aversive tasks). It is not wise to offer rewards as primary incentives to motivate students to do things that you would like to see them do on their own, such as watch educational television programs, read quality books, or participate in civic affairs or community improvement efforts.

Rewards can act as motivators only for those students who believe that they have a chance to get the rewards if they put forth reasonable effort. Therefore, if you wish to create incentives for the whole class and not just for your high achievers, you will need to ensure that all students have equal (or at least reasonable) access to the rewards. This may require performance contracting or some less formal method of individualizing criteria for success.

For example, MacIver and Reuman (1993/94) described an incentives program in which students were rewarded either for maintaining high performance or for improving less satisfactory performance. Each week, students attempted to beat their current "base score" on the week's most important quiz, test, project, assignment, or performance task. They were rewarded according to the "improvement points" they earned. Those who turned in perfect tests or papers or beat their current base score by more than nine points were awarded 30 improvement points; those who scored within five points of a perfect paper or beat their current base score by five to nine points were awarded 20 improvement points; those who scored within four points of their current base score were awarded 10 improvement points; and those who scored more than four points below their current base score were not awarded any improvement points in that subject for that week.

Midgley and Urdan (1992) offered useful suggestions about the kinds of accomplishments that you might emphasize in providing students with recognitions or other symbolic rewards. First, recognize the quality of students' accomplishments rather than the quantity, and in particular recognize students for taking on challenging work or stretching their abilities (even if they make mistakes). Also, recognize them for coming up with different or unusual ways to solve problems. These priorities give powerful messages about what is valued in your classroom.

Midgley and Urdan also suggested that you use multiple criteria that allow you to adapt your recognitions to individual differences, rather than using the same criteria for all students and thus ending up comparing them directly. However, make sure that your recognitions are for genuine accomplishments (given what is reasonable to expect from the student). Finally, although you may want to provide recognition to students in a variety of domains (athletics, good citizenship, etc.), make sure that every student has the opportunity to earn recognition in the academic domain.

How to Reward

Deliver rewards in ways that provide students with informative feedback and encourage them to appreciate their developing knowledge and skills, not just to think about the rewards. If you offer rewards in advance as incentives, emphasize your major instructional goals in setting criteria for judging performance and determining reward credits. Reward students for mastering key ideas and skills (or showing improvement in their mastery levels), not merely for participating in activities or turning in assignments. Include provisions for redoing work that does not meet minimum standards.

In explaining and following through on incentive systems, emphasize the importance of the learning and help students to appreciate and take pride in their accomplishments. Portray the rewards as verifications of significant and worthwhile achievements, not as the whole point of their efforts. This is less crucial with surprise rewards not announced in advance as incentives, but even when delivering surprise rewards it is wise to cast them as expressions of appreciation for your students' efforts and accomplishments, without making too much of the "big surprise."

Additional guidelines about rewarding students are implied in the following section on praising effectively. These guidelines focus on praising students in ways that emphasize providing them with informative feedback rather than exercising control over their behavior. Most of what is said about praise also applies to other forms of rewards, and in particular to what you might say to students in the process of delivering the rewards.

Praising Your Students Effectively

Praise is widely recommended as a way to reward students, although it does not always have this effect (Brophy, 1981; Schwieso & Hastings, 1987). Sometimes a teacher's praise is not even intended as a reward for a specific accomplishment, as when the praise is used in an attempt to build a social relationship with an alienated student (i.e., "I like your new shirt, John."). Even when praise is intended as a reward, some students will not perceive it that way. For one thing, some students do not attach much value to teacher praise and thus do not feel particularly rewarded when they receive it (Ware, 1978). Also, many students appreciate praise that is communicated in private but are less enthused about being praised in front of their classmates (Caffyn, 1989).

Students may find it embarrassing to be singled out, humiliating to be praised for some minor accomplishment, or irritating to have classmates' attention called to their neatness, punctuality, or conformity behaviors rather than to more clearly noteworthy achievements. For example, a teacher's statement that "I like the way Susie is sitting up straight and ready to listen" is almost certain to embarrass Susie. It may even alienate her if she is sophisticated enough to realize that the statement is not really praise of her but an attempt to cue the behaviors of some of her classmates.

As related examples, consider the following expressions of teacher praise:

"John, I really enjoyed your story, especially the machine that converts peanut butter into energy. I'd like you to read it to the class later today. Also, how about drawing a picture of what that machine might look like?"

"Mary, you did a fine job. I especially liked the way you wrote your story so neatly—centered headings, no smudges, writing carefully on the lines—keep up the good work!"

In these examples, the teacher's praise of John's work focuses on its substance and is likely to be appreciated because it identifies genuinely noteworthy accomplishments. By drawing attention to a particular detail of John's story, the teacher shows that she has paid attention to its content and appreciates its creativity. In contrast, her praise of Mary's work focuses on form and neatness rather than its substantive content or the creativity of her writing. She did not mention any of the particulars of Mary's story or even give any clear indication that she remembered any of it. Although well intended and apparently sincere, such praise is unlikely to be pleasing to Mary because it will cause her to suspect that the teacher did not like her story or does not think highly of her writing abilities.

Public praise can be problematic even when it is recognized as praise and appreciated as such both by the recipient and by classmates. Students who are eager for teacher attention may begin clamoring for it, and students who believe that they are just as deserving as classmates who have been praised may begin to feel slighted (Ollendick & Shapiro, 1984).

Praise Should Be Appreciative Rather than Controlling

Sometimes this is easier said than done. As Kohn (1993, p. 102, original italics) observed, "the most notable aspect of a positive judgment is not that it is positive but that it is a *judgment*." Therefore, it is important to phrase praise statements as communication of informative feedback rather than as evaluation. Effective praise expresses appreciation for students' efforts or admiration for their accomplishments, in ways that call attention to the efforts or accomplishments themselves rather than to their role in pleasing the teacher. This helps students learn to attribute their *efforts* to their own intrinsic motivation rather than to external incentives supplied by the teacher, and to attribute their *successes* to their own abilities and efforts rather than to external supports. You might express such praise as part of a "celebration" of what has been learned or accomplished as you bring a unit or series of activities to closure.

Effective Praise Also Is Genuine

Brophy and Evertson (1981) found that teachers were credible and spontaneous when praising students whom they liked, often smiling as they spoke and praising genuine accomplishments. These teachers praised students whom they disliked just as frequently, but usually without accompanying spontaneity and warmth and often with reference to appearance or conduct rather than accomplishments. Some teachers praise poor responses as part of a well-intentioned attempt to encourage low achievers (Nafpaktitis, Mayer, & Butterworth, 1985; Natriello & Dornbusch, 1985). This tactic often backfires, however, because it undermines the teacher's credibility and confuses or depresses the students (to the extent that they realize that they are being treated differently from their classmates).

Students need informative feedback to support their learning efforts, but they do not need more intensive expressions of praise. Correlations between teachers' rates of praise and their students' achievement gains are low in magnitude and mixed in direction, suggesting that the most effective teachers are sparing rather than effusive in their praise (Brophy & Good, 1986). However, most teachers enjoy delivering praise and most students enjoy receiving it, at least when it is delivered as spontaneous, genuine reaction to student accomplishment rather than as part of a calculated attempt to manipulate the student. Keep this in mind when deciding when and how to praise students. Other guidelines for praising effectively are given below and in Table 5.1.

1. Praise simply and directly, in a natural voice, without gushing or dramatizing.
2. Praise in straightforward, declarative sentences (e.g., "I never thought of that before") instead of gushy exclamations (e.g., "Wow!") or rhetorical questions (e.g., "Isn't that terrific?"). The latter are condescending and more likely to embarrass than reward.

TABLE 5.1. Guidelines for Effective Praise

Effective Praise	Ineffective Praise
1. Is delivered contingently	1. Is delivered randomly or unsystematically
2. Specifies the particulars of the accomplishment	2. Is restricted to global positive reactions
3. Shows spontaneity, variety, and other signs of credibility; suggests clear attention to the student's accomplishment	3. Shows a bland uniformity that suggests a conditioned response made with minimal attention
4. Rewards attainment of specified performance criteria (which can include effort criteria, however)	4. Rewards mere participation, without consideration of performance processes or outcomes
5. Provides information to students about their competence or the value of their accomplishments	5. Provides no information at all or gives students information about their status
6. Orients students toward better appreciation of their own task-related behavior and thinking about problem solving	6. Orients students toward comparing themselves with others and thinking about competing
7. Uses students' own prior accomplishments as the context for describing present accomplishments	7. Uses the accomplishments of peers as the context for describing students' present accomplishments
8. Is given in recognition of noteworthy effort or success at difficult tasks	8. Is given without regard to the effort expended or the meaning of the accomplishment
9. Attributes success to effort and ability, implying that similar success can be expected in the future	9. Attributes success to ability alone or to external factors such as luck or (easy) task difficulty
10. Fosters endogenous attributions (students believe that they expend effort on the task because they enjoy the task and/or want to develop task-relevant skills)	10. Fosters exogenous attributions (students believe that they expend effort on the task for external reasons—to please the teacher, win a competition or reward, etc.)
11. Focuses students' attention on their own task-relevant behavior	11. Focuses students' attention on the teacher as an external authority figure who is manipulating them
12. Fosters appreciation of, and desirable attributions about, task-relevant behavior after the process is completed	12. Intrudes into the ongoing process, distracting attention from task-relevant behavior

Source: Brophy, J. (1981). Teacher praise: A functional analysis. *Review of Educational Research, 51,* 5–32.

3. Specify the particular accomplishment being praised and recognize any noteworthy effort, care, or perseverance (e.g., "Good! You figured it out all by yourself. I like the way you stuck with it without giving up" instead of "Good"). Call attention to new skills or evidence of progress

(e.g., "I notice you've learned to use different kinds of metaphors in your compositions. They're more interesting to read now.").

4. Use a variety of phrases for praising students. Overused stock phrases soon begin to sound insincere and give the impression that you have not paid much attention to the accomplishments you are praising.

5. Combine verbal praise with nonverbal communication of approval. "Good job!" is rewarding only when delivered with a smile and a tone that communicates appreciation or warmth.

6. Avoid ambiguous statements that students may take as praise for compliance rather than for learning (e.g., "You were really good today."). Instead, be specific in praising their accomplishments (e.g., "I'm very pleased with your reading this morning, especially the way you read with so much expression. You made the conversation between Billy and Mr. Taylor sound very real.").

7. Ordinarily, students should be praised privately. This communicates that the praise is genuine and avoids the problem of sounding as though you are holding the student up as an example to the rest of the class.

Wlodkowski (1985) summarized many of these same principles in his "3S-3P" guidelines: Praise (or other rewards) should be Sincere, Specific, Sufficient (adapted to the accomplishment), and Properly attributed for genuinely Praiseworthy accomplishments, in a manner Preferred by the learner.

CALL ATTENTION TO THE INSTRUMENTAL VALUE OF LEARNING

Often it is possible to make students aware of naturally existing extrinsic incentives for mastering academic content or skills instead of offering them artificial rewards for doing so. A good curriculum is constructed as a means rather than an end in itself, so that all of its components are intended as vehicles for moving students toward outcomes that will enrich their lives and equip them to function successfully in our society. At least in theory, it is in a student's best interest to engage in any academic activity seriously and complete it successfully, so as to obtain the benefits that it was designed to yield.

However, school activities differ in the degree to which their life application potential is immediate and obvious to students. Some knowledge and skills taught in school can be applied in the students' current lives or obviously will be needed as life skills later. These natural consequences of task mastery can be powerful incentives for motivating learning efforts. Therefore, whenever you see the opportunity to do so, help your students to appreciate that the knowledge or skills developed by an activity are useful in enabling them to meet their own current needs, providing them with a means to social advancement, or preparing them for occupational or other success in life. In the process, cite examples by relating your own personal experiences or telling anecdotes about individuals with whom your students can identify (such as famous people that they look up to or former students from your school).

The strategy of calling students' attention to the life application value of what they are learning is not used as often as it could be, and when it is, it is often used in self-defeating ways. Rather than stress the present or future application value of what is being learned in positive terms, many teachers only mention negative outcomes that may result from failure to learn it. These include personal embarrassment (e.g., "You don't want people to think you are ignorant.") or future educational or occupational disasters (e.g., "You'll never get through the sixth grade."; "How are you going to get a job if you can't do basic math?"). Other teachers use variations that cast the student in a more positive light but portray society as a hostile environment (e.g., urging students to learn to count so that merchants don't shortchange them or to learn to read so that they don't get cheated when signing contracts).

Rather than distract your students with such worries, be more positive in helping them appreciate the potential applications of what they are learning. Basic language arts and mathematics skills are used daily when shopping, banking, driving, reading instructions for using some product, paying bills, carrying on business correspondence, and planning home maintenance projects or family vacations. Scientific knowledge is useful for everything from coping effectively with minor everyday challenges to making good decisions in emergency situations. Knowledge of history and related social studies topics provides a basis for making personal, social, and civic decisions. In general, a good working knowledge of the information, principles, and skills taught in school prepares people to make well-informed decisions that can save time, trouble, expense, or even lives. It also empowers people by preparing them to appreciate and take advantage of the opportunities that society offers.

Help your students to recognize such connections between classroom learning and life outside of school, so that they come to see academic activities as enabling opportunities to be valued rather than as unwelcome impositions. More generally, help your students to appreciate that schools are established by society for their benefit. In this regard, you might note that the educational opportunities we have come to take for granted in our country are available only to the privileged few in many countries. The idea here is not to preach to your students or make them feel guilty but to heighten their awareness of education as opportunity and to underscore the idea that conscientious learning efforts are in their own best interests, not just duties that they must perform in order to please you or their parents.

OCCASIONALLY STRUCTURE APPROPRIATE FORMS OF COMPETITION

The opportunity to compete can add excitement to classroom activities, whether the competition is for prizes or merely for the satisfaction of winning. Competition may be either individual (i.e., students compete in pairs or as individuals working against everyone else) or group (i.e., students are divided into teams that compete with one another). Traditionally, competitions have been structured around test scores or other performance measures, but it also is possible to build competitive elements into ordinary instruction by including activities such as argumentative essays, debates, or simulation games that involve competition (Keller, 1983).

Despite its popularity among many teachers and its considerable motivational potential, *most motivational theorists oppose the use of competition or place heavy qualifications on its applicability as a motivational strategy.* There are several good reasons for this.

First, participating in classroom activities already involves risking public failure and a great deal of competition is already built into the grading system. Therefore, it may be counterproductive to introduce additional competitive elements.

Second, competition is even more salient and distracting than rewards for most students. For example, Ames & Ames (1981) found that students working on their own tended to evaluate their progress with reference to their prior performance, noting and appreciating developments in knowledge and skill. In contrast, students working in competitive structures were so focused on comparisons and winning/losing that they paid little or no attention to what they were learning.

Third, the qualifications that apply to the use of rewards as incentives also apply to competition. In particular, competition is more appropriate for use with routine practice tasks than with tasks calling for discovery or creativity, and it can be effective only if everyone has a good (or at least an equal) chance of winning. To ensure this, it may be necessary to use team competition in which the teams are balanced by ability profiles or to use individual competition in which a handicapping system enables each student to compete with his or her own previous performance rather than with classmates.

Finally, a root problem with competition is that it creates losers as well as winners (and usually many more losers than winners). Even when there is no rational reason for it, a loser's psychology tends to develop whenever individuals or teams lose competitions. Individuals may suffer at least temporary embarrassment, and those who lose consistently may suffer more permanent losses in confidence, self-concept, and enjoyment of school (Epstein & Harackiewicz, 1992; Moriarty et al. 1995; Reeve & Deci, 1996). Members of losing teams may devalue one another and scapegoat those whom they hold responsible for the team's loss (Ames, 1984; Johnson & Johnson, 1985).

In combination, these considerations should give you pause about introducing competition as a motivational strategy. If you are thinking about doing so, plan to minimize its risks by making sure that all students have an equal chance to win, that winning is determined primarily by degree of effort (and perhaps a degree of luck) rather than by level ability, that attention is focused more on the task than on who wins and who loses, and that reactions to the outcome emphasize the positive (i.e., winners are congratulated but losers are not criticized or ridiculed; the accomplishments of the class as a whole, not just of the winners, are acknowledged).

There are ways to depersonalize competition. For example, you might divide the class into several teams and ask each team to develop a campaign speech based on specified criteria. Next, the class would use these criteria to critique the speeches. Then, each team would take the best features from all of the initial versions and produce an improved speech that represents the class's best thinking. This series of activities involves competitive elements, but it focuses on the content rather than the competition.

Student Team Learning Methods

One way to exploit the motivational potential of competition while avoiding most of its undesirable effects is to use student team learning methods in which students cooperate in addition to competing. These methods feature both a handicapping system to supply individual criteria for scoring each student's work and an incentive system that offers group rewards to teams whose combined individual scores enable them to win competitions against other teams (Slavin, 1990).

TGT

The original student team learning method was called Teams-Games-Tournament (TGT). In TGT, students work together in four- or five-member, heterogeneously composed teams to help one another master content and prepare for competitions against other teams. The teacher first presents the material to be learned, then team members work together filling out worksheets. They discuss the material, tutor one another, and quiz one another to assess mastery. These forms of cooperative learning continue throughout the week in preparation for tournaments held on Fridays.

For the tournaments, students are assigned to three-person tables composed of students from different teams who are similar in achievement level. The three students compete at academic games covering the content taught that week and practiced during team meetings. Most of these games are simply numbered questions on a handout. A student picks a number card and attempts to answer the corresponding question. Students can earn points by responding to questions correctly or by successfully challenging and correcting the answers of the other two students at the table. These points are later summed to determine each team's score, and the teacher prepares a newsletter that recognizes successful teams and unusually high scores attained by individuals. The newsletter may also contain cumulative team scores if tournaments last longer than one week.

Prior to the next tournament, the teacher may assign certain students to different tournament tables in order to keep the competition at each table as even as possible. This ensures that even though the teams are heterogeneous in composition and team membership remains the same, all students begin each tournament with an equal chance to earn points for their teams because they are competing against peers whose achievement levels are similar to theirs. This incentive structure motivates students not only to master the material on their own but also to help their teammates master it.

STAD

Student Teams-Achievement Divisions (STAD) is a simplification of TGT. STAD follows the same heterogeneous grouping and cooperative learning procedures as TGT but replaces the games and tournaments with a quiz. Quiz scores are translated into team competition points based on how much students have improved their performance over past averages.

Both TGT and STAD combine cooperative learning with team competition and use group rewards for cumulative individual performance; however, STAD depersonalizes the competition. Rather than compete face-to-face against classmates at tournament tables, students in STAD classrooms try to do their best on quizzes taken individually. STAD is generally considered an improvement on TGT because it is easier to implement and it reduces the salience of the competition.

Jigsaw II

Jigsaw II is an adaptation of the original Jigsaw (described in Chapter 6), a cooperative learning method that ensures that students interact with and learn from one another because each team member possesses unique information that must be communicated to the others. Jigsaw II combines competitive elements with these cooperative elements. Students begin by reading a narrative (such as a chapter in a history text or a biography of an accomplished person) to provide them with a common base of information. Then, to develop the material, each member of a team is given a separate topic on which to become an "expert." Students from different teams who have been assigned to the same topic meet in "expert groups" to discuss their topics. Then they return to their teams to teach what they have learned to their teammates.

Except for the topic on which they have become expert, students must depend on their classmates to provide them with information that is not included in the base narrative. Furthermore, as team members, students have responsibilities not only to master the material themselves but to teach it effectively to teammates so that all team members can be successful in the competition. At the end of the week, students take a quiz, their individual scores are summed to compute team scores, and team accomplishments are recognized through the class newsletter.

TAI

Team-Assisted Individualization (TAI) is an adaptation of individualized mathematics instruction that introduces cooperative learning methods and team competition with group reward, as in STAD. TAI combines direct instruction by the teacher (to small, homogeneously formed groups), follow-up practice using programmed instructional materials, and a student team learning approach to seatwork management.

Student team learning methods consistently show positive effects on achievement. These achievement benefits are related to the use of group rewards based on team scores computed by adding the team members' individual performance scores. Methods that ensure the accountability of individual group members to their group mates produce higher achievement than methods that allow one or two students to do the work while the others take more passive roles. The highest achievement outcomes result from methods that combine group goals with individual accountability (Slavin, 1988).

Note that the achievement advantages of student team learning methods reside in their group reward and individual accountability features, not their competitive features. There is no evidence that group competition offers advantages over other cooperative learning methods so long as arrangements are made to provide group rewards based on the cumulative performance of individual group members. Besides using direct competitions (as in TGT and STAD), good results have been obtained by giving teams certificates for meeting preset standards (independently of the performance of other teams) and by using task specialization to motivate students to encourage their teammates. Thus, although the effects of student team learning on achievement appear to be primarily motivational, the key is not motivation to win competitions against other teams but motivation to assist one's teammates to meet their individual goals and thus ensure that the team will do well.

Like other forms of cooperative learning, student team learning methods have produced positive effects on outcomes other than achievement. These methods promote friendships and prosocial interaction among students as well as positive outcomes on individual affective variables such as self-esteem, academic self-confidence, and liking for the class and for classmates.

CONCLUSION

Extrinsic motivational strategies can be effective in certain circumstances, but you should not rely on them too heavily. If your students become preoccupied with rewards or competition, they may not pay enough attention to what they are supposed to be learning or develop much appreciation for its value. The quality of task engagement and of ultimate achievement tends to be higher when students perceive themselves to be engaged in activities for their own reasons rather than in order to please an authority figure, obtain a reward, or escape punishment (Deci & Ryan, 1985; Flink et al., 1992; Lepper, 1983).

Your students are unlikely to become preoccupied with extrinsic rewards or pressures if you confine your extrinsic motivational strategies to noting the instrumental value of what is being learned or offering after-the-fact praise or rewards to show appreciation for their learning efforts and achievements. There is danger of such preoccupation, however, whenever you announce your intentions to implement an incentive system, so that students know beforehand that they will be trying to earn a reward or win a competition as they engage in classroom activities.

What can happen was shown in a study by Meece and Holt (1993), who interviewed students about their goals and correlated this information with other measures of motivation and achievement. They found that students who emphasized only mastery goals showed better achievement and more desirable patterns on other motivational measures than students who mentioned both mastery goals and ego/social goals (demonstrate high ability, please the teacher). This is another reminder that "more" motivation doesn't necessarily translate into better or optimal motivation, especially if it leads to the use of effort-minimizing strategies instead of more active learning strategies.

Under some circumstances, however, performance goals can supplement learning goals, especially if they translate into hard work to get good grades (rather than into a preoccupation with self-worth protection). For example, Bouffard et al. (1995) reported that college students, especially males, who were highly invested in both learning and performance goals showed higher academic achievement than peers who were highly invested in only one type of goal. In turn, the latter students outperformed peers who were not highly invested in either type of goal. Even this study suggested that learning goals are preferable to performance goals, however, because they were associated with better scores on other measures of motivation and on measures of the students' use of cognitive and metacognitive strategies for regulating their learning.

In conclusion, if you use rewards and other extrinsic incentives, use them in ways that encourage students to commit themselves to your instructional goals, so that they engage in academic activities with the intention of acquiring the knowledge and skills that these activities are meant to develop, and in doing so, to obtain extrinsic rewards as well. This may produce a form of motivation to learn that is comparable to that produced by intrinsic motivation, or at least close enough to serve your purposes. To the extent that students focus primarily on obtaining rewards rather than on accomplishing learning goals, less satisfactory results can be expected. If students perceive themselves as performing a task solely to obtain a reward, they tend to concentrate on meeting minimum standards for performance rather than on doing a high-quality job. As a result, they may write 300-word essays containing exactly 300 words or read only those parts of the text that they need to read in order to answer the questions on an assignment. You can minimize these dangers by (1) using extrinsic motivation approaches sparingly, (2) keeping in mind the qualifications on when they might be used, and (3) implementing the methods and delivering the rewards in ways that reflect the guidelines for praising effectively given in Table 5.1.

SUMMARY

This has been the first of four chapters on the value aspects of motivation, which focus on people's reasons for engaging in activities and the benefits that they expect to derive from such engagement. The chapter described strategies for addressing value issues by supplying extrinsic incentives to motivate task engagement. These strategies do not attempt to increase the value that students place on the task itself, but instead link successful completion of the task to delivery of consequences that the students do value.

Three general strategies for supplying extrinsic motivation were discussed: (1) rewarding students for good performance, (2) calling attention to the instrumental value of academic activities, and (3) occasionally structuring appropriate forms of competition. The discussion emphasized using these extrinsic incentives in ways that are compatible with other motivational principles, rather than incorporating them within a behavioral control approach to classroom management.

Extrinsic motivational methods are more suited to increasing the intensity of effort than improving the quality or creativity of performance. They also are more suited to motivating steady performance on tasks requiring following a clear strategy to reach a clear goal than on more open, divergent, or complex tasks. If you announce rewards in advance to create an incentive system, make sure that the system motivates students to focus on accomplishing your instructional goals (not just on obtaining the rewards) and that each student has an equal (or at least reasonable) opportunity to earn the rewards. When delivering praise or rewards, help students to appreciate and take pride in their accomplishments, both as a class and as individuals. Praise of individual students ordinarily should be done in private, should be appreciative rather than controlling, and should display the characteristics summarized in Table 5.1.

Where appropriate, call students' attention to naturally existing extrinsic incentives for mastering academic content or skills. More generally, infuse your everyday teaching with modeling and socialization designed to build students' appreciation of the fact that schools are established to prepare them for life in our society and that the curriculum was designed with this in mind.

Competition provides another potential source for extrinsic motivation. However, it is even more salient and distracting than rewards and it adds higher stakes to classroom activities that already involve risk of public failure and competition for grades. Consequently, if you use competition at all, use it in ways that depersonalize the competition and focus students primarily on learning goals. This may be accomplished through methods that combine competition with cooperative learning, including the student team learning methods that have produced positive effects on measures of achievement, affect, and social and motivational outcomes.

Extrinsic motivational strategies can be used in ways that complement the strategies described in other chapters in this book, provided that (1) they are not overemphasized; (2) they are implemented in ways that focus students' attention primarily on what they are learning rather than on rewards or other incentives; and (3) they preserve and support intrinsic motivation by avoiding incentive systems or explanations that lead students to infer that they engage in academic activities only to please you or to obtain rewards.

REFERENCES

Ames, C. (1984). Competitive, cooperative, and individualistic goal structures: A cognitive-motivational analysis. In R. Ames & C. Ames (Eds.), *Research on motivation in education. Volume 1: Student motivation* (pp. 177–208). New York: Academic Press.

Ames, C., & Ames, R. (1981). Competitive versus individualistic goal structures: The salience of past performance information for causal attributions and affect. *Journal of Educational Psychology, 73,* 411–418.

Barrett, M., & Boggiano, A. (1988). Fostering extrinsic orientations: Use of reward strategies to motivate children. *Journal of Social and Clinical Psychology, 6,* 293–309.

Berndt, T., & Miller, K. (1990). Expectancies, values, and achievement in junior high school. *Journal of Educational Psychology, 82,* 319–326.

Boggiano, A., Barrett, M., Weiher, A., McClelland, G., & Lusk, C. (1987). Use of the maximal operant procedure to motivate children's intrinsic interest. *Journal of Personality and Social Psychology, 53,* 866–879.

Bouffard, T., Boisvert, J., Vezeau, C., & Larouche, C. (1995). The impact of goal orientation on self-regulation and performance among college students. *British Journal of Educational Psychology, 65,* 317–329.

Brophy, J. (1981). Teacher praise: A functional analysis. *Review of Educational Research, 51,* 5–32.

Brophy, J., & Evertson, C. (1981). *Student characteristics and teaching.* New York: Longman.

Brophy, J., & Good, T. (1986). Teacher behavior and student achievement. In M. Wittrock (Ed.), *Handbook of research on teaching* (3rd ed., pp. 328–375). New York: Macmillan.

Caffyn, R. (1989). Attitudes of British secondary school teachers and pupils to rewards and punishments. *Educational Research, 31,* 210–220.

Cameron, J., & Pierce, W.D. (1994). Reinforcement, reward, and intrinsic motivation: A meta-analysis. *Review of Educational Research, 64,* 363–423.

Cameron, J., & Pierce, W.D. (1996). The debate about rewards and intrinsic motivation: Protests and accusations do not alter the results. *Review of Educational Research, 66,* 39–51.

Chance, P. (1993). Sticking up for rewards. *Phi Delta Kappan, 74,* 787–790.

Condry, J., & Chambers, J. (1978). Intrinsic motivation and the process of learning. In M. Lepper & D. Greene (Eds.), *The hidden costs of reward: New perspectives on the psychology of human motivation* (pp. 61–84). Hillsdale, NJ: Erlbaum.

Deci, E., & Ryan, R. (1985). *Intrinsic motivation and self-determination in human behavior.* New York: Plenum.

Eccles, J., & Wigfield, A. (1985). Teacher expectations and student motivation. In J. Dusek (Ed.), *Teacher expectancies* (pp. 185–226). Hillsdale, NJ: Erlbaum.

Epstein, J., & Harackiewicz, J. (1992). Winning is not enough: The effects of competition and achievement orientation on intrinsic interest. *Personality and Social Psychology Bulletin, 18,* 128–138.

Flink, C., Boggiano, A., Main, D., Barrett, M., & Katz, P. (1992). Children's achievement-related behaviors: The role of extrinsic and intrinsic motivational orientations. In A. Boggiano & T. Pittman (Eds.), *Achievement and motivation: A social-developmental perspective* (pp. 189–214). Cambridge: Cambridge University Press.

Heckhausen, H. (1991). *Motivation and action* (2nd ed.). New York: Springer-Verlag.

Johnson, D., & Johnson, R. (1985). Motivational processes in cooperative, competitive, and individualistic learning situations. In C. Ames & R. Ames (Eds.), *Research on motivation in education. Volume 2: The classroom milieu* (pp. 249–286). Orlando, FL: Academic Press.

Keller, J. (1983). Motivational design of instruction. In C. Reigeluth (Ed.), *Instructional-design theories and models: An overview of their current status* (pp. 383–434). Hillsdale, NJ: Erlbaum.

Kohn, A. (1993). *Punished by rewards: The trouble with gold stars, incentive plans, A's, praise, and other bribes.* Boston: Houghton Mifflin.

Lepper, M. (1983). Extrinsic reward and intrinsic motivation: Implications for the class-room. In J. Levine & M. Wang (Eds.), *Teacher and student perceptions: Implications for learning* (pp. 281–317). Hillsdale, NJ: Erlbaum.

Lepper, M., & Greene, D. (Eds.). (1978). *The hidden costs of reward: New perspectives on the psychology of human motivation.* Hillsdale, NJ: Erlbaum.

MacIver, D., & Reuman, D. (1993/94). Giving their best: Grading and recognition practices that motivate students to work hard. *American Educator, 17*(4), 24–31.

Meece, J., & Holt, K. (1993). A pattern analysis of students' achievement goals. *Journal of Educational Psychology, 85,* 582–590.

Midgley, C., & Urdan, T. (1992). The transition to middle level schools: Making it a good experience for all students. *Middle School Journal, 24,* 5–14.

Moriarty, B., Douglas, G., Punch, K., & Hattie, J. (1995). The importance of self-efficacy as a mediating variable between learning environments and achievement. *British Journal of Educational Psychology, 65,* 73–84.

Nafpaktitis, M., Mayer, G., & Butterworth, T. (1985). Natural rates of teacher approval and disapproval and their relation to student behavior in intermediate school classrooms. *Journal of Educational Psychology, 77,* 362–367.

Natriello, G., & Dornbusch, S. (1985). *Teacher evaluative standards and student effort.* New York: Longman.

Ollendick, T., & Shapiro, E. (1984). An examination of vicarious reinforcement processes in children. *Journal of Experimental Child Psychology, 37,* 78–91.

Pintrich, P., Marx, R., & Boyle, R. (1993). Beyond cold conceptual change: The role of motivational beliefs and classroom contextual factors in the process of conceptual change. *Review of Educational Research, 63,* 167–199.

Reeve, J. (1996). *Motivating others: Nurturing inner motivational resources.* Boston: Allyn & Bacon.

Reeve, J., & Deci, E. (1996). Elements of the competitive situation that affect intrinsic motivation. *Personality and Social Psychology Bulletin, 22,* 24–33.

Schwieso, J., & Hastings, N. (1987). Teachers' use of approval. In N. Hastings & J. Schweiso (Eds.), *New directions in educational psychology: 2. Behaviour and motivation in the classroom* (pp. 115–136). London: Falmer.

Slavin, R. (1988). Cooperative learning and student achievement. *Educational Leadership, 46*(2), 31–33.

Slavin, R. (1990). *Cooperative learning: Theory, research, and practice.* Englewood Cliffs, NJ: Prentice-Hall.

Ware, B. (1978). What rewards do students want? *Phi Delta Kappan, 59,* 355–356.

Wlodkowski, R. (1985). *Enhancing adult motivation to learn.* San Francisco: Jossey-Bass.

CHAPTER 6

Connecting with Students' Intrinsic Motivation

That children can be regulated by external constraints and controls is without dispute. The question is whether this describes the atmosphere and goals of education to which we as educators, and as a culture, aspire.

An alternative perspective, more complex and subtle than the one just described, considers the motivation to learn to be a developmental issue. While learning can be wholly controlled and prompted from the outside (i.e., externally regulated), the goal of education is, from the alternative view, the development of self-regulation for learning. This is conceptualized as a movement away from heteronomy and toward autonomy in the acquisition of knowledge, away from reliance on others for the incentives to learn and toward internal satisfaction with accomplishment and the learning process itself.

(Ryan, Connell & Grolnick, 1992, p. 168) (original italics)

The extrinsic motivation strategies described in Chapter 5 are designed to stimulate students to engage in classroom activities effortfully because completing these activities successfully will bring them valued rewards. In a purely extrinsic approach, the activity itself is not valued except as an instrument that students can use to obtain rewards that they do value. In contrast, intrinsic motivational strategies apply when students value (or can learn to value) participation in the activity itself. These strategies are based on the idea that teachers should emphasize academic activities that students find inherently interesting and enjoyable so that they engage in these activities willingly without any need for extrinsic incentives.

For reasons described in Chapter 1, it is not feasible to base your all-day, everyday motivational strategies on the principle of connecting with students' existing intrinsic motivation. Within what is feasible, however, you can use three general sets of strategies to increase the role of intrinsic motivation in your students' classroom experiences: (1) use classroom management and teaching styles that address students' needs for autonomy, competence, and relatedness; (2) plan learning activities that students are likely to find enjoyable or intrinsically rewarding; and (3) modify the design of other learning activities to include features that will enhance the activities' appeal. These approaches to connecting with the intrinsic motivation potential that your students bring with them into your classroom are discussed in this chapter, along with the theoretical principles that underlie them and the views of teachers concerning their applications.

CONCEPTIONS OF INTRINSIC MOTIVATION

Some treatments of intrinsic motivation emphasize the *affective* quality of students' engagement in an activity—the degree to which they enjoy or derive pleasure from the experience. This kind of intrinsic motivation is more typical of play or recreational activities than learning activities. Other treatments of intrinsic motivation place more emphasis on its *cognitive* aspects—the degree to which students find participation in the activity to be self-actualizing, competence-enhancing, or otherwise meaningful and worthwhile. To the extent that these cognitive aspects predominate, intrinsic motivation begins to resemble motivation to learn as defined in Chapter 7.

Most intrinsic motivation theorists do not directly address distinctions between its affective/fun aspects and its cognitive/learning aspects. Instead, they focus on the issue of control, emphasizing that actions must be experienced as self-determined if intrinsic motivation is to develop. This emphasis is seen in the quotation that begins the chapter.

Until recently, intrinsic motivation theorists tended to depict intrinsic motivation and extrinsic motivation as incompatible opposites, and to caution teachers against using extrinsic incentives lest they erode their students' intrinsic motivation to learn. This tendency to portray a simple dichotomy has receded in favor of the idea that *relative autonomy* increases by degrees along a dimension that extends from purely extrinsic motivation through mixed forms to purely intrinsic motivation. Most intrinsic motivation theorists now concede that extrinsic incentives can be used in ways that complement other motivational strategies and do not undermine students' intrinsic motivation. Even so, these theorists still argue that intrinsic motivational approaches to teaching are preferable to extrinsic approaches. Deci and Ryan (1994) reviewed several studies indicating that self-determined learning tends to be of higher quality than extrinsically motivated learning.

The concept of intrinsic motivation began as a reaction to drive-reduction or need theories. Its emergence was part of the attempt to balance the notion that people are driven to respond to felt needs with the notion that we often engage in activities because we want to rather than because we feel a need to (Collier, 1994).

Abraham Maslow (1962) spoke of self-actualization needs that we begin to express when our lower needs are satisfied. These include needs for creative self-expression, satisfaction of curiosity, and other exploratory or skill-enhancing activities that appear to be intrinsically motivated.

Robert White (1959) suggested that we often act out of competence motivation: We want to deal effectively with the environment and master and control the things around us. This energizes activities such as exploration, attention, thought, and play. It also causes us to seek new challenges rather than wait for events to happen, and to experience such challenges as intrinsically motivating.

Recently, leading intrinsic motivation theorists, notably Edward Deci and Richard Ryan, have begun to define intrinsic motivation in terms of the presence of subjective perceptions of self-determination rather than in terms of the absence of extrinsic incentives (Condry & Stokker, 1992; Deci & Ryan, 1991). That is, if we *feel* self-determined, then for all practical purposes we *are* self-determined, even if extrinsic incentives are in effect.

Other conceptions of intrinsic motivation also emphasize our subjective experiences during task engagement. In discussing flow, for example, Csikszentmihalyi (1993) emphasized the experience of becoming absorbed in a task. He noted that this can occur with any task that offers challenges that are well matched to our current knowledge and skill (see Chapter 1). Eckblad (1981) defined extrinsically motivated activity as activity where there is a clear differentiation in awareness between means and ends. In contrast, intrinsically motivated activity is not experienced as a means undertaken to achieve some goal. In a pure state of intrinsic motivation, there is no awareness of means–end separation, of the self, or of striving to achieve some goal separate from the ongoing activity.

Most of these themes, but especially the emphasis on developing competence through self-initiated activity, are included in the self-determination theory put forth by Deci and Ryan (1991, 1994). They defined intrinsically motivated actions as performed out of interest and requiring no external prods, promises, or threats. These actions are experienced as wholly self-determined, as representative of and emanating from our sense of self. We pursue them out of interest when we are free from external pressures. In contrast, extrinsically motivated actions are performed instrumentally to attain some separate consequence. These actions usually would not occur spontaneously and therefore must be prompted by incentives or other external pressures.

Deci and Ryan (1994) suggested that three factors promote self-determination in classrooms: (1) providing students with meaningful rationales that will enable them to understand the purpose and personal importance of each learning activity; (2) acknowledging students' feelings when it is necessary to require them to do something that they don't want to do (i.e., by letting them know that you are aware of their feelings and taking time to explain why the requirement is needed); and (3) managing the classroom and instructing students using a style that emphasizes choice rather than control.

Levels of Extrinsic Regulation That Increasingly Overlap With Intrinsic Motivation

Deci and Ryan have elaborated their original version of self-determination theory to include a developmental analysis of extrinsic motivation. This analysis differentiates subtypes of extrinsic motivation and explains how extrinsically motivated actions can become self-determined through the developmental processes of internalization and integration. *Internalization* refers to the transformation of an externally prescribed regulation or value into an internally adopted one. *Integration* is the process through which internalized regulations and values become integrated into the self (Ryan, 1993).

Some types of internalization are more adaptive than others and result in forms of extrinsic regulation of behavior that include certain aspects of intrinsic motivation. Deci and Ryan identified four types of extrinsic regulation that can be ordered along a continuum from external control to autonomous self-regulation.

External regulation occurs when our actions are regulated by external rewards, pressures, or constraints. In the classroom, students are externally regulated when they attend to lessons or work on assignments solely because they will be rewarded if they do or punished if they do not.

Introjected regulation occurs when we act as we do because we think we should or would feel guilty if we did not. Such regulation is internal in the sense that we no longer require external prodding to perform the action. However, we are responding to felt pressure that is still external to our sense of self. In the classroom, introjected regulation is seen in students who attend to lessons or work on assignments primarily because they know that they will get bad grades and disappoint their parents if they do not.

Identified regulation occurs when the regulation or value is adopted by the self as personally important and valuable. In the classroom, identified regulation is seen in students who attend to lessons and work on assignments because they view these activities as important for their self-selected goal of attending college or entering a particular occupation.

Integrated regulation is the most self-determined form of extrinsic motivation. It results from the integration of identified values and regulations into one's coherent sense of self. Any conflicts between different values and associated action tendencies (e.g., the desire to be both a good student and a rock musician) are eliminated by making whatever adjustments might be needed to achieve harmonious coexistence.

Actions that are higher on the continuum from external regulation to integrated regulation are increasingly self-determined and thus more like intrinsically motivated actions. They are still extrinsically motivated, however, because they are performed as means to attain separate goals. In contrast, intrinsically motivated actions are done "for their own sake."

Deci and Ryan's suggestions to teachers emphasize socializing and instructing students in ways that encourage self-determined learning initiatives and thus result in intrinsically motivated learning. To the extent that this goal is not fully attained and extrinsic motivation enters the picture, they favor socializing and teaching students in ways that produce higher-level rather than lower-level forms of extrinsic regulation. Their ideas, presented in the following section, overlap considerably with the principles involved in orienting students toward learning goals rather than performance goals (see Chapter 3).

Deci and Ryan: Autonomy, Competence, and Relatedness as Bases for Intrinsic Motivation

Deci and Ryan believe that social settings promote intrinsic motivation when they satisfy people's needs for autonomy, competence, and relatedness. That is, people are inherently motivated to feel connected to others within the setting, to function effectively in it, and to feel a sense of personal initiative while doing so. When teachers and classroom climates support satisfaction of these needs, students will feel self-determined and intrinsically motivated; when they do not, students will feel controlled and extrinsically motivated.

At first glance, there appears to be a contradiction between the need for autonomy and the need for relatedness. That is, to the extent that a teacher requires students to do things that they would not choose to do spontaneously, the students' desire to please the teacher (which is part of their need for relatedness) would motivate them to adopt the teacher's agenda rather than pursue their own. However, keep in mind that the key feature of intrinsic motivation is the students' subjective sense of self-determination, not the degree to which extrinsic incentives or pressures may be present. Hodgins, Koestner, and Duncan (1996) have shown that when the need for autonomy is expressed as a tendency to experience self-determination of one's behavior (rather than as a tendency to prefer acting independently without any influence from others), it actually promotes connectedness with others and positive perceptions of social experiences.

RESPONDING TO STUDENTS' AUTONOMY NEEDS

Despite recent advances in their theorizing and broadening of their purview on motivation, most of the advice to teachers offered by Deci, Ryan, and their colleagues continues to focus on supporting students' sense of self-determination in the classroom by offering them opportunities for autonomy and choice and by avoiding overtly controlling behaviors.

Encourage Students to Function as Autonomous Learners

Grolnick and Ryan (1987) suggested that *autonomy-supportive teachers* believe that it is important for their students to learn to solve their own problems. These teachers see their role as facilitating independent thought and decision making. They try to involve students in the process of learning by giving them choices. They support students' problem-solving attempts by using discussion and other autonomy promoting techniques rather than by imposing their own solutions on the students. In contrast, *control-oriented teachers* overmanage their students using detailed directions backed by rewards, grades, and threats. These techniques lead students to experience their learning in school as instrumental (i.e., as means to good grades) rather than as self-determined.

Valas and Sovik (1994) painted a similar picture of autonomy-supporting teachers. These teachers provide their students with choices, minimize extrinsic performance pressures (e.g., grades and normative comparisons, competition, continuous close monitoring), encourage students to solve problems in their own ways rather than insisting on a single method, and invite students to ask questions and suggest ideas for individual learning projects.

Allow Students to Make Choices

Offer your students choices of alternative tasks or opportunities to exercise autonomy in pursuing alternative ways to meet requirements. For example, allow them to select topics for book reports, composition assignments, and research projects, and perhaps also to select from alternative ways of reporting to you or the class as a whole (work with a partner to present a biography as an interview of the person about his or her life, present a book review using a "Siskel and Ebert" format, etc.). If they are likely to make undesirable choices when left completely on their own, provide them with a menu of choices to select from or require them to get their choices approved before going ahead with their projects. Take students' interests into account when considering choice options (see Box 6.1).

Many instructional goals involve the acquisition and use of processes rather than the learning of specific content. In these situations, many different information sources and instructional materials or media may be useful as means for accomplishing the learning goals. In addition, if you invite them to do so, your students might suggest additional means that you had not considered but would be willing to approve as equivalent alternatives. By offering such choices, you provide students with opportunities to assume responsibility for regulating their own learning and to experience a sense of self-determination as they do so.

Offer autonomy and choice opportunities to all students, not just higher achievers. Research on teacher expectation phenomena indicates that some teachers provide frequent autonomy and choice opportunities for their higher achievers but micromanage the learning efforts of their lower achievers. Lower achievers often need more explicit directions and more structuring and scaffolding of their learning efforts, but they also need opportunities to experience self-determination and self-regulation of their learning.

One way to build in choice opportunities for all students is to set up *learning centers* where students can work individually or in collaboration with peers on a variety of projects. Some of the projects may be required because they are essential to the accomplishment of your unit goals in one or more subject areas, but others might be optional—viewed as enrichment activities and included at least in part because most students find them interesting or enjoyable.

For example, a language arts or social studies center might include children's literature selections relating to the topic of the current social studies

---

Box 6.1.   Connecting with Students' Interests

Students develop abiding interests in certain domains of knowledge (e.g., pioneer life, dinosaurs). They also discover that they enjoy certain activities that provide bases for learning (e.g., reading certain literary genres, writing poetry, acting in plays or simulations, conducting experiments, doing research). The reasons for unique patterns of interest development are not clear. Most theorists assume that interests begin when children are exposed to a knowledge domain or type of activity and discover that they value it because they identify with it in some fashion or because it meets some salient need. As interests take hold and develop, they begin to motivate action sequences that incorporate the experience of flow as described by Csikszentmihalyi (1993). That is, as people pursue their interests they develop domain-specific knowledge and skills, leading them to seek out interest-related activities that fea-

ture optimal matches between their current knowledge and skill levels and the levels of challenge embedded in the activities.

To the extent that doing so is feasible given your instructional goals, you may find it worthwhile to incorporate your students' interests into your curriculum (or at least to point out connections between the curriculum and those interests), as well as to offer students choice options that allow them to pursue their interests as they work on reading, research, and writing assignments. Researchers who have studied the role of interest in learning have found that students sustain their attention more continuously and process information at deeper levels when they have a personal interest or investment in the knowledge domain (Alexander, Kulikowich, & Jetton, 1994; Renninger, Hidi, & Krapp, 1992; Schiefele, 1991).

---

unit. The collection would include a variety of genres of children's literature written at a range of reading levels, although it would be limited to books considered suitable as content sources for enriching students' knowledge about the unit topic (e.g., pioneer life or the Civil War). Students might be required to read and write their reactions to one or more of these books, but they would be allowed to decide which books to read. They also might be allowed at least some autonomy (although perhaps also with some degree of guidance) concerning the content and organization of their reports.

Morrow (1992, 1993) developed a writing and reading appreciation program that included significant provisions for student autonomy and choice in working on language arts projects. Students worked on these activities several times each week when they were assigned to the literacy center in a corner of the classroom. At any given time, the center contained five to eight books per child, including picture story books, poetry, informational books, magazines, biographies, and other fictional and nonfictional sources. Selections were changed periodically, especially to create collections relating to topics being taught concurrently in science or social studies.

The center also included six types of manipulative materials that students might use with their projects: (1) felt-board stories (characters from a book made of oaktag or construction paper that could be used when retelling a story by displaying them on a felt board); (2) audio-taped stories that children could listen to through headsets as they followed along in the accompanying book; (3) roll movies (illustrated stories that could be advanced scene by scene by scrolling them through a viewing apparatus); (4) prop stories (collections of materials for use in retelling a story, such as three stuffed bears, three bowls, and a yellow-haired doll for telling the story of *Goldilocks*); (5) puppet stories (various types of puppets to use in retelling stories); and (6) chalk talks (materials for drawing a story on a chalkboard or sheet of paper while the story is being read or told). While in the literacy center, students could use these or other materials to: read a book, magazine, or newspaper; read to a friend; listen to someone read to them; listen to a taped story and follow the words in the book; use the felt board with a storybook and felt characters; use the roll movie with its storybook; write a story; draw a picture about a story they had read; write a story and then make it into a book; make a felt story or a tape for a book they had read or a story they had written; write and perform a puppet show; record activities in the log; check out books to take home and read; or follow directions on a task card for some other selected activity.

The teacher demonstrated how to use these materials and carry out activity choices, then moved students toward independent and collaborative functioning. Students chose whether they wanted to work alone or with peers. If they chose to work with peers, the group decided who would act as leader and what tasks they would pursue. The students operated mostly independently of the teacher in deciding what tasks to work on and how to complete them. However, they were encouraged to select activities that included both reading and writing, to try activities they had not tried before and work with classmates they had not worked with before, and to take on significant projects and follow them through to completion rather than flit from one thing to another (unfinished projects could be stored for resumption when the students next returned to the literacy center).

Students involved in this program expressed more interest in reading and writing than students in classes restricted to more traditional activities. They also performed better on tests of reading comprehension and oral and written literacy. Note that this approach not only responded to students' autonomy needs but also responded to their relatedness needs by allowing them to work together with classmates of their own choosing. A variation that might be used with any subject matter is to divide students into self-selected interest groups and allow them to do worthwhile content-related research projects.

RESPONDING TO STUDENTS' COMPETENCE NEEDS

Intrinsic motivation theorists have pointed out that people tend to enjoy and become absorbed in activities that are well matched to their current levels of knowledge and skill and thus provide optimal challenges that allow them to develop their competence. This principle has several potential applications in classrooms.

First, as a prerequisite, make sure that learning activities are in fact well matched to your students' levels of knowledge and skill. If necessary, use the strategies presented in Chapters 3 and 4 to help students recognize and appreciate optimal challenges. If activities are ill matched to your students' levels, and especially if they are too difficult for them, there will be no potential for intrinsic motivation.

Within the range of activities that are optimally challenging, some are especially enjoyable or absorbing because they offer good opportunities for students to satisfy their competence needs. Examples include activities that (1) allow students to make active responses and get immediate feedback, (2) incorporate gamelike features that most students find enjoyable, and (3) incorporate features that are associated with job satisfaction in the work place.

Emphasize Activities that Offer Opportunities to Make Active Responses and Get Immediate Feedback

Active Responses

Students tend to prefer activities that allow them to respond actively—to interact with you or with one another, manipulate materials, or do something else other than just listen or read. Routine recitation, boardwork, or seatwork activities provide only limited potential for active response. Students should get frequent opportunities to go beyond the simple question–answer formats of these routine activities in order to do projects, experiments, discussions, role play, simulations, computerized learning activities, educational games, or creative applications.

Even within traditional lesson formats, you can create opportunities for more active student involvement by going beyond factual questions to stimulate students to discuss or debate issues, offer opinions about cause-and-effect relationships, speculate about hypothetical situations, or think creatively about problems. Students need to master basic facts, concepts, and definitions, but they also need frequent opportunities to address higher-level objectives by applying, analyzing, synthesizing, or evaluating what they have learned at the knowledge or comprehension level.

Also, avoid overemphasis on convergent questions that admit to only a single correct answer. In leading a discussion of a story or text chapter, for example, include questions that invite students to tell what they thought were the most interesting or important aspects, and why (Sansone & Morgan, 1992). Questions asked during everyday lessons should include frequent opportunities for students to state opinions, make predictions, suggest sources of action, formulate solutions to problems, or engage in other forms of divergent thinking.

Language arts instruction should include dramatic readings and prose and poetry composition; mathematics instruction should include problem-solving exercises and realistic application opportunities; science instruction should include experiments and other laboratory work; social studies instruction should include debates, research projects, and simulation exercises; and art, music, and physical education instruction should include opportunities to use developing skills in authentic application activities, not just to practice the skills in isolation. Such activities allow students to feel that school learning involves *doing* something.

Research on students' attitudes toward academic activities consistently shows that they prefer active over passive forms of learning. For example, 11- and 12-year old students interviewed by Cooper and McIntyre (1994) associated effective teaching with methods that produced high levels of imaginative and practical involvement in lesson activity. Examples included storytelling by the teacher (which the students found engaging even though it is primarily a listening activity), drama and role-play exercises, use of visual stimuli (e.g., photographs, drawings, diagrams, videos), whole-class and small-group discussion, and opportunities to collaborate in pairs and groups in brainstorming, problem solving, or developing some group product.

Immediate Feedback

Activities that offer the greatest potential for student enjoyment and for flow experiences are those that allow students not only to respond actively but also to get immediate feedback that they can use to guide subsequent responses. This feedback feature is an important reason for the popularity of computer games and other pastimes featured in arcades (Malone & Lepper, 1987). Automatic feedback features also are built into many educational games and computerized learning systems.

You can provide such feedback yourself when leading the class or a small group through a lesson or when circulating to supervise progress during independent work times. When you are less available for immediate response (such as when you are teaching a small group), you can still arrange for students who are working independently to get feedback by consulting answer keys; following instructions about how to check their work; consulting with an aide, adult volunteer, or appointed student helper; or discussing their work in pairs or small groups.

Although it is not always necessary for learning purposes, *immediate* feedback enhances the psychological impact of an activity. Most students are eager to receive and respond to immediate feedback when learning something for the first time, but much less enthused about the prospect of going back to try to relearn something that "we did already."

Incorporate Gamelike Features into Learning Activities

Many learning and application activities can be structured to include features typically associated with games or recreational pastimes (Keller, 1983; Lepper & Cordova, 1992; Malone & Lepper, 1987). With a bit of imagination, ordinary seatwork assignments can be transformed into "test yourself" challenges, puzzles, or brain teasers that allow students to satisfy their competence needs. Some such activities involve clear goals but require students to solve problems, avoid traps, or overcome obstacles in order to reach the goals. For example, students might be asked to suggest possible solutions to a science or engineering problem or to find a shortcut for a tedious mathematical procedure. Or, the activity might challenge students to find the problem by identifying the goal itself and then developing a method for reaching it. Many explore and discover activities follow this model.

For example, McKenzie (1975) described three ways to introduce mystery to inquiry or problem solving in social studies or science. First, as a way to engage students in inquiry leading to discovery of a concept or generalization, provide students with different examples or illustrations of phenomena that seem to be unrelated at first. Then inform the students that all of the cases are alike in some way and challenge them to discover the similarity or pattern. The resultant discovery will be a definition of a concept or a statement of a generalization. For example, pictures of pioneers on the frontier, the Wright brothers with their airplane, black students integrating a segregated school, and an astronaut might be presented along with the challenge, "All of these people are pioneers. Can you figure out what pioneers have in common?"

A variation on this is to provide a set of clues—such as artifacts, divergent historical accounts of an event, or other data arranged to tell some story—then ask students to reconstruct the event by acting as a detective (or an archaeologist or historian). A third technique is to present some situation that seems familiar and ask students what they think will happen. After they make predictions, demonstrate that in fact something unexpected happens. Then challenge the class to try to explain why the unexpected event occurred. You might use this technique to introduce the concept of gravity, for example, by dropping pairs of objects together to illustrate that a smaller, lighter object such as a coin will reach the floor just as quickly as a larger, heavier object such as a baseball (contrary to most students' expectations).

Some gamelike activities involve elements of suspense or hidden information that emerges as the activity is completed (i.e., puzzles that convey some message or provide the answer to some question once they are filled in). Still other gamelike activities involve a degree of randomness or uncertainty about the outcome of one's performance on any given trial (i.e., knowledge games that cover a variety of topics at several difficulty levels and assign questions according to card draws or dice rolls—Trivial Pursuit is an example).

Covington (1992) described games and simulations that engage students in cooperative learning and higher-order thinking as they work to develop explanations for puzzling phenomena (e.g., how birds can migrate for thousands of miles and yet keep returning to the same place each year) or solutions to technical problems (e.g., how to use X-rays to destroy a cancerous tumor without harming the surrounding healthy tissue). When designed as opportunities to apply principles developed through instruction in school subjects, these gamelike activities can have powerful motivational as well as instructional value.

Note that most of these gamelike features involve presenting intellectual challenges to individuals working alone or to groups working cooperatively. This illustrates that *gamelike features* has a much broader meaning than *games,* a term that most teachers associate specifically with *competitions.* The gamelike features described here are less distracting from learning objectives and more effective in promoting student motivation to learn than are games, especially competitive games that emphasize speed in supplying memorized facts rather than thoughtful integration or application of learning.

Ideas from Research on Job Characteristics

Industrial psychologists have studied workplace conditions and job character-istics that affect workers' job satisfaction and work motivation (Kanfer, 1990; Katzell & Thompson, 1990; Pinder, 1984). Their findings concerning leadership and workplace conditions overlap considerably with classroom findings con-cerning teacher leadership style and classroom climate. Their findings concern-ing job satisfaction also overlap with much of what has been said already about characteristics of school tasks that support intrinsic motivation (autonomy, ac-tive responses that yield immediate feedback, collaboration with peers, etc.).

However, the job characteristics literature also points to certain features of work that have not yet received much attention in educational research. In particular, three job characteristics emphasized by Hackman and Oldham (1980) are skill variety, task identity, and task significance. Their findings have implications for designing school activities that respond to students' compe-tence needs.

Skill Variety

Skill variety refers to the range of different activities needed to carry out a task, as well as the range of skills that these activities entail. Workers tend to enjoy jobs that include a variety of activities and provide them with opportu-nities to use a variety of skills. In contrast, most workers find jobs that involve constant repetition of the same task to be boring and aversive. Students show the same preferences.

Alleman and Brophy (1993–94) interviewed college students about learn-ing activities that they remembered from K–12 social studies. Their responses were coded for what they said about the cognitive and affective outcomes of the activities. Desirable affective outcomes were coded when the students re-ported that an activity had produced interesting learning or enabled them to empathize with the people being studied and see things from their point of view. Negative assessments were coded when the students disparaged activi-ties as pointless (e.g., learning about state birds) or as boring and repetitive (e.g., worksheets or assignments such as reading a chapter in the text and then answering questions about it).

Analyses indicated that the students frequently mentioned desirable affec-tive outcomes, and never expressed negative assessments, when describing thematic units (such as on pioneer life or a foreign country) that included a variety of information and activities, field trips, class discussion and debate activities, or pageant or role-enactment activities. They expressed less enthusiastic, but still generally positive, reactions to simulation activities, research projects, construction projects, and lecture/presentation activities. Finally, seatwork was in a class by itself because it yielded practically no descriptions of desirable affective outcomes but frequent negative assessments (especially complaints about boring, repetitive seatwork that had to be done individually and silently).

Task Identity

Task identity refers to the opportunity to do a complete job from beginning to end. Workers tend to enjoy jobs that allow them to create a product that they can point to and identify with more than jobs that do not yield such tangible evidence of the fruits of their labor. Students probably respond similarly to academic tasks. That is, they are likely to prefer tasks that have meaning or integrity in their own right over tasks that are mere subparts of some larger entity, and are likely to experience a satisfying sense of accomplishment when they finish such tasks. Ideally, task completion will yield a finished product that students can use or display (i.e., a map, diagram, or other illustration; an essay or report; a scale model; or something other than just another ditto or workbook page).

Many writers concerned with motivation in education have pointed out that knowledge is decontextualized in school. Abstract principles and skills that have wide application are taught in circumstances far removed from those in which they will be used. Also, much school knowledge is modularized—that is, broken into component parts taught separately. One result of this decontextualization and modularization of school knowledge is to remove much of the intrinsic motivation potential from school learning. You can recapture some of this intrinsic motivation potential by creating learning situations in your classroom that resemble the situated learning that occurs in out-of-school settings.

Scholars who have studied learning in home and job settings believe that it is a mistake to separate knowing from doing, or what is learned from how it is learned and used (Brown, Collins, & Duguid, 1989; Lave & Wenger, 1991; Rogoff, 1990). They believe that learning is *situated*; that is, that knowledge is adapted to the settings, purposes, and tasks to which it is applied (and for which it was constructed in the first place). Consequently, they argue, if we want students to learn and retain knowledge in a form that makes it usable for application, we need to make it possible for them to develop that knowledge in the natural setting, using methods and tasks suited to that setting. In this view, the ideal model for schooling is on-the-job training that occurs as experienced mentors work with novices or apprentices.

Obviously, there are limits to the degree to which in-school learning can be shifted to out-of-school settings. However, the notion of situated learning has implications for the design of in-school instruction as well. In particular, it implies that we need to be more conscious of potential applications when we select and plan our teaching of curricular content, and that we should empha-size those applications in presenting the content to students.

Also, as much as possible, we should allow students to learn through en-gagement in authentic tasks. *Authentic tasks* require using what is being learned for accomplishing the very sorts of life applications that justify the in-clusion of this learning in the curriculum in the first place. If it is not possible to engage students in the actual life applications that the curriculum is sup-posed to prepare them for, then at least engage them in realistic simulations of these applications.

Theory and research on task identity as a job characteristic and on situated learning and authentic tasks in education lead to similar ideas about the kinds of learning activities that students are likely to find intrinsically motivating. In particular, they underscore the value of engaging students in authentic life ap-plications of the knowledge and skills they are learning in school, especially applications that yield some conclusion or product that students can appreci-ate as a significant accomplishment.

Task Significance

Task significance refers to the degree of impact that the job has on the lives of other people, both immediately within the workplace and potentially in other contexts. This concept also connects with educators' notions of task authenticity and with the principle of teaching school subjects with an eye to-ward applications to life outside of school.

RESPONDING TO STUDENTS' RELATEDNESS NEEDS

You can go a long way toward meeting your students' relatedness needs by establishing your classroom as the kind of learning community described in Chapter 2. Be a supportive teacher who cares about your students as persons and helps them succeed as learners. In addition, teach your students to act as members of a learning community by listening carefully and responding thoughtfully during lessons and discussions and by supporting one another's learning when working in pairs or small groups.

In this kind of collaborative classroom climate, students will be able to please both you and their classmates (and thus meet their relatedness needs) simply by acting in accordance with learning community values. The prevail-ing norm of "we're all in this together, learning and helping one another learn" creates alignment among the actions needed to satisfy needs for autonomy, competence, and relatedness. Therefore, students can meet all of these needs simultaneously by asking and answering questions, working collaboratively on assignments, and engaging in other everyday learning activities. This alignment does not exist in competitive or hostile climates, where students may be unable to meet their relatedness needs or able to meet them only at cost to their sense of autonomy, their self-concept, or other components of their motivational systems.

Provide Frequent Opportunities for Students to Collaborate With Peers

In classrooms that feature a positive interpersonal climate and learning community norms of collaboration, students are likely to experience enhanced intrinsic motivation when they participate in learning activities that allow them to interact with their classmates. You can build some of this into whole-class activities such as discussion, debate, role-play, or simulation. In addition, you can shift many of the practice and application components of your curriculum from solitary seatwork to collaborative activities that allow students to work together in pairs or small groups to tutor one another, discuss issues, develop solutions to problems, or work as a team to produce a report, display, or some other group product. Such cooperative learning activities offer potential motivational benefits because they respond directly to students' relatedness needs, as well as potential learning benefits because they engage students in the social construction of knowledge.

Emphasize Purely Cooperative Learning Formats

The student team learning methods described in Chapter 5 allow for cooperative learning among teammates, but they also involve competing against other teams and focus learning efforts on preparing for tests. Consequently, they are primarily extrinsic approaches to motivation. However, there are other approaches to paired or small-group learning that are purely cooperative and thus likely to enhance students' intrinsic motivation. Three of the best known of these methods are Learning Together, Group Investigation, and Jigsaw.

Learning Together

The Learning Together model was developed by David and Roger Johnson (Johnson & Johnson, 1975; Johnson et al., 1984). In this model, students work on assignments in four- or five-member groups, ultimately turning in a single product that represents the group's effort. The Learning Together model incorporates four key features:

1. *Positive interdependence:* Students are interdependent with other members of their group in achieving a successful group product. Positive interdependence can be structured through mutual goals (goal interdependence); division of labor (task interdependence); dividing materials, resources, or information among group members (resource interdependence); assigning students unique roles (role interdependence); or giving group rewards (reward interdependence).
2. *Face-to-face interaction among students:* Activities that call for significant interaction among group members are preferred over activities that can be accomplished by having group members work on their own.
3. *Individual accountability:* Mechanisms are needed to ensure that each group member has clear objectives for which he or she will be held

accountable and receives any needed assessment, feedback, or instructional assistance.

4. *Instructing students in appropriate interpersonal or small-group skills:* Students cannot merely be placed together and told to cooperate. They need instruction in skills such as asking and answering questions, ensuring that everyone participates actively and is treated with respect, and assigning tasks and organizing cooperative efforts.

Group Investigation

Group Investigation methods were developed by Shlomo Sharan and his colleagues in Israel (Sharan & Sharan, 1976; Sharan et al., 1984). In this model, students form their own two- to six-member groups to work together using cooperative inquiry, group discussion, and planning and carrying out of projects. Each group chooses a topic from a unit studied by the whole class, breaks this topic into individual tasks, and carries out the activities needed to prepare a group report. Eventually, the group makes a presentation or display to communicate its findings to the class and is evaluated based on the quality of this report.

Jigsaw

Developed by Elliot Aronson and his colleagues (1978), the Jigsaw approach ensures active individual participation and group cooperation by arranging tasks so that each group member possesses unique information and has a special role to play. The group product cannot be completed unless each member does his or her part, just as a jigsaw puzzle cannot be completed unless each piece is included. For example, information needed to compose a biography might be broken into early life, first accomplishments, major setbacks, later life, and world events occurring during the person's lifetime. One member of each group would be given the relevant information and assigned responsibility for one of the five sections of the biography, and other group members would be assigned to other sections. Members of different groups who were working on the same section would meet together in expert groups to discuss their sections. Then they would return to their regular groups and take turns teaching their group mates about their sections. Because students can only learn about sections other than their own by listening carefully to their group mates, they are motivated to support and show interest in one another's work. The students then prepare biographies or take quizzes on the material individually.

A variation entitled Jigsaw II was developed by Robert Slavin (1983). One feature of Jigsaw II is that the teacher does not need to provide each student with unique materials. Instead, all students begin by reading a common narrative and then each group member is given a separate topic on which to become an expert. This adaptation also can be used with the original Jigsaw. If it is adopted without also incorporating the team competition features of Jigsaw II (see Chapter 5), it will simplify Jigsaw but still preserve its purely cooperative format.

Research on small-group cooperative learning methods indicates that they do indeed respond to students' relatedness needs. These methods have been shown to promote friendships and prosocial interaction among students who differ in achievement, gender, race, ethnicity, and handicapping conditions. In addition, they tend to have positive effects on outcomes such as self-esteem, academic self-confidence, liking for the class, liking and feeling liked by classmates, and dispositions toward empathy and social cooperation (Slavin, 1990; Miller & Hertz-Lazarowitz, 1992).

Certain qualifications on the use of cooperative learning methods should be noted, however. First, although most students prefer to collaborate with peers, some prefer to work alone. You may have good reasons for requiring the latter students to work together with peers under some circumstances, but whenever you are using cooperative learning purely for intrinsic motivation reasons, you should allow students who want to work alone to do so. Second, even if all of the students in a group enjoy working in the cooperative format, they may become distracted from learning goals if they begin to socialize, have difficulty negotiating roles, or begin to become concerned that some members of the group are not fulfilling their responsibilities. Third, bear in mind that the intrinsic motivational benefits of cooperative formats do not guarantee accomplishment of your instructional goals. To ensure that cooperative approaches yield acceptable learning outcomes, you will need to make sure that the tasks you assign are suited to the cooperative learning format that you want your students to follow, to prepare the students to collaborate effectively, and to monitor group interactions and intervene if necessary (Good, McCaslin & Reys, 1992; McCaslin & Good, 1996).

Pairs/Partners

Although most research attention has focused on cooperative learning in small-group formats, some formats call for pairs of students to work together as partners. Many language arts programs, for example, include components calling for pairs of students to listen to each other read or spell and provide corrective feedback or to read and respond to each other's written compositions. Also, many teachers assign pairs of students to act as study partners who correct and provide feedback concerning each other's work on mathematics assignments, to act as laboratory partners in carrying out science experiments, or to collaborate in "study buddy" relationships in working on homework assignments. Less formally, they may invite students to seek help from seatmates or friends in the classroom (within certain guidelines, such as that helpers should not merely give answers but provide helpees with whatever clues or explanations they may need in order to move forward on their own and eventually accomplish the learning goal).

Techniques have been developed to create interdependence between partners and encourage them to collaborate fruitfully. One such technique is *scripted cooperation* (Dansereau, 1988; O'Donnell, 1996; O'Donnell & Dansereau, 1992). As applied to a text study assignment, for example, the scripted cooperation method begins with breaking down the text into sections.

Both partners read the first section of the text, then put the material away. One partner plays the role of recaller and states all of the information that he or she can remember. The other partner plays the role of listener–detector by listening carefully and attempting to detect errors or omissions in the recall. Both partners then share ideas about how to elaborate the information to make it more memorable (e.g., by developing analogies or generating images). When both partners can restate the gist of this section successfully, they move on to the next section but switch roles. They proceed in this manner, switching roles each time they start a new section, until they complete the material to be studied. Research indicates that pairs of students using the scripted cooperation method tend to learn more than students who study alone or pairs of students who are asked to study together but are not instructed to use the scripted cooperation techniques of alternation of roles, overt rehearsal, active listening, and collaborative elaboration on the content.

ADAPTING ACTIVITIES TO STUDENTS' INTERESTS

To the extent that doing so will support your instructional goals, you can select expository reading assignments and design your classroom presentations to feature elements that enhance their interest value for students. For example, Hidi and Baird (1988) found that students' interest was enhanced when the main ideas in an expository text were elaborated through insertions that featured one of the following motivational principles: (1) character identification (information about people with whom the students could identify, such as those whose inventions or discoveries led to the knowledge under study); (2) novelty (content that was interesting to the students because it was new or unusual); (3) life theme (applications or other connections to things that were important to the students in their lives outside of school); and (4) activity level (content that included reference to intense activities or strong emotions).

Whenever instructional goals can be accomplished using a variety of examples or activities, incorporate content that students find interesting or activities that they find enjoyable. People, fads, or events that are currently prominent in the news or the youth culture, for example, can be worked into everyday lessons as examples or applications of the concepts being learned. For example, a history teacher pointed out that the Ark of the Covenant mentioned in the ancient history text was the same ark featured in the movie *Raiders of the Lost Ark*. Similarly, a geography teacher sparked interest in studying the coordinates (latitude and longitude) by noting that the sunken remains of the *Titanic* can easily be located again, even though they lie on the ocean floor hundreds of miles out to sea, because the discoverers fixed the location precisely using the coordinates.

Another way to incorporate students' interests into activities is to encourage them to ask questions and make comments about the topic. Relevant questions and comments create "teachable moments" that you can pursue by temporarily suspending the planned sequence of events in order to address issues raised by students. Such questions or comments indicate interest on the part of students who make them, and chances are good that other students will share this interest.

It also is helpful, both from instructional and from motivational points of view, to plan lessons and assignments that include divergent questions and opportunities for students to express opinions, make evaluations, or in other ways respond personally to the content. For example, after reviewing information about the Christians and the lions, the gladiators, and other excesses of the Roman circuses, a history teacher asked his students why they thought such practices had developed in Roman society and how otherwise cultured people could take pleasure in such cruelty. This led to a productive discussion in which students made contributions and developed insights about issues such as violence in sports and in contemporary society generally, the role of peer pressure in escalating aggression once conflict flares up, and the difference between enjoyment of pleasures and indulgence in excesses. This same teacher, after describing life in Athens and Sparta, asked students which city they would rather live in and why. Again, this led to a lively discussion that included parallels among modern nations and contrasted societies that focus on building military strength (at a cost in quality of civilian life) with societies that have more balanced priorities.

EMBELLISHING THE DESIGN OF TRADITIONAL LEARNING ACTIVITIES TO ENHANCE THEIR INTRINSIC MOTIVATION POTENTIAL

Mark Lepper and Thomas Malone developed theory and research on ways in which conventional school learning activities might be altered or embellished to increase their intrinsic motivation potential (Lepper & Malone, 1987; Malone & Lepper, 1987). In particular, they suggested making adjustments to enhance one or more of the following four sources of intrinsic motivation: (1) *challenge* (adjust difficulty levels so that tasks are optimally challenging); (2) *curiosity* (include elements that will stimulate curiosity); (3) *control* (offer choices or in other ways encourage students to experience a sense of autonomy or self-determination when they engage in the activities); and (4) *fantasy* (embellish activities in ways that encourage students to engage in them with a playful set, an identification with fictional characters, or an involvement in a world of fantasy).

Challenge and control issues were discussed previously in this chapter. Curiosity issues will be discussed in Chapter 7. This section focuses on the strategy of embellishing learning activities with fantasy elements, drawing on studies by Lepper and his colleagues (Lepper & Cordova, 1992; Lepper & Hodell, 1989). This research has been done in computerized learning situations, but its implications should apply to more conventional learning activities as well.

One study was done with a mathematics program designed to teach students about Cartesian coordinates. In the unembellished version, students were asked to find a hidden dot lying beneath one of the intersections of an 11×11 Cartesian grid, with axes labeled from –5 to +5. Students were to find the dot by guessing its location. After each incorrect guess, they were provided with written and visual feedback (in the form of an arrow) indicating the direction in which the hidden dot lay relative to the point guessed. When they eventually guessed correctly, they were given congratulatory feedback.

In the embellished version of this activity, the same problems were presented within a fantasy context designed to heighten intrinsic interest. Students were invited to help a fantasy character hunt for hidden treasures buried on a desert island. When correct guesses were made, small icons representing a treasure (e.g., an ivory comb, a silver goblet, or a rusty hook) appeared on the screen, accompanied by sound effects.

In another study, students learned to work with a computerized graphics program by completing activities calling for them to (1) draw lines connecting objects on the screen, (2) negotiate passage through a series of mazes, and (3) construct a series of geometric shapes. The unembellished versions of these activities simply called for the students to construct the necessary lines or geometric shapes. The embellished versions involved constructing the same lines or shapes, but presented these tasks within one of three fantasy contexts: (1) a pirate in search of buried treasure, (2) a detective hunting down criminals, or (3) an astronaut seeking out new planets in space.

Schank and Cleary (1995) have developed even more elaborately embellished computerized learning opportunities that incorporate simulation-based learning by doing, incidental learning, learning by reflection, case-based teaching, or learning by exploring. For example, a program for teaching foreign languages through simulation-based learning by doing leads students through scenarios that require them to use the language they are learning in realistic situations (e.g., arriving in the country by plane and going through customs, finding transportation, and checking in at a hotel). At each step, students interact with simulated people who appear in video clips and respond to what they say. When these communications are successful, the program moves the students on to the next scenario. When communication breaks down, the program offers them various options for getting help and then returning to the situation.

An incidental learning program teaches US geography and map skills by allowing students to take simulated car trips around the United States. They begin with a map of the country, zoom in on a particular state by clicking on that state, then see a state map that allows them to zoom in further by clicking on a city. Students then can travel from city to city along the interstate highway system. When they reach a chosen destination, they can watch video clips that feature sports highlights, movie clips, music videos, amusement parks, or historical footage associated with the location. In the process, they familiarize themselves with US states and cities and learn to plan travel using maps.

A case-based approach to teaching biological principles invites students to create their own animal by taking an existing animal and changing it in some way. They begin by selecting possibilities from lists of animals and potential changes, then explore the ramifications of the created animal by answering questions. If they select a fish that has wings, for example, the program might ask them to reflect on why the ability to fly would be useful to a fish, when this ability might be used, or what might be some limitations on its use. In the process, they view videos relating to these questions.

An elaborate simulation activity called Broadcast News allows groups of high school social studies students to produce their own news shows on current events, working with real news sources from a day in the recent past. Students follow actual television news procedures and use video equipment to research, write, and edit stories; prioritize and sequence the stories for inclusion in the newscast; then put it all together under "live taping" conditions.

Research on embellishments of conventional learning activities has shown that students prefer the embellished versions and usually show improved learning outcomes as well. Fantasy elements appear to add intrinsic interest to activities because they allow students to identify with fantasy characters, feel emotional reactions, and vicariously experience situations that may not be open to them in real life. Fantasy environments can evoke mental images of physical or social situations that are not actually present and thus produce the cognitive advantages that accrue from linking the known to the unfamiliar. Especially useful are fantasy elements that provide helpful metaphors for learning new skills (e.g., the family metaphor for mathematical set concepts) or provide real-world contexts within which the skills can be used (e.g., simulating running a lemonade stand).

However, Lepper and Cordova (1992) cautioned that motivational embellishment strategies do not always have such beneficial effects. The best results can be expected when the embellishments draw students' attention to the key ideas or processes that the activity is designed to teach, and when students must learn these key ideas or processes in order to complete the activity successfully and thus accomplish its fantasy goal. Where fantasy elements do not support learning in this fashion, they may function merely as "bells and whistles" that enhance the affective aspects of intrinsic motivation but do not engage the cognitive aspects that produce desired learning outcomes. Students may learn no more, or even less, from these embellished versions than they would from conventional versions of the same activities. Similar cautions apply to attempts to revise texts to make them more interesting (see Box 6.2).

Fantasy embellishments do not need to be as elaborate as the ones already described. For example, Anand and Ross (1987) showed that both motivational and learning benefits resulted when problems on division of fractions were personalized by incorporating references to the students or to people or things with whom they identified (the teacher, their friends, their favorite foods, etc.). You can introduce fantasy or imagination elements into your everyday instruction that will engage your students' emotions or allow them to experience events vicariously. In studying poems or stories, for example, you can encourage students to debate the authors' motives in writing the works or to learn about formative experiences in the authors' lives. In studying scientific or

---

Box 6.2.   Attempts to Make Texts More Interesting

For a time, it was believed that the interest potential and even the comprehensibility of textbooks could be improved significantly by revising them into a zesty, magazine-style of writing. This approach focused on making the content more dramatic by adding vivid anecdotes and details focused more around people than events. It also involved writing more engaging prose that featured fewer passive sentences and abstract words; more memorable images and colorful picture words; strong, vivid verbs; and added colloquialisms and metaphors. Early experiments with these revised texts appeared promising.

However, findings accumulated over time by several different teams of investigators indicated that these magazine-style texts usually did not produce higher student ratings of interest or enjoyment, and that even when they did, they reduced students' learning of key ideas. The magazine-style writing tended to reduce the coherence of text passages (making it harder for students to recognize and remember linkages among key ideas). Also, the inserted anecdotes and interesting details often proved to be more seductive than instructive (because they focused students' attention on minor or side issues at the expense of attention to important content). Eventually, it became clear that the best combination of motivational and learning outcomes can be expected from texts that structure content into networks of connected information that cohere around important ideas (Britton et al., 1989; Duffy et al., 1989; Garner et al., 1991; Graves et al., 1991; McKeown & Beck, 1994; Wade et al., 1995).

These findings concerning the content and organization of texts probably also apply to the content and organization of presentations made by teachers or conveyed through instructional media. The larger principle involved is that content representations or embellishments made for motivational purposes are likely to have desirable effects if they help students to recognize and remember key ideas, but not if they distract students' attention from key ideas by focusing them on trivia. Similarly, motivational embellishments of learning activities should be designed to support students' accomplishment of your instructional goals and not be distracting bells and whistles.

---

mathematical principles and methods, you can help students to appreciate the practical problems that needed to be solved or the personal motives of the discoverers that led to development of the knowledge or skills being taught.

Alternatively, you can set up role-play or simulation activities that allow students to identify with real or fictional characters or to deal with academic content in direct, personalized ways. Rather than just assign students to read history, for example, you can make it come alive by arranging for them to role play Columbus and his crew debating what to do after 30 days at sea (or at the secondary level, by arranging for them to take the roles of the American, British, and Russian leaders meeting at Yalta).

To dramatize the importance of a genuinely secret ballot, you might have students act out an election scene in a totalitarian state where one must get a pencil from the election supervisors (i.e., officials of the ruling party) if one wishes to write in names instead of voting for the single slate of candidates. To demonstrate the efficiency of assembly lines, you might organize some of your students into an assembly line in which each participant performs one step in the process of making sandwiches or collating information packets.

Elaborate simulations have been developed for teaching many social studies topics, particularly economics. For example, Kourilsky (1983) designed the Mini-Society program to teach 7–12 year-olds primarily about economics and secondarily about government, career, consumer, and value issues through participation in economic activities followed by debriefing of what was learned. The learning experiences involve participation in a market economy couched within a democratic society. Students learn that scarcity is the problem posed when limited resources are balanced against relatively unlimited wants, and they study the advantages and disadvantages inherent in various economic systems. Then they create within their classroom a mini-society based on market mechanisms. The society includes a name, a flag, a currency system, civil servants, and some initial mechanisms through which citizens can earn money by meeting criteria of good citizenship or accomplishment (as a way to introduce money into circulation). The main activities of the mini-society, however, involve setting up and running businesses that offer goods or services in exchange for mini-society money. In the process, students collaborate with partners to plan and run businesses; vote on taxes, government services, and other policy issues; and engage in a great deal of analysis and decision making on issues in economics and government.

A popular economics simulation for secondary students acquaints them with investing principles by inviting them to establish a simulated investment portfolio. They allocate a given sum to an initial set of investments of their own choosing, then manage the portfolio throughout the rest of the school year by making any desired changes and updating the associated bookkeeping. The simulated investments are tracked and discussed periodically so that students can understand what would have happened if they had been investing real money and try to determine why some investment decisions worked out better than others. Other economics-based experiential learning activities go beyond simulation by engaging students in developing and running actual businesses, with participation in profits or losses.

Simulation activities are not confined to full-scale drama, role play, simulation games, and other "major productions." More modest simulation exercises can be incorporated into everyday instruction. You can invite students to briefly project themselves into fictional or nonfictional situations under study by asking them, "If you were (the story's hero, the president of the US, a homeless person, etc.), what would you think or feel when that happened? What actions might you take?" In teaching a mathematical procedure, you might ask students to identify problems in everyday living that the procedure might be used to solve (and then list these on the board). Material on totalitarian societies might be brought home by asking students to imagine and talk about what it would be like to seek housing in a country where the government owned all of the property or to get accurate information about world events in a country where the government controlled all of the media. Reports on states, nations, or cultures might be written as travel brochures or newspaper articles, with students asked to keep their chosen purpose and audience in mind when deciding what to include and how to present it. Such fantasy or simulation exercises do not take much time or require special preparations, but they can stimulate students to relate to the content more personally and to take greater interest in it.

INSTRUCTIONAL APPROACHES THAT REFLECT MULTIPLE PRINCIPLES WORKING IN COMBINATION

Several broad educational philosophies incorporate principles for connecting with students' existing intrinsic motivation or for supporting its development by engaging them in learning activities designed to be intrinsically motivating (progressive education, discovery learning, open education, whole language). These principles also are emphasized in certain more focused models for incorporating motivational principles in curriculum and instruction. The TARGET program described in Chapter 2 is one example. Two others are the motivated literacy approach to language arts instruction and the project-based learning approach to social studies and science instruction.

Motivated Literacy

Julianne Turner (1993, 1995) described what she called the Motivated Literacy approach to beginning literacy instruction, defining it as an emphasis on open tasks over closed tasks. Teachers who emphasized *closed tasks* taught a literacy curriculum focused heavily on teacher-directed skills lessons followed by seatwork assignments on which students worked individually, attempting to provide correct answers to closed-ended questions. In contrast, teachers who favored a motivated literacy approach emphasized more open and authentic tasks. *Open tasks* included interactive–constructive tasks, in which students could manipulate materials to reach an outcome (such as in a game) or arrange words to reconstruct a nursery rhyme; partner reading, in which two students shared the oral reading of a story; composition, in which students wrote on self-selected topics; and tradebook reading, in which they read self-selected books.

Open tasks allow students to decide what information to use and how they want to use it to solve some larger problem. These tasks feature characteristics emphasized by Lepper and Hodell (1989) as associated with intrinsic motivation: challenge and self-improvement, student autonomy, the pursuit of personal interests, and social collaboration. Emphasis on such open tasks promoted significantly greater student engagement in literacy activities, as indicated by increased reading strategy use, persistence, and following through to task completion and accomplishment of learning goals. In general, teachers who emphasized the motivated literacy approach followed the principles of teaching for understanding, appreciation, and life application of knowledge described in Chapter 2. Some examples of the open tasks that they used were as follows.

Several teachers reproduced texts from stories or nursery rhymes on oak-tag, cutting the sentences into individual words. Then they invited their students to reconstruct the sentences in meaningful ways. This was a challenging activity for even the best readers, yet still accessible to readers at lower levels. It required students to use a sophisticated array of strategies including designing a plan, rehearsing, decoding, monitoring for upper- and lowercase letters and punctuation, sequencing, and backtracking for comprehension. Errors prompted them to try other word sequences. Frequently they tried many arrangements, rereading each time to determine if they were satisfied with their construction.

Other teachers designed multiple activities that supported their instructional goals and then allowed students to select from among them. For example, one classroom featured a week-long celebration of *Clifford's Birthday Party* (Bridwell, 1988) which embedded activity options including writing about the party described in the book, writing about a parallel party held in their classroom, writing party invitations, making a list of party supplies, drawing and labeling Clifford's gifts, and reading other Clifford books. In carrying out these activities, the students produced products that showed care, planning, and originality, and sparked task-oriented conversations. Turner attributed this in part to the students' opportunities to select activities that they found most interesting.

Several teachers allowed their students to work with selected partners to choose learning tasks and then sequence their learning activities. These teachers helped each pair of partners to think through their choices, make decisions about how to plan and monitor their work, evaluate their completed products, and note things to keep in mind for the future.

Some teachers connected with students' interests by allowing them to select books to read. The added incentive of choosing an intriguing book supported students' engagement during oral reading times and encouraged them to persist in reading difficult texts. Similarly, frequent composition opportunities allowed students to explore topics of importance to them. In one class, for example, all of the students wrote on the theme of butterflies, but responses ranged from discussions of the life cycle to pretend fantasies.

Students in motivated literacy classrooms often worked in pairs or small groups, which allowed them to pique one another's curiosity, share interests, and model expertise that classmates could emulate. This reflected the fact that open tasks are more flexible and conducive to student collaboration than closed tasks that allow for only one approach or answer.

Anderman (1993) described a motivating approach to writing instruction. In this study, third and fourth graders were asked to spend time each day writing in journals about any topic they wished to address. They also participated in weekly feedback sessions in which they read their writings to the teacher and other students. Over time, these students not only developed their writing abilities but also acquired a continuing desire to engage in journal writing. Their writing became more communicative, consisting of letters and stories rather than lists. It also revealed a broader understanding of the uses of writing, greater persistence at writing tasks, and increased creativity.

Project-Based Learning

Phyllis Blumenfeld and her colleagues (1991) described Project-Based Learning, a comprehensive approach to classroom teaching and learning that incorporates several principles for capitalizing on students' intrinsic motivation. It calls for engaging students in *projects:* relatively long-term, problem-focused, and meaningful units of instruction that integrate concepts from a number of disciplines or fields of study. Within the framework, students pursue solutions to authentic problems by asking and refining questions, debating ideas, making predictions, designing plans or experiments, collecting and analyzing data, drawing conclusions, communicating their ideas and findings to others, asking new questions, and creating products.

There are two essential components to projects: (1) they require a question or problem that organizes and drives activities, and (2) the activities result in a series of products that culminate in a final product that addresses the driving question. The final products represent the students' problem solutions, organized and presented in a form (e.g., a model, report, videotape, or computer program) that can be shared with others and critiqued. Feedback from others permits students to reflect on and extend their emergent knowledge and to revise their products if necessary. Project-based learning incorporates the following motivational features: tasks are varied and include novel elements, problems are authentic and challenging, students exercise choice in deciding what to do and how to do it, they collaborate with peers in carrying out the work, and the work leads to closure in the form of production of the final product.

These motivational features of project work do not guarantee that students will acquire needed information, generate and test solutions, and evaluate their findings carefully. Teachers using project-based learning need to make sure that students possess whatever subject-matter knowledge and research skills are required to complete their projects successfully, that the projects cause students to learn key ideas and skills in the process of carrying them out, and that students view the projects as authentic and value the products they create.

Howard Gardner (1991) proposed a radical restructuring of K–12 schooling in which students would spend most of their time engaged in project-based learning, in and out of classroom settings. Projects can be developed for any subject, although they are especially well suited to science and social studies. Blumenfeld et al. (1991) suggested ways in which projects can be designed to maximize their motivational impact. Some of these involve using emerging technology that enables students to work with computerized databases in conducting their research or to use computerized design, video technology, and other innovations in developing their products.

TEACHERS' EXPERIENCE-BASED MOTIVATIONAL STRATEGIES

When inservice teachers are asked to describe the strategies they use to motivate their students, the experience-based strategies that they report mostly resemble the theory- and research-based intrinsic motivational strategies presented in this chapter. For example, Hootstein (1995) interviewed eighth-grade teachers about the strategies they used to motivate students to learn US history. The 10 most frequently mentioned strategies were as follows:

1. Having students role play characters in historical simulations (mentioned by 83 percent of the teachers).
2. Organizing projects that result in the creation of products (60 percent).
3. Playing games with students as a way to review material for tests (44 percent).
4. Relating history to current events or to students' lives (44 percent).
5. Assigning students to read historical novels (44 percent).
6. Asking thought-provoking questions (33 percent).
7. Inviting guest speakers from the community (33 percent).
8. Showing historical videos and films (28 percent).
9. Organizing cooperative learning activities (28 percent).
10. Providing small-scale hands-on experiences (28 percent).

Hootstein also gathered responses from the eighth graders taught by these teachers. He showed them the strategies mentioned by their teachers and asked them to identify the single strategy that would most motivate them to want to learn US history. Role playing historical characters was the strategy mentioned most often. However, the next most frequently mentioned strategy was participating in group discussions of the textbook or other material. The students also mentioned teacher attempts to make the subject interesting to them, to relate it to current events or their own interests, or to inject humor through jokes, stories, or anecdotes. Here is additional evidence that students do not necessarily need technology, games, or various bells and whistles to enjoy learning, and that they even enjoy relatively passive forms of learning if the teacher makes the material interesting to them.

Zahorik (1996) asked 30 elementary and 35 secondary teachers enrolled in a graduate course to write papers on (1) what makes for a good learning experience, (2) a very interesting activity they had used, (3) how they created interest, and (4) subject-matter facts and concepts they had found to be interesting to students. The teachers' papers once again emphasized the intrinsic motivational strategies described in this chapter, although in ways that underscore the limitations as well as the strengths of these strategies.

The actions that teachers reported taking for generating interest in learning were concentrated in eight categories. The most popular category, mentioned by 100 percent of the teachers, was *hands-on activities*. Examples included manipulatives such as pattern blocks in mathematics; playing games of all kinds; simulations, role play, and drama; projects such as growing seedlings in science or making television commercials in Spanish; and solving problems or puzzles such as determining the sugar content of chewing gum.

Personalized content was mentioned by 65 percent of the teachers. These responses took three forms: (1) tying content to students' prior knowledge, experiences, or interests (e.g., beginning a unit on weather by having students discuss their experiences with tornados); (2) allowing students to generate the content to be studied, often through teacher–student planning; (3) selecting from the required curriculum that content which is likely to interest students (e.g., appealing novels, rules for how married names are composed in Spanish).

Also mentioned by 65 percent of the teachers were *student trust* techniques that show respect for students' intelligence, integrity, and pride. These techniques permit students to share their ideas and experiences through dialogue, reporting, debating, and displaying work; to make decisions for themselves and use their creativity; or to develop ownership of classroom events through involvement in planning units and choosing tasks.

Group tasks were mentioned by 55 percent of the teachers. These were activities that students carried out cooperatively in small groups, such as performing a group science demonstration on water evaporation and condensation.

The remaining categories included using a *variety of materials* (29 percent), *teacher enthusiasm* (28 percent), *practical tasks that involve students in activities that have utility outside of school or produce a useful product* (17 percent), and using a *variety of activities* (11). In speaking of variety, the teachers especially mentioned materials, resources, or activities that were atypical in some way, such as field trips, guest speakers, artifacts, or animals. Examples of teacher enthusiasm included being humorous and emphasizing fun, describing personal experiences to students, participating in tasks as an equal group member, showing excitement, and communicating a sense of purpose, direction, or organization to students. One teacher, for example, dressed up as a story character. Another told her students about her recent trip to Spain. Practical activities included artwork that could be used as gifts, producing a book for others to read, learning how to read a menu, planning a trip to a national park, and discussing contraception.

Among activities that they avoided for motivational reasons, teachers mentioned: (1) *sedentary activities* (i.e., explaining, giving directions, reviewing, testing, reading textbooks, doing workbooks, taking notes); (2) *unsuitable tasks* (i.e., too difficult or extensive, or too easy or redundant); (3) *artificial tasks* that have no perceived practical utility or application outside of school; (4) *student distrust* (i.e., unilateral actions taken by the teacher in areas where student choice could have been provided); and (5) *teacher insipidity* (i.e., the teacher displaying lack of enthusiasm, caring, fun, or involvement).

The teachers had disappointingly little to say about putting students into contact with inherently interesting content. Most of what they did say involved adding interesting elements to the content base rather than helping students to develop interest in or appreciation for the content base itself. Also, the teachers' content-related responses focused more on topics than ideas. The teachers reported that their students were interested in the following categories of topics: *human* (anything that has to do with people or culture, such as the skeleton, food, family, diseases, pets, weapons, holidays, sex, death, violence, or money); *now* (topics of current importance in the students' lives, such as television, drugs, fashion, music, gangs, shopping malls, and slang); *nature* (topics relating to the physical and biological world, such as dinosaurs, giraffes, the sea, ecology, wolves, and weather); and *functional* (any topic that could be shown to be practical or useful, such as safety, consumerism, map reading, the stock market, or computers).

When the teachers did mention ideas embedded in the content that could provide a basis for capturing students' interest, many of their responses referred to very limited ideas or specific facts (such as that Van Gogh cut off his own ear). However, some teachers, especially secondary teachers, did mention more broadly applicable ideas (no country exists that does not need another country for something; plants and animals exist in symbiotic relationships; the passive voice is used in Spanish to shift blame away from persons).

In discussing these findings, Zahorik expressed concern that many of the teachers seemed to treat hands-on activities more as ends than as means. At least a third of their reported hands-on activities seemed gratuitous—likely to generate interest but not to lead to important learning. For example, a fifth-grade social studies unit on the 1950s included activities calling for singing Elvis Presley songs, impersonating Elvis, writing essays speculating on whether Elvis was still alive, and critiquing Elvis's movies. Like others who have commented on this point, Zahorik cautioned that *hands-on* activities will not produce important learning unless they include *minds-on* features that engage students in thinking about powerful ideas (Duckworth, Easley, Hawkins, & Henriques, 1990; Flick, 1993; Loucks-Horsley et al., 1990; Roth, 1992).

Zahorik concluded by suggesting that *the key to the minds-on aspect of learning activities is getting students in touch with the powerful ideas that anchor content structures, reflect major instructional goals, and provide the basis for authentic applications.* This is another way of saying that in order to support significant learning, intrinsic motivation needs to include the cognitive/learning aspects associated with motivation to learn, not just the affective/fun aspects associated with interest or enjoyment.

Middleton (1995) studied the motivational beliefs of teachers and students in middle-school mathematics classes. He found that both groups emphasized both expectancy and value issues when discussing motivation, although high-achieving students placed more emphasis on value (they wanted tasks to be interesting) and low-achieving students placed more emphasis on control (they wanted tasks that they could handle without difficulty).

Teachers' beliefs about what makes mathematics intrinsically motivating to students were associated not only with the teachers' motivational practices but also with their students' motivational ideas. For example, one teacher believed that involving his students in applications to real-life problems was the key to motivation in mathematics. His students were especially likely to report that application activities were more fun than other mathematics activities. In contrast, another teacher believed that her students were most motivated when they found the work easy, and in fact this is what her students reported. A third teacher placed relatively equal emphasis on task difficulty and challenge, learning with understanding, and hands-on activities, and her students showed a similar variety and balance in talking about what makes mathematical activities fun.

This research was done in a small and relatively homogeneous rural school district, so there is no reason to believe that the students brought these contrasting views with them into these teachers' classes. Instead, it appears that the students acquired these different notions about what makes different mathematics activities worthwhile or enjoyable because they were exposed to systematic socialization messages from their teachers. Here again is evidence that teachers can shape their students' motivational orientations, not just react to them.

This same point was emphasized by Mitchell (1993), who followed up on an idea originally suggested by John Dewey in distinguishing between *catching* students' interest and *holding* their interest. Mitchell's research in secondary mathematics classrooms suggested that motivational techniques such as presenting students with brain teasers or puzzles, allowing them to work on computers, or allowing them to work in groups were effective in catching the students' interest in mathematical learning activities but not necessarily in holding that interest in ways that led to accomplishment of significant learning goals. Instead, the latter outcome was associated with content emphases that reflected the principle of meaningfulness (students could appreciate the content's applications to life outside of school) and instructional methods that reflected the principle of involvement (students spent most of their time engaged in active learning and application activities, not just watching and listening).

CONCLUSION

Schooling should be as enjoyable as it can be for both teachers and students. Therefore, whenever your instructional objectives can be met through a variety of activities, emphasize activities that students find rewarding and avoid ones that they find boring or aversive. However, bear in mind that there are two important limitations on what you can accomplish through intrinsic motivational strategies.

First, your opportunities to use these strategies are limited. You have to teach the whole curriculum, not just the parts that appeal to students or lend themselves to application of the principles presented in this chapter. Even when intrinsic motivation is present and activities are enjoyable to students, learning still requires concentration and effort.

Second, although intrinsic motivational strategies should increase students' enjoyment of classroom activities, they do not directly stimulate intentions to accomplish the activities' learning goals. Therefore, even when you are able to use intrinsic motivational strategies, you will need to supplement these with strategies for stimulating students' motivation to learn (see Chapter 7). Otherwise, students may enjoy your activities but fail to derive the intended knowledge or skills from them.

In this regard, note that our colloquial language for discussing intrinsic motivation is misleading. We commonly describe certain topics or tasks as "intrinsically interesting" and speak of engaging in activities "for their own sake." Such language implies that motivation resides in activities rather than in people. In reality, *people generate intrinsic motivation;* it is not somehow built into topics or tasks. When we are intrinsically motivated we study or do something not for *its* sake but for *our* sake—because doing so provides us with enjoyable stimulation or satisfaction.

The motives, goals, and strategies that your students develop in response to learning activities will depend both on the nature of the activities themselves and on how you present them. Students who are motivated solely by grades or other extrinsic rewards are likely to adopt goals and strategies that concentrate on meeting minimum requirements that entitle them to acceptable reward levels. They will do what they must to prepare for your tests, then forget most of what they learned.

It is better when students find academic activities intrinsically rewarding. Even then, however, students may not learn what you would like them to learn if the basis for their intrinsic motivation is primarily affective (they enjoy the activity) rather than cognitive (they find it interesting, meaningful, or worthwhile to learn what the activity is designed to teach). Consequently, it will be important for you to use strategies designed to *motivate students to learn* from academic activities—to seek to gain the intended knowledge and skill benefits from these activities and to set goals and use cognitive strategies that will enable them to do so.

SUMMARY

Recent theorizing has shifted from portraying intrinsic and extrinsic motivation as incompatible opposites. It is now recognized that they lie on a continuum such that relative autonomy increases as one moves from purely extrinsic motivational situations to purely intrinsic ones. Furthermore, the notion that extrinsic motivational strategies will necessarily erode intrinsic motivation has receded in favor of recognition that extrinsic strategies can be used in ways that complement intrinsic strategies. Even so, most motivational theorists argue that intrinsic strategies are preferable because they lead to higher quality task engagement and support the development of continuing intrinsic interest in the topic or activity.

Definitions of intrinsic motivation focus on the perception that one's actions are self-determined, so suggestions to teachers emphasize motivational strategies designed to encourage students to maintain or develop this perception. Elaborating on this idea, Deci and Ryan recommend avoiding actions that might lead students to infer that they engage in academic activities solely to please their teachers or to earn rewards, and instead emphasizing strategies that respond to students' needs for autonomy, competence, and relatedness.

You can respond to your students' autonomy needs by encouraging them to function as autonomous learners and allowing them frequent opportunities to make choices. Learning centers provide one way to build autonomy and choice opportunities into your students' everyday classroom experiences.

You can respond to your students' competence needs by making sure that learning activities are well matched to their current levels of knowledge and skill, by emphasizing activities that offer opportunities for them to make active responses and get immediate feedback, by incorporating gamelike features into learning activities, and by emphasizing authentic activities and life applications that feature skill variety, task identity, task significance, and related characteristics that tend to make work enjoyable, whether it occurs in the classroom or on the job.

You can respond to your students' relatedness needs primarily by establishing your classroom as the kind of learning community described in Chapter 2. In addition, you can provide frequent opportunities for your students to collaborate with one another, especially by using purely cooperative small-group learning formats (i.e., Learning Together, Group Investigation, or Jigsaw) or by allowing students to work together in pairs.

Other approaches to intrinsic motivation involve adapting activities to students' interests or embellishing them to enhance their intrinsic motivation potential. Whenever doing so is compatible with your instructional goals, it is a good idea to feature content that students find interesting or activities that they find enjoyable. In addition, conventional activities can be cast within a fantasy format that allows students to take the role of fantasy characters in carrying out some goal-oriented series of tasks. Many computerized games and learning programs take this approach. Less elaborately, you can incorporate drama, simulation, role-play, and other fantasy elements into everyday activities in ways that make these activities more personalized and emotionally engaging for students.

Certain broad educational philosophies have been built around the principle of engaging students in learning activities designed to be intrinsically motivating. Recently, more focused models for incorporating motivational principles into curriculum and instruction have been developed, including the TARGET program described in Chapter 2 and the Motivated Literacy and Project-Based Learning models described in this chapter.

Research on teachers' experience-based strategies for motivating students indicates that they emphasize intrinsic motivational strategies. However, teachers sometimes implement these strategies in ways that appear likely to generate interest but not to engage students with powerful ideas. Hands-on activity does not guarantee minds-on learning.

In the interest of making school as enjoyable as it can be for your students, emphasize activities that they find rewarding and avoid ones that they find boring or aversive. However, apply these strategies in ways that will allow you to address the entire curriculum and to ensure that your students accomplish your instructional goals. Even intrinsically motivated students may not do so if their motivation is primarily active/fun oriented rather than cognitive/learning oriented. Consequently, even when you are able to use the intrinsic motivational strategies described in this chapter, you also will need to use the motivation to learn strategies described in Chapter 7.

REFERENCES

Alexander, P., Kulikowich, J., & Jetton, T. (1994). The role of subject-matter knowledge and interest in the processing of linear and nonlinear text. *Review of Educational Research, 64,* 201–252.

Alleman, J., & Brophy, J. (1993–94). Teaching that lasts: College students' reports of learning activities experienced in elementary school social studies. *Social Science Record, 30*(2), 36–48; *31*(1), 42–46.

Anand, P., & Ross, S. (1987). A computer-based strategy for personalizing verbal problems in teaching mathematics. *Educational Communication and Technology Journal, 35,* 151–162.

Anderman, E. (1993). *The zone of proximal development as a context for motivation.* Educational Resource Information Center (ERIC) Document No. Ed 374 631.

Aronson, E., Blaney, N., Stephan, C., Sikes, J., & Snapp, M. (1978). *The jigsaw classroom.* Beverly Hills, CA: Sage.

Blumenfeld, P., Soloway, E., Marx, R., Krajcik, J., Guzdial, M., & Palincsar, A. (1991). Motivating project-based learning: Sustaining the doing, supporting the learning. *Educational Psychologist, 26,* 369–398.

Bridwell, N,. (1988). *Clifford's birthday party.* New York: Scholastic.

Britton, B., VanDusen, L., Gulgoz, S., & Glynn, S. (1989). Instructional texts rewritten by five expert teams: Revision and retention improvement. *Journal of Educational Psychology, 81,* 226–239.

Brown, J., Collins, A., & Duguid, P. (1989). Situated cognition and the culture of learning. *Educational Researcher, 18*(1), 32–42.

Collier, G. (1994). *Social origins of mental ability.* New York: Wiley.

Condry, J., & Stokker, L. (1992). Overview of special issue on intrinsic motivation. *Motivation and Emotion, 16,* 157–164.

Cooper, P., & McIntyre, D. (1994). Patterns of interaction between teachers' and students' classroom thinking, and their implications for the provision of learning opportunities. *Teaching and Teacher Education, 10,* 633–646.

Covington, M. (1992). *Making the grade.* Cambridge: Cambridge University Press.

Csikszentmihalyi, M. (1993). *The evolving self: A psychology for the third millennium.* New York: HarperCollins.

Dansereau, D. (1988). Cooperative learning strategies. In C. Weinstein, E. Goetz, & P. Alexander (Eds.), *Learning and study strategies: Issues in assessment, instruction, and evaluation* (pp. 103–120). San Diego: Academic Press.

Deci, E., & Ryan, R. (1991). A motivational approach to self: Integration in personality. In R. Dienstbier (Ed.), *Nebraska Symposium on Motivation, Volume 38, Perspectives on motivation* (pp. 237–288). Lincoln: University of Nebraska Press.

Deci, E., & Ryan, R. (1994). Promoting self-determined education. *Scandinavian Journal of Educational Research, 38,* 3–14.

Duckworth, E., Easley, J., Hawkins, D., & Henriques, A. (1990). *Science education: A minds-on approach for the elementary years.* Hillsdale, NJ: Erlbaum.

Duffy, T., Higgins, L., Mehlenbacher, B., et al. (1989). Models for the design of instructional text. *Reading Research Quarterly, 24,* 434–456.

Eckblad, G. (1981). *Scheme theory: A conceptual framework for cognitive-motivational processes.* New York: Academic Press.

Flick, L. (1993). The meanings of hands-on science. *Journal of Science Teacher Education, 4,* 1–8.

Gardner, H. (1991). *The unschooled mind: How children think and how schools should teach.* New York: Basic Books.

Garner, R., Alexander, P., Gillingham, M., Kulikowich, J., & Brown, R. (1991). Interest and learning from text. *American Educational Research Journal, 28,* 643–659.

Good, T., McCaslin, M., & Reys, B. (1992). Investigating work groups to promote problem solving in mathematics. In J. Brophy (Ed.), *Advances in research on teaching* (Vol. 3, pp. 115–160). Greenwich, CT: JAI Press.

Graves, M., Prenn, M., Earle, J., Thompson, M., Johnson, V., & Slater, W. (1991). Improving instructional text: Some lessons learned. *Reading Research Quarterly, 26,* 111–121.

Grolnick, W., & Ryan, R. (1987). Autonomy support in education: Creating the facilitating environment. In N. Hastings & J. Schwieso (Eds.), *New directions in educational psychology: 2. Behaviour and motivation in the classroom* (pp. 213–231). London: Falmer.

Hackman, J.R., & Oldham, G. (1980). *Work redesign.* Reading, MA: Addison-Wesley.

Hidi, S., & Baird, W. (1988). Strategies for increasing text-based interest and students' recall of expository texts. *Reading Research Quarterly, 23,* 465–483.

Hodgins, H., Koestner, R., & Duncan, N. (1996). On the compatibility of autonomy and relatedness. *Personality and Social Psychology Bulletin, 22,* 227–237.

Hootstein, H. (1995). Motivational strategies of middle school social studies teachers. *Social Education, 59,* 23–26.

Johnson, D., & Johnson, R. (1975). *Learning together and alone.* Englewood Cliffs, NJ: Prentice-Hall.

Johnson, D., Johnson, R., Holubec, E., & Roy, P. (1984). *Circles of learning: Cooperation in the classroom.* Alexandria, VA: Association for Supervision and Curriculum Development.

Kanfer, R. (1990). Motivation theory in industrial and organizational psychology. In M. Dunnette & L. Hough (Eds.), *Handbook of industrial and organizational psychology* (2nd ed., Vol. 1, pp. 75–170). Palo Alto, CA: Consulting Psychologists Press.

Katzell, R., & Thompson, D. (1990). Work motivation: Theory and practice. *American Psychologist, 45,* 144–153.

Keller, J. (1983). Motivational design of instruction. In C. Reigeluth (Ed.), *Instructional-design theories and models: An overview of their current status* (pp. 383–434). Hillsdale, NJ: Erlbaum.

Kourilsky, M. (1983). *Mini-Society: Experiencing real-world economics in the elementary school classroom.* Menlo Park, CA: Addison-Wesley.

Lave, J., & Wenger, E. (1991). *Situated learning: Legitimate peripheral participation.* Cambridge: Cambridge University Press.

Lepper, M., & Cordova, D. (1992). A desire to be taught: Instructional consequences of intrinsic motivation. *Motivation and Emotion, 16,* 187–208.

Lepper, M., & Hodell, M. (1989). Intrinsic motivation in the classroom. In C. Ames & R. Ames (Eds.), *Research on motivation in education. Volume 3: Goals and cognitions* (pp. 73–105). San Diego: Academic Press.

Lepper, M., & Malone, T. (1987). Intrinsic motivation and instructional effectiveness in computer-based education. In R. Snow & M. Farr (Eds.), *Aptitude, learning, and instruction: III. Conative and affective process analysis* (pp. 255–286). Hillsdale, NJ: Erlbaum.

Loucks-Horsley, S., Capitan, R., Carlson, M., Kuerbis, P., Clark, R., Melle, G., Sachse, T., & Walton, E. (1990). *Elementary school science for the '90s.* Alexandria, VA: Association for Supervision and Curriculum Development.

Malone, T., & Lepper, M. (1987). Making learning fun: A taxonomy of intrinsic motivation for learning. In R. Snow and M. Farr (Eds.), *Aptitude, learning, and instruction: III. Conative and affective process analysis* (pp. 223–253). Hillsdale, NJ: Erlbaum.

Maslow, A. (1962). *Toward a psychology of being.* Princeton, NJ: VanNostrand.

McCaslin, M., & Good, T. (1996). *Listening in classrooms.* New York: HarperCollins.

McKenzie, G. (1975). Some myths and methods on motivation social study. *The Social Studies, 66,* 24–28.

McKeown, M., & Beck, I. (1994). Making sense of accounts of history: Why young students don't and how they might. In G. Leinhardt, I. Beck, & C. Stainton (Eds.), *Teaching and learning in history* (pp. 1–26). Hillsdale, NJ: Erlbaum.

Middleton, J. (1995). A study of intrinsic motivation in the mathematics classroom: A personal constructs approach. *Journal for Research in Mathematics Education, 26,* 254–279.

Miller, N., & Hertz-Lazarowitz, R. (Eds.). (1992). *Interaction in cooperative groups: The theoretical anatomy of group learning.* New York: Cambridge University Press.

Mitchell, M. (1993). Situational interest: Its multifaceted structure in the secondary school mathematics classroom. *Journal of Educational Psychology, 85,* 424–436.

Morrow, L. (1992). The impact of a literature-based program on literacy achievement, use of literature, and attitudes of children from minority backgrounds. *Reading Research Quarterly, 27,* 250–275.

Morrow, L. (1993). *Developing literacy in the early years: Helping children read and write.* Boston: Allyn & Bacon.

O'Donnell, A. (1996). Effects of explicit incentives on scripted and unscripted cooperation. *Journal of Educational Psychology, 88,* 74–86.

O'Donnell, A., & Dansereau, D. (1992). Scripted cooperation in student dyads: A method for analyzing and enhancing academic learning and performance. In N. Miller & R. Hertz-Lazarowitz (Eds.), *Interaction in cooperative groups: The theoretical anatomy of group learning* (pp. 121–140). New York: Cambridge University Press.

Pinder, C. (1984). *Work motivation: Theory, issues, and applications.* Glenview, IL: Scott, Foresman, & Co.

Renninger, K., Hidi, S., & Krapp, A. (Eds.). (1992). *The role of interest in learning and development.* Hillsdale, NJ: Erlbaum.

Rogoff, B. (1990). *Apprenticeship in thinking: Cognitive development in social context.* New York: Oxford University Press.

Roth, K. (1992). Science education: It's not enough to "do" or "relate." In M. Pearsall (Ed.), *Scope, sequence, and coordination of secondary school science: Relevant research* (Vol. 2, pp. 151–164). Washington, DC: National Science Teachers Association.

Ryan, R. (1993). Agency and organization: Intrinsic motivation, autonomy and the self in psychological development. In J. Jacobs (Ed.), *Nebraska Symposium on Motivation: Developmental perspectives on motivation* (Vol. 40, pp. 1–56). Lincoln: University of Nebraska Press.

Ryan, R., Connell, J., & Grolnick, W. (1992). When achievement is *not* intrinsically motivated: A theory of internalization and self-regulation in school. In A. Boggiano & T. Pittman (Eds.), *Achievement and motivation: A social-developmental perspective* (pp. 167–188). Cambridge: Cambridge University Press.

Sansone, C., & Morgan, C. (1992). Intrinsic motivation and education: Competence in context. *Motivation and Emotion, 16,* 249–270.

Schank, R., & Cleary, C. (1995). *Engines for education.* Hillsdale, NJ: Erlbaum.

Schiefele, U. (1991). Interest, learning, and motivation. *Educational Psychologist, 26,* 299–323.

Sharan, S., & Sharan, Y. (1976). *Small-group teaching.* Englewood Cliffs, NJ: Educational Technology Publications.

Sharan, S. et al. (1984). *Cooperative learning in the classroom: Research in desegregated schools.* Hillsdale, NJ: Erlbaum.

Slavin, R. (1983). *Cooperative learning.* New York: Longman.

Slavin, R. (1990). *Cooperative learning: Theory, research, and practice.* Englewood Cliffs, NJ: Prentice-Hall.

Turner, J. (1993). A motivational perspective on literacy instruction. In D. Leu & C. Kinzer (Eds.), *Examining central issues in literacy research, theory, and practice: Forty-second Yearbook of the National Reading Conference* (pp. 153–161). Chicago: National Reading Conference, Inc.

Turner, J. (1995). The influence of classroom contexts on young children's motivation for literacy. *Reading Research Quarterly, 30,* 410–441.

Valas, H., & Sovik, N. (1994). Variables affecting students' intrinsic motivation for school mathematics: Two empirical studies based on Deci and Ryan's theory on motivation. *Learning and Instruction, 3,* 281–298.

Wade, S., Alexander, P., Schraw, G., & Kulikowich, J. (1995). The perils of criticism: Response to Goetz and Sadowski. *Reading Research Quarterly, 30,* 512–515.

White, R. (1959). Motivation reconsidered: The concept of competence. *Psychological Review, 66,* 297–333.

Zahorik, J. (1996). Elementary and secondary teachers' reports of how they make learning interesting. *Elementary School Journal, 96,* 551–564.

CHAPTER 7

Stimulating Students' Motivation to Learn

In short, intrinsic motivation cannot constitute a sufficient and stable motivational basis for schooling in general or a predesigned curriculum in particular. It will . . . encourage an orientation toward activity based on immediate satisfaction rather than on values. Contrary to claims made by some psychologists, intrinsically motivated students will not be consistently motivated. Certain aspects of the curriculum will interest them, while others will not; at times they will study, and at times they will not. Thus, students who rely exclusively on intrinsic motivation are likely to neglect a large part of their schoolwork.

Most students, however, do not do this. The average student in a good school tends to do the work . . . even when a subject does not arouse high intrinsic motivation and even when rewards and punishments are not salient. What, then, is the source of such students' hard work? . . . the students share the belief of the curriculum designers that the program is desirable and valuable.

NISAN (1992, PP. 129–130)

MOTIVATION TO LEARN

I share the view expressed by Mordecai Nisan in this quotation, which is why I place more emphasis on motivation to learn than on intrinsic motivation. By *motivation to learn,* I mean a student's tendency to find academic activities meaningful and worthwhile and to try to get the intended learning benefits from them. In contrast to intrinsic motivation, which is primarily an affective response to an activity, motivation to learn is primarily a cognitive response involving attempts to make sense of the activity, understand the knowledge it develops, and master the skills that it promotes (Brophy, 1983; Brophy & Kher, 1986).

Students may be motivated to learn from an activity whether or not they find its content interesting or its processes enjoyable. They may not get to choose the activity, but they can choose to make the most of the learning opportunities it presents (see Box 7.1).

Box 7.1.   Motivation to Learn as a Felt Obligation

Intrinsic motivation and motivation to learn often go together and operate in mutually supportive fashion. However, each can occur independently of the other, which is one reason why they need to be distinguished. Lee and Brophy (1996) described students with contrasting motivational patterns that illustrate the combinations that occur. These students were observed in sixth-grade science classes and described in terms of their motivation to learn science.

Students who were intrinsically motivated to learn science displayed both intrinsic interest in the subject and motivation to learn it. Jason was inquisitive, curious, and active in his attempts to construct scientific knowledge. He expanded lesson content to relate it to his prior knowledge or personal experience. He paid close attention to lessons and pointed out mistakes, ambiguities, or places where further elaboration was needed in the curriculum unit or the teacher's explanations. Sometimes he posed challenging questions or engaged in debates until he convinced the teacher of his ideas or was convinced by the teacher's explanations. He contributed to class discussions by proposing alternative or novel ideas and demonstrated leadership in small-group work. When he had extra time he helped other students, checked and elaborated his answers in the activity book, or pursued his interest and curiosity in the subject. He also expanded class activities to connect to science experiences outside of class, as when he reported growing sugar crystals on a paper clip at home after having watched the activity demonstrated on a televised science program.

Other students demonstrated cognitive engagement with the goal of understanding science, but did not show the intrinsic motivation or self-initiation seen in students like Jason. Sara's cognitive engagement was confined to the lesson content and activity requirements assigned by the teacher. In the process of undergoing conceptual change, Sara recognized conceptual conflicts and tried to modify misconceptions into scientific conceptions. When she didn't understand something said in class she would say so and ask for clarification or further explanation. She volunteered during lessons and did her assignments conscientiously, seeking to understand the material rather than just to get correct answers. She was clearly motivated to learn science with understanding and willing to invest the time, effort, and strategies needed to do so. However, she and other students who shared her pattern did not demonstrate intrinsic interest in science or enjoyment in carrying out scientific activities. Instead, they seemed to be motivated by a duty-bound sense of obligation or commitment to understanding academic content and mastering skills.

Neil displayed the inconsistency that results when a student's pattern includes intrinsic motivation but not motivation to learn. He sometimes engaged in learning activities to satisfy his personal interest in learning science, but this interest waxed and waned. He displayed keen interest and initiative in some situations but was inattentive and uninvolved in others. In interviews, he described the former activities as fun (e.g., experiments on water evaporation and condensation), but said that he didn't enjoy the latter activities (e.g., writing in the activity book). Thus, the quality of Neil's engagement depended

(Continued)

Box 7.1.   Motivation to Learn as a Felt Obligation—*Concluded*

on his interest (intrinsic motivation). He did not display any consistent motivation to learn science independently of his interest in particular topics or activities.

Finally, some students were unmotivated to learn science and thus seldom cognitively engaged in activities designed to develop such learning. For example, Kim was often inattentive to lessons and prone to use strategies designed to minimize her effort in completing work. She rarely volunteered to respond in class, and when called on as a nonvolunteer she made feeble responses or said, "I don't know." In small-group activities, her interactions were social rather than academic. She readily accepted other students' ideas and copied their answers instead of trying to make sense of what was being taught. Instead of attempting to answer activity book questions before engaging in class discussions of them, she usually waited until the discussions began and then wrote down answers given by other students. She also left some questions unanswered. She and other task-avoidant students (as well as one task-resistant student) displayed both a lack of intrinsic motivation and a lack of motivation to learn science.

Thorkildsen, Nolen, and Fournier (1994) interviewed 7–12 year-old students about the fairness of selected practices that teachers might use to motivate their students to learn. One group favored practices that would help students to find the material more interesting, challenging, and intrinsically meaningful, and thus promote the desire to understand new ideas. Their responses suggested a combination of intrinsic motivation and motivation to learn. A second group favored practices that encouraged students to work diligently to get a good education. These students appeared to possess a dutiful commitment to education and thus to display motivation to learn, but not intrinsic motivation. Finally, a third group favored extrinsic incentive systems that would reward students for their efforts or accomplishments. These students did not seem to possess either intrinsic motivation or motivation to learn as defined in this book, although they did express a willingness to work on the teacher's agenda in exchange for extrinsic rewards.

RELATED MOTIVATIONAL CONCEPTS

Motivation to learn overlaps considerably with the "learning" or "mastery" orientations described by goal theorists and summarized in Table 3.1. It is a somewhat broader concept, however, meant to apply not only to achievement situations that involve specific goals but also to other situations in or out of school that offer the potential for learning. This learning may be incidental rather than intentional—that is, discovered in the process of task engagement rather than acquired systematically through goal-directed behavior.

This definition of motivation to learn harks back to the distinction between learning and performance: *Learning* refers to the information processing, sensemaking, and advances in comprehension or mastery that occur
while one is acquiring knowledge or skill; *performance* refers to the demonstration of such knowledge or skill after it has been acquired. Strategies for stimulating students' motivation to learn apply not only to their performance (work
on tests or assignments) but also to the information-processing strategies that
they use in learning content or skills in the first place (attending to lessons,
reading for understanding, comprehending explanations, putting things into
their own words). These strategies encourage students to use thoughtful information-processing and skill-building strategies when they are learning. This is
quite different from merely offering them incentives for good performance
later.

The learning taught in schools is mostly cognitive learning—abstract concepts and verbally coded information. In order to make good progress in such
academic learning, students need to develop and use *generative learning strategies* (Weinstein & Mayer, 1986). That is, they need to process information actively, relate it to their existing knowledge, put it into their own words, make
sure that they understand it, and so on. Therefore, motivating students to
learn means not only stimulating them to take an interest in and see the value
of what they are learning, but also providing them with guidance about how
to go about learning it.

My conception of student motivation to learn also overlaps with the learning orientation described by Hermine Marshall (1994). In classes with a *learning orientation*, emphasis is placed on the learning purposes of schools and assignments and on the effort and strategies required to figure things out. In
these classes, teachers frame lessons and assignments in terms of what students will learn from them and emphasize the importance of thinking and understanding over supplying right answers and completing worksheets. The
students in these classes come to see themselves as learners or problem solvers
who are expanding their understanding of the world and themselves with
guidance from their teachers.

Marshall contrasted these learning orientation classes with classes that
featured a *work orientation*. Here, students tended to view assignments as tasks
to be completed so that they could receive a reward or go out to recess. They
frequently did not understand the purposes of academic activities, and they
engaged in these activities using surface-level rather than deeper-level information processing and retention strategies. Their teachers made frequent references to "work" and the need to get work finished, and their curricula emphasized dittos and workbooks. In contrast, the learning-oriented students'
teachers tended to speak in terms of purposeful and reflective learning, and
their curricula featured many more open-ended and authentic tasks.

In discussing literacy learning, Penny Oldfather emphasized the concept
of *the continuing impulse to learn.* She described it as an ongoing engagement
with learning that is propelled and focused by the thoughts and feelings that

emerge when students construct meaning. It is characterized by intense involvement, curiosity, and a search for understanding. The continuing impulse to learn goes well beyond situational interest in a topic or activity. Developing it requires creating classroom cultures in which students discover what they care about, create their own learning agendas, and most importantly, connect who they are to what they do in school (Oldfather & Dahl, 1994).

Phyllis Blumenfeld and her colleagues (Blumenfeld, Puro, & Mergendoller, 1992) developed a concept of student motivation to learn, which they described as combining motivation and cognitive engagement. They contrasted fifth- and sixth-grade science classes in which students reported higher levels of motivation to learn with classes in which they reported lower levels. In the former classes, teachers stressed ideas rather than facts, highlighted the value of science through stories about scientists or about how science connects to everyday events, and expressed their own enthusiasm for the subject by relating stories of their personal scientific experiences. These teachers also made conceptual material more concrete and interesting by providing examples and by connecting the material to their students' experiences or to current events. They assigned more varied tasks and encouraged students to cooperate in small groups. In contrast, in science classes in which students reported lower motivation to learn, the teachers focused more on recitation, quizzes, and grades.

Four factors characterized the teachers' practices in the classes in which students reported higher levels of motivation to learn:

Opportunities to Learn: The teachers (1) focused lessons around mid-level concepts that were substantive but not overwhelming to students; (2) made the main ideas evident in presentations, demonstrations, discussions, and assignments; (3) developed concepts by presenting concrete illustrations of scientific principles and relating unfamiliar information to their students' personal knowledge; (4) made explicit connections between new information and things that students had learned previously, and pointed out relationships among new ideas by stressing similarities and differences; (5) elaborated extensively on textbook readings rather than allowing the book to carry the lesson; (6) guided students' thinking when posing high-level questions; and (7) asked students to summarize, make comparisons between related concepts, and apply the information they were learning. In combination, these methods provided students with frequent opportunities to learn, and where necessary, with assistance in helping them do so.

Press: The teachers pressed for thinking through their feedback and expectations for lesson participation. They (1) required students to explain and justify their answers; (2) prompted, reframed the question, or broke it into smaller parts when students were unsure, and probed students when their understanding was unclear; (3) monitored for comprehension rather than procedural correctness during activities; (4) encouraged responses from all students through such techniques as asking for votes or for students to compare their responses and debate the merits of different ideas (rather than allowing a small subgroup to dominate the lessons); and (5) supplemented the short answer assignments in the commercial workbooks by adding questions that required their students to write explanations of results or alternative representations of information in the form of diagrams or charts. These methods required their students to actively think about what they were hearing or reading, instead of just monitoring it passively or trying to memorize it.

Support: These teachers supported their students' attempts to understand through modeling and scaffolding. They (1) modeled thinking, suggested strategies, and worked with students to solve problems when the students had difficulty (instead of just providing answers); (2) reduced the procedural complexity of manipulative tasks by demonstrating procedures, highlighting problems, providing examples, or allowing for planning time; and (3) encouraged collaborative efforts by requiring all students to make contributions to the group. Thus, besides exerting a consistent press for thinking and learning through the demands they made on their students, these teachers gave the students whatever help they needed to enable them to meet those demands.

Evaluation: These teachers' evaluation and accountability systems emphasized understanding and learning rather than work completion, performance, comparison, or right answers. They used mistakes as ways to help students check their thinking, and they explicitly encouraged students to take risks. Finally, they allowed students who had done poorly to redo assignments or retake quizzes.

All four of these factors need to be present and working together in order to develop motivation to learn that includes high levels of cognitive engagement in the content and learning activities. This was illustrated in the case of a teacher whose students reported high levels of motivation but significantly lower levels of cognitive engagement. This teacher typically spent several minutes at the beginning of each lesson attempting to pique students' interest by using humor, showing dramatic visual aids, connecting the topic to students' experiences, or expressing his own enthusiasm. He also usually made a statement about the lesson's purpose, but confined it to brief remarks that did not specify what students would be able to do with the information.

Unfortunately, this teacher did not follow up his good motivational beginnings by using teaching techniques that encourage high cognitive engagement. His questions tended to be low level, generally requiring only recall. He rarely checked to make sure that students understood main ideas before moving on to the next segment. He did not call on many students to respond and usually provided elaboration himself rather than eliciting it from students. Nor did he ask students to make and justify predictions, to relate points under discussion to prior knowledge, or to summarize or extend their learning. Instead, he relied heavily on information presentation, often reading from the textbook or calling on students to read aloud, then asking questions that required only repetition or simple paraphrasing of the reading. He sometimes inserted comments or asked questions designed to sustain students' interest in the material, but he did not provide them with opportunities to synthesize or apply what they were learning.

In summarizing these findings, Blumenfeld, Puro, and Mergendoller stated that teachers need to do two things in order to motivate their students to learn and to think carefully about what they are learning: (1) *bring the lesson to the students* by providing opportunities for them to learn and enhancing the interest value of the learning to them, and (2) *bring the students to the lesson* by requiring them to think about and use the material and supporting their efforts to do so. The teacher just described did a good job of enhancing the interest value of his lessons, but he did not consistently provide his students with quality opportunities to learn. He did not bring them to the lesson by requiring them to think about the material and supporting their learning efforts.

SOCIALIZING MOTIVATION TO LEARN AS A GENERAL DISPOSITION

Each person has a unique motivational system, developed in response to experiences and to socialization from significant others in his or her life. In the case of students developing motivation to learn academic knowledge and skills, teachers are important significant others. Therefore, rather than just accommodate classroom activities to students' existing motivational patterns, teachers can *shape* those patterns through socialization designed to develop students' motivation to learn.

As noted in Chapter 1, motivation to learn can be viewed as either an enduring disposition (to value learning and thus to approach learning situations thoughtfully and purposefully) or a situation-specific state (the intention to engage purposefully in a given activity by adopting its goal and trying to learn the concepts or master the skills that it develops). The rest of this chapter suggests ways for you to socialize your students' motivation to learn as a general disposition and stimulate it in particular teaching situations by bringing it to the forefront relative to other motives that may be operating at the time.

I begin with three general strategies for establishing a learning environment that creates a favorable context in which to socialize students' motivation to learn. These strategies involve helping students come to understand that classrooms are primarily places for learning and that acquiring knowledge and skills contributes to their quality of life (not just their report card grades).

Model Your Own Motivation to Learn

Model interest in learning throughout all of your interactions with your students. This modeling will encourage students to value learning as a rewarding, self-actualizing activity that produces personal satisfaction and enriches their lives. Besides teaching what is in the textbooks, share your interests in current events and items of general knowledge (especially as they relate to the subjects you teach). Call attention to current books, articles, television programs, or movies on these subjects and to examples or applications in everyday living, in the local environment, or in current events.

Modeling means more than just calling your students' attention to examples or applications of concepts taught in school. It means acting as a model by *sharing your thinking* about such examples or applications—showing your students how educated people use information and concepts learned in school to understand and respond to everyday experiences in their lives and to news about events occurring elsewhere.

Without being preachy about it, you can relate personal experiences illustrating how you use language arts knowledge to communicate or express yourself effectively in important life situations, how you use mathematical or scientific knowledge to solve everyday household-engineering or repair problems, or how you use social studies knowledge to help you appreciate things that you see in your travels or to understand the significance of events in the news. Through such modeling, help your students come to see how it is both stimulating and satisfying to understand (or even just to think, wonder, or make predictions about) what is happening in the world around us.

Much of your modeling will occur in the process of carrying out everyday instruction. Such modeling may be subtle or indirect, but if it is displayed consistently it will have cumulative effects on your students' attitudes and beliefs. One important place to model curiosity and interest in learning is when responding to students' questions, especially questions that are not covered in the textbook. Questions usually indicate that students are interested in the topic and thinking actively about it rather than just listening passively. Consequently, be prepared to respond in ways that show that you value such questions. First, acknowledge or praise the question itself: "That's a good question, Latonya. It does seem strange that the people of Boston would throw the tea into the water, doesn't it?" Then, answer the question or refer it to the class: "How about it, class? Why would they throw the tea into the water instead of taking it home with them?"

You also can model curiosity in responding to questions for which you do not have ready answers: "I never thought about that before. Why didn't they take the tea home with them? They must have decided not to steal it but to throw it into the water instead. How come?" At this point, you could continue to think aloud in this vein or else invite suggestions from the class. If no one is prepared to answer the question, adopt some strategy to address it. You might promise to get the answer for the student, or better yet, invite the student to go to the library (or another resource) to find the answer and then report back to the class.

Other occasions for modeling curiosity and interest in learning arise when you convey information to students about your life outside of school. If you read a book, magazine article, or newspaper item of interest, mention it so that students can read it for themselves if they wish (better yet, make the item available for loan). Also, announce television programs, museum exhibits, or other special events of educational or cultural value.

You can also model your own curiosity and interest in learning through comments made in passing during class. Without belaboring the point, you can communicate that you regularly read the newspaper ("I read in the paper that . . . "), watch the news ("Last night on the news they showed . . . "), and participate in various educational and cultural pursuits. Your students should be aware that you think carefully about and participate in elections, keep abreast of current events, and otherwise show evidence of an active, inquiring mind.

For example, a junior high school teacher used modeling effectively in connection with an assignment involving reading about current events in the newspaper. He began by noting that he read the editorial page regularly, sometimes agreeing and sometimes disagreeing, but always finding the ideas thought provoking. He went on to discuss the newspaper's position and his own position on a forthcoming summit meeting, noting that he was initially pessimistic about the likely outcome of this meeting but that he had become more interested and optimistic about it as he became better informed by reading the paper and watching news programs. This led to a stimulating discussion that clarified for the students, and provoked many questions about, the position of the United States and the Soviet Union on major issues to be discussed at the meeting. The teacher went on to provoke further interest and curiosity by noting that, although he was sharing his own position on the issues discussed that day, he usually withheld his positions on issues discussed in class to encourage students to think for themselves and avoid inhibiting those who might disagree with him. This teacher probably increased his students' interest in newspaper articles and television programs about current events, as well as giving them a model to follow in responding to those news sources in active, thoughtful ways.

Communicate Desirable Expectations and Attributions

In your everyday teaching, routinely project attitudes, beliefs, expectations, and attributions (statements about the reasons for your students' behavior) implying that students share your enthusiasm for learning. To the extent that you *treat students as if they already are eager learners,* they will be more likely to become eager learners. Let them know that they are expected to be curious, to want to learn with understanding, and to want to apply what they are learning to their everyday lives (Marshall, 1987).

Minimally, this means avoiding suggestions that students will dislike academic activities or work on them only to get good grades. More directly, it means treating students as active, motivated learners who care about their learning and are trying to learn with understanding (Blumenfeld & Meece, 1988).

For example, an elementary teacher communicated positive expectations by announcing at the beginning of the year that she intended to make her students into social scientists. She referred to this idea frequently throughout the year in comments such as, "Since you are social scientists, you will recognize that the description of this area as a tropical rain forest has implications about what kinds of crops will grow there," or "Thinking as social scientists, what conclusions might we draw from this information?" Besides cueing her students to use disciplinary conventions for handling evidence and drawing conclusions, such comments encouraged them to identify with the social science disciplines and to connect what they were learning with their lives outside of school.

As another example, consider this teacher's treatment of division with remainders:

TEACHER: We started out with 18 links and divided them into groups of 3, so how many groups are we going to get?

ANTHONY: Six.

TEACHER: Six groups. You're right. We could say six groups of three make 18, right? OK, this time let's say I'm going to take away one. How many would I have then? [Several students say 17.] Seventeen. I want someone to come up and put these 17 links into groups of two. How many groups do you end up with?

BRENDA: Eight groups plus one left over.

TEACHER: Can't you put it in with one of the others? [Brenda shakes her head.] No. So we counted 8 groups of 2, but what else do we have?

BRENDA: One left over.

TEACHER: One left over. OK, in math, what do we call a leftover?

LYLE: A remainder.

TEACHER: Right. So this problem is a little more interesting—we have a remainder.

In the process of teaching about division with remainders, this teacher is also socializing attitudes about mathematics. She presents the concept of remainders in a positive and problem-solving fashion that encourages students to view mathematics with interest and confidence. Another teacher might have introduced this new level of complexity with a sense of futility or irritation ("You don't know what to do now, do you?" "This problem has a remainder, so it's more difficult"). If made consistently, such comments would lead students to view division as complicated and frustrating.

Minimize Performance Anxiety

Motivation to learn is likely to develop most fully when students are goal oriented but relaxed enough to be able to concentrate on the task at hand without worrying about whether they can meet performance expectations. You can encourage this by making clear distinctions between instructional activities designed to promote learning and tests designed to evaluate performance. Most classroom activities should be structured as learning experiences rather than as performance assessments.

To the extent that learning activities include testlike events (i.e., recitation questions, practice exercises), portray these as opportunities for your students to work with and apply what they are learning rather than as opportunities for you to test their mastery. If you want your students to engage in academic activities with motivation to learn (which implies a willingness to take intellectual risks and make mistakes), you will need to protect them from anxiety or premature concern about performance adequacy.

Eventually you will have to evaluate their performance and assign grades using tests or other assessment devices. Until that point, however, emphasize teaching and learning rather than performance evaluation, and encourage students to respond to performance demands in terms of Let's assess our progress and learn from our mistakes, rather than Let's see who knows it and who doesn't. If necessary, add statements such as, We're here to learn, and you can't do that without making mistakes, or caution students against laughing at the mistakes made by classmates.

STIMULATING STUDENTS' MOTIVATION TO LEARN IN SPECIFIC LEARNING SITUATIONS

If the three general strategies just described pervade the learning environment that you establish in your classroom, they will subtly encourage your students to develop motivation to learn as a general disposition. You then can supplement these general strategies by using one or more of the following specific strategies during each of the learning situations that you create each day. These specific strategies are designed to stimulate students' motivation to learn what an activity is designed to teach. They are described within three categories: (1) strategies for shaping students' expectations about the learning, (2) strategies for inducing motivation to learn, and (3) strategies for scaffolding students' learning efforts.

STRATEGIES FOR SHAPING STUDENTS' EXPECTATIONS ABOUT THE LEARNING

Students are more likely to respond positively to your attempts to induce motivation to learn if they expect the learning to be interesting or important. You can foster and maintain this expectation by being enthusiastic when introducing and implementing learning activities and by shifting into an intense communication style when explaining things that are especially important.

Be Enthusiastic (Regularly)

Students take cues from their teachers about how to respond to school activities. If you present a topic or assignment with enthusiasm, suggesting that it is interesting, important, or worthwhile, your students are likely to adopt this same attitude (Bettencourt et al., 1983).

Projecting enthusiasm does not mean pep talks or phony theatrics. Instead, it means identifying good reasons for viewing a topic as interesting, meaningful, or important and then communicating these reasons to your students when teaching about the topic. You can use dramatics or forceful salesmanship if you are comfortable with these techniques, but if not, low-key but sincere statements of the value that you place on a topic or activity will be just as effective (Cabello & Terrell, 1994). Even a brief comment showing that a topic is food for thought or illustrating how it is interesting, unique, or different from previously studied topics may be sufficient. The primary objective of projecting enthusiasm is to induce students to value the topic or activity, not to amuse, entertain, or excite them.

A history teacher generated a great deal of interest (and also pulled together a great many concepts) by enthusiastically explaining to his students that during the Middle Ages, the Mediterranean Sea was the center of the world. Mediterranean seaports were major trade centers and places like England were outposts of civilization, but this changed drastically with discovery of the New World and the emergence of new centers of trade and culture. His presentation included references to maps, reminders about the primary modes of transportation at the time, and characterizations of the attitudes of the people and their knowledge about other countries and trade possibilities.

Another teacher brought ancient Israel alive by enthusiastically telling his students about David as the slayer of Goliath and ancestor of Jesus, Abraham leading his people to the Promised Land, Solomon as a wise man and builder of the temple, and Moses as the man who presented the Ten Commandments and led the people out of the wilderness. This lesson included locating Jerusalem, Israel, and the Sinai peninsula on a map and speculating about whether the temple might be rebuilt in modern Jerusalem (noting that a major Moslem temple is located next to the spot occupied by Solomon's temple). In each of these examples, the teacher was able to parlay personal interest and detailed knowledge about a topic into an effective presentation that sparked interest and elicited many questions and comments.

The potential power of teacher enthusiasm is captured in the following quotation explaining why certain teachers find a permanent place in their students' memories:

> What intrigues students most about these teachers is their enthusiasm for subjects that seemed boring and purposeless in other teachers' classes. Memorable teachers challenge students to expect more than just recognition or a paycheck from the work they choose. Why is Mr. Phillips so fired up about differential equations? How could Ms. Patrelli get so excited about the Crusades? Sometimes it is an encounter with just such a teacher that inspires students to reconsider the intrinsic rewards of exploring a domain of knowledge. (Csikzentmihalyi, Rathunde, & Whalen, 1993, pp. 184–85)

Be Intense (Selectively)

Learn to use timing, nonverbal expressions and gestures, and cueing and other verbal techniques to project a level of intensity that tells students that material is important and deserves close attention. Often, an intense presentation will begin with a direct statement of the importance of the message ("I'm going to show you how to invert fractions—now pay close attention and make sure that you understand what this involves, when and why you do it, and how you do it"). Then, present the message itself using verbal and nonverbal public speaking techniques that convey intensity and cue attention: a slow-paced, step-by-step presentation during which you emphasize key words, use unusual voice modulations or exaggerated gestures that focus attention on key terms or procedural steps, and intensely scan the group following each step to look for signs of understanding or confusion (and to allow anyone with a question to ask it immediately). In addition to your words, everything about your tone and manner should communicate to students that what is being said is important and that they should give it full attention and ask questions about anything they do not understand.

Pick your spots for using such an intense communication style. You cannot be so intense all the time, and even if you could, your students would adjust to it so that it would lose much of its effectiveness. Therefore, reserve intensity for times in which you want to communicate, This is especially important; pay close attention. Likely occasions include introduction of important new terms or definitions, especially those that might be confusing to students; demonstration of procedures (preparing paint in an art class, serving a volleyball, or handling scientific equipment); modeling of problem-solving techniques, especially when giving instructions for assignments; and any instruction that is intended to eliminate misconceptions (and thus requires making students aware that although they think they already understand the point at issue, their "knowledge" is incorrect). Exaggerated intensity is less appropriate for more routine instructional situations, although it is wise to slow the pace and be alert for signs of confusion or student desire to ask a question whenever you are covering new or complex material.

STRATEGIES FOR INDUCING MOTIVATION TO LEARN

Regardless of extrinsic incentives, intrinsic interest, or whatever other motivational influences may be operating, you will need to motivate your students to learn what your lessons and activities are designed to teach. This requires introducing and carrying out lessons and activities in ways that keep both you and the students *goal oriented*—developing key knowledge and skills in ways that support understanding, appreciation, and life applications.

Awareness of goals should guide both your teaching and your students' learning. You will need to stay aware of the primary learning outcomes that a lesson or activity is designed to develop and how these fit within the bigger picture composed by the curriculum as a whole. This will enable you to make good decisions about what content to emphasize, how to frame it so that students can appreciate its value, and how to develop it so that they will not only learn it but be able to use it in application situations in and out of school.

Similarly, clarity about learning goals will help your students to focus on key ideas and applications and thus to learn with a sense of purpose. To the extent that students are aware that the point of their efforts is not just to please you or prepare for a test, they will be more likely to monitor their progress, seek help if they need it, and persist until they have learned what they are supposed to learn.

All of this assumes that your lessons and activities are focused on major instructional goals, phrased in terms of desired student outcomes. To ensure this, you will need to implement the principles outlined in Chapter 2 concerning goal-oriented planning, adapting instructional materials in the light of your major instructional goals, structuring content around powerful ideas developed in depth, and emphasizing authentic activities and assignments. Within the context created by this approach to teaching school subjects for understanding, appreciation, and life application, you can use the following strategies to induce motivation to learn in particular situations.

Induce Curiosity or Suspense

Student curiosity is the driving force that underlies many motivational theorists' suggestions for (1) capitalizing on students' existing intrinsic motivation (by introducing content or activities that allow them to satisfy existing curiosity) or (2) motivating students to learn (by saying or doing things that pique their curiosity). Consequently, strategies for inducing curiosity could have been addressed either previously in Chapter 6 or here in Chapter 7. They are addressed here because I believe that successful use of these strategies involves stimulating curiosity in ways that foster development of continuing interest in broad topics or knowledge networks, especially interest in the key ideas around which these networks are structured. Otherwise, students may focus their curiosity on seductive but trivial details or may lose interest in the topic once their initial curiosity is satisfied (Friedlander, 1965; Loewenstein, 1994).

Some teachers have not only developed techniques for stimulating students' curiosity or whetting their anticipation but also incorporated these techniques within frequently used routines. For example, a mathematics teacher began most classes with an intriguing problem which was written on the board but covered by a rolled down map. His students quickly learned to notice when the map was pulled down and anticipate the moment when he would roll it up with a flourish and "allow" them to see the problem. When he did, he usually had their full attention. Another teacher achieved a similar effect by concealing props within a large box that she placed on her desk for use on days when she was going to do some interesting demonstration. Again, all eyes were on her when she opened that box.

Karmos and Karmos (1983) described a mathematics teacher who periodically started a lesson by saying, "Last night I went down to my basement and I found . . . " The first time, he told of finding a tree that doubled its number of branches each hour on the hour, and then used this "discovery" as the basis for posing interesting mathematics problems. Things "found in his basement" on other occasions included alligators and a diesel train. It wasn't long before whenever this teacher said, "Last night, I went down to my basement . . . ," his students knew that they could anticipate some preposterous claim followed by some interesting problems.

A topic or activity need not be new in order to generate curiosity. In fact, we often develop curiosity about aspects of topics with which we are familiar and knowledgeable. Such curiosity usually develops when we experience doubt or confusion because we have become aware that our existing ideas appear to be contradictory or incomplete (unable to account for some phenomenon). This motivates us to want to sort things out or acquire more information that will allow us to resolve the gaps or discrepancies in our thinking (Berlyne, 1960).

You can stimulate curiosity or suspense by posing questions or doing setups that make students feel the need to resolve some ambiguity or obtain more information about a topic. To prepare students to read material about Russia, for example, you could ask them if they know how many time zones there are in Russia or how the United States acquired Alaska. Such questions help make new information food for thought and convert "just another reading assignment" into an interesting learning experience. It is mind-boggling for most students to discover that one country encompasses 11 time zones or that the United States purchased Alaska from Russia. These are just two basic facts found in most treatments of the history or geography of Russia.

Whether students find such facts interesting and think about them rather than merely attempt to memorize them depends largely on the degree to which their teachers stimulate curiosity about them and provide contexts for thinking about their associations with prior knowledge or beliefs. This example further illustrates two important points made earlier: Interest resides in people rather than in topics or activities, and the motivation that develops in particular situations does so as a result of interactions among persons, tasks, and the larger social context.

You can stimulate your students' curiosity about a topic and encourage them to generate interest in it by (1) asking them to speculate or make predictions about what they will be learning; (2) raising questions that successful completion of the activity will enable them to answer; and (3) where relevant, showing them that their existing knowledge is not sufficient to enable them to accomplish some valued objective, is internally inconsistent, is inconsistent with new information, or is currently scattered but can be organized around certain general principles or powerful ideas (Malone & Lepper, 1987).

Keller (1983) noted that one general way to stimulate curiosity in your students is to put them into an active information-processing or problem-solving mode as you introduce learning activities. You can do this by posing interesting questions or problems that the students will address as they engage in the activity. For example, the scientific concept of condensation might be introduced by calling students' attention to the water that begins to appear on the outside of a glass of ice water and asking them to explain this phenomenon. If necessary, you could prompt their thinking by suggesting seemingly plausible possibilities (e.g., "Is the water seeping through the glass?")

Reeve (1996) suggested five strategies for stimulating curiosity: (1) suspense, (2) guessing and feedback, (3) playing to students' sense of knowing, (4) controversy, and (5) contradiction.

Suspense strategies focus students' attention on competing hypotheses or problems with uncertain conclusions. By inviting students to consider competing answers to questions such as what caused the Civil War or why the dinosaurs became extinct, you can create within them a sense of mental struggle that Reeve compared to the struggles experienced by heroes in dramatic plots. Students, especially those prone to say "just tell us the answer," can learn to value the process of seeking answers to challenging intellectual questions, as well as to experience the satisfactions of doing so.

The strategy of *guessing and feedback* involves introducing a topic by giving students a pretest or leading them through a prior knowledge assessment activity that requires them to answer specific questions about the topic. The questions should be usefully connected to key ideas but also likely to produce a variety of responses, so that most students will find that they have answered some of them incorrectly (e.g., Which is the northernmost state: Colorado, Kansas, or Nebraska?). Reeve argued that the knowledge that one has guessed incorrectly piques one's curiosity to learn more about the topic.

Playing to students' sense of knowing is a related strategy that applies when students already possess considerable prior knowledge about the topic. For example, by the time they reach junior high school, most students have had a great deal of exposure to U.S. maps and geography. If they have begun to respond to these topics with boredom or complacency, a question such as, "Name the eight states that border one of the Great Lakes," might restimulate their curiosity and interest, because most of them will be able to identify many but not all of these states correctly.

Controversy strategies involve eliciting divergent opinions on an issue and then inviting students to resolve these discrepancies through sustained discussion. In the process, students may recognize the need to consult textbooks or reference materials or conduct other research to obtain needed information.

The *contradiction* strategy is used after students have assimilated a body of information that has led them to formulate a conclusion. At this point, you introduce additional information that contradicts this conclusion, forces students to recognize that the issue is more complicated than they thought, and stimulates them to develop more complete understandings. For example, in teaching science, you might first establish that sodium and chloride are both human poisons, then point out that when combined as sodium chloride, they constitute basic table salt. Or, having established that humans "sit atop the evolutionary developmental ladder," you might point out that there are more insects than any other species and that their combined weight exceeds that of all animals.

Induce Dissonance or Cognitive Conflict

If a topic is familiar, students may think that they already know all about it and thus may listen to presentations or read texts with little attention or thought. You can counter this tendency by pointing out unexpected, incongruous, or paradoxical aspects of the content; by calling attention to unusual or exotic elements; by noting exceptions to general rules; or by challenging students to solve the mystery that underlies a paradox. One teacher implemented several of these principles when he introduced a unit on the Middle Ages by telling students that they would learn about "our ancestors" who chose to remain illiterate and ignorant and who persecuted people who did not share their religion. Later he contrasted the Moslem advances in mathematics, science, and the construction of libraries with the illiteracy of most Christian kings and lords during the Middle Ages. This stimulated his mostly Christian students to develop empathy with and appreciation for the culture of the Moslems of the Middle Ages, instead of viewing them only as faceless enemies of Christian crusaders.

Another teacher used dissonance to stimulate curiosity about the Persian empire by noting that Darius was popular with the people he conquered and asking students to anticipate reasons why this might be so. Another teacher introduced a selection on the Trojan War by telling students that they would read about "how just one horse enabled the Greeks to win a major battle against the Trojans." Another introduced a video on the fall of the Roman Empire by saying, "Some say that the factors that led to the decay of the Roman Empire are currently at work in the United States—as you watch the video, see if you notice parallels."

United States history is full of opportunities to create dissonance, especially in students whose prior exposures have been confined to overly sanitized and patriotic versions of the subject. Exposure to topics such as the Trail of Tears, the Japanese Internment during World War II, or post-war involvement by the CIA in undermining foreign governments can be startling eye openers for students, especially if approached not just as past history but as grist for discussions about whether such things might still happen today or what their implications might be for current and future government policy.

The school curriculum includes a great many strange-but-true phenomena, especially in mathematics and science. By calling attention to these phenomena, you can get your students to begin asking themselves, How can that be? Otherwise, students may treat the material as just more information to be absorbed without giving it much thought or even noticing that it seems to contradict their previous learning.

Conceptual Change Teaching

Sometimes students' prior learning includes misconceptions about important concepts. For example, science units on plants typically emphasize their roles as food producers via the photosynthesis process. Students enter these courses knowing little about photosynthesis but a great deal about food, especially food for people. They know that food is something that you consume or eat, that it is taken in from the outside environment, and that there are many different kinds of food. This knowledge produces distorted understandings in students who assume that food for plants is similar to food for people, because plants make their own food. Neither soil nor water nor fertilizers (even if called "plant food") are taken in as food or consumed for energy. Plants' only source of food is that which they manufacture themselves by transforming light energy from the sun into chemical potential energy stored in food by combining the light energy with carbon dioxide, water, and soil minerals.

Science educators have found that in order to understand the food production function of plants, students must restructure their thinking about the nature of food, focusing on its scientific definition as potential energy for metabolism rather than on reasoning by analogy from their prior experiences with food for humans. Posner and his colleagues (1982) suggested that four conditions must be satisfied if students are to be induced to change their understandings of key concepts: (1) dissatisfaction with existing concepts must be induced and the new concepts must (2) be intelligible to the students, (3) be initially plausible, and (4) appear fruitful. These ideas underlie what has become known as *conceptual change teaching*.

Anderson and Roth (1989) developed a version of conceptual change teaching to teach middle school students about plants' food production function. They began by asking students to define food—and food for plants—and to respond to a problem. This provided information about the students' conceptions and made the students more aware of them. Next, students were given explanations about different ways of defining food, including its scientific definition. Then they were asked to address questions that allowed them to appreciate how this new definition of food could explain everyday phenomena (e.g., Is water food? Juice? Vitamin pills? Can people live on vitamin pills alone? Why or why not?). Students also were asked to write their ideas about how plants get food, to write about what kind of food plants use, and to draw pictures on a diagram to show how they think food moves inside a plant.

As the unit progressed and students were exposed to scientific information about plants and food production, the instruction frequently referred back to these early exercises, drawing direct contrasts between scientific explanations and the explanations that students offered based on their prior knowledge. In addition, students engaged in experimental observations of plants, discussion of similarities and differences between plants and animals, comparisons of materials taken into plants with materials made by plants during photosynthesis, and comparisons between energy-containing and non-energy-containing materials that people consume. These activities encouraged students to make connections between their own ideas and scientific concepts, as well as to use their newly structured conceptions to make predictions and develop more satisfying explanations of familiar, everyday phenomena.

Kathleen Roth (1996) has extended the conceptual change teaching model to history teaching, and noted that it can be used with any subject. In her version, the key steps include (1) eliciting students' current ideas, (2) challenging those ideas to create cognitive dissonance, (3) presenting new ideas in ways that make sense given the students' perspectives, and (4) supporting the students in finding the new ideas useful in a variety of real-world application contexts.

Make Abstract Content More Personal, Concrete, or Familiar

Definitions, principles, and other abstract information may have little meaning for students unless made more concrete. One way to accomplish this is to relate experiences or anecdotes illustrating how the content applies to the lives of individuals that your students are interested in or likely to identify with.

For example, a junior high teacher read aloud a brief selection about Spartacus in order to personalize his instruction about slavery in ancient times. When covering the crusades, this same teacher gave particular emphasis to the Children's Crusade, noting that the children involved were "your age and younger" and that most of them died before the crusade ultimately ended in failure. He also made poignant connections to contemporary Iran, where religion-based zeal led preadolescents to volunteer to go to war. Another teacher brought the medieval guilds alive for her students by describing them in detail and soliciting the students' reactions to the fact that if they had lived during the Middle Ages, to become a journeyman they would have had to leave their homes as children and spend seven years apprenticed to a master craftsman.

You can make abstractions concrete by conducting demonstrations or by showing objects, pictures, or videos. In studying another country, for example, teach about its people and culture in addition to its physical features and products. Show students what the country looks like and help them to imagine what it would be like to live there. Perhaps include children's literature sources that offer stories set in the country or follow members of a representative family through a typical day or week in their lives.

You also can help your students to relate new or strange content to their existing knowledge by using examples or analogies that refer to familiar concepts, objects, or events. For example, teachers involved in my research have made the following connections:

- The Nile River flooding and its effects on Egyptian customs compared to the spring flooding in Michigan rivers and its effects on local customs.
- The Washington Monument as a modern example of an obelisk.
- Three times the size of the Pontiac Silverdome as the size of the largest Roman colosseums.
- Identification of students in the class (or failing that, famous personalities) descended from the ancient peoples or the geographical areas being studied.
- Linking of students' family names to the guilds (Smith, Tanner, Miller, Baker).

- Similarities in climate and potential for flower raising and dairy farming as reasons why the Dutch were drawn to the Holland, Michigan, area.
- Similarities in the customs associated with the Roman Saturn Festival compared to those associated with modern Christmas festivities.
- Explaining how the medieval social and political systems worked by describing the local (rural central Michigan) area as part of the outlying lands surrounding a manor based in Lansing, which in turn would be under the protection of and would pay taxes to "the king of Detroit."

Sometimes the problem is not that content would be too abstract or unfamiliar for students to understand if it were explained sufficiently, but that the text simply does not provide enough explanation (Brophy, 1992). This is one reason why it is wise to view your texts as outlines to be elaborated on, not as the entire curriculum. For example, one text that I studied explained Russia's exit from World War I by saying only that "the revolution came and a new government was established." This brief statement does not supply enough details to enable students to understand and visualize the events surrounding the Russian revolution. To make these events more understandable, you would need to elaborate on the text by explaining why and how the communists and others organized political and eventual military resistance to the Czar's regime, killed or expelled the Czar's family and key officials, and established a new government. Such elaboration on the text transforms the relatively meaningless statement that "the revolution came and a new government was established" into a meaningful story that students can explain in their own words because they can relate it to their prior knowledge and visualize the events to which it refers. Thus, they can actively process the content instead of just trying to memorize it.

The preceding example also illustrates another technique for making content more concrete and personal for students: Dramatize it by telling stories or at least representing the content within narrative formats. In contrast to analytic or impersonal explanatory formats, narrative formats contain the key features of stories: a focus on particular hero figures pursuing some goal, a plot that involves conflict or some barriers to accomplishment of the goal, and a resolution that includes reference to success or failure in accomplishing the goal and the implications of this for subsequent events. Egan (1990) has written extensively about the power of narratives for capturing students' imaginations. He has suggested that 8–15-year olds in particular are highly responsive to the narrative format, and especially to dramatic stories featuring inspiring hero figures struggling to accomplish great feats or to right the wrongs of the world. This narrative approach can be applied not only in language arts and history, but in mathematics and science as well (in stories about how individuals or small groups struggled to solve mathematical problems, unlock scientific mysteries, or develop important inventions).

You may need to adapt your curriculum to make sure that it features gender equity and suitable connection to the ethnic and cultural backgrounds of your students. Even when content is selected and taught effectively in other respects, certain students may feel excluded and lose interest if they come to believe that a school subject is about "them" rather than "us" (Alton-Lee, Nuthall, & Patrick, 1993). Consequently, your treatment of history should include sufficient attention to social history, women's roles, and the lives of everyday people along with political and military events, and should include multiple perspectives on their meanings and implications. Similarly, your material on literature, biography, and contributions to the arts and sciences or to society and culture should include sufficient attention to contributions by women and members of minority groups, especially groups represented in your class.

Research assignments connected with this content should include opportunities for students to choose biographical subjects, literature selections, or historical events on which to focus. In this way, those who wish to do so can pursue their interests in content with which they identify in part because of its relevance to gender or cultural identity issues that are important to them (see Chapter 9 for more about adapting to gender and cultural differences).

Induce Task Interest or Appreciation

You can induce appreciation for a topic or activity by verbalizing reasons why students should value it. If it has connections with something that your students already recognize as interesting or important, note these connections. If the knowledge or skills to be taught have applications to everyday living, point out these applications, especially any that will allow students to solve problems or accomplish goals that are important to them. Also, mention any new or challenging aspects of activities that students can anticipate.

Sometimes, instead of just telling students why the content they are about to learn is valuable, you can arrange for them to discover this for themselves by engaging them with a question or problem that requires the content for its solution. This approach is most applicable with mathematical or scientific principles and procedures. Most of these principles were developed in the first place as a by-product of attempts to understand some important phenomenon or solve some practical problem, and since their development other important applications have accumulated. You can make use of these applications in introducing and developing the content.

Arts and humanities knowledge usually lacks such direct linkages to practical applications, but it has value as grist for developing insights into the human condition and advances in personal identity and self-actualization. Stories, for example, whether fictional or historical, usually can be framed with reference to enduring dilemmas or common problems with which your students can identify. When properly framed and developed, stories have value not just as entertainment or cultural literacy knowledge but as case studies and food for thought about the trade-offs involved in alternative ways of responding to situations that provoke fear, rage, jealousy, conflicting loyalties, moral dilemmas, or other powerful emotions. In exposing your students to such stories, encourage them to put themselves in the place of the hero or another key character and think about how they might have handled the situations depicted as the story develops. In considering works of art, help your students not only to appreciate the artist's interpretation of the theme but also to develop their own interpretation and think about how they might express it artistically.

Information about people in the past or in other cultures can be rendered more meaningful and potentially significant to students by helping them to appreciate how these people's experiences contrast in insight-producing ways with their own geographical and cultural experiences. For example, a junior high teacher motivated students to read about the ancient Greek legal system by noting that it was similar to our own system in many ways but that it called for 501 jurors. This teacher also motivated his students to study the map of Greece with interest and appreciation by explaining that even though no place in Greece is more than 40 miles from the sea, its jagged contours give it far more coastline than most larger countries.

Sivan and Roehler (1986) studied teachers' introductions to activities conducted during small-group reading instruction. They found that when the teachers introduced activities with emphasis on the value of the activities themselves or of the knowledge or skills that the activities would develop, students engaged in the activities with an enhanced sense of their usefulness and with greater metacognitive awareness of their learning strategies and progress.

Induce Students to Generate Their Own Motivation to Learn

You can induce your students to generate their own motivation to learn by asking them to think about topics or activities in relation to their own interests or preconceptions. For example, you can ask them to identify questions about a topic that they would like to get answered or to note things that they find to be surprising as they read. These techniques help students to understand that motivation to learn must come from within themselves—that it is a property of the learner rather than of the task to be learned.

Ortiz (1983) developed techniques for inducing this insight with respect to reading assignments. She emphasized to students that their motivational responses to a text—whether interest or boredom—are generated by them and not inherent in the text itself. To illustrate this, she engaged students in activities such as thinking of ways to make reading a page from the phone book interesting, having them read a text in common and then share reasons why they did or did not find it interesting, and having them note and analyze what was going through their minds at times when they did or did not find a text interesting. These exercises helped students to realize that they need to generate interest themselves and to acquire a repertoire of strategies for doing so.

One popular way to induce students to generate their own motivation to learn is to use the K-W-L technique (Ogle, 1986). Developed originally as a way to facilitate reading comprehension, K-W-L promotes learning by helping students to retrieve relevant background knowledge and learn with awareness of purpose and accomplishment. The technique unfolds through several steps. First, as they are about to begin study of a topic, students write down what they already *Know* (or think they know) about the topic and what they *Want* to learn about it. Alternatively, this step can be done as a teacher-led group activity, in which students' responses are listed on the board, the chartstand, or the overhead projection screen.

The next steps occur during study of the topic. Here, you address any misconceptions that emerged in your students' "K" responses and provide answers (or arrange for the students themselves to get answers) to the questions they raised in their "W" responses.

Finally, as a culmination of their study of the topic, students write what they *Learned* about it. At this time, they also revisit their earlier "K" and "W" responses. They may see a need to change some of these earlier statements, if they have discovered that part of what they thought they knew was incorrect. The K-W-L technique is useful not only for its originally intended purpose of helping students to read content selections with greater interest and understanding, but also for developing productive learning sets when introducing new topics in science, social studies, and other content areas.

Conti, Amabile, and Pollak (1995) described a method of inducing an active cognitive learning set that incorporates fantasy elements and creativity. Prior to reading a text section on the psychology of dreaming, students read a paragraph that described a dream. Some of them were asked to imagine having this dream the day before they were going to speak with a panel of experts on dreaming. They were to write the three most interesting and unusual questions that came to mind about this dream or about dreams in general. Other students were asked to use the dream paragraph to complete a word substitution exercise that did not engage them in thinking creatively about the dream or about the topic of dreaming. The researchers found that students who completed the creative pretask showed more intrinsic interest in the topic and greater long-term retention for the content of the longer instructional passage.

You can use variations of this technique with a broad range of content. The key elements are (1) placing students within a fantasy context that calls for them to address some problem or take advantage of some opportunity and (2) asking them to act out this role in a way that involves thinking creatively about the topic to be studied.

STRATEGIES FOR SCAFFOLDING STUDENTS' LEARNING EFFORTS

Scaffolding strategies are needed to complement motivational strategies because, as Blumenfeld, Puro, and Mergendoller (1992) noted, motivating students to learn requires not only bringing them to the lesson but bringing the lesson to them. You are off to a good start if you present students with worthwhile learning activities and introduce the activities in ways that help students to appreciate their value. You need to follow this up, however, by

asking questions or assigning tasks that will require students to (1) think critically and creatively about the content, (2) apply it in activities calling for inquiry, problem solving, or decision making; and (3) get feedback. In the
process, you can support and scaffold your students' efforts to respond to
these challenges by providing them with learning objectives and advance organizers, modeling task-related thinking and problem solving, and helping
them to learn with metacognitive awareness and control of their own learning
strategies.

State Learning Goals and Provide Advance Organizers

Instructional theorists have shown that learners retain more information when
their learning is goal directed and structured around key concepts. They commonly advise teachers to introduce activities by stating learning goals and by
providing advance organizers that characterize what will be learned in general terms. These techniques help students to know what to expect and to prepare to learn efficiently.

Learning goals and advance organizers also serve motivational purposes.
These techniques call students' attention to the benefits that they should receive from engaging in an activity and help them to establish a learning set to
use in guiding their responses to it (Lane, Newman, & Bull, 1988; Marshall,
1987). As used here, the term "learning goal" is meant to have a broader
meaning than "behavioral objective," "instructional objective," or other terms
that suggest a performance standard that students are expected to reach
when their mastery is assessed. The kinds of learning goals likely to contribute to students' motivation to learn are broader and phrased in terms of
the added capacities (knowledge, insights, coping strategies) that students
will acquire, preferably with reference to their potential application to life
outside of school.

Learning goals and advance organizers ordinarily are communicated in
the process of introducing a lesson or activity to students. It seems natural to
use these occasions to make sure that students understand what they will be
doing and why they will be doing it. However, classroom research suggests
that few teachers systematically take advantage of these opportunities.

For example, Newby (1991) observed 30 first-year elementary teachers
over a four-month period, developing thick-description records of the classroom discourse and activities that occurred during the observation times.
These data were later analyzed for the presence of motivational strategies, cat-
egorized into four types: focusing attention, emphasizing relevance, building
confidence, or imposing rewards and punishments. Data from 168 hours of
observation yielded 1,748 instances of teacher behavior coded as one of these
motivational strategies, or about 10.4 strategies per hour by each teacher.
However, 58 percent of these were reward or punishment strategies, and most
of the rest (27 percent) were attention-focusing strategies. Only 7.1 percent of
the strategies involved building students' confidence in their abilities to handle the work, and only 7.5 percent were relevance strategies that involved

explaining the value of the learning or why it was being taught. Thus, these teachers mentioned the purpose or value of learning less than once per hour.

Anderson and her colleagues (1985) found that first-grade teachers' presentations of assignments to their students typically included procedural directions or special hints (e.g., pay attention to the underlined words), but seldom called attention to the purposes and meanings of the work. Only five percent of the teachers' presentations explicitly described the purpose of the assignment in terms of the content being taught, and only 1.5 percent included explicit descriptions of the cognitive strategies to use. In these classrooms, the work was mostly low-level and repetitive, the directions seldom included statements about what would be learned or how it related to other learning, and the teachers' monitoring focused on the students' work completion progress rather than on their levels of understanding.

What can result from this was summarized in what one student was heard to say to himself as he finished a worksheet: "I don't know what it means, but I did it." The data from this study indicated that many students (especially low achievers) did not understand how to do their assignments. Rather than ask their teachers or get help in other ways, they often were content to respond randomly or rely on response sets (such as alternating or using geometrical patterns for circling multiple choice answers or picking one from a list of new words to fill the blank in a sentence without reading the sentence itself). Low achievers tended to be more concerned about finishing their assignments than about understanding the content they were supposed to be learning. High achievers completed most assignments successfully and showed less concern about finishing on time, but even they showed little evidence of understanding the content-related purposes of the assignments. No student consistently explained assignments in terms of their curricular content. Instead, most responses were vague generalities (e.g., "It's just our work" or "We learn to read").

These findings are not unique. Rohrkemper and Bershon (1984) interviewed elementary students about what was on their minds when they worked on assignments. They found that of 49 students who gave codable responses, 2 were concerned only about getting finished, 45 were concerned about getting the answers correct, but only 2 mentioned trying to understand what was being taught.

If we want students to be aware of the learning goals of classroom activities and to appreciate the potential of these activities for promoting personal growth and enhancing quality of life, we will need to draw the students' attention to these goals and potentials. Unfortunately, it appears that most teachers, even those who are effective in other respects, do not introduce learning activities in ways that are likely to stimulate their students' motivation to learn (see Box 7.2).

Plan Questions and Activities to Help Students Develop and Apply Powerful Ideas

Once you have clarified the purposes and goals of an activity and provided any needed introduction to its content base, ask questions and engage

Box 7.2.   Teachers' Task Introductions

Brophy, Rohrkemper, Rashid, and Goldberger (1983) observed reading and mathematics instruction in inter-mediate-grade classrooms to test predictions about the relationships between the expectations that teachers established when introducing tasks to their students and the apparent levels of engagement displayed by the students once the tasks were begun. As expected, low levels of student engagement were observed on tasks that the teachers had introduced by communicating negative expectations (that the tasks would be boring or that the students would not enjoy them). However, task introductions in which teachers communicated positive expectations were not associated with the highest levels of student engagement. Instead, student engagement was highest when the teachers launched directly into tasks without making introductory statements about them.

Later analyses of these data by Brophy and Kher (1986) suggested that these teachers' positive task introductions did not have much impact on their students' motivation to learn because (1) they did not occur often enough; (2) when they did occur, they usually were too short or sketchy to do much good; and (3) whatever good they might have done was probably negated by other statements likely to undermine their students' motivation to learn.

Only about a third of the teachers' task introductions included comments judged likely to have positive effects on student motivation, and most of these were brief predictions that the students would enjoy the task or would do well on it. In about 100 hours of classroom observation, only 9 task introductions were noted that included substantive information about motivation to learn:

These are not elementary, high school, or college words; these are living-level words. You'll use them every day in life. If you plan to be a writer or enjoy reading, you'll need these words.

Remember, the essential thing is to do them correctly, not to be the first to finish.

I think you will like this book. Someone picked it out for me, and it's really good.

This is a really strange story. It's written in the first person, so that the person talking is the one who wrote the story about his experience. It has some pretty interesting words in it. They are on the board.

The stories in this book are more interesting than the ones in the earlier level books. They are more challenging because the stories and vocabulary are more difficult. Reading improves with practice, just like basketball. If you never shoot baskets except when you are in the game, you are not going to be very good. Same with reading. You can't do without it.

Answer the comprehension questions with complete sentences. All these stories are very interesting. You'll enjoy them.

You girls should like this story because it is a feminist story. You boys will enjoy yours too. Your story is especially interesting. I want you to be sure to read it. It's a mystery, and you'll enjoy it.

(Continued)

Box 7.2.   Teachers' Task Introductions—*Concluded*

Percent is very important. Banks use it for interest loans, and so on. So it is important that you pay attention.

You're going to need to know fractions for math next year. You will need fractions in the world to come.

Notice how minimal and essentially barren most of these remarks are. They do not go into enough detail to be very meaningful or memorable for most students, and many have a perfunctory quality suggesting that the teacher was going through the motions without much enthusiasm or conviction. Also, most of the teachers' remarks to students concerned procedural demands and evaluations of work quality or progress rather than description of the task itself or what the students might get out of it. No teacher was ever observed to suggest that a task had self-actualization value (i.e., that students could develop knowledge or skills that would bring them pleasure or personal satisfaction). Middleton (1995) reported the same finding for middle school mathematics classes.

Furthermore, any desirable effects that the teachers' occasional positive task introductions may have had were probably undercut by remarks such as the following:

Today's lesson is nothing new if you've been here.

If you get done by 10 o'clock, you can go outside.

Your scores will tell me whether we need to stay with multiplication for another week. If you are talking, I will deduct 10 points from your scores.

This penmanship assignment means that sometimes in life you just can't do what you want to do.

The next time you have to do something you don't want to do, just think, Well, that's part of life.

Get your nose in the book, otherwise I'll give you a writing assignment.

You don't expect me to give you baby work every day, do you?

You've been working real hard today, so let's stop early.

You'll have to work real quietly, otherwise you'll have to do more assignments.

My talkers are going to get a third page to do during lunch.

We don't have a huge amount to do, but it will be time consuming.

This test is to see who the really smart ones are.

It is important to note that the teachers observed in this study were all experienced and, if anything, better than average as a group. Yet, they seldom took advantage of opportunities to stimulate their students' motivation to learn in the process of introducing academic activities; when they did, their positive task introductions were too short and sketchy to be very effective. Furthermore, they frequently violated important motivational principles by bribing or threatening students to create extrinsic work pressures, portraying tasks as boring or pointless, or even treating them as if they were punishments in themselves. To avoid displaying such patterns yourself, it will be important for you to monitor your teaching consistently enough to allow you to notice and initiate corrective actions if you begin to drift into counterproductive habits (see Good & Brophy, 1997, concerning developing awareness of your classroom teaching).

students in activities designed to help them develop their understanding of the content by processing and applying it. In developing your plans, emphasize questions and activities that will stimulate students to reflect on what they are learning and engage in thoughtful discussion of its meanings and implications. You may occasionally need to use drill activities to reinforce learning that must be memorized, as well as recitation activities to check and correct understanding of basic knowledge that must be in place to anchor subsequent learning activities. However, most of your questions should be asked not just to monitor comprehension but to stimulate students to think about the content, connect it to their prior knowledge, and begin to explore its applications.

Thus, questioning ordinarily should not take the form of rapidly paced drills or attempts to elicit right answers to miscellaneous factual questions. Instead, use questions as means for engaging students with the content they are learning. Stimulate students to process that content actively and "make it their own" by rephrasing it into their own words and considering its meanings and implications. Focus your questions on the most important elements of the content and guide students' thinking in ways that move them systematically toward key understandings. The idea is to build an integrated network of knowledge structured around powerful ideas, not to stimulate rote memorizing of miscellaneous information.

For each subtopic to be developed, ask questions in sequences designed to help students construct connected understandings. Use different kinds of question sequences to accommodate different instructional goals. To develop an unfamiliar topic, for example, you might begin with questions designed to stimulate interest in the topic or help students connect it to their prior experiences, then move to questions designed to elicit key ideas, then move to questions calling for reflection on or application of these ideas. Where students already have prior knowledge about a topic, you might wish to place them into an application mode immediately, such as by posing a problem, eliciting alternative solution suggestions and rationales, and then engaging the class in a reflective discussion of these ideas.

It is not possible to develop complete scripts for question sequences and proceed through them rigidly, because students' responses to questions are only partially predictable in advance. It would not be wise to attempt this in any case, because you will want to adapt lesson plans to developing situations and take advantage of teachable moments that students create by asking questions or making comments that are worth pursuing. Nevertheless, an important part of goal-oriented planning is the planning of purposeful sequences of questions designed to help students construct key understandings. Such planned question sequences are much more likely to yield thoughtful classroom discourse than the inefficient patterns of questioning that occur when teachers have not thought through their purposes for developing a particular topic.

Certain aspects of questioning technique can enhance the power of your questions to stimulate student thinking. First, address most of your questions to the entire class rather than to a single designated student. This will encourage all students, and not just the designated individual, to think about the question. Second, before calling on anyone to respond, allow sufficient wait time to enable students to process and formulate responses to the question. You may need to emphasize to students that you are more interested in thoughtfulness and quality than in speed of response, as well as to discourage overly eager students from blurting out answers. Finally, distribute response opportunities widely rather than allow a few students to answer most of your questions. Students learn more if they are actively involved in discussions than if they sit passively without participating, and distributing response opportunities helps keep all students attentive and accountable.

Using questions that call for content-based thinking and problem solving, initiate patterns of discourse that evolve into exchanges of views in which students respond to one another as well as to you, and in which they respond to statements as well as to questions. Dillon (1988, 1990) has shown that teachers' statements can be just as effective as their questions for producing lengthy and insightful responses during discussions. Questions may even impede discussions at times, especially if they are perceived as attempts to test students rather than to solicit their ideas. Instead of continuing to ask questions, you sometimes can sustain discussions nicely by simply remaining silent; by asking students to respond to what their classmates have said; by probing for elaboration (e.g., "Tell us more about that" or "Perhaps you could give some examples"); by asking indirect questions (e.g., "I wonder what makes you think that"); by summarizing or restating what a student has said; or simply by making some declarative statement that adds to the discussion and indirectly invites further comment from students.

When collecting responses to a problem-solving or decision-making question, record the responses (list them on the board, a chart, or an overhead screen, etc.), but do not evaluate them immediately. Continue collecting and recording suggested solutions or courses of action as long as anyone has new suggestions to contribute, then invite students to develop arguments for or against selected alternatives. Such discussions should be conducted within the norms of the learning community described in Chapter 2. That is, students should understand that the purpose of reflective discussion is to work collaboratively to deepen their understandings of the meanings and implications of content. They will need to listen carefully, respond thoughtfully, and participate assertively but respectfully in discussions. Both in advancing their own ideas and in responding critically to those of classmates, they should build a case based on relevant evidence and arguments and avoid divisive or other inappropriate behavior.

Classroom discourse patterns that are desirable from both an instructional and a motivational perspective develop in students a set of dispositions that together constitute what Newmann (1990) called *thoughtfulness:* a persistent desire that claims be supported by reasons (and that the reasons themselves be scrutinized), a tendency to be reflective by taking time to think through problems rather than acting impulsively or automatically accepting the views of others, a curiosity to explore new questions, and a flexibility to entertain alternative and original solutions to problems. Based on observations in high school social studies classes, Newmann identified six key indicators of thoughtfulness:

1. Classroom discourse focuses on sustained examination of a few topics rather than superficial coverage of many.
2. The discourse is characterized by substantive coherence and continuity.
3. Students are given sufficient time to think before being required to answer questions.
4. The teacher presses students to clarify or justify their assertions, rather than accepting and reinforcing them indiscriminately.
5. The teacher models the characteristics of a thoughtful person (showing interest in students' ideas and their suggestions for solving problems, modeling problem-solving processes rather than just giving answers, and acknowledging the difficulties involved in gaining clear understandings of problematic topics)
6. Students generate original and unconventional ideas in the course of the interaction.

Classes that display these characteristics are demanding, so Newmann and his colleagues were not surprised to find that students in such classes viewed them as more difficult and challenging than most of their other classes. However, these investigators also reported a less predictable finding that connects with the topic of this book: Even though the students described these classes as more difficult and challenging, they also described them as more engaging and interesting. Here again is evidence that the key to motivation to learn is minds-on engagement with powerful ideas.

Model Task-Related Thinking and Problem Solving

The information-processing and problem-solving strategies needed for thinking about particular content or responding to particular tasks may be unknown to many of your students unless you make them overt and observable by modeling them. Such modeling should include the thinking that goes into selecting the general approach to use, deciding on what options to take at choice points that arise during the process, checking on progress as one goes along, and making certain that one is on the right track. It also should include recovery from false starts and from use of inappropriate strategies, so that students can see how to develop a successful strategy even after getting off to a bad start (Schunk & Hanson, 1985).

This kind of cognitive modeling is powerful not just as an instructional device but as a way to show students what it means to approach a task with motivation to learn. That is, it allows you to model the attitudes, beliefs, and strategies that are associated with such motivation. These include: patience, confidence, persistence in seeking solutions through information processing and rational decision making, benefiting from the information supplied by mistakes rather than giving up in frustration, and concentrating on the task and how to respond to it rather than focusing on the self and worrying about one's limitations (see Chapter 4).

Induce Metacognitive Awareness and Control of Learning Strategies

When motivated to learn, students do not merely let information wash over them and hope that some of it will stick. Instead, they process the information actively by concentrating their attention, making sure that they understand, integrating new information with existing knowledge, and encoding and storing this information in a form that will allow them to remember it and use it later. Students are most likely to do these things effectively if they do them with *metacognitive awareness*—conscious selection of appropriate strategies, monitoring of their effectiveness, noting and correcting their mistakes, and shifting to new strategies if necessary.

You can help your students remain aware of their goals and strategy decisions by structuring and scaffolding their engagement in learning activities. To the extent needed, such structuring and scaffolding might include pre-activity instructions that emphasize the purposes and goals of the activity, questions or cues offered during the activity to help keep students aware of the processes they are using in responding to it, and post-activity debriefing that focuses on analyzing and appreciating what has been accomplished (Brophy & Alleman, 1991; Jones & Idol, 1990; Markova, Orlov, & Fridman, 1986; Rosenshine & Guenther, 1992).

A complete activity might include the following stages:

1. *Introduction:* Communicate the goals of the activity and cue relevant prior knowledge and response strategies.
2. *Initial scaffolding:* Explain and demonstrate procedures if necessary, then ask questions to develop key ideas and make sure that students understand what to do before releasing them to work on their own.
3. *Independent work:* Release students to work individually or in collaboration with peers, but monitor their progress and intervene when necessary.
4. *Debriefing/reflection/assessment:* Revisit the activity's primary goals with the students and assess the degree to which they have been accomplished.

This sequence operationalizes the point that effective activities require not just physical actions or time on task but cognitive engagement with important ideas. Even an inductive or discovery learning activity will require an optimal type and amount of structuring and scaffolding to maximize its impact.

Introduction

Students will need to understand the intended purposes of the activity and what these imply about how they should respond to it. Good introductions to activities fulfill at least four functions: (1) stimulating students' interest in or recognition of the value of the activity; (2) communicating its purposes and goals; (3) cueing relevant prior knowledge and response strategies; and (4) establishing a learning set by helping students to understand what they will be doing, what they will have accomplished when they are finished, and how these accomplishments will be communicated or evaluated. Information about purposes and goals should emphasize cognitive and affective engagement with powerful ideas, not just instructional objectives in the narrower sense. Cueing of relevant prior knowledge might include comparing or contrasting with previous activities, asking students to use their knowledge to make predictions about the upcoming activity, explaining where the activity fits within a sequence or bigger picture, or helping students make connections between its content and their personal knowledge or experiences. To guide students' thinking during a presentation, video, or film, you might distribute a partial outline for them to fill in or a series of questions for them to answer as the lesson unfolds.

Initial Scaffolding

Before releasing students to work mostly on their own, provide whatever explicit explanation and modeling they may need in order to understand what to do, how to do it, and why it is important. To the extent that the activity calls for skills that need to be taught rather than merely cued, your scaffolding should include explicit explanation and modeling of strategic use of the skills for accomplishing the tasks that are embedded in the activity.

Independent Work

Once students have been released to work individually or collaboratively, monitor their efforts and provide any additional scaffolding or responsive elaboration on the instructions that may be needed to structure or simplify the task, clear up confusion or misconceptions, or help students to diagnose and develop repair strategies when they have made mistakes or used inappropriate strategies. These interventions should not involve doing tasks for students or simplifying the tasks to the point that they no longer engage students in the cognitive processes needed to accomplish the activity's goals. Instead, intervene by scaffolding within the students' zones of proximal development in ways that allow them to handle as much of the task as they can handle at the moment but also to progress toward fully independent and successful performance.

Students will need feedback—not only information about correctness of responses but also diagnosis of the reasons for errors and explanation of how their performance might be improved. To the extent possible, provide such feedback immediately as you circulate to monitor students' progress.

Debriefing/Reflection/Assessment

Bring activities to closure in ways that link them back to their intended goals and purposes. Provide students with opportunities to assess their performance and to correct and learn from their mistakes. Ordinarily, you should include a post-activity debriefing or reflection that reemphasizes the activity's purposes and goals, reflects on how (and how well) they have been accomplished, and reminds students about where the activity fits within the larger unit or curriculum strand.

Teach Skills for Self-Regulated Learning and Studying

Many of your students will need instruction in cognitive and metacognitive skills for learning and studying effectively. You can teach them to become more aware of their goals during task engagement, to monitor their selection of strategies to use in pursuing those goals, to note the effects of these strategies and adjust them if necessary, and to control their affective responses to these unfolding events (Pressley & Beard El-Dinary, 1993).

Actively Preparing to Learn

Teach your students to prepare to learn actively by mobilizing their resources and approaching tasks in thoughtful ways: getting ready to concentrate, previewing tasks by noting their nature and objectives, and in the case of complex tasks, developing plans before trying to respond to them.

Committing Material to Memory

If material must be memorized, teach your students techniques for memorizing efficiently. Such techniques include active rehearsal; repeating, copying, or underlining key words; making notes; or using imagery or other mnemonic strategies.

Encoding or Elaborating on the Information Presented

Ordinarily you will not want students to memorize information but instead to retain its gist and be able to apply it later. Teach them strategies for identifying and retaining main ideas: paraphrasing and summarizing information to put it into their own words, relating it to what they already know, and assessing their understanding by asking themselves questions.

Organizing and Structuring the Content

Students also need to learn to structure extensive content by dividing it into sequences or clusters. Teach your students to note the main ideas of paragraphs, outline the material, and notice and use the structuring devices built into it. Also, teach them strategies for effective note-taking (Devine, 1987; Kiewra et al., 1991).

Monitoring Comprehension

In giving instructions for assignments, remind your students to remain aware of the learning goals, the strategies they use to pursue those goals, and the corrective efforts they undertake if the strategies have not been effective. Also, teach them strategies for coping with confusion or mistakes: backing up and rereading, looking up definitions, identifying places in the text where the confusing point is discussed, searching the recent progression of topics for information that has been missed or misunderstood, retracing steps to see whether the strategy has been applied correctly, and generating possible alternative strategies.

Maintaining Appropriate Affect

Finally, model and instruct your students in ways of approaching academic activities with desirable affect (i.e., relaxed but alert and prepared to concentrate, ready to enjoy or at least take satisfaction in engaging in the task). Also, teach them ways to avoid undesirable affect (anger, anxiety, etc.). Such instruction should include taking satisfaction in accomplishments and using coping skills to respond to frustration or failure (i.e., reassuring self-talk, refocusing of attention on the task at hand, and use of the comprehension-monitoring strategies listed at the end of the previous paragraph).

A literacy program developed by a team of university researchers and elementary school teachers illustrates application of many of the strategies suggested here for scaffolding students' learning efforts. This program is described in Box 7.3.

Teach Volitional Control Strategies

In many learning situations, some students begin with goal clarity and motivation to learn and possess the strategies needed to do so, but fail to follow through because they become distracted, fatigued, or preoccupied with competing goals. In recognition of this, some motivational theorists distinguish between motivation and volition (Corno, 1993; Corno & Kanfer, 1993; Kuhl & Beckmann, 1985).

These theorists use the term *motivation* to refer to the adoption of goals and the development of goal-related plans, then use the term *volition* to refer to actions taken to follow through on those plans and make sure that they are implemented. Such actions include concentrating on the task at hand, buckling down to get to work, resisting distractions, and persisting in the face of difficulties. People who display these volitional characteristics in most of what they do are typically described as conscientious, disciplined, self-directed, resourceful, or striving.

Volitional striving that takes the form of single-minded pursuit of particular goals is not always adaptive, as when goals are situationally inappropriate or the student is persisting in focusing on a given task as a way to avoid evaluation or more difficult tasks (McCaslin & Good, 1996). Assuming appropriate goals, however, volitional striving is usually adaptive and needed to ensure that initial goal commitment leads to eventual goal attainment.

You may need to teach at least some of your students volitional control strategies such as the following:

1. Metacognitive control (thinking of initial steps to take in order to get started right away; going back over work to check it and making revisions before turning it in).

Box 7.3. Concept-Oriented Reading Instruction

Developed by a team consisting of university professors and teachers from two elementary schools, Concept-Oriented Reading Instruction (CORI) is an approach to teaching reading, writing, and science that incorporates principles for motivating students and scaffolding their use of learning strategies (Guthrie et al., 1996). The program incorporates four general phases:

1. *Observe and personalize:* The first step in engaging students in literacy was to provide them with opportunities to observe concrete objects and events in the natural world (a tree, flower, cricket, caterpillar, or bird nest, for example). Following such observations, students brainstormed to identify questions they would like to explore with additional observations, data collecting, reading, writing, and discussing.

2. *Search and retrieve:* Through teacher modeling and scaffolded practice, students learned how to conduct research by clarifying the questions to be pursued, collecting and organizing observations and resource materials, extracting relevant information, and recording it in a form that supported later use.

3. *Comprehend and integrate:* The students also were taught strategies for processing the source materials they used: noting and summarizing main topics and critical details, drawing comparisons, relating illustrations to texts, evaluating texts, and taking into account the author's point of view. They also learned strategies for elaborating on texts by looking up additional information, combining material from separate sources, and recording notes and reflections.

4. *Communicate to others:* Finally, students learned to synthesize and communicate information to others through forms that included a written report, a class-authored book, dioramas, charts, and informational stories.

Students in the CORI program showed concurrent developments in their intrinsic motivation for reading and the quality of their literacy engagement. They became more involved, curious, and social in their literacy activities; read about a broader range of topics; and displayed developments in literacy engagement strategies such as searching for information in multiple texts, representing ideas through drawing and writing, and transferring conceptual knowledge to new situations. The authors concluded that classroom contexts that support development of intrinsic motivation and literacy engagement are: (1) observational, encouraging students to initiate learning by generating their own questions from real-world observations; (2) conceptual, focusing on substantive topics rather than reading skills; (3) self-directing, supporting student autonomy and choice of topics, books, and collaborating peers; (4) metacognitive, with explicit teaching of reading strategies, problem solving, and composing; (5) collaborative, emphasizing social construction of meaning within communities of learners; (6) expressive, creating opportunities for self-expression through writing, debating, and group interaction; and (7) coherent, emphasizing connections between classroom activities and tasks across the day, week, and month.

2. Motivation control (reminding oneself to concentrate and focus on task goals; generating ways to carry out the task that will make it more enjoyable, challenging, or reassuring; imagining completing the task successfully and enjoying the satisfaction of doing so).
3. Emotion control (reassuring oneself when bothered by fear of failure or doubts about one's ability; activating strategies that one has learned for coping when confused or frustrated).
4. Controlling the task situation (developing and revising a step-by-step plan for getting complex tasks accomplished; moving away from noise and distractions; gathering all needed materials before beginning the work).
5. Controlling others in the task setting (asking for help from teacher or classmates; asking others to stop bothering or interrupting).

With highly distractible students, you may need to provide study carrels or other distraction-reduced work environments in addition to teaching them strategies for maintaining their engagement in learning activities.

Self-Regulated Learning

Rohrkemper and Corno (1988; see also Corno & Rohrkemper, 1985) suggested that the highest form of cognitive engagement that students can use to learn in classrooms is *self-regulated learning*—active learning in which students assume responsibility for motivating themselves to learn with understanding. Self-regulated learning should be the ultimate goal of your motivational efforts.

Rohrkemper and Corno suggested that you can set the stage for development of self-regulated learning by using teaching strategies that foster intrinsic motivation and motivation to learn: using a variety of learning activities and teaching methods; frequently offering students choices to accommodate their individual preferences and interests; structuring classroom discourse that features both teacher–student and student–student discussion of content; pursuing topics in depth through activities that develop understanding and application of significant networks of knowledge; and providing timely, informative, and encouraging feedback that is oriented toward private support of learning rather than public comparison of performance.

Within this context, you then can promote self-regulated learning more directly by (1) clarifying goals, modeling strategies, and otherwise working to ensure that students' learning is meaningful and strategic, and (2) withdrawing these learning supports when they are no longer needed and providing opportunities for students to work with increasing autonomy on tasks that challenge them to integrate and apply what they are learning.

Teaching learning skills and strategies empowers students by helping them to truly understand what they are learning (which should improve their attitudes toward it) and to generalize and apply it to tasks of their own choosing. Students' need for instruction in strategy use recedes as their expertise develops. At first they may need interventions designed to increase their awareness and deliberate use of learning strategies, but this kind of assistance can be

faded as they begin to acquire the skills of expert learners (e.g., abilities to diagnose the reasons for learning problems and to focus immediately on the
most likely solutions rather than working systematically through a larger
repertoire, to develop short cuts through longer processes, and to use certain
strategies automatically without having to make conscious decisions to do so).

Along with the findings of Blumenfeld, Puro, and Mergendoller (1992)
concerning classroom factors that foster student motivation to learn, the ideas
put forth by Rohrkemper and Corno (1988) concerning classrooms that foster
self-regulated learning again remind us that there are intimate connections between teachers' motivational strategies and their approaches to curriculum
and instruction.

CONCLUSION

The motivational strategies developed throughout this book are potentially
quite powerful, especially if used systematically and in complementary ways.
This entails establishing your classroom as a learning community as described
in Chapter 2, then infusing motivational elements into your unit, weekly, and
daily planning. Units should be structured around powerful ideas and include
a variety of learning activities and formats. Individual activities should be appropriately challenging and scaffolded so as to address the expectancy aspects
of students' motivation, and the combination of the activity itself, its content
base, and the way that you introduce and scaffold it should address the value
aspects of your students' motivation in multiple ways.

The idea here is to create what Ford (1992) called *motivational insurance*
when designing activities and social contexts for your classroom. Ford
noted that the most motivating activities and experiences in life are those
that afford opportunities for simultaneous pursuit and attainment of many
different kinds of goals. Adapted to the classroom context, this principle
implies that, from a motivational standpoint, the most desirable classroom
activities are those that make it possible for students to accomplish the
teacher's instructional goals while at the same time accomplishing many of
their own personal and social goals. Designing learning experiences so that
they allow attainment of as many different kinds of goals as possible (so
long as this includes attaining your instructional goals) provides some motivational insurance against the possibility that no relevant goal will be
activated.

SUMMARY

Various conceptions of motivation to learn, including my own, emphasize its cognitive
elements—the information processing, sensemaking, and advances in comprehension
or mastery that occur when students are seeking to gain the intended learning benefits

from a classroom activity. The term connotes minds-on cognitive engagement with powerful ideas. Motivation to learn in this sense is not guaranteed by interest in a topic or hands-on involvement in an activity. It requires opportunities to learn through exposure to curriculum content and learning activities, teacher pressure and support for such learning, and follow through in the form of evaluation and accountability systems that lead to additional learning opportunities if necessary.

As a significant person in your students' lives, you can socialize their motivation to learn. Three general strategies for socializing enduring dispositions to value learning and thus to approach learning situations thoughtfully and purposefully are modeling motivation to learn in your own everyday teaching, communicating related expectations and attributions about your students by treating them as if they already are eager learners, and avoiding practices that create performance anxiety and thus distract students from learning goals to performance goals. These strategies may be viewed as elaborations on the notion of establishing your classroom as a learning community (as described in Chapter 2).

Within the context established by these general strategies, you can use more specific techniques to stimulate your students' motivation to learn in the specific learning situations that you create each day. These include strategies for shaping students' expectations about the learning, for inducing motivation to learn, and for scaffolding their learning efforts.

Two strategies for shaping students' expectations about the learning are being enthusiastic (regularly) and being intense (selectively). You should routinely project enthusiasm for lessons and activities. You may be dramatic or entertaining in the process, but the point is to induce students to value the topic or activity. At times when you are communicating something particularly important, use relevant communication techniques to project a level of intensity that alerts students to the need to pay especially close attention.

Strategies for inducing motivation to learn are designed to help your students focus on learning goals and become cognitively engaged with the key ideas that lessons and activities are designed to develop. These include inducing curiosity or suspense or inducing dissonance or cognitive conflict when introducing the lesson or activity; making abstract content more personal, concrete, or familiar to students by linking it to their experience; inducing task interest or appreciation; and inducing students to generate their own motivation to learn.

Strategies for scaffolding students' learning efforts are needed to help students understand the purpose and nature of an activity and then support their efforts to accomplish its goals (to the extent that such support is needed). Scaffolding strategies include stating learning goals and providing advance organizers when introducing the activity, modeling task-related thinking and problem solving whenever these are not already familiar to students, inducing metacognitive awareness and control of learning strategies, and teaching skills for volitional follow through, studying, and other self-regulated learning skills.

The motivational picture is never complete without inclusion of these strategies for motivating students to learn. Even in learning situations in which students are confident that they can achieve success with reasonable effort, are aware of opportunities to earn rewards, and are motivated to engage in the activity because they are interested in the topic or enjoy the processes involved, they will not necessarily be motivated to learn unless you also stimulate and scaffold their learning efforts using some of the strategies presented in this chapter.

REFERENCES

Alton-Lee, A., Nuthall, G., & Patrick, J. (1993). Reframing classroom research: A lesson from the private world of children. *Harvard Educational Review, 63,* 50–84.

Anderson, C., & Roth, K. (1989). Teaching for meaningful and self-regulated learning of science. In J. Brophy (Ed.), *Advances in research on teaching* (Vol. 1, pp. 265–309). Greenwich, CT: JAI.

Anderson, L., Brubaker, N., Alleman-Brooks, J., & Duffy, G. (1985). A qualitative study of seatwork in first-grade classrooms. *Elementary School Journal, 86,* 123–140.

Berlyne, D. (1960). *Conflict, arousal, and curiosity.* New York: McGraw-Hill.

Bettencourt, E., Gillett, M., Gall, M., & Hull, R. (1983). Effects of teacher enthusiasm training on student on-task behavior and achievement. *American Educational Research Journal, 20,* 435–450.

Blumenfeld, P., & Meece, J. (1988). Task factors, teacher behavior, and students' involvement and use of learning strategies in science. *Elementary School Journal, 88,* 235–250.

Blumenfeld, P., Puro, P., & Mergendoller, J. (1992). Translating motivation into thoughtfulness. In H. Marshall (Ed.), *Redefining student learning: Roots of educational change* (pp. 207–239). Norwood, NJ: Ablex.

Brophy, J. (1983). Conceptualizing student motivation. *Educational Psychologist, 18,* 200–215.

Brophy, J. (1992). The de facto national curriculum in U.S. elementary social studies: Critique of a representative example. *Journal of Curriculum Studies, 24,* 401–447.

Brophy, J., & Alleman, J. (1991). Activities as instructional tools: A framework for analysis and evaluation. *Educational Researcher, 20*(4), 9–23.

Brophy, J., & Kher, N. (1986). Teacher socialization as a mechanism for developing student motivation to learn. In R. Feldman (Ed.), *Social psychology applied to education* (pp. 257–288). New York: Cambridge University Press.

Brophy, J., Rohkemper, M., Rashid, H., & Goldberger, M. (1983). Relationships between teachers' presentations of classroom tasks and students' engagement in those tasks. *Journal of Educational Psychology, 75,* 544–552.

Cabello, B., & Terrell, R. (1994). Making students feel like family: How teachers create warm and caring classroom climates. *Journal of Classroom Interaction, 29,* 17–23.

Conti, R., Amabile, T., & Pollak, S. (1995). The positive impact of creative activity: Effects of creative task engagement and motivational focus on college students' learning. *Personality and Social Psychology Bulletin, 21,* 1107–1116.

Corno, L. (1993). The best-laid plans: Modern conceptions of volition and educational research. *Educational Researcher, 22,* 14–22.

Corno, L., & Kanfer, R. (1993). The role of volition in learning and performance. In L. Darling-Hammond (Ed.), *Review of research in education* (Vol. 19, pp. 301–341). Washington, DC: American Educational Research Association.

Corno, L., & Rohrkemper, M. (1985). The intrinsic motivation to learn in classrooms. In C. Ames & R. Ames (Eds.), *Research on motivation in education. Vol. 2: The classroom milieu* (pp. 53–90). Orlando, FL: Academic Press.

Csikzentmihalyi, M., Rathunde, K., & Whalen, S. (1993). *Talented teenagers: The roots of success and failure.* New York: Cambridge University Press.

Devine, T. (1987). *Teaching study skills: A guide for teachers* (2nd ed.). Boston: Allyn & Bacon.

Dillon, J. (Ed.). (1988). *Questioning and teaching: A manual of practice.* London: Croom Helm.

Dillon, J. (Ed.). (1990). *The practice of questioning*. New York: Routledge.

Egan, K. (1990). *Romantic understanding: The development of rationality and imagination, ages 8–15*. New York: Routledge.

Ford, M. (1992). *Motivating humans: Goals, emotions, and personal agency beliefs*. Newbury Park, CA: Sage.

Friedlander, B. (1965). A psychologist's second thoughts on concepts, curiosity, and discovery in teaching and learning. *Harvard Educational Review, 35*, 18–38.

Good, T., & Brophy, J. (1997). *Looking in classrooms* (7th ed.). New York: Longman.

Guthrie, J., Van Meter, P., McCann, A., Wigfield, A., Bennett, L., Poundstone, C., Rice, M., Faibisch, F., Hunt, B., & Mitchell, A. (1996). Growth of literacy engagement: Changes in motivations and strategies during concept-oriented reading instruction. *Reading Research Quarterly, 31*, 306–332.

Jones, B., & Idol, L. (Eds.). (1990). *Dimensions of thinking and cognitive instruction*. Hillsdale, NJ: Erlbaum.

Karmos, J., & Karmos, A. (1983). A closer look at classroom boredom. *Action in Teacher Education, 5*, 49–55.

Keller, J. (1983). Motivational design of instruction. In C. Reigeluth (Ed.), *Instructional-design theories and models: An overview of their current status*, (pp. 383–434). Hillsdale, NJ: Erlbaum.

Kiewra, K., Dubois, N., Christian, D., McShane, A., Meyerhoffer, M., & Roskelley, D. (1991). Note-taking functions and techniques. *Journal of Educational Psychology, 83*, 240–245.

Kuhl, J., & Beckmann, J. (Eds.). (1985). *Action control: From cognition to behavior*. New York: Springer-Verlag.

Lane, D., Newman, D., & Bull, K. (1988). The relationship of student interest and advance organizer effectiveness. *Contemporary Educational Psychology, 13*, 15–25.

Lee, O., & Brophy, J. (1996). Motivational patterns observed in sixth-grade science classrooms. *Journal of Research in Science Teaching, 33*, 303–318.

Loewenstein, G. (1994). The psychology of curiosity: A review and reinterpretation. *Psychological Bulletin, 116*, 75–98.

Malone, T., & Lepper, M. (1987). Making learning fun: A taxonomy of intrinsic motivation for learning. In R. Snow & M. Farr (Eds.), *Aptitude, learning, and instruction: III. Conative and affective process analysis* (pp. 223–253). Hillsdale, NJ: Erlbaum.

Markova, A., Orlov, A., & Fridman, L. (1986). Motivating schoolchildren to learn. *Soviet Education, 28*, 8–88.

Marshall, H. (1987). Motivational strategies of three fifth-grade teachers. *Elementary School Journal, 88*, 135–150.

Marshall, H. (1994). Children's understanding of academic tasks: Work, play, or learning. *Journal of Research in Childhood Education, 9*, 35–46.

McCaslin, M., & Good, T. (1996). The informal curriculum. In D. Berliner & R. Calfee (Eds.), *Handbook of educational psychology* (pp. 622–670). New York: Macmillan.

Middleton, J. (1995). A study of intrinsic motivation in the mathematics classroom: A personal constructs approach. *Journal for Research in Mathematics Education, 26*, 254–279.

Newby, T. (1991). Classroom motivation: Strategies of first-year teachers. *Journal of Educational Psychology, 83*, 195–200.

Newmann, F. (1990). Qualities of thoughtful social studies classes: An empirical profile. *Journal of Curriculum Studies, 22*, 253–275.

Nisan, M. (1992). Beyond intrinsic motivation: Cultivating a "sense of the desirable." In F. Oser, A. Dick, & J. Patry (Eds.), *Effective and responsible teaching: The new synthesis* (pp. 126–138). San Francisco: Jossey-Bass.

Ogle, D. (1986). K-W-L: A teaching model that develops active reading of expository text. *Reading Teacher, 39,* 564–570.

Oldfather, P., & Dahl, K. (1994). Toward a social constructivist reconceptualization of intrinsic motivation for literacy learning. *Journal of Reading Behavior, 26,* 139–158.

Ortiz, R. (1983). Generating interest in reading. *Journal of Reading, 27,* 113–119.

Posner, G., Strike, K., Hewson, K., & Gertzog, W. (1982). Accommodation of a scientific conception: Toward a theory of conceptual change. *Science Education, 66,* 211–228.

Pressley, M., & Beard El-Dinary, P. (guest editors). (1993). Special issue on strategies instruction. *Elementary School Journal, 94,* 105–284.

Reeve, J. (1996). *Motivating others: Nurturing inner motivational resources.* Boston: Allyn & Bacon.

Rohrkemper, M., & Bershon, B. (1984). Elementary school students' reports of the causes and effects of problem difficulty in mathematics. *Elementary School Journal, 85,* 127–147.

Rohrkemper, R., & Corno, L. (1988). Success and failure on classroom tasks: Adaptive learning and classroom teaching. *Elementary School Journal, 88,* 297–312.

Rosenshine, B., & Guenther, J. (1992). Using scaffolds for teaching higher level cognitive strategies. In J. Keefe & H. Walberg (Eds.), *Teaching for thinking* (pp. 35–47). Reston, VA: National Association of Secondary School Principals.

Roth, K. (1996). Making learners and concepts central: A learner-centered, conceptual change approach to fifth-grade American history planning and teaching. In J. Brophy (Ed.), *Advances in research on teaching* (Vol. 6, pp. 115–182). Greenwich, CT: JAI.

Schunk, D., & Hanson, A. (1985). Peer models: Influence on children's self-efficacy and achievement. *Journal of Educational Psychology, 77,* 313–322.

Sivan, E., & Roehler, L. (1986). Motivational statements in explicit teacher explanations and their relationship to students' metacognition in reading. *National Reading Conference Yearbook, 35,* 178–184.

Thorkildsen, T., Nolen, S., & Fournier, J. (1994). What is fair? Children's critiques of practices that influence motivation. *Journal of Educational Psychology, 86,* 475–486.

Weinstein, C., & Mayer, R. (1986). The teaching of learning strategies. In M. Wittrock (Ed.), *Handbook of research on teaching* (3rd ed., pp. 315–327). New York: Macmillan.

CHAPTER 8

Socializing Uninterested or Alienated Students

Apathy, not discouragement, is the ultimate motivational problem facing teachers. Students who display learned helplessness, failure syndrome, or related performance concerns frequently lose their focus on learning and require special motivational treatment beyond what is needed for the class as a whole (see Chapter 4). However, these students usually value learning and would like to be able to complete learning activities successfully.

In contrast, *apathetic students* are uninterested in or even alienated from school learning: They don't find it meaningful or worthwhile, don't want to engage in it, don't value it even when they know that they can achieve success with reasonable effort, and may even resist it if they fear that it will make them into something that they do not want to become. You will need to make sustained efforts to resocialize such students' attitudes and beliefs. More specifically, you will need to show them what it means to engage in academic activities with motivation to learn, nurture their desire to do so, and follow up with appropriate structuring and scaffolding of their learning efforts.

In this regard, it is helpful to view motivation to learn as a *schema*—a network of connected insights, skills, values, and dispositions that enable students to understand what it means to engage in academic activities with the intention of accomplishing their learning goals and with metacognitive awareness of the strategies they use in attempting to do so. Students in whom this motivation-to-learn schema has not developed tend to view school tasks as imposed demands rather than as learning opportunities, and thus to engage in them (if at all) with work-avoidance goals and perhaps performance goals, but not learning goals. They participate in lessons and work on assignments only to the extent needed to garner acceptable grades and stay out of trouble. They give little consideration to learning goals, let alone to appreciating the value of the learning or taking pride in their accomplishments.

In contrast to the rich literature on strategies for dealing with students whose problems lie in the expectancy aspects of motivation, there is a dearth of theory-based research on strategies for dealing with uninterested or alienated students. However, it is possible to suggest several sets of principles based on what is known about the development and socialization of value-based motivation in homes, schools, and work settings (Baumrind, 1991; Damon, 1995; Epstein, 1989; Grusec & Goodnow, 1994; Perry & Perry, 1983).

CONSIDER CONTRACTING AND INCENTIVE SYSTEMS

In many respects, students who find no value in school activities are ideal candidates for the use of contracting or other approaches that involve offering incentives in exchange for specified accomplishments. Most motivation theorists urge caution in using such incentive systems because they can undermine students' intrinsic motivation to engage in the rewarded activities. Where such intrinsic motivation is lacking, however, there is nothing to undermine. Thus, at least in areas where apathetic students clearly have no intrinsic motivation, you have nothing to lose by using extrinsic incentives.

However, the qualifications and guidelines on how to use extrinsic incentives (see Chapter 5) still apply if you want to move apathetic students away from dependence on these incentives and toward self-regulated motivation to learn. Therefore, avoid offering incentives in ways that reinforce these students' tendencies to view lessons and assignments as unwelcome impositions that must be endured for extrinsic reasons. Instead, use contracting approaches that include collaborative goal setting, and take advantage of the opportunities provided by the goal-setting negotiations to help the students begin to appreciate the value of what they are learning.

Emphasize authentic activities, phrase goal statements in terms of learning accomplishments rather than tasks completed, and use qualitative criteria for assessing progress. Revisit these goals and assessment criteria during post-activity debriefings, and as much as possible, elicit summaries and critiques of accomplishments from the students themselves. If the activity has yielded some noteworthy product, offer to display it in the classroom or suggest that the student share it with classmates or family members.

The point here is not merely to deflect attention from extrinsic rewards and their role in motivating these students' efforts, but to provide the students with concepts and language that they can use to appreciate and take pride in their accomplishments. Students can't appreciate what they don't see or understand. They need concepts and language to help them articulate learning goals, assess progress, and think about end products in terms of understandings, skills, or accomplishments (not merely task completion or compliance with minimal requirements).

Richly descriptive language is especially important for practice activities in subjects such as grammar, computation, or penmanship. To begin with, students should be aware that such practice is important because the ultimate goals—writing and problem solving in life situations—cannot be accomplished efficiently until key subskills are mastered to levels of smooth, accurate performance, such that they can be integrated and applied effortlessly when needed. Analogies to the importance of skill practice in preparing for integrated athletic or musical performance might be useful here.

In addition, though, students will need concepts and language to describe the immediate outcomes of their learning efforts. It is more meaningful and motivating to think about a reading assignment in terms of "understanding why slavery flourished in the south but not in the north" rather than "studying history," to "learn to divide when there is both a decimal point and a remainder" rather than to "do your math problems," or to "learn to adjust your writing position so that you stay on the line and maintain the same slant as you move across the page" rather than to "practice your penmanship." Use richly descriptive goal characterizations like these when introducing such activities. As students begin to work on them, phrase your feedback with reference to these goals. In assessing their completed work, refer to specific, qualitative aspects of their performance instead of confining yourself to grades or general evaluative comments.

It *may* be helpful to explain to apathetic students why learning can be empowering and self-actualizing. However, it almost certainly *will* be helpful to arrange conditions that allow them to experience these outcomes directly. Therefore, whether or not you use performance contracts or other incentive systems, be sure to negotiate goals and provide feedback to these students in language that they can use to plan and assess their learning. By engaging them in the processes of setting goals and reflecting on their work, you lead them through first-hand experiences in what it means to engage in academic activities with motivation to learn.

As these processes become more familiar, the students can begin to engage in them more naturally without feeling pressed to respond to unfamiliar demands. This will leave more of their cognitive resources free to think about the purposes, meanings, and potential applications of what they are learning. Eventually they should begin to do this spontaneously and thus start to generate and build on their own motivation to learn (Thorkildsen, 1988; Vallacher & Wegner, 1987).

DEVELOP AND WORK WITHIN A CLOSE RELATIONSHIP WITH THE STUDENT

Chapter 2 emphasizes that you can become your own most valuable motivational tool by building close relationships with students and establishing yourself as a supportive and helpful resource person. It is important to do this with all students, but especially with uninterested or alienated students who don't find much value in school learning. These students are already moving in undesirable directions, so they need to be turned around. This will require exerting counterpressures against, and ultimately prevailing over, whatever forces have led them to become apathetic or resistant learners. If failure syndrome problems are also present, you will have to work on these too, using the techniques described in Chapter 4. Sometimes students dismiss a content area or type of learning activity as boring or useless because they fear failure and want to establish an excuse for not trying hard.

Whether or not they are compounded by failure syndrome problems, well-established apathy or resistance problems will not be cleared up quickly with a brief talk or a single key experience. You will need to work for and accept gradual progress, and to stay patient and supportive even if you encounter skepticism or resistance. Be prepared for such reactions, at least from students whose apathy has hardened into a well-articulated belief system. After all, why should these students take seriously your attempts to portray school learning as worthwhile if their own prior experiences, and perhaps the messages they get from their peers or even their parents, tell them otherwise?

To establish a potential for succeeding with apathetic students, (1) show them that you care about them personally as individuals and are trying to get through to them primarily because you are concerned about their present and future best interests, not just because you want to get them to comply with your demands, and (2) help them to see that their prior experiences have been limited or distorted—that despite the grading system and other performance incentives, the basic reason for engaging in learning activities is to acquire the empowerment and self-actualization potential that these activities are designed to develop (see Box 8.1). A great deal of modeling, socialization, and reflective discussion of learning experiences will be required to accomplish this agenda. For these efforts to have much effect, your relationships with these students will have to be such that they value your opinions and want to please you.

In getting to know apathetic students, take note of the situations in which they do or do not accomplish learning goals, and adjust accordingly. Also, get them talking about their school experiences in ways that help you to capitalize on their existing motivation. In particular, ask them about situational features (i.e., content areas, types of activities, types of learning formats) that they find conducive to learning, and about ways that other learning experiences might be made more worthwhile or helpful. Simply providing such students with opportunities for input is likely to improve your relationships with them and their attitudes toward learning, and their responses may include specific suggestions that you are willing to accept and that actually lead to improved performance.

DISCOVER AND BUILD ON EXISTING INTERESTS

Another reason for developing good relationships with apathetic students as individuals is to learn about their values and interests. Students who are not motivated to learn are pursuing other goal-oriented agendas. Some of these agendas will be incompatible with your own but others might provide motivational bases to use as starting points in working with these students while

---

Box 8.1.   Self-Actualization Motives for School Learning

Furst and Steele (1986) interviewed older adults who had enrolled (not necessarily for credit) in courses at universities, asking them why they had done so. Their responses are interesting because most of them focused on self-actualization rather than extrinsic reasons for course enrollment. Based on statistical analyses, Furst and Steele grouped the reasons into nine categories.

1. *Keeping up/becoming involved:* To keep up with what is going on in the world; reexamine my perspectives on contemporary issues; become better able to cope with the challenges of daily living; become more effective as a citizen; become better acquainted with congenial people; improve my ability to participate in community work; participate in group activity; satisfy an inquiring mind; or share a common interest with my spouse or friend.

2. *Fulfillment:* To develop an unfulfilled talent; supplement a narrow previous education; pursue earlier interests that I could not get around to before; or complete some previously unfinished learning.

3. *Stimulation and self-maintenance:* To get relief from boredom; get a change from the routine of home or work; maintain or enhance my self-respect; keep my mind active and alert by making intellectual demands on it; or feel a sense of achievement.

4. *Practical achievement:* To acquire knowledge on a particular subject; learn a specific skill; feel a sense of achievement; prepare myself for retirement living; or satisfy a desire to develop new interests.

5. *Self-understanding/personal adjustment:* To gain insight into personal problems; get help with a crisis in my personal life; or reexamine myself and my role in life.

6. *Formal attainment and recognition:* To comply with the recommendations or urging of someone else; help me earn a degree, diploma, or certificate; or increase others' respect for me.

7. *Qualifying for privileges:* To qualify for privileges such as use of library or swimming pool, or to participate in group activities.

8. *Prerequisite knowledge:* To acquire knowledge to help with other educational courses or to gain insight into human relations.

9. *Intellectual stimulation and enjoyment:* To learn just for the joy of learning or to satisfy an inquiring mind.

Most of these reasons for learning appear just as applicable to K–12 students as to older learners. You can cultivate their development in your students by frequently making reference to them and by asking questions that lead students to discover them.

---

you nurture their motivation to learn. Almost any substantive interest, for example, can become the basis for developing language arts skills. Students might read books or magazines about sports and entertainment personalities, automobile customizing, computer games, or other topics popular in the youth culture, then write reports summarizing and reflecting on what they read. This may be less desirable than having them read and write about science or social studies topics, but at least it provides opportunities for applying language arts skills and perhaps for developing some important dispositions (i.e., reading for key ideas, reflecting on and communicating about them).

As another example, certain apathetic students might possess social motivation that you could use to substitute in part for their lack of motivation to learn. Such students might learn little or nothing if left to work individually but accomplish some important learning goals if paired with classmates who are more oriented toward learning. You might make frequent use of partner learning formats with these students in the short run, while working toward the long-run goal of developing their capacities as self-regulated learners.

John Dewey (1913) believed that interest, if construed properly, is basic to good curriculum and instruction. He saw no value in attempting to dress up or sugar coat something that has no fundamental relevance to students, because this will create only momentary or fleeting interest. However, he saw great value in creating genuine interest by helping students to see connections between the school curriculum and their own spontaneously developed interests, goals, and abilities. He believed that curriculum content and learning activities should be selected in relation to students' current experience, abilities, and needs, and should be represented in ways that enable the students to appreciate their relevance and value in relation to what already has significance for them.

Genuine interest implies absorption in the process of learning, not just interest in its final products. It also implies recognition of long-term goals, monitoring of progress toward these goals, and willingness to strive to reach them. The interest-related payoff to the learner is some form of development or self-actualization.

Dewey's ideas about interest connect to what was said in Chapter 6 about intrinsic motivation residing in persons rather than objects or events. To develop genuine interests in apathetic students and use these as bases for motivating their learning, you need to go beyond inducing curiosity or temporary interest. In addition or instead, induce these students to identify with the whole idea of learning the content or skills you are teaching—to view acquisition of the content or skills as worth the effort for reasons that they can understand. In other words, *help these students to see that it is in their own best interests to learn what you are trying to teach them.*

Mordecai Nisan (1992) made a similar point in stating that schooling does not aim to provide satisfaction of what is *desired* by students but instead to cultivate in them what the culture construes as *desirable.* Ultimately, schooling is based on values rooted in images of a state of human perfection that is worth aspiring to attain. Apathetic students need help in understanding that school attendance and the demands of the educational system are part of a set of cultural expectations that are legitimate and desirable because they are designed to help students develop toward the culture's image of the ideal human being. Therefore, students owe it to themselves, as well as to the culture, to take advantage of the opportunities that schooling offers to develop well-differentiated and self-actualized personal identities, as well as the knowledge, skills, values, and dispositions that they will need to function effectively in society.

When phrased in such language, the sense of the desirable sounds like a very abstract value that would be difficult to convey to K–12 students, let alone to cultivate in apathetic students who see no value in schooling. However, Nisan's research with first-, fourth-, and seventh-graders showed that these students already possessed at least intuitive versions of this value. The students were asked to express opinions about several scenarios, one of which involved a child who did not attend school. Large majorities of students at all three grade levels viewed failure to attend school as bad behavior, even when the child was depicted as living in a country in which school attendance was not required and not common. Most of the students believed that there should be laws requiring school attendance, and they justified their opinions on the basis of concern about children's long-term well-being. They viewed schooling as desirable and necessary for proper development.

These findings imply that, at some level, most if not all students understand that it is in their own best interests not only to attend school but to strive to accomplish learning goals. Apathetic students have suppressed this realization, so you will have to help them rediscover it and confront its implications through sympathetic yet persistent comments and questions. Both your and their efforts should emphasize securing their long-run best interests by promoting their progress in all aspects of the curriculum, not just pursuing their current interests in particular topics or activities.

HELP STUDENTS TO DEVELOP AND SUSTAIN MORE POSITIVE ATTITUDES TOWARD SCHOOL WORK

Just as interest and other forms of intrinsic motivation reside in persons, not activities, the same is true of negative reactions to school learning experiences. Emphasize this when working with students who view learning activities as aversive. Assuming that the activities are well suited to the students' current learning abilities and needs, their aversive experiences are caused by their own negative attitudes and expectations, rather than by anything inherent to the activities themselves. Other students find these activities meaningful, worthwhile, and even enjoyable; they will too if they learn to approach the activities with a more positive mindset.

Csikzentmihalyi (1993) has noted that people can learn to experience flow even in routine activities if they seek out challenges and relish stretching their limits. For example, they might "complexify" an otherwise boring activity by trying to do it artistically, seeking to increase their efficiency, or setting goals that convert the activity into something more challenging and interesting.

Theorists writing about self-regulation and volition have noted that students can develop strategies for managing their affective responses to learning activities. They then can use these strategies to maintain task focus and avoid becoming distracted by boredom, anger, frustration, or other negative emotions. You can assist such development by making your students more aware and able to make efficient use of the coping strategies they have developed on their own, as well as by teaching them new ones.

Oldfather (1992) interviewed fifth- and sixth-graders about the strategies they had developed for getting started and staying focused on tasks that they found boring or unrewarding. Several emphasized accepting the teacher's assurances that the task was worth doing (or more generally, the idea that there was a significant purpose behind everything that they were asked to do in school). For example, Suki found her science project boring but believed that "I have to think of it as important, because if you thought it wasn't important, you wouldn't do anything about it." Phil identified two factors that helped him overcome resistance to a task: (1) observing peers enjoying the task ("Seeing that everybody else likes it in there, I must like it too, once I figure it out.") and (2) gaining a sense of competence (recognizing that he could "figure it out" if he applied himself to the activity, and thus expand his repertoire of knowledge and skills).

McCaslin and Good (1996) spoke of scaffolding students' motivation and volition by asking them questions such as the following:

Do you like the unit we have been studying? How come? (Why not?) What about _____ interests (bores) you?

Do you think that when you like something or find it interesting it is easier to learn? Is it easier to remember?

Are there ways that you can try to make work more interesting or fun for you?

What are some of the things you do?

Does that seem to help you learn?

Why do you suppose that is?

Have you ever tried _____ ?

Besides calling students' attention to useful strategies, such scaffolding encourages honest communication because it legitimizes the students' view that engagement in learning activities is sometimes boring or aversive. It doesn't endorse this view, but it acknowledges that the students believe it and makes it OK to talk about it.

Making Work More Enjoyable or Satisfying

Many suggestions have been made to adults who would like to derive more satisfaction from their jobs. You can adapt these suggestions as ways to help apathetic students learn to take more satisfaction from their school work.

Waitley and Witt (1985) emphasized that the nature of work resides at least as much in the worker's attitude as in the work itself. To illustrate this, they told of three construction workers who were asked to talk about their jobs. The first worker mostly complained about negative aspects of the job (i.e., demanding boss, frustrations caused by bad weather or poor materials). The second worker talked more descriptively, but emphasized the steps involved in carrying out discrete tasks (i.e., mixing mortar, positioning a brick properly, troweling mortar around the brick and then scraping off the excess). The third worker, who derived the most satisfaction from the job, explained that he was building a cathedral!

Waitley and Witt identified several techniques used by workers to make their jobs more rewarding and enjoyable:

- Adopt positive attitudes and expectations by focusing more on what you expect to accomplish than on the difficulties you expect to encounter.
- Develop plans and goal sequences to guide your work but also get feedback and be prepared to revise plans when necessary.
- Emphasize perseverance and flexibility over attempts to be perfect from the beginning.
- Make routine work more interesting by treating it as a game, trying to surpass self-imposed quotas, trying to do individual portions perfectly, or discovering how you can add personal creativity to it.
- Learn to enjoy the challenge of solving problems and to take satisfaction in a job well done.
- Congregate with people who share similar attitudes and expectations, while avoiding people who lack goals or who are more into complaining than coping.

Cameron and Elusorr (1986) also offered suggestions for making work more interesting. Most are based on psychological principles but some are based on Zen philosophy, especially the notion of present focus.

Present Focus

If you stay absorbed in what you are doing, you won't be watching the clock. Therefore, when you show up for a task, really show up—be there, pay close attention to what you are doing, focus on it, and do it fully. If you catch your mind wandering, notice where it went and why. Make a note of any business that needs to be attended to later so that you can put your concerns on hold and refocus on the task at hand.

Ritual

Starter rituals help you to get into present focus. For example, a "clearing ritual" in which you set up your equipment or clear your desk and arrange your papers might be a useful transition from other activities into getting ready to study or work.

Ride the Waves

Don't let situations that are imperfect or do not work out well gnaw at you. Care about what you do, do your best, analyze and try to deal with problems, but don't give up or do less than your best merely because you know that things are not going to be perfect.

A Personalized Approach

Bring creativity to the job. If you must deal with certain recurring difficulties, stop looking at them as built-in handicaps and begin to view them as opportunities or challenges. If things are going so smoothly that you get bored, get off of automatic pilot and return to present focus by finding ways to make the job less routine or more demanding (i.e., by striving to meet personally set goals or varying your routines).

Make a Game of It

Turn work into play by creating a game that you can play while doing the job. A medical technician might occasionally take time out to view slides as if she were an art critic, a bartender might become a connoisseur of cliches that he hears from boring customers, a grocery bagger might try to pack items so that they come out level at the fill line, and a waitress might learn the ordering habits of regulars and make bets with herself on their behavior.

See Your Work as an Art Form

Any action can be performed with a sense of aesthetics—seek ways to do your work gracefully or to produce an end product that is visually or otherwise pleasing in addition to functional.

See Your Work as a Teacher

Analyze the work to discover what there is to learn about it. If you get bored, figure out at what point you became bored, why you did the same task yesterday without getting bored, or whether something else is irritating you. Analyze differences between when you are bored and when you are not bored for ideas about how to minimize boredom. Also, learn more about the work itself (i.e., possibilities for using any equipment involved, ways to do the job more efficiently, shortcuts to use and cues for recognizing when they are relevant).

Find a Rhythm to Your Work

Finding natural rhythms or cycles in work can help make it more enjoyable and reduce the sense that it "never lets up." If possible, take time away from some continuous task so as to vary it with another task and give yourself a chance to relax from that particular form of effort. Pay attention to natural rhythms in work cycles to help keep you aware of the variation that is built into tasks and the progress you are making toward goals.

Unwind

When pressure gets to you, let your mind slip into something more comfortable (but not into doubts, worries, or irritations). Alternate periods of intense concentration and activity with brief periods of relaxation. If you can't walk around or take a break, sit back, close your eyes, and meditate briefly. Sharing jokes and finding humor on the job helps too.

Seek Excellence

Learn to seek excellence in doing your work and taking satisfaction from doing so. In the process of seeking excellence, use the following techniques:

1. *Just the details:* Pay attention to each detail of the job and do it fully and carefully. This combines present focus with the notion of taking pride in each separate small piece of the job as part of what is involved in completing the job as a whole successfully.
2. *Your life depends on it:* Do the work as if your life depended on doing it well. Think of it as something that you are going to dedicate to people you care about or are going to sign with your name when you finish.

Students develop some of these techniques on their own, although often only the less adaptive ones (see Box 8.2). You might teach them some of the more adaptive techniques, which should help them to derive satisfactions in the process of carrying out assignments and to sustain the volitional control needed to see the work through to completion. Techniques for making work more enjoyable should go a long way toward reducing apathy and resistance. However, they apply more to routine tasks calling for expert performance than to tasks designed as learning experiences for novices. As Marshall (1988) has emphasized, classrooms are better described as learning settings than as work settings. Consequently, even if you do all of the things already suggested in this chapter, you will still need to socialize apathetic students' motivation to learn.

SOCIALIZE APATHETIC STUDENTS' MOTIVATION TO LEARN

Values and attitudes ordinarily are acquired primarily through exposure to respected *models* who exhibit them, rather than through more typical instruction. However, they also can be socialized through *persuasive communication* (if students accept the message) and developed through *participation in powerful learning experiences* that foster them. You can socialize motivation to learn indirectly through modeling, persuasion, and scaffolding of students' learning experiences, but you cannot transmit it directly through instruction because it includes elements of emotional involvement and personal commitment that can come only from the students themselves (Gagné, Briggs, & Wager, 1988).

The task of socializing motivation to learn is difficult with apathetic students who have not had much exposure to experiences that help them understand what it means to engage in learning activities with the intention of gaining the benefits they were designed to develop. The task is even more challenging with alienated students who have come to view schooling as aversive, because it requires changing existing attitudes and values in addition to building new ones.

Box 8.2.   Students' Coping Strategies

Students develop strategies for coping with situations in which they find schoolwork aversive or discouraging. For example, McCaslin (1990) interviewed sixth graders about how they handled the "hard stuff" in mathematics. The following excerpts are from interviews with two girls who were best friends and were viewed by their teacher as sharing a tendency to be persistent and effortful in working on assignments. Despite this teacher-perceived similarity, the girls were quite different in their approach to difficult math problems. Both girls persistently tried to solve the problems, but the first one did so mostly in order to get the assignment finished so that she could interact with her friends. She made strategic use of fantasies connected with this goal as a way to help her get through the rough spots:

A lot of times I get sick of things so I just want to stop. And I do . . . I always, whenever I'm working and I just get sick of working, I just stop because I can't stand it anymore. I think of things that I like to do. Like in school, I'm going to play with my friends, I think of all the things that are fun that we do, and stuff. But I have to get this done and *right* before I can go to do that.

In contrast, her friend was more focused on learning with understanding (not just getting correct answers), but was less successful in avoiding the frustration and worry that accompanied failure to solve difficult problems easily. Not having developed her friend's ability to use fantasy strategically, she had to distract herself by engaging in alternative activities.

Well, I think I'm going to get them all wrong. And I kind of feel like I have to get up and walk around and think about it. I feel like I have to stop and work on something else for a little bit. I might get up and work on spelling for a minute 'cause that's pretty easy and I don't have to think about it, 'cause spelling I just know the answers and they're right there. I can't think about the math and what I'm going to do . . . (It's time for a break) when I get pretty frustrated, I think to myself "You can't do this," and I start tearing, I start biting my pencil. Then I know I have to get up and do something else. I just get so frustrated with it I can't think. . . . I start to fiddle with my hands, go like that. I know I have to do something else. 'Cause I really get mad. I don't take a real long (break) time, maybe just 10 minutes. Then I come back to work again. Just to get it out of my mind for a minute.

McCaslin's analyses and other recent studies indicate that students differ dramatically in the motivational patterns that they bring to the classroom and in the related strategies that they employ for setting goals, addressing task demands, and seeking to make "repairs" when their initial efforts do not succeed.

You can help your apathetic or discouraged students learn to cope with situational pressures by teaching them strategies for doing so. From a motivational standpoint, however, it would be better to emphasize strategies that help students to see value and take satisfaction in the work over strategies that merely provide temporary relief from what they continue to view as an aversive situation.

You cannot force students to change their attitudes and values, not even with sanctions such as punishments or failing grades. You may be able to force them to do at least a minimum amount of work by requiring them to complete assignments during recess periods, after school, or in in-school detention programs. However, getting work out of students is not the same as motivating them to learn. Therefore, it is better to minimize your reliance on coercive methods and instead build and work within more productive teacher–student relationships.

Apathetic students need consistent application of the strategies described in Chapter 7, supplemented by more individualized treatment tailored to their personal characteristics and needs. Attempts to develop their motivation to learn need to be relentless, yet subtle. They won't get far if the students perceive you as nagging them, manipulating them, or attempting to force your will on them. Instead, you will need to be seen as enabling or empowering them by opening doors to self-actualization and teaching them to exploit potentials that have lain dormant because the students were not aware of them.

Apathetic students need the same curiosity-, interest-, and reflection-stimulating experiences that other students do, but they need to encounter them more frequently and carry them out in more personal, intense, and sustained ways. They especially need to be stimulated to reflect on and communicate about their learning. Therefore, keep focusing them on the self-actualizing potential of learning experiences by asking them questions about the content or by making assignments that require them to think about and appreciate new insights, to form and explain opinions, to develop explanations, or to make connections or applications. Scaffold their engagement in learning activities and their post-activity reflections to make sure that they experience empowering or self-actualizing outcomes. Your goal is to induce them to *identify* with these experiences—to connect learning experiences with their self-concepts and to begin to develop images of their ideal selves that cast them as open-minded, active learners (see Box 8.3).

To the extent that apathetic students are open to considering it and capable of understanding it, consider trying a "hard sell" approach to socializing their motivation to learn. Perhaps begin by informing them that they have missed the boat on some important opportunities for self-actualization, and that you want to give them a second chance or a chance to catch up.

Ask them questions to initiate discussions about why schools and libraries exist, why people go to museums or watch educational programs, why they read newspapers and magazines, and why they travel and seek other opportunities to broaden their lives. Also, model and provide examples of ways that people with active minds can bring the world to themselves by using their own resources without depending on other people or media to bring things to them. For example, you might draw on examples from your own life to illustrate motivation to learn and the self-talk that accompanies it, while articulating values such as the following:

Get Worthwhile Payoffs from Your Investments of Time and Effort. Whenever you invest in some activity (and *especially* when your engagement in the

Box 8.3.   Develop Students' Self-Schemas as Motivated Learners

Markus and Nurius (1986) have developed the concept of *possible selves*—cognitive representations of oneself in the future. Possible selves represent the selves that a person could become, would like to become, or is afraid of becoming. To the extent that people have developed clear notions of possible selves, they can mobilize their energies toward becoming their ideal selves and avoiding movement in the direction of possible selves that they do not want to develop.

Overall movement toward ideal possible selves is supported by the development of *self-schemas* in particular domains of functioning. Cross and Markus (1994) showed that competent functioning in a domain requires both domain-specific ability and a self-schema for this ability. Optimal progress in mathematics, for example, requires both steady development of needed mathematical knowledge and recognition that one possesses this knowledge and can use it to solve problems.

Self-schemas represent one's domain-specific abilities and one's experiences in the domain. *Schematic* students possess well-developed self-schemas in a domain. They can use these self-schemas to make quick and confident judgments, to adapt flexibly to different information-processing goals, and to accurately retrieve information relevant to the domain. They are sensitive to schema-relevant information and pay close attention to it. As a result, they are attuned to schema-relevant situations and ready to exercise schema-relevant abilities when needed. They value these self-schemas, assigning them critical personal importance.

In contrast, students who are *aschematic* in that same domain have not developed well-articulated and valued self-schemas. They may possess as much domain-specific ability as schematic students and may even display equivalent competence when pressured or motivated to do so. However, they are not as likely as schematic students to seek out opportunities to activate their domain-specific competencies, recognize these opportunities when they arise, or exploit them as fully or persistently.

These ideas about possible selves and self-schemas apply well to the ideas presented in this book about the development of motivation to learn as a general disposition. Learning situations (in or out of school) constitute one important domain of functioning in life. People who develop well-articulated self-schemas relating to this domain will tend to recognize and value learning situations and to engage in them with motivation to learn. More generally, their possible selves will include ideals featuring an open, active mind and a tendency to be reflective about their experience. They will also recognize passive or closed-minded individuals as possible selves to be avoided.

In contrast, the kinds of apathetic students discussed in this chapter are aschematic in the domain of motivation to learn. Their experiences and the socialization influences that have shaped their development have not led them to understand what it means to engage in learning activities with motivation to learn, or to value doing so as part of becoming a fully self-actualized person. To change them significantly, you will need to provide them with opportunities for these experiences, scaffold their engagement in the experiences, and induce them to reflect on what they have accomplished and its implications for their self-schemas and future possible selves.

activity is required), do so in ways that produce useful outcomes and do not leave you feeling that you have wasted time and effort. If you are going to study, learn. Get the most out of the experience by using generative learning strategies that focus on the meanings and potential applications of key ideas.

Take Satisfaction in Gaining Understanding. Learn to take pleasure in acquiring information and to experience satisfaction in coming to understand how things work. Take time to appreciate the minor epiphanies represented by "aha" reactions, "so that's how it works" insights, or "I never knew that—I'll bet that's why ____" connections.

Enjoy the Stimulation of Novel or Surprising Input. New input stimulates the cognitive juices, especially when it extends knowledge of things that we are already highly interested in or when it violates our expectations, contrasts with what we are familiar with, or in some other way surprises us or makes us aware that our knowledge is incomplete. It is fascinating to learn about lifestyles or actions that we have never considered or thought possible.

Enjoy Vicarious Experiences. Especially in reading fiction, but also in keeping up with current events or reading in the social sciences, there are opportunities to identify with focal characters or project ourselves into the situations being depicted. This allows us to vicariously experience what happens to the characters or people in these situations, and to think about how we would respond in their place.

Appreciate Expansion of Self-Knowledge. Whenever we learn about particular people or about the human condition in general, we learn more about ourselves. This includes similarities and contrasts with other people as well as information about the motives and intentions that underlie behavior, about different ways of handling life situations, and so on.

Take Pride in Becoming a Well-Informed Person and Citizen. Expanding our knowledge and using our cognitive abilities is unique to the human condition and an important part of what it means to be a fully functioning person. Engagement in these activities provides bases for us to take satisfaction in feeling that we are aware of what is going on in the world, that we can follow news and current events knowledgeably, that we are informed voters, and that we have developed well-articulated opinions on policy issues or matters that come up in social discussion.

Along with providing such modeling and expectations yourself, expose your apathetic students to peers or people with whom they identify who can model active minds at work. For example, in an intervention study designed to encourage 7–11 year-old students to become more intrinsically motivated learners, Hennessey, Amabile, and Martinage (1989) had the students watch videotapes that included the following dialogue:

ADULT: Tommy, of all the things your teacher gives you to do in school, think about the one thing you like to do best and tell me about it.

TOMMY: Well, I like social studies the best. I like learning about how other people live in different parts of the world. It's also fun because you get to do lots of projects and reports. I like doing projects because you can learn a lot about something on your own. I work hard on my projects and when I come up with good ideas, I feel good. When you are working on something that you thought of, and that's interesting to you, it's more fun to do.

ADULT: So, one of the reasons you like social studies so much is because you get to learn about things on your own. And it makes you feel good when you do things for yourself; it makes it more interesting. That's great! (p. 216).

As part of your attempt to socialize motivation to learn in apathetic students, you might expose these students to selected videotapes from television talk shows (or at least make reference to certain common types of participants on these shows) in order to draw contrasts between active and passive or closed minds. In the process, draw distinctions between the content and style of communication displayed by interesting, well-informed, and obviously reflective guests and the guests who defeat their own best interests by impulsively blurting out ill-considered ideas, loudly repeating counterproductive arguments, undermining their own credibility, and causing other guests and onlookers to respond to them with derision or irritation. Point out that these people did not have to become the way they are—most of them are not stupid but are passive, unreflective, willfully ignorant, or defensively aggressive rather than open to new information or ideas. They never learned to ask what things mean, why they are important, or what their implications might be for personal or social decision making.

Where it may be productive to do so, you might go on to point out that despite the diversity and richness of the self-actualization opportunities that the modern world presents, some people maintain very restricted mental lives. They think only about work, daily needs, and popular culture. They are not desirable as spouses, parents, friends, or coworkers because they have nothing to say, prattle on about trivia, or aggressively spout uninformed opinions rather than engage in mutually satisfying conversations. They got this way by passing through school without taking advantage of the opportunities it offers, rationalizing by finding everything to be boring or stupid.

The point to emphasize with apathetic students is that schooling is not intended just to teach them basic skills and prepare them for jobs; in addition, it is intended to help them realize their human potential more fully in all aspects of their lives. To put it bluntly, schooling is intended to help them become the kinds of people that others admire rather than the kinds that are mostly ignored because they just pass their time like cows chewing cud or are mostly looked down upon because they act like the people who embarrass themselves on television talk shows.

CONCLUSION

Apathetic students do not value what schooling has to offer and thus are indifferent or resistant to it. You can use threats and sanctions to compel them to perform to some minimum standard, but if you want to get through to them and resocialize their values, you will have to do it by modeling, communicating attitudes, expectations, and attributions, and arranging for them to engage in experiences that foster the development of motivation to learn.

Assuming appropriate curriculum and instruction, there are many good reasons for taking advantage of what school has to offer. Unfortunately, the reasons typically emphasized to apathetic students tend to focus on "tickets" to advancement in society (i.e., you need knowledge, skills, diplomas, etc. to get good jobs). These are valid reasons and probably should be emphasized to some degree, but they focus on extrinsically imposed requirements rather than learning. Also, they are easy for apathetic students to dismiss because these students can always point to people who dropped out of school but nevertheless achieved at least material success in our society.

Consequently, your best chances of getting through to apathetic students lie in helping these students to appreciate the empowerment and self-actualization outcomes that result from consistently engaging in school learning activities with motivation to learn. These ideas may be abstract, but even elementary students have at least an intuitive understanding of what they mean and recognition of their validity. Students can recognize the differences between people who are admired because they are thoughtful, well-informed, and open-minded and people who are ignored because they are passive or are rejected because they are boorish.

The key is to help unmotivated and resistant students see that these personal qualities are rooted in values and dispositions toward learning. This realization should encourage them to develop values and dispositions relating to motivation to learn, not only to help ensure their success in school but also to help them become fully functioning in all aspects of their lives.

SUMMARY

This chapter suggested strategies for working with apathetic students who are uninterested in or alienated from school learning. Many of these students also display expectancy-related motivational problems and therefore also require treatment using the strategies described in Chapter 4. Whether or not expectancy-related problems are present, apathetic students need modeling, socialization, and engagement in experiences that develop their motivation to learn.

Apathetic students require the same strategies for addressing the value-related aspects of motivation that were recommended for use with the class as a whole—the strategies described in Chapters 5 and 6 and especially in Chapter 7. However, these strategies will need to be applied more insistently and in more personalized ways in an attempt to get through to these students.

Contracting and incentive systems are widely recommended for use with apathetic students, in part because there is less need to fear undermining intrinsic motivation. These strategies can be helpful, but if they are to function as motivation builders rather than mere performance incentives, they will need to be implemented in ways that focus students' attention on learning goals and on the empowerment and self-actualization satisfactions that may be derived from attaining them.

It is important to develop and work within close relationships with apathetic students. For one thing, you will need to display patience and determination in pushing for steady progress despite setbacks or resistance, and this is difficult to do if you don't have a good relationship with the student. Also, your modeling and socialization efforts will be more successful if the student likes you and wants to please you.

In an effort to make schooling more intrinsically rewarding for apathetic students, discover and build on their existing interests, especially topical interests that might provide a basis for assignments or social interests that might sustain their learning efforts. Also, make sure that these students understand the purpose and value of learning activities and assignments. At some level, most of them realize that school activities are designed with their own best interests in mind, but many of them will not appreciate the relevance or potential application value of learning unless it is pointed out to them.

To help apathetic students develop and sustain more positive attitudes toward school work, teach them strategies for making work more enjoyable or satisfying and for sustaining their efforts through volitional control. If they experience learning activities as aversive even though these activities are well suited to their current abilities and needs, help them to understand that they are causing their own problems—that their negative experiences flow from their own negative attitudes rather than from anything inherent in the work.

Finally, make determined efforts to socialize apathetic students' motivation to learn. With many of these students, you will need to work not only to induce them to *value* motivation to learn, but also to *understand* what this concept means and what it feels like as it is experienced in the process of engaging in learning activities. In this regard, explanations are likely to be helpful and exposure to and discussion of modeled examples (positive and negative) are likely to be even more helpful, but the most helpful strategies of all involve providing apathetic students with opportunities to engage in activities that promote motivation to learn and scaffolding their engagement in those activities in ways that develop their appreciation of learning as empowering and self-actualizing.

REFERENCES

Baumrind, D. (1991). Effective parenting during the early adolescent transition. In P. Cowan & M. Hetherington (Eds.), *Family transitions* (pp. 111–164). Hillsdale, NJ: Erlbaum.

Cameron, C., & Elusorr, S. (1986). *Thank God it's Monday: Making your work fulfilling and finding fulfilling work.* Los Angeles: Jeremy P. Tarcher, Inc.

Cross, S., & Markus, H. (1994). Self-schemas, possible selves, and competent performance. *Journal of Educational Psychology, 86,* 423–438.

Csikzentmihalyi, M. (1993). *The evolving self: A psychology for the third millennium.* New York: HarperCollins.

Damon, W. (1995). *Greater expectations: Overcoming the culture of indulgence in America's homes and schools.* New York: The Free Press.

Dewey, J. (1913). *Interest and effort in education.* Boston: Houghton-Mifflin.

Epstein, J. (1989). Family structures and student motivation: A developmental perspective. In C. Ames & R. Ames (Eds.), *Research on motivation in education* (Vol. 3, pp. 259–295). San Diego: Academic Press.

Furst, E., & Steele, B. (1986). Motivational orientations of older adults in university courses described by factor and cluster analyses. *Journal of Experimental Education, 54,* 193–201.

Gagné, R., Briggs, L., & Wager, W. (1988). *Principles of instructional design* (3rd ed.). New York: Holt, Rinehart & Winston.

Grusec, J., & Goodnow, J. (1994). Impact of parental discipline methods on the child's internalization of values: A reconceptualization of current points of view. *Developmental Psychology, 30,* 4–19.

Hennessey, B., Amabile, T., & Martinage, M. (1989). Immunizing children against the negative effects of reward. *Contemporary Educational Psychology, 14,* 212–227.

Markus, H., & Nurius, P. (1986). Possible selves. *American Psychologist, 41,* 954–969.

Marshall, H. (1988). In pursuit of learning-oriented classrooms. *Teaching and Teacher Education, 4,* 85–98.

McCaslin, M. (1990). Motivated literacy. In J. Zutell & S. McCormick (Eds.), *Literacy theory and research: Analyses for multiple paradigms* (39th yearbook, pp. 35–50). Rochester, NY: National Reading Conference, Inc.

McCaslin, M., & Good, T. (1996). *Listening in classrooms.* New York: HarperCollins.

Nisan, M. (1992). Beyond intrinsic motivation: Cultivating a "sense of the desirable." In F. Oser, A. Dick, & J. Patry (Eds.), *Effective and responsible teaching: The new synthesis* (pp. 126–138). San Francisco: Jossey-Bass.

Oldfather, P. (1992, April). *My body feels completely wrong: Students' experiences when lacking motivation for academic tasks.* Paper presented at the annual meeting of the American Educational Research Association, San Francisco.

Perry, D., & Perry, L. (1983). Social learning, causal attribution, and moral internalization. In J. Bisanz, G. Bisanz, & R. Kail (Eds.), *Learning in children: Progress in cognitive development research* (pp. 105–136). New York: Springer-Verlag.

Thorkildsen, T. (1988). Theories of education among academically able adolescents. *Contemporary Educational Psychology, 13,* 323–330.

Vallacher, R., & Wegner, D. (1987). What do people think they're doing? Action identification and human behavior. *Psychological Review, 94,* 3–15.

Waitley, D., & Witt, R. (1985). *The joy of working.* New York: Dodd, Mead, & Co.

CHAPTER 9

Adapting to Differences in Students' Motivational Patterns

And there is the poignant story of Sandy and math baseball. It appears that Sandy's fears about mathematics began in the third grade when her teacher's favorite mathematics game was a variant on the spelling bee called math baseball. Two captains were appointed from the class, and they chose teams for the game. The teams lined up on either side of the room, lead-off batters closest to the blackboard. The teacher "pitched" a problem and the lead-off batters ran to the blackboard and solved it as fast as they could. The one who came to the correct solution in the shortest time scored a run.

Sandy wasn't a fast runner, so she was usually at a disadvantage before she even started the calculation. And although she was very accurate in doing arithmetic calculations, Sandy was slower than a lot of the other children. So she could never score a run for her team. Even though other pupils didn't say anything to her, Sandy knew she was a liability to her friends, and she grew to dread these episodes of public problem solving. Sandy never recovered her initial enjoyment of mathematics. She couldn't take comfort in the fact that she got the right answers and did well on tests, because in the most important area—respect among friends—she didn't feel successful at all.

(BRUSH, 1990, P. 14)

Sandy's story illustrates two points that are noted later in this chapter in the section on gender differences in motivational patterns: Compared to boys, girls are less likely to be motivated by involvement in competitions and more likely to question their abilities in mathematics. Such gender differences complicate your motivational efforts: Some strategies work well with boys but not with girls, or vice versa. Similar complications can arise when students differ in developmental levels, cognitive or learning styles, or cultural backgrounds.

The math baseball game used in Sandy's classroom violates several important motivational principles, so it is not surprising that it had negative effects on Sandy and probably other students as well. If you avoid such ill-considered "motivational" strategies, you are unlikely to have significant negative effects on students. However, the strategies that you do use may have uneven positive effects because of individual and group differences in students' motivational patterns. To the extent that such differences exist, they may lead you to use different motivational strategies with different students.

THEORETICAL POSITIONS ON GROUP AND INDIVIDUAL DIFFERENCES

A longstanding truism of educational psychology is that learners are individuals and must be treated as such if we expect to optimize their motivation and learning. As an abstract proposition, this statement is compelling. However, we immediately encounter complexities when we seek to apply it to particular students or situations. Over time, a great many claims have been made that teachers need to accommodate this or that dimension of difference among students, but few of these claims have been backed by a significant research base establishing that (1) differences on the dimension are important enough to justify the effort it would take for teachers to assess students and provide differentiated curriculum and instruction to different subgroups; (2) the suggestions made to teachers about differentiating instruction are feasible for implementation under normal classroom conditions; and (3) if provided, such differentiated treatment would serve the long-run best interests of all of the students involved.

For the most part, the motivational strategies suggested in this book are based on psychological principles believed to apply to people in general, regardless of age, gender, social class, race, cultural background, or personal characteristics. Many motivational theorists would expect these strategies to affect all students similarly rather than to produce contrasting reactions in different subgroups. Certain principles might be more relevant to certain situations (e.g., introducing an activity versus providing feedback to students' responses), but the principles would apply to all students.

Other motivational theorists would maintain that efforts to implement motivational principles need to be tailored not only to situations but to students. They might agree that you can use the same basic set of motivational strategies with all students but argue the need to use some strategies more frequently or intensively with students who belong to certain subgroups or have developed certain personal characteristics.

Still other motivational theorists would argue that you face a more complex situation: different students need different motivational strategies because application of any given strategy is likely to increase motivation in some students but decrease it in others. For example, anxious and dependent students respond well to praise and encouragement but not to challenge or criticism, whereas confident and independent students show the opposite pattern. Some students prefer material rewards, others prefer symbolic rewards, and still others prefer special privilege or teacher rewards.

Eden (1975) developed a model that incorporated this idea. His model assumes that, for a given person in a given situation, certain motives are relevant but others are not. Therefore, the effect of tying task engagement to a motive will depend on the relevance of that motive to the person at the time. If task engagement produces a relevant motivational consequence, there is likely to be a (probably substantial) increase in motivation to perform the task. However, if task engagement produces some irrelevant motivational outcome, there is likely to be a (probably small but real) decrease in motivation to perform the task. Eden presented some evidence in support of this model (although not evidence based on students' behavior in classrooms).

Intrinsic motivational theorists might interpret Eden's work as further evidence of the need to provide students with choices of what assignments to do and when and how to do them. Extrinsic motivational theorists might interpret it as further evidence that teachers should not rely on a few incentives but instead offer students a variety of rewards from which to choose, so that all of them will be able to work toward incentives that they find appealing.

These implications are valid as far as they go, but they don't take into account the arguments developed earlier in this book about (1) the limited applicability of intrinsic and extrinsic motivational approaches in classrooms and (2) the need to move beyond catering to students' existing motivational systems in order to develop new ones, especially values and dispositions relating to motivation to learn.

A PERSPECTIVE ON ACCOMMODATING STUDENTS' PREFERENCES

I have already noted that *accommodating students' existing motivational systems does nothing to move them in directions that you would like to see them move.* In addition, there are two other reasons for proceeding cautiously when adapting motivational strategies to student differences. First, *accommodating students' preferences is not the same as meeting their needs.* Several studies have shown that allowing students to choose their own learning methods or arranging to teach them as they prefer to be taught may produce *less* achievement than teaching them in some other way, even if it improves their attitudes toward learning (Clark, 1982; Dorsel, 1975; Hannafin & Sullivan, 1996; Schofield, 1981; Solomon & Kendall, 1979; Trout & Crawley, 1985).

Second, *accommodating students' existing personal characteristics may reinforce those characteristics, including ones that you would prefer to change if possible.* For example, it is tempting to respond reciprocally to passive or alienated students by minimizing your interactions with them—never calling on them during lessons unless they raise their hands and avoiding them during independent work times unless they indicate a need for help. This might maximize both your comfort and that of the students involved, but it would not be in their best interests.

Even where it may be desirable to treat different students differently, your opportunities to do so will be limited unless you teach in a special education resource room or some other setting with a very low student/teacher ratio. If you teach a typical class of 20 or more students, you will have to focus most of your curriculum and instruction on the class as a whole and work at the margins to adapt to individual differences.

With respect to students' motivation, the most important individual differences lie in the degree to which they value what schooling has to offer (and the reasons why they do so), the degree to which they believe that they can meet the demands of schooling if they invest reasonable effort, and the degree to which they emphasize learning goals versus less desirable goals. These aspects of students' motivation have been the focus of the first eight chapters of the book, with Chapters 4 and 8 describing strategies for students who need more intensive or personalized treatment beyond what is recommended for the class as a whole.

The remainder of this chapter will focus on other dimensions that may provide a basis for differentiating your treatment of different individuals or subgroups in your classes. As you read this and any other advice about differentiating your motivational strategies, however, keep in mind that your primary responsibility is to induce your students to move in desirable directions, not just to cater to their current preferences and interests.

In considering the claims and suggestions made to teachers for differentiating curriculum and instruction, I begin with one of the better researched variables: the cognitive style dimension of psychological differentiation.

DIFFERENCES IN PSYCHOLOGICAL DIFFERENTIATION

Cognitive style refers to the ways that people process information and use strategies to respond to tasks. People differ, for example, in their tendencies to attend to global features versus fine details of stimuli, to classify stimuli into a few large categories versus many smaller ones, or to make quick, impulsive decisions versus employing a slower, more painstaking approach to problem solving. Cognitive styles are called styles rather than abilities because they refer to *how* people process information and solve problems, not *how well.*

A cognitive-style dimension that has implications for motivation is *psychological differentiation,* also known as *field dependence versus field independence* or as *global versus analytic perceptual style* (Witkin et al., 1977). People who are low in psychological differentiation *(field dependent)* have difficulty differentiating stimuli from the contexts in which they are embedded, so their perceptions are easily affected by manipulations of the surrounding context. In contrast, people who are high in psychological differentiation *(field independent)* perceive more analytically. They can separate stimuli from context, so their perceptions are less affected when changes in context are introduced.

These differences apply to social perceptions as well as to perceptions of the physical world. Consequently, field-dependent people's perceptions and opinions are strongly affected by those of other people, whereas field-independent people are more likely to resist social pressures and make up their minds on the basis of their own perceptions. In ambiguous social situations, field-dependent people are more attentive to and make more use of prevailing social frames of reference, monitor the faces of others for cues as to what they are thinking, attend more to verbal messages with social content, and get physically closer to and interact more with others. As a result, they tend to be liked by other people and perceived as warm, tactful, considerate, socially outgoing, and affectionate. In contrast, field-independent people have a more abstract, theoretical, analytical, and impersonal orientation. This makes them more able to resist external pressures toward conformity, but also more likely to be perceived as cold, distant, or insensitive.

In classrooms, field-dependent students tend to prefer to learn in groups and to interact frequently with teachers, whereas field-independent students prefer more independent and individualized learning opportunities. They also tend to prefer and do better in mathematics and science, whereas field-dependent students tend to prefer and do better in the humanities and social sciences.

Most students do not consistently reflect these extremes of psychological differentiation, but they may tend more toward one set of attributes than the other. To the extent that they do, they are likely to be happier in school if they spend most of their time focusing on content and learning within formats matched to their preferences. However, it is not clear that such differentiated treatment would serve their long-run best interests. Extremely field-independent students have social adjustment problems, and extremely field-dependent students are conforming to the point that they seem to lack minds of their own. These students might be better off in the long run if they could learn to appreciate and function more frequently in their nonpreferred orientation.

Therefore, learn to recognize and respect both orientations and to build on students' strengths but also work on their areas of weakness. You might structure field-dependent students' learning experiences enough to enable them to cope effectively, provide frequent encouragement and praise, be supportive when noting their mistakes, and allow them to learn in collaboration with peers most of the time. Field-independent students do not need as much personal support and encouragement, although they will require explicit feedback. With these students, it may be more important for you to respect their needs for privacy and distance, to avoid penalizing them unreasonably for low social participation, and to allow them frequent opportunities to operate autonomously.

LEARNING STYLE DIFFERENCES

Much attention has been focused on the notion of learning styles, especially by people who offer workshops or sell materials purported to help teachers assess their students' learning styles and follow up with differentiated curriculum and instruction. Learning style inventories address questions such as the following: Are the students "verbal learners" who prefer to listen to information or "visual learners" who prefer to read it or see it displayed graphically? Do they prefer to learn alone or with others? Do they prefer to study for frequent short periods or fewer longer periods? Do they like to study in silence, with soothing musical or white noise backgrounds, or in potentially distracting environments (i.e., amid people who are conversing or next to a playing radio or television)?

For example, McCarthy (1980, 1990) identified four learning style types by locating students on two dimensions: perceiving (concrete sensing/feeling versus more abstract thinking) and processing (active doing versus reflective watching). Combinations of high and low scores on these dimensions produce the following four learning styles:

1. *Imaginative learners* perceive information concretely and process it reflectively. They listen, share, and seek to integrate school experience with self experience.
2. *Analytic learners* perceive information abstractly and process it reflectively. They appreciate both details and ideas, tend to think sequentially, and value ideas more than people.
3. *Commonsense learners* perceive information abstractly and process it actively. They tend to be pragmatic learners who value concrete problem solving and like to "tinker" and experiment to learn by discovery.
4. *Dynamic learners* perceive information concretely and process it actively. They tend to integrate experience and application, are enthusiastic about new learning, ready to engage in trial-and-error learning, and adept at risk taking.

McCarthy designed the 4MAT system of instruction as a way to accommodate these differences in students' preferences and strengths and thus to improve their motivation and achievement. She reported positive results from an intervention done with elementary students.

The 4MAT system is a model for designing units of study that accommodate the four learning styles as well as the supposed hemispheric (left- versus right-brain) preferences of students. Intended to be applicable to any content area or grade level, it calls for an eight-step cycle of instruction and learning activities relating to the unit topic. Each of the four learning styles is represented by two steps in the cycle, one designed to facilitate right-brain learning and the other to facilitate left-brain learning. According to McCarthy, if the teacher follows the full cycle, each individual student's learning style will be addressed during at least one-fourth of the instructional time. During other parts of the cycle the learner will be "stretched," learning other ways to solve problems and thus developing a broader repertoire of problem-solving skills.

Wilkerson and White (1988) tested the 4MAT system against a more conventional treatment of a science unit on machines taught to third graders. The 4MAT version was constructed by taking the lessons and activities from the teacher's edition of the textbook and reworking them into the eight-step 4MAT cycle as follows:

Step 1: Students visualize machines they have experienced in everyday life, then draw pictures of these mental images (right mode lesson for innovative learners).

Step 2: Students work in small groups to discuss how the machines they have drawn make their work easier (left mode lesson for innovative learners).

Step 3: Students view a filmstrip depicting six simple machines used in everyday life, then draw pictures of the machines. Also, teacher holds up various objects (e.g., fishing reel, scissors) and students point to pictures of the same types of machines as the objects being shown (right mode lesson for analytic learners).

Step 4: Using the overhead projector, the teacher explains characteristics of each of the six simple machines. Then, students use a flannel board to match new words from the unit with their definitions (left mode lesson for analytic learners).

Step 5: Teacher reads students a book about machines. Then the students complete three worksheets reviewing concepts taught in Steps 4 and 5 (left mode lesson for commonsense learners).

Step 6: Wooden models of simple machines, examples of compound machines, and task cards are placed at work stations. Working in groups of three or four, students examine the machines and discuss potential responses to questions written on the task cards (right mode lesson for commonsense learners).

Step 7: Each student is given a plastic bag containing 11 word cards. The teacher asks questions about machines and the students answer by holding up one of their word cards. Then, each student is given a piece of transparency film and asked to draw a compound machine that would make work easier (left mode lesson for dynamic learners).

Step 8: The pieces of transparency film are used to make a film strip that is shown to the class. As their drawings come up, individual students explain to the class how the machines they drew would work (right mode lesson for dynamic learners).

While the 4MAT group was working through this cycle, students in the conventional group read from the textbook, provided oral and written responses to questions based on this material, and engaged in activities that included making a lever, conducting an experiment on inclined planes, completing a crossword puzzle that reviewed the six simple machines, making a bar graph showing the numbers of machines found in their homes, and watching a commercial filmstrip about machines. Assessment data indicated that both groups of students enjoyed the unit, although the 4MAT students tended to like more of the activities they experienced. Also, the 4MAT students showed higher scores on an objective test measuring achievement of content knowledge, comprehension, application, and analysis objectives. However, there were no significant group differences on a test of synthesis and evaluation abilities that required students to draw a compound machine that would crack an egg or feed goldfish, list steps involved in operating the machine, and state reasons why someone would or would not want to purchase it. Thus, the

4MAT approach produced modest but favorable effects on students' attitudes and achievement.

McCarthy and the 4MAT system are relatively unusual within the learning styles literature, for at least three reasons. First, intervention studies based on the system were done with elementary students and encompassed a significant portion of the curriculum and instruction that they experienced. In contrast, most learning style studies have been done at the high school and (especially) the college level and many interventions have been restricted to variations in study or test environments.

Second, reports of research on the 4MAT system have been published in respected research journals. Unfortunately, most of the sources cited by advocates of learning styles are either position pieces unsupported by classroom research or dissertations and other unpublished studies (Bennett, 1995; Dunn & Dunn, 1992; Dunn et al., 1995). Critics have noted that the credibility of learning styles enthusiasts is questionable because of their tendency to make outlandish claims for the effectiveness of the measurement inventories and instructional models they sell, that most of the studies purporting to support learning style approaches are too flawed to survive the peer review standards of research journals, and that most of these studies have been conducted by people with vested interests in positive results who gave instructions to the participants in learning style treatment groups designed to maximize their enthusiasm and positive expectations (Curry, 1990; Kavale & Forness, 1990; O'Neil, 1990).

Finally, McCarthy noted the need for teachers to help students stretch themselves to function in learning modes that they use infrequently. Unfortunately, the advice offered by most learning style advocates only emphasizes catering to students' existing preferences, without recognizing that this might not be in their long-run best interests.

Like most other reviewers who pay close attention to the research literature, I do not see much validity in the claims made by those who urge teachers to assess their students with learning style inventories and follow up with differentiated curriculum and instruction. First, the research bases supporting these urgings tend to be thin to nonexistent. Second, a single teacher working with 20 or more students does not have time to plan and implement much individualized instruction. With respect to student motivation, much more is to be gained by focusing on students' learning goals, values, and expectancies than on the variables emphasized in learning style inventories.

Similar comments apply to schemes for differentiating instruction according to student profiles developed using supposed measures of cognitive styles, brain hemisphere preferences, or multiple intelligences. These individual difference concepts can be useful to teachers if adopted only loosely and used primarily as reminders of the value of including a variety of learning activities and formats in the curriculum. However, scientific validity and practical feasibility problems arise if such concepts are emphasized to the extent of seeking to develop individual curricular prescriptions for each student.

However, it is worth keeping your students' preferences in mind and accommodating them by providing opportunities for autonomy and choice whenever doing so would support progress toward learning goals. Sometimes such accommodation is not feasible or advisable. For example, in order to attain certain learning goals students must engage in processes that they might prefer to avoid (e.g., presentations to the class, debates, cooperative work on a group project). Or, you might have to limit certain students' opportunities to pursue favorite topics or learn in their preferred mode, because if the students spent too much time indulging these preferences they would fail to develop knowledge or skills needed in school or in life generally. You can accommodate such preferences much of the time, however, and doing so will increase your students' opportunities to experience intrinsic motivation in your classroom (see Box 9.1).

CHANGES WITH AGE IN STUDENTS' MOTIVATIONAL PATTERNS

Different grade levels present somewhat different motivational challenges to teachers because of age-related changes in students' motivational patterns. Most students begin schooling enthusiastically, but then show progressive deterioration on measures of school-related attitudes, curiosity, and intrinsic motivation (Engelhard & Monsaas, 1988; Harter, 1992; Wigfield, 1994).

In addition, most students in the early grades show positive (actually, unrealistically high) self-concepts and success expectations. These inflated self-perceptions of ability persist until about age seven, when they begin to show more consistent relationships with test scores and other more objective measures. As students become better at understanding and interpreting the feedback they receive, and as they begin to compare themselves with peers, their self-assessments become more accurate or realistic (Stipek, 1984a; Stipek & MacIver, 1989). To the extent that they begin to experience failure and understand its implications, they become susceptible to learned helplessness and other failure syndrome problems. However, even students who doubt their abilities usually do not begin to give up consistently when they encounter difficulties until they are about 10 years old (Nicholls & Miller, 1984).

Young children's unrealistically positive self-perceptions reflect more than mere childish egocentricity. Developments in their processing of performance feedback and related attributional thinking lead to shifts from intrinsic motivation to a focus on grades, from carefree optimism to social comparison and realism in judging achievement, and (for many students) from an emphasis on effort and an incremental view of ability to an emphasis on ability viewed as a stable entity. Younger students attend primarily to their own accomplishments rather than to those of classmates, so they tend to feel competent and successful if they complete a task or show improvement in their work. They tend to attribute success more to effort than ability, and to believe that they can increase their levels of ability by investing the effort needed to do so. As they develop, however, they begin to see effort and ability as inversely related.

Box 9.1.   Preferences Identified as Elements of Learning Styles

One problem with the notion of learning styles and its potential application in classrooms is the seemingly limitless variety of learner preferences and other potential bases for learning styles. Listed below are just some of the dimensions identified in the learning styles literature:

- Type of lighting (natural, incandescent, fluorescent).
- Brightness of lighting.
- Sound (quiet, various types of music, radio or TV, ambient noise in social settings).
- Room temperature and humidity.
- Seating accommodations (desks, straightbacked chairs, easy chairs, pillows on floor, etc.).
- Body position while studying (standing, sitting, reclining).
- Need for imposed structure versus desire to do things in one's own way.
- Preferring to learn alone, with a partner, in a small group, as part of a team, or with an adult or expert tutor.
- Preferring an adult or expert tutor to act in an authoritative versus a collegial manner.
- Preference for routine and predictability versus variety and unpredictability.
- Preference for certain learning modalities over others (visual, auditory, tactile, kinesthetic).
- Variations in alertness levels and readiness to study connected to time of day.
- Preferring to sit still versus move around while learning.
- Global versus analytic information processing style.
- Right- versus left-brain information processing style.

- Impulsive versus reflective style of processing information or making decisions.
- Preference for sustained study periods versus shorter periods interspersed with frequent breaks.
- Opportunity to eat, drink, or chew on something while studying.
- Working on one thing at a time until it is finished versus enjoying working on several things simultaneously and leaving many things unfinished.
- Conforming versus resistant to authority.
- Preferring to be taught directly versus to discover for self.
- Preferring to develop a close relationship with the teacher versus to maintain a distance.
- Relying on intuition and insight versus inductive or deductive reasoning.
- Getting started right away versus requiring warm-up.
- Evaluation mode preferences (short answer tests, essay tests, portfolios, projects).
- Preferring individual versus cooperative versus competitive task structures.
- Oriented toward extrinsic rewards versus intrinsic satisfactions.
- Confident, exploratory, willing to learn from mistakes versus anxious, teacher-dependent, perfectionistic.
- Focusing on the big picture versus the details.
- Preferring deductive, rule-example sequence versus inductive, example-rule sequence.
- Focusing on people using narrative approaches versus focusing on things using analytic approaches.
- Preferring whole versus part learning of complex skills (observing demonstrations of the complete sequence

(Continued)

Box 9.1.   Preferences Identified as Elements of Learning Styles—*Concluded*

and then attempting to duplicate it versus taking one step at a time).

- Preferring receptive learning by watching and listening versus active learning by doing.
- Emphasizing rote memorizing versus generative learning strategies.

For most of these variables (and many others that could have been listed), there is little or no classroom-based research to support claims that matching instruction to student preferences will produce significant improvements in learning outcomes. Even if there were an abundance of such evidence, however, few teachers would have the time and resources needed to assess students on these so-called learning style variables, develop individual prescriptions, and proceed accordingly.

However, you can accommodate many of these preferences by avoiding unnecessarily rigid behavioral requirements and by providing students with opportunities to exercise autonomy and make choices in self-regulating their learning. Within limits, for example, rules regulating behavior when working on assignments might allow students to move around the room, collaborate with peers, or leave their desk to work somewhere else. Choice options might include variations not only in topics but in the kinds of information processing required (visual versus auditory input or output, focus on the big picture versus attention to detail, etc.). In general, unless you become aware of good reasons not to, you probably should accommodate students' requests or demonstrated preferences for opportunities to engage in certain kinds of learning or styles of working.

By the time they reach seventh grade, most are well aware that the need to expend considerable effort on a task implies limitations in domain-related abilities (Shell, Colvin, & Bruning, 1995).

Young children's inflated perceptions of their own competence and lack of sophistication in making social comparisons and interpreting feedback provide certain advantages to primary-grade teachers. For one thing, their students are less susceptible to learned helplessness problems because failure does not faze them the way it fazes older students who are more aware of its potential implications (Miller, 1985; Rholes et al., 1980). Also, younger students are less likely to feel embarrassed or to infer that their teacher believes that they lack ability if they are encouraged or praised for effort (Barker & Graham, 1987; Lord, Umezaki, & Darley, 1990).

These findings imply that primary-grade teachers can afford to be more spontaneous in scaffolding their students' learning, giving them feedback, and praising both their efforts and their accomplishments. Even so, teachers in these grades should follow the praising guidelines given in Chapter 5. They also should provide primarily informative rather than evaluative feedback and focus their students' attention on appreciating their accomplishments to date and building on them in the future, not on comparisons with classmates. If feedback emphasizes social comparisons or normative evaluations, even kindergarten students will experience failure and begin to lower their self-evaluations of ability (Butler, 1990; Licht, 1992; Stipek & Daniels, 1988).

Transitional Grades

Within the general trend of steady decreases in intrinsic motivation and self-perceptions of ability, there is a tendency for noteworthy drops to occur when students shift from elementary to middle or junior high schools, or from middle or junior high schools to high schools. Negative effects on motivation are especially likely following the first shift, because it entails movement from a more supportive to a less supportive learning environment (Anderman & Maehr, 1994; Eccles, 1993; Eccles et al., 1993; Harter, Whitesell, & Kowalski, 1992; Mergendoller, 1993). Compared to elementary classrooms, middle school and junior high classrooms confront students with greater emphasis on teacher control and discipline; fewer opportunities to engage in decision making, choice, or self-management; less personal and positive teacher–student relationships; more frequent use of practices such as whole-class teaching, ability grouping, and public evaluation of work; and more stringent standards for grading. The enhanced salience of performance feedback and social comparison, within the context of a new reference group, causes many students to reevaluate their academic abilities.

Adjustments to new levels of schooling need not be so stressful or destructive to students' motivation. When middle and junior high schools provide more personalized and supportive environments suited to their students' psychological needs, the students do not demonstrate the same declines in motivation or increases in rates of misconduct seen in more traditional schools (Bryk, Lee, & Smith, 1990; Dreyfoos, 1990; Eccles & Midgley, 1989).

School-level changes such as creating schools within schools and smaller learning environments, block scheduling and flexible use of time, and assigning an adult advisor to each student can help ease transitions to higher levels of schooling. Even more importantly, teachers can establish their classrooms as learning communities and incorporate the strategies built into the TARGET program, as described in Chapter 2. In particular, teachers at higher school levels who work with transitional students just entering from lower levels should go out of their way to welcome these students, make them feel comfortable in their new surroundings, and scaffold their learning efforts in ways that help them to feel confident that they will be able to meet the challenges that face them.

Developments in Children's Interests

Educators have studied children's interests because connecting with those interests is one way to stimulate intrinsic motivation and perhaps motivation to learn. Jersild and Tasch (1949) conducted a massive survey of the interests of students in Grades 1–12, and numerous smaller studies have also been conducted (Hurlock, 1964). These studies indicated that interests become differentiated with age, so that younger students have more interests in common than older students. At all ages, however, students tend to be more interested in stories and other content dealing with people than in content dealing with impersonal topics, and to prefer learning experiences that involve active doing over those that are confined to watching and listening.

Students' responses to questions about their interests are heavily influenced by their prior experiences. Consequently, these responses say more about the students' past exposure to interest-generating experiences than about their probable responses to potential future experiences. Even so, certain documented trends are worth noting.

Primary-grade students' interests center on themselves and their personal and family experiences. In school, they tend to prefer language arts, mathematics, and art over science, social studies, and local or world news. For reading, they tend to enjoy stories about other children and familiar experiences; tales of fantasy, fun, and humor; and narratives featuring acts of kindness or bravery.

Students in the intermediate grades tend to be more interested in realistic stories—tales of adventure, sportsmanship, or the work of inventors. They also develop interests in nature study and natural science, and more generally, in science and social studies topics. They tend to become interested in subjects in which they are successful, but develop negative attitudes toward subjects that are difficult for them. Whereas younger students talk mostly about their own play and recreation or their family and home activities, students in the middle grades talk more about family vacations and other trips away from the local setting, books they have been reading, and television, movies, and other entertainment and youth culture activities.

These trends continue as students progress through secondary schools but their interests broaden to include topics from history and the social sciences and current events in the news, including events occurring in other parts of the world. High school students also develop interests in self-improvement, self-understanding, and vocations. The emergence of these interests reflects progression from a primary focus on competence (i.e., What are my areas of strength and weakness?) to a primary focus on identity issues (i.e., What kind of person do I want to become, in terms of personal values, lifestyle, occupation, etc.?).

The curriculum scope and sequence followed in most school districts is reasonably well matched to students' developing knowledge and interests. Even so, you can generate additional opportunities to connect with their interests by administering and following up on interest inventories and by allowing for choices of topics for reading assignments and learning projects. Authors of children's literature tend to be well attuned to the interests and imaginations of the age groups that they write for, as do many authors of educational software. Consequently, it is worth your while to familiarize yourself with literature selections and computerized learning programs that are especially appealing to students at your grade level. Also, keep in touch with other teachers and with librarians for suggestions in these areas.

Developments in Students' Preferences Regarding Curriculum and Instruction

Many younger students find it difficult to sustain attention to lengthy activities, especially information presentations. Consequently, it is wise to emphasize hands-on learning activities in the early grades, to keep presentations and discussions relatively short, and to intersperse them with activities that call for more active forms of learning.

Older students can sustain attention to longer presentations and discussions, and they often enjoy doing so. However, they become increasingly impatient with presentations that mostly require them to commit transmitted information to memory. Instead, they want more interactive discussion of curricular topics, including discussion of their controversial aspects (Nicholls, Nelson, & Gleaves, 1995).

GENDER DIFFERENCES

As children develop in our society, they are exposed to *gender role socialization* suggesting that certain family and social roles, occupations, personal attributes, and ways of dressing and behaving are primarily feminine, while others are primarily masculine. Gender role socialization pervades most children's experiences. It is modeled by the individuals they encounter in their personal lives and in the media, expressed directly in the messages they receive from their parents and peers (and sometimes their teachers), and reinforced through communication of expectations concerning such things as the toys and games they will want to play with, the books they will enjoy reading, or the things that they will want to do in school or in their free time.

In response to the Women's Movement and other social forces, there has been a loosening of the more restrictive aspects of traditional gender roles in the U.S. over the last 50 years. Even so, many activities are still associated primarily with one gender or the other. To the extent that an activity is gender typed, teachers' and students' attitudes and expectations are likely to be affected. They may anticipate gender differences in interest and enjoyment in the activity, and perhaps also in success expectancies and performance attributions (if the gender typing is based on notions of gender differences in ability). Such gender typing has been noted in several aspects of schooling.

One of these involves subject-matter preferences and related motivational responses. Most studies find that boys value and enjoy mathematics and science more than language arts, but girls show the opposite pattern (Brush, 1980; Wigfield, 1993). Some researchers view these differences merely as carry-overs from traditional socialization designed to prepare boys primarily to be breadwinners but girls primarily to be wives and mothers. They point to evidence of reductions in gender differences in recent years and suggest that further reductions can be expected to occur naturally in response to continued reductions in gender role specialization in the home and workplace.

Others urge teachers to try to reduce gender differences in response to school subjects, especially if the differences encompass not only preferences or value perceptions but also beliefs about ability and related attributional inferences. Concern is greatest with respect to science and especially mathematics, where several investigators have found that girls believe themselves to possess less domain-specific ability than boys, or that girls are more likely than boys to attribute their successes to luck or other external factors but to attribute their failures to lack of ability (Bornholt, Goodnow, & Cooney, 1994; Eccles et al., 1989; Ryckman & Peckham, 1987; Stipek, 1984b; Stipek & Gralinski, 1991).

This pattern of subject-matter differences in gender-related attitudes and beliefs develops over time, so it is more noticeable in junior high and high school students than in elementary students. Occasionally, somewhat different patterns appear. For example, Licht, Stader, and Swenson (1989) found that fifth-grade girls rated themselves as less smart than boys in social studies and science, but not in mathematics or reading. They attributed this finding to the fact that at fifth grade, the performance feedback that students receive for social studies and science is less frequent and more ambiguous than the feedback they receive for mathematics and reading, so the students' self-ratings of ability are more dependent on their general assumptions or beliefs than on specific data.

This interpretation is supported by other studies showing that, especially in the early grades, boys are more likely to have higher (although not necessarily more accurate) ability perceptions and future success expectations than girls. Boys also are more likely to credit their successes to high ability but attribute their failures to bad luck, lack of interest, low effort, or other causes that do not imply a lack of ability (Blatchford, 1992; Eccles, 1987; Miller, 1986; Nicholls, 1979). These differences make girls more vulnerable to learned helplessness and other failure syndrome problems than boys, especially in subjects like mathematics or science where the girls might suspect limitations in their domain-specific abilities.

In any case, it is clear that starting around fifth grade and continuing thereafter, girls' ability beliefs and expectancies for future success in mathematics and science tend to drop below those of boys, even though their grades in these subjects are as good or better than boys' grades. Girls also are more likely to opt out of mathematics and science classes when they begin to get the opportunity to do so, thus cutting themselves off from future career opportunities that require academic preparation in these subjects. These patterns develop at least as much among brighter girls as among other girls.

Boys generally place less value on engaging in academic activities than girls do, so that the quality of their engagement is more variable. They are more likely than girls to adopt work-avoidant goals or display task resistance. When they adopt learning or performance goals, however, they are likely to focus on achieving mastery or competitive success. In contrast, girls are more likely to focus on consistently putting forth their best efforts and pleasing their teachers (Berndt & Miller, 1990; Blatchford, 1992; Boggiano, Main, & Katz, 1991; Bouffard et al., 1995; Harter, 1975; Meece & Holt, 1993; Van Hecke & Tracy, 1983). Again, these differences do not always appear (Urdan & Maehr, 1995; Van Hecke et al., 1984). However, they show up often enough to be cause for concern because they further contribute to girls' vulnerability to learned helplessness (because girls more consistently put forth their best efforts and therefore tend to attribute failures to lack of ability, whereas boys more consistently credit their successes to high ability but explain away their failures).

Other research has focused on gender differences in student behavior and teacher–student interaction patterns in classrooms (Brophy, 1985; Good & Brophy, 1995). These studies indicate that boys are more active and salient in the classroom than girls. They have more of almost every kind of interaction that occurs between students and teachers, although the differences are greatest for interactions that boys initiate themselves by calling out answers or by misbehaving and drawing some form of teacher intervention. However, teachers also initiate interactions more frequently with boys, especially to give them procedural instructions, check their progress on assignments, or generally monitor and control their activities.

Along with differences in the quantity of teacher–student interaction, researchers have identified qualitative differences in the ways in which teachers interact with boys versus girls. In particular, words of encouragement or feedback directed to boys tend to focus exclusively on their achievement striving and accomplishments, but some of what is said to girls in parallel situations focuses instead on neatness, following directions, speaking clearly, or showing good manners. Teachers sometimes pay more attention to, ask more thought-provoking questions of, or provide more extensive feedback to boys in mathematics or science classes but to girls in language arts classes. When groups of students work on computers or carry out scientific experiments, boys are more likely to take active roles but girls are more likely to act as recorders or just observers.

These trends are observed in varying degrees in almost all classrooms, regardless of whether the teachers are male or female. Thus, they are rooted in the gender role expectations that most people acquire through socialization into our culture. Sadker and Sadker (1994) suggested that many of these differences reflect gender differences in styles of participation in social conversation that are pervasive in our society and thus carry over into classrooms: (1) men speak more often and frequently interrupt women; (2) listeners pay more attention to male speakers, even when female speakers use similar styles and make similar points; (3) women participate less actively in conversations but do more gazing and passive listening; and (4) women often transform declarative statements into more tentative statements that reduce their ability to influence others (e.g., "We could solve this problem using the Pythagorean Theorem, couldn't we?").

Clear-cut teacher favoritism of one gender over the other is rare. Gender differences in teacher–student interaction patterns tend to be relatively small in quantity and subtle in quality. Furthermore, most of them reflect gender differences in student behaviors that impact on teachers, rather than consistent teacher tendencies to treat boys and girls differently in parallel situations. Even so, it is wise to remain conscious of gender issues and to monitor your interactions with boys versus girls. This will help you not only to avoid inappropriate gender discrimination but also to take advantage of opportunities to free your students from some of the counterproductive restrictions built into traditional gender role concepts.

With regard to subject matter, help your boys to take full advantage of reading and writing opportunities, and in particular, to appreciate poetry and other forms of literature that they might view as feminine. Similarly, help your girls to value and develop their full potential in mathematics and science. Stimulate their interest in and willingness to take courses in these subjects and help them to realize that they have the abilities to enable them to be successful in these subjects if they apply reasonable effort.

Also, where necessary, encourage girls to become more active in the classroom. Make systematic efforts to observe and get to know each girl as an individual (especially girls who achieve satisfactorily and appear to be well adjusted but rarely initiate contact with you or assert themselves in the classroom). Encourage these girls to speak their minds, call on them to participate if they do not volunteer, assign them to leadership roles for group projects, and take other actions to encourage them to become more assertive. Broaden their perspectives by helping them to realize that the full spectrum of career opportunities is open to them and by using learning experiences such as stories involving females in leadership positions or discussions or assignments focusing on the work of female scientists.

DIFFERENCES IN FAMILY AND CULTURAL BACKGROUNDS

Students from lower social class backgrounds or from racial or ethnic minority groups may experience difficulties at school to the extent that the values, language, behavioral expectations, and other aspects of the school culture contrast with what these students have been exposed to in their families and local subcultures. However, these difficulties can be minimized by teachers who are knowledgeable about and respectful of their students' home cultures and who work with the assets that the students bring to school with them rather than treating these as deficiencies or problems.

Theory and research on these issues have developed in ways that reflect these distinctions. Early studies focused on group comparisons and yielded conclusions suggesting, for example, that lower-class students preferred material rewards whereas middle-class students preferred intrinsic rewards, that Hispanic students were oriented toward cooperative learning, that Native American students responded negatively to public praise, and that African-

American students had lower success expectations and less favorable attribution patterns than other students.

Subsequent research indicated that these and other sweeping statements about group differences were either incorrect or exaggerated, and that in any case, general sociological categories such as social class, race, ethnicity, or minority group membership were not nearly as useful as knowledge about individual students' family backgrounds and home cultures for understanding and suggesting ways to improve their adjustment to schooling. When researchers focused on specific families, and especially on the frequency and nature of the interactions that children had with their parents, they discovered many dimensions of family life and home culture that affect the degree to which children are comfortable at school, prepared to meet its challenges successfully, and confident in their ability to do so (Ginsburg & Bronstein, 1993; Grolnick & Ryan, 1989; Hess & Holloway, 1984; Hokoda & Fincham, 1995).

Many of these family factors that affect students' motivation at school are included in Joyce Epstein's (1989) TARGET model that led to Carole Ames's TARGET intervention model described in Chapter 2. Epstein referred to the TARGET variables as family structures. The six structures and some of their influences on student motivation are as follows.

Task structure: The task structure includes all activities conducted at home that may be related to school learning (e.g., household chores, play and hobby activities, school assignments done as homework, learning opportunities designed by the parents). Some families do much more than others to prepare their children for school and support their schooling experiences. They interact with their children frequently in cognitively stimulating ways, provide them with instruction and learning opportunities suited to their developmental levels (e.g., reading to them, teaching them to tell time and tie shoe laces, or teaching them the letters of the alphabet or how to write their names during the preschool years, and discussing their school work with them in later years), expose them to educational games and media at home, take them to museums and zoos, and encourage their talents and interests. Interaction around these activities builds important knowledge and skills and also has positive effects on children's developing curiosity, interest, attitudes toward school, acceptance of challenge, and tendency to engage in activities with learning goals rather than less desirable goals.

Authority structure: The authority structure concerns the types and frequencies of children's responsibilities, self-directed activities, and opportunities to participate in family decision making. Families support their children's development of desirable motivational patterns by using authoritative childrearing methods that include age-appropriate sharing of authority, negotiation of rules and expectations, and opportunities for children to make their own decisions. These home experiences develop desirable motivational patterns on variables such as locus of control, personal responsibility, efficacy perceptions, tendency to seek success and not fear failure, and orientation toward self-regulated learning (but with readiness to interact effectively with teachers and participate in discussions and projects with other students). Families that rely on authoritarian or laissez-faire childrearing methods develop less desirable motivational patterns in their children.

Reward structure: The reward structure refers to the degree to which parents pay attention to and reward their children's efforts and accomplishments. Parents support their children's school motivation by emphasizing encouragement and reward over threat and punishment, and by focusing their encouragement and rewards on school-related accomplishments (not just accomplishments in sports or other areas). It also helps if parents recognize improvement as well as excellence, cooperative as well as competitive behavior, and intrinsic satisfactions as well as extrinsic rewards.

Grouping structure: Students' readiness to get along and collaborate with peers is affected by the degree to which their families encourage them to display nurturing behavior (in caring for younger siblings or elderly family members, for example), monitor their interactions with peers and teach them to negotiate plans and resolve disagreements productively, model tolerance and appreciation of diversity, and help them to balance responsibilities to peers with responsibilities to parents, teachers, and others in their lives.

Evaluation structure: The evaluation structure concerns the standards set for learning and behavior, the procedures used for monitoring and evaluating attainment of those standards, and the methods used to provide feedback about accomplishments and needed improvements. Supportive parental activities within this structure include emphasizing private and informative feedback over public and evaluative judgments, being flexible in adjusting standards to accommodate developments in children's abilities, and discussing the reasons for and implications of these developments in ways that help children to appreciate their accomplishments and set appropriate goals in the future.

Time structure: The time structure concerns the schedules that families set for their children's activities and assignments. Especially when children have busy schedules (music lessons, sports, homework, chores, etc.), it is important for them to learn to develop realistic plans and manage their time effectively. Parents need to see that their children have sufficient time to do all of the things that they are expected to do, but also to see that these things are in fact accomplished and that a high priority is placed on school-related tasks if time is tight.

When parents fail to do these things that help prepare children for school and support their progress as students, it is usually because they do not realize their importance or know how to do them. Most parents care about their children's success at school and will respond positively to information sharing and requests from teachers. Furthermore, one of the distinctive features of the teachers and schools that are most effective with students at risk for school failure is that they reach out to these students' families, get to know them, keep them informed of what is going on at school, and involve them in decision making.

It is important to establish collaborative relationships with all of your students' parents, but especially with the parents of students who are struggling, apathetic, or resistant to you or your curriculum. The parents may have had similar problems in school themselves, may feel guilty about their child's problems, or may be inhibited or suspicious at first in dealing with you (if they view teachers primarily as authority figures capable of getting their child into trouble). However, they are likely to be grateful and become more responsive if they see that you care about their child and want to work with them to pursue the child's best interests, not merely to give them bad news and then expect them to "do something."

The same is true of their child. Minority students and others whose family backgrounds place them at risk for school failure do especially well with teachers who share warm, personal interactions with them but also hold high expectations for their academic progress, require them to perform up to their capabilities, and see that they progress as far and as fast as they are able. These teachers break through social-class differences, cultural differences, language differences, and other potential barriers to communication in order to form close relationships with at-risk students, but they use these relationships to maximize the students' academic progress, not merely to provide friendship or sympathy to them (Delpit, 1992; Hayes, Ryan, & Zseller, 1994; Kleinfeld, 1975; Siddle-Walker, 1992).

At-risk students also do especially well in classrooms that offer warm, inviting social environments. Therefore, help your students to value diversity, learn from one another, and appreciate different languages and traditions. Treat the cultures that they bring to school as assets that provide students with foundations of background knowledge to support their learning efforts and provide you with opportunities to enrich the curriculum for everyone. Think in terms of helping minority students to become fully bicultural rather than in terms of replacing one culture with another. If you are unfamiliar with a culture that is represented in your classroom, educate yourself by reading about it, talking with community leaders, visiting homes, and most importantly, talking with students to learn about their past history and future aspirations.

For example, Moll (1992) interviewed the families of students enrolled in a bilingual education class to identify resources available in the community that might be capitalized upon at the school, which was located in a primarily Spanish-speaking minority community. He identified the following "funds of knowledge" possessed by members of these households: ranching and farming (horsemanship, animal husbandry, soil and irrigation systems, crop planting, hunting, tracking, dressing game); mining (timbering, minerals, blasting, equipment operation and maintenance); economics (business, market values, appraising, renting and selling, loans, labor laws, building codes, consumer knowledge, accounting, sales); household management (budgets, child care, cooking, appliance repairs); material and scientific knowledge (construction, carpentry, roofing, masonry, painting, design and architecture); repairs (airplane, automobile, tractor, house maintenance); contemporary medicine (drugs, first-aid procedures, anatomy, midwifery); folk medicine (herbal knowledge, folk cures); and religion (catechism, baptisms, bible studies, moral knowledge and ethics).

Moll noted that teachers could usefully integrate these funds of knowledge into classrooms through such activities as having students do research on community issues, understanding the architectural principles used in building community houses, or developing awareness of how the community functioned socially. He also emphasized the value of integrating parents intellectually into the life of the school. Similarly, Leacock (1969) noted that opportunities for connecting the curriculum to the students' home backgrounds often are missed because instruction stays too close to what is in the textbooks. As an example, she noted "community helpers" lessons in elementary social studies classes. Usually at least some students in a class, and frequently a great many students, have parents who are police officers, fire fighters, postal workers, and other service workers studied in these units, but few teachers think to invite these parents to come to the classroom and speak with the students about their jobs.

If necessary, modify your curricula to infuse a multicultural perspective and feature the cultures represented by your students. Modifications might include a somewhat different selection of content (especially in history and literature) as well as treatment of many more topics as issues open to multiple perspectives rather than as bodies of factual information that admit to only a single interpretation. In covering cultures and customs, emphasize instructional materials that focus on universal human experiences and parallels between comparable cultural practices over materials that encourage chauvinism by focusing on exotic practices. Expose students to literature or multimedia content sources that not only feature models who come from minority groups represented in your classroom but also portray these models in ways that encourage all students to identify with them. In addition, expose your students to actual, living models by arranging for classroom speakers, field trips, or current events discussions that will raise minority students' consciousness of roles and accomplishments to which they might aspire.

Knapp (1995) analyzed ways in which teachers working in ethnically heterogeneous classrooms responded to the cultural diversity of their students. Some teachers did not respond constructively because they held negative stereotypes of certain ethnic or socioeconomic groups. These stereotypes led them to treat students from these groups in ways that limited their learning opportunities and communicated low expectations.

In contrast, constructive teachers held more positive expectations of their students and possessed a basic knowledge of their cultures. The most effective ones explicitly accommodated the students' cultural heritages by communicating to them that their cultural backgrounds were not problems to be overcome but rather strengths to be acknowledged and drawn upon in schooling. For example, here is Knapp's description of a bilingual teacher of a combined first- and second-grade class composed of a mixed population of Hispanic, African-American, and white students:

> Mr. Callio holds high expectations for his students and demands strict accountability for the work assigned to them. He recognizes that his students do not arrive at school with all the skills he would like them to have and plans his instruction accordingly. At the same time, his approach builds in a respect for the strengths and backgrounds of the students in his class. For example, Mr. Callio's classroom is alive with pictures from different parts of the world, showing the different ethnic, racial, and cultural groups represented in his students. One display reads "Yo soy Latin y orgulloso" ("I am Latin and proud of it") in big letters surrounded by pictures of pyramids, indigenous Mesoamericans, and other Latino faces. Another reads "I am African American and proud" and displays pictures of African people, places, and artifacts. Mr. Callio argues that it is imperative to provide positive self-images and role models if a teacher expects students to be driven to succeed. Mr. Callio uses his Spanish extensively in the classroom—and not simply to help those students with limited English proficiency. Rather, he argues that Spanish is an important language to know and encourages his monolingual English speakers to try to learn it. One of the top students in the class, an African-American male, regularly tries to piece together Spanish sentences. (Knapp, 1995, p. 39)

COUNTERACTING PEER PRESSURES

A positive approach that honors diversity and focuses on helping all students to achieve their potentials should carry you a long way in motivating your students to learn, regardless of their social class, racial, or ethnic backgrounds. However, you may encounter consistent resistance to adoption of learning goals by alienated students who have come to view putting forth consistent effort in school as "selling out," "sucking up to teachers," or "acting white" (as well as sporadic resistance by other students who are being pressured by alienated peers). You will need to take actions designed to turn around the alienated students, and in the meantime, to minimize their negative influences on classmates.

The most effective way to turn around resistant students is to put them in contact with respected models with whom they identify and ask the models to help these students see that their attitudes undermine their own best interests. Ideal models might be teenagers and young adults who formerly attended your school and could tell your students true stories about local people that illustrate how life paths begin to diverge when students their age decide either to take advantage of or to reject what schooling has to offer them.

In addition, try to resocialize resistant students' attitudes, whatever your (and their) social class and ethnic backgrounds may be. Toward this end, I recommend three strategies. First, do not scoff at the students' ideas (about "acting white," etc.) or dismiss them out of hand. Accept them as genuinely held beliefs, although beliefs that you do not share. If you try to undermine these beliefs using persuasion methods, make sure that everything about your tone and manner and all of the arguments that you present to the students communicate your concern about their best interests. If they view your behavior as an attempt to manipulate them for your own purposes, your persuasion attempts will backfire. In the case of minority group students, even if they concede your good intentions, they may not accept your arguments if they believe that you essentially are pressuring them to give up their cultural heritage in exchange for economic opportunities in the larger society (Secada & Lightfoot, 1993).

Second, draw these students out by using active listening, reflection, and related counseling techniques. In private conversations, ask them to elaborate on their views and listen carefully as they do so. Occasionally, paraphrase or reflect to show that you have heard and understood what the student is saying (e.g., "So, your friends taunt you when you contribute good ideas to class discussion or get good grades on tests. How does that make you feel?"). If you continue in this vein, the student may begin to see for himself that he doesn't really believe what peers are telling him, that the peers are pursuing their own questionable agendas rather than acting as true friends concerned about his best interests, that they are pressuring him to subvert his own values, and that he needs to find ways to resist this peer pressure without significant cost to his social relationships (or perhaps to cultivate friendships with more compatible peers).

Third, with students who begin to develop such insights, you might use the inoculation techniques that have been developed for helping people to cope with stressful situations. For example, techniques for helping timid children to become more assertive include role playing or discussing vignettes in which someone ignores or mistreats them, then analyzing how the situation might be handled effectively or how the role-played response might have been improved. Similar techniques can be used to help socially pressured students plan ahead for and practice possible responses to situations in which peers taunt them for displaying motivation to learn at school.

Along with your own efforts, improvements in the school's culture and in school–community relations will be needed to turn around the most hostile and resistant students, especially if they belong to a local subculture that detests or distrusts schooling as an institution. You cannot simply wait for these improvements to occur, however, because you must work with your students each day, dealing with them and the school milieu as they are at the moment. You may not be able to eliminate resistant students' negative attitudes toward the school as a whole, but at least you can get them to view you as an exception and begin to "go along with the program" in your classroom. Whatever the apparent odds against you, you will maximize your chances to succeed with these students if you follow the suggestions made in this book, especially those calling for making yourself and your classroom attractive to students, modeling motivation to learn, communicating positive expectations and attributions, and connecting with students' home cultures.

CONCLUSION

You may have noticed that even though this chapter deals with individual and group differences, it frequently reemphasizes strategies presented in previous chapters and recommends individualizing along the margins of a general motivational approach to the class as a whole rather than using very different methods with different students. There are three reasons for this. First, psychological theory and research, both on motivation in particular and on the human condition in general, indicates that humans are much more similar than different. A particular motive might be less relevant for some people than for others, but to the extent that the motive is applicable in a given situation, research-based principles relating to the motive should apply to everyone.

Second, empirical research bears out these theoretical expectations. Discouraged students may need more attention to the expectancy-related aspects of motivation whereas apathetic students may need more attention to the value-related aspects, boys may need more encouragement in language arts and girls more encouragement in mathematics and science, members of minority groups may have a greater need for exposure to models with whom they can identify, and so on. However, these distinctions lie in the details of implementation of motivational principles, not in the principles themselves. What has been said in this book about the desirability of learning goals relative to performance or work avoidant goals, about the value of inducing students to attribute their successes to the combination of sufficient ability and reasonable effort but to attribute their failures to insufficient effort or strategy knowledge, about helping students to see that schooling is designed to empower them to pursue their own best interests and achieve self-actualization goals, and so on, are principles that you can apply with all of your students, whoever they may be.

Finally, much of my own research has focused on the dynamics of teacher–student interactions, particularly as they are affected by teachers' and students' attitudes, beliefs, and expectations. This work has sensitized me to the problems of rigid expectations, labeling effects, and stereotyping that often result when teachers think of their classes as collections of subgroups (blacks versus whites, boys versus girls, high achievers versus low achievers, cooperative students versus troublemakers, etc.) or think of individual students in terms of stereotyped labels (gifted, learning disabled, hyperactive, low functioning, emotionally disturbed, etc.). Up to a point, descriptive categories and labels are necessary and help us to understand students and plan to meet their needs. However, if we lose sight of students' individuality and begin to think about them primarily in terms of category labels, we may begin to notice only those things about them that fit our stereotypes and drift into patterns of interacting with them that cause our expectations to function as self-fulfilling prophecies.

Thus, there is danger in pigeonholing students and thinking about motivation in terms of the contrasting needs of different subgroups or student types. I believe that you will be a more successful motivator if you learn general principles and strategies and use these to establish your classroom as a learning community, then supplement by providing individual students with whatever special emphases or motivational extras they may need.

SUMMARY

Motivational theorists differ in the relative emphasis they place on general principles assumed to apply universally versus specialized principles intended for use with particular subgroups or student types. Most such theorists, including myself, emphasize principles that are believed to apply universally but may have more relevance in certain situations or with certain students than others. However, some theorists have called for using different strategies with different students.

Some schemes for differentiating motivational strategies amount to nothing more than accommodating students' content or activity preferences. There are at least three reasons for proceeding with caution in adopting such strategies: (1) accommodating students' existing preferences does nothing to develop their motivation to learn or in other ways to move them in directions you would like to see them move; (2) accommodating their preferences is not the same as meeting their needs; and (3) accommodating their preferences may have the effect of reinforcing personal characteristics that ought to be changed. Consequently, any plans for individualizing motivational strategies should be designed to meet the students' needs and long-run best interests, not just to accommodate their current preferences. In addition to these theoretical concerns, there is also the important practical constraint of feasibility: Teachers working with 20 or more students need to focus their curriculum and instruction on the class as a whole. They do not have the time or resources to plan a unique program for each individual student.

Within this perspective, the chapter considers claims and suggestions made to teachers for differentiating curriculum and instruction so as to optimize students' motivation. One of the better-researched bases for planning contrasting approaches is the cognitive style dimension of psychological differentiation. Field-dependent students are people-oriented in their content interests and prefer to learn in close collaboration with others. Field-independent students have more theoretical and analytic interests and prefer to learn more autonomously and individually. You might want to accommodate these preferences most of the time, although students who represent the extremes of this dimension need to learn to function effectively in situations that call for their non-preferred cognitive style.

Much of what you hear about individualizing your approaches to motivation will be based on the notion of learning styles. Often these ideas will be presented by people who are eager to sell you learning style inventories and other assessment devices or manuals outlining their learning style models. They are likely to imply that implementing these models will quickly produce remarkable improvements in students' motivation and achievement. In fact, the research base supporting these models is thin to nonexistent (depending on the model) and characterized by questionable scientific procedures and interpretations of findings.

One model that does have some support is the 4MAT system, which is a method of planning instructional units to ensure that each of four learning styles is represented. Other variables proposed as bases for learning style differentiations are shown in Box 9.1. You probably should accommodate students' preferences on most of these variables whenever there is no good reason not to. However, there is little reason to believe that it will be worth your while to purchase assessment instruments and seek to implement elaborate models of differentiated instruction based on these learning style notions. The same is true of models based on supposed multiple intelligences or brain hemisphere preferences.

Developmental differences in children's cognitive abilities and motivational needs and interests make certain strategies more or less relevant at particular grade levels. Young children's inattention to social comparisons and limited understanding of the implications of failure feedback make them less likely than older students to emphasize performance goals over learning goals or to develop learned helplessness problems. Such problems can develop even in these students, however, if teachers fail to follow the guidelines in Chapters 2–4. Teachers at higher levels of schooling who deal with transitional students coming in from lower levels should go out of their way to make sure that these students adjust smoothly to the new school and do not suffer dramatic drops in their self-perceptions of ability.

Motivational problems relating to rigid gender roles are less serious than they used to be. Nevertheless, many activities are still gender typed, and this may inhibit some students' interest in them. All students need help in overcoming the rigidities of traditional gender roles and learning to develop their potentials in areas that they associate with the opposite gender. In addition, some students (especially girls with respect to mathematics or science) need to be helped to realize that claims of large gender differences in ability in different subject areas are incorrect, and that they have the ability to succeed if they apply reasonable effort in subjects traditionally associated with the opposite gender.

Early research on student social class, race, and ethnicity produced sweeping generalizations which have come to be recognized as incorrect, exaggerated, or misinterpreted. Subsequent research has shifted attention from these general sociological labels to investigation of individual students' family and cultural experiences as factors influencing the students' readiness for and successful functioning in school. Also, investigations of minority groups have shifted from identifying supposed deficits to developing understanding of the prior experiences and cultural backgrounds that children bring to school and how these may be used as strengths to build on.

Students may be anxious or conflicted at school if the expectations and culture they encounter there contrast with what the students experience in the rest of their lives. Teachers who are successful with minority-group and other at-risk students develop good personal relationships with these students and their families and embrace their languages and cultures. However, they also work to maximize the students' academic progress, not merely to provide them with friendship or sympathy. You are most likely to help each of your students to get maximal empowerment and self-actualization benefits from being in your class if you think in terms of using the same basic motivational principles to pursue the same basic learning goals with all of them, rather than in terms of using different principles to pursue different goals with different subgroups or individuals.

REFERENCES

Anderman, E., & Maehr, M. (1994). Motivation and schooling in the middle grades. *Review of Educational Research, 64,* 207–309.

Banks, W., McQuater, G., & Hubbard, J. (1978). Toward a reconceptualization of the so-
    cial-cognitive bases of achievement orientations in blacks. *Review of Educational Re-
    search, 48*, 381–397.
Barker, G., & Graham, S. (1987). Developmental study of praise and blame as attribu-
    tional cues. *Journal of Educational Psychology, 79*, 62–66.
Bennett, C. (1995). *Comprehensive multicultural education: Theory and practice* (3rd ed.).
    Boston: Allyn & Bacon.
Berndt, T., & Miller, K. (1990). Expectancies, values, and achievement in junior high
    school. *Journal of Educational Psychology, 82*, 319–326.
Blatchford, P. (1992). Academic self-assessment at 7 and 11 years: Its accuracy and asso-
    ciation with ethnic group and sex. *British Journal of Educational Psychology, 62*,
    35–44.
Boggiano, A., Main, D., Katz, P. (1991). Mastery motivation in boys and girls: The role
    of intrinsic versus extrinsic motivation. *Sex Roles, 25*, 511–520.
Bornholt, L., Goodnow, J., & Cooney, G. (1994). Influences of gender stereotypes on
    adolescents' perceptions of their own achievement. *American Educational Research
    Journal, 31*, 675–692.
Bouffard, T., Boisvert, J., Vezeau, C., & Larouche, C. (1995). The impact of goal orienta-
    tion on self-regulation and performance among college students. *British Journal of
    Educational Psychology, 65*, 317–329.
Brophy, J. (1985). Interactions of male and female students with male and female teach-
    ers. In L. Wilkinson & C. Marrett (Eds.), *Gender influences in classroom interaction*
    (pp. 115–142). Orlando, FL: Academic Press.
Brush, L. (1980). *Encouraging girls in mathematics: The problem and the solution.* Cam-
    bridge, MA: Abt.
Bryk, A., Lee, V., & Smith, J. (1990). High school organization and its effects on teachers
    and students: An interpretive summary of the research. In W. Klune & J. Witte
    (Eds.), *Choice and control in American education* (Vol. 1, pp. 135–226). Philadelphia:
    Falmer.
Butler, R. (1986). The role of generalized expectancies in determining causal attribu-
    tions for success and failure in two social classes. *British Journal of Educational Psy-
    chology, 56*, 51–63.
Butler, R. (1990). The effects of mastery and competitive conditions on self-assessment
    at different ages. *Child Development, 61*, 201–210.
Clark, R. (1982). Antagonism between achievement and enjoyment in ATI studies. *Edu-
    cational Psychologist, 17*, 92–101.
Cooper, H., & Dorr, N. (1995). Race comparisons on need for achievement: A meta-
    analytic alternative to Graham's narrative review. *Review of Educational Research,
    65*, 483–508.
Curry, L. (1990). A critique of the research on learning styles. *Educational Leadership,
    48*(2), 50–56.
Delpit, L. (1992). Acquisition of literate discourse: Bowing before the master? *Theory
    Into Practice, 31*, 296–302.
Dorsel, T. (1975). Preference-success assumption in education. *Journal of Educational
    Psychology, 67*, 514–520.
Dreyfoos, J. (1990). *Adolescents at risk: Prevalence and prevention.* London: Oxford Univer-
    sity Press.
Dunn, R., & Dunn, K. (1992). *Teaching elementary students through their individual learning
    styles.* Boston: Allyn & Bacon.

Dunn, R., Gorman, B., Griggs, S., Olson, J., & Beasley, M. (1995). A meta-analytic validation of the Dunn and Dunn model of learning-style preferences. *Journal of Educational Research, 88,* 353–362.

Eccles, J. (1987). Gender roles and women's achievement related decisions. *Psychology of Women Quarterly, 11,* 135–172.

Eccles, J. (1993). School and family effects on the ontogeny of children's interests, self-perceptions, and activity choices. In J. Jacobs (Ed.), *Nebraska symposium on motivation. Volume 40. Developmental perspectives on motivation* (pp. 145–208). Lincoln: University of Nebraska Press.

Eccles, J., & Midgley, C. (1989). Stage/environment fit: Developmentally appropriate classrooms for early adolescents. In R. Ames & C. Ames (Eds.), *Research on motivation in education* (Vol. 3, pp. 139–186). San Diego: Academic Press.

Eccles, J., Wigfield, A., Flanagan, C., Miller, C., Reuman, D., & Yee, D. (1989). Self-concepts, domain values, and self-esteem: Relations and changes at early adolescence. *Journal of Personality and Social Psychology, 57,* 283–310.

Eccles, J., Wigfield, A., Midgley, C., Reuman, D., MacIver, D., & Feldlaufer, H. (1993). Are traditional middle grades schools undermining the academic motivation of early adolescents? *Elementary School Journal, 93,* 553–574.

Eden, D. (1975). Intrinsic and extrinsic rewards and motives: Replication and extension with Kibbutz workers. *Journal of Applied Social Psychology, 5,* 348–361.

Engelhard, G., & Monsaas, J. (1988). Grade level, gender, and school-related curiosity in urban elementary schools. *Journal of Educational Research, 82,* 22–26.

Epstein, J. (1989). Family structures and student motivation: A developmental perspective. In C. Ames & R. Ames (Eds.), *Research on motivation in education. Vol. 3: Goals and cognitions* (pp. 259–295). San Diego: Academic Press.

Ginsburg, G., & Bronstein, P. (1993). Family factors related to children's intrinsic/extrinsic motivational orientation and academic performance. *Child Development, 64,* 1461–1474.

Good, T., & Brophy, J. (1995). *Contemporary educational psychology* (5th ed.). White Plains, NY: Longman.

Graham, S. (1994). Motivation in African Americans. *Review of Educational Research, 64,* 55–117.

Grolnick, W., & Ryan, R. (1989). Parent styles associated with children's self-regulation and competence in school. *Journal of Educational Psychology, 81,* 143–154.

Hannafin, R., & Sullivan, H. (1996). Preferences and learner control over amount of instruction. *Journal of Educational Psychology, 88,* 162–173.

Harter, S. (1975). Developmental differences in the manifestation of mastery motivation on problem-solving tasks. *Child Development, 46,* 370–378.

Harter, S. (1992). The relationship between perceived competence, affect, and motivational orientation within the classroom: Processes and patterns of change. In A. Boggiano & T. Pittman (Eds.), *Achievement and motivation: A social-developmental perspective* (pp. 77–114). New York: Cambridge University Press.

Harter, S., Whitesell, N., & Kowalski, P. (1992). Individual differences in the effects of educational transitions on young adolescents' perceptions of competence and motivational orientation. *American Educational Research Journal, 29,* 777–807.

Hayes, C., Ryan, A., & Zseller, E. (1994). The middle school child's perceptions of caring teachers. *American Journal of Education, 103,* 1–19.

Hess, R., & Holloway, S. (1984). Family and school as educational institutions. In R. Parke (Ed.), *Review of child development research, Vol. 7: The family* (pp. 179–222). Chicago: University of Chicago Press.

Hokoda, A., & Fincham, F. (1995). Origins of children's helpless and mastery achievement patterns in the family. *Journal of Educational Psychology, 87,* 375–385.

Hurlock, E. (1964). *Child development* (4th ed.). New York: McGraw-Hill.

Jersild, A., & Tasch, R. (1949). *Children's interests and what they suggest for education.* New York: Bureau of Publications, Teachers College, Columbia University.

Kavale, K., & Forness, S. (1990). Substance over style: A rejoinder to Dunn's animadversions. *Exceptional Children, 56,* 357–361.

Kleinfeld, J. (1975). Effective teachers of Indian and Eskimo students. *School Review, 83,* 301–344.

Knapp, M. (1995). *Teaching for meaning in high-poverty classrooms.* New York: Teachers College Press.

Leacock, E. (1969). *Teaching and learning in city schools.* New York: Basic Books.

Licht, B. (1992). The achievement-related perceptions of children with learning problems: A developmental analysis. In D. Schunk & J. Meece (Eds.), *Student perceptions in the classroom* (pp. 247–264). Hillsdale, NJ: Erlbaum.

Licht, B., Stader, S., & Swenson, C. (1989). Children's achievement-related beliefs: Effects of academic area, sex, and achievement level. *Journal of Educational Research, 82,* 253–260.

Lord, C., Umezaki, K., & Darley, J. (1990). Developmental differences in decoding the meanings of the appraisal actions of teachers. *Child Development, 61,* 191–200.

McCarthy, B. (1980). *The 4MAT system.* Oakbrook, IL: Excel.

McCarthy, B. (1990). Using the 4MAT system to bring learning styles to school. *Educational Leadership, 48,* 31–37.

Meece, J., & Holt, K. (1993). A pattern analysis of students' achievement goals. *Journal of Educational Psychology, 85,* 582–590.

Mergendoller, J. (guest ed.). (1993). Middle grades research and reform [Special Issue]. *Elementary School Journal, 93,* 443–658.

Midgley, C. (1993). Motivation and middle level schools. In P. Pintrich & M. Maehr (Eds.), *Advances in motivation and achievement* (Vol. 8, pp. 217–274). Greenwich, CT: JAI.

Miller, A. (1985). A developmental study of the cognitive basis of performance impairment after failure. *Journal of Personality and Social Psychology, 49,* 529–538.

Miller, A. (1986). Performance impairment after failure: Mechanism and sex differences. *Journal of Educational Psychology, 78,* 486–491.

Moll, L. (1992). Bilingual classroom studies and community analysis. *Educational Researcher, 21,* 20–24.

Nicholls, J. (1979). Development of perception of own attainment and causal attributions for success and failure in reading. *Journal of Educational Psychology, 71,* 94–99.

Nicholls, J., & Miller, A. (1984). Development and its discontents: The differentiation of the concept of ability. In J. Nicholls (Ed.), *The development of achievement motivation* (pp. 185–218). Greenwich, CT: JAI.

Nicholls, J., Nelson, J., & Gleaves, K. (1995). Learning "facts" versus learning that most questions have many answers: Student evaluations of contrasting curriculum. *Journal of Educational Psychology, 87,* 253–260.

O'Neil, J. (1990). Making sense of style. *Educational Leadership, 48*(2), 4–9.

Rholes, W., Blackwell, J., Jordan, C., & Walters, C. (1980). A developmental study of learned helplessness. *Developmental Psychology, 16,* 616–624.

Ryckman, D., & Peckham, P. (1987). Gender differences in attributions for success and failure situations across subject areas. *Journal of Educational Research, 81,* 120–125.

Sadker, M., & Sadker, D. (1994). *Failing at fairness: How America's schools cheat girls.* New York: Scribner.

Schofield, H. (1981). Teacher effects on cognitive and affective pupil outcomes in elementary school mathematics. *Journal of Educational Psychology, 73,* 462–471.

Schultz, C., & Sherman, R. (1976). Social class, development, and differences in reinforcer effectiveness. *Review of Educational Research, 46,* 25–59.

Secada, W., & Lightfoot, T. (1993). Symbols and the political context of bilingual education in the United States. In M. Arias & U. Casanova (Eds.), *Bilingual education: Politics, practice, and research* (pp. 36–64). Chicago: University of Chicago Press.

Shell, D., Colvin, C., & Bruning, R. (1995). Self-efficacy, attribution, and outcome expectancy mechanisms in reading and writing achievement: Grade-level and achievement-level differences. *Journal of Educational Psychology, 87,* 386–398.

Siddle-Walker, E. (1992). Falling asleep and failure among African-American students: Rethinking assumptions about process teaching. *Theory Into Practice, 31,* 321–327.

Solomon, D., & Kendall, A. (1979). *Children in classrooms: An investigation of person-environment interaction.* New York: Praeger.

Stipek, D. (1984a). The development of achievement motivation. In R. Ames & C. Ames (Eds.). *Research on motivation in education. Vol. 1. Student motivation* (pp. 145–174). New York: Academic Press.

Stipek, D. (1984b). Sex differences in children's attributions for success and failure on math and spelling tests. *Sex Roles, 11,* 969–981.

Stipek, D., & Daniels, D. (1988). Declining perceptions of competence: A consequence of changes in the child or in the educational environment? *Journal of Educational Psychology, 80,* 352–356.

Stipek, D., & Gralinski, J. (1991). Gender differences in children's achievement-related beliefs and emotional responses to success and failure in mathematics. *Journal of Educational Psychology, 83,* 361–371.

Stipek, D., & MacIver, D. (1989). Developmental change in children's assessment of intellectual competence. *Child Development, 60,* 521–538.

Trout, J., & Crawley, F. (1985). The effects of matching instructional strategy with selected student characteristics on ninth-grade physical science students' attitudes and achievement. *Journal of Research in Science Teaching, 22,* 407–419.

Urdan, T., & Maehr, M. (1995). Beyond a two-goal theory of motivation and achievement: A case for social goals. *Review of Educational Research, 65,* 213–243.

Van Hecke, M., & Tracy, R. (1983). Sex differences in children's responses to achievement and approval. *Child Study Journal, 13,* 165–173.

Van Hecke, M., Tracy, R., Cotler, S., & Ribordy, S. (1984). Approval versus achievement motives in seventh-grade girls. *Sex Roles, 11,* 33–41.

Voelkl, K. (1993). Academic achievement and expectations among African-American students. *Journal of Research and Development in Education, 27,* 42–55.

Wigfield, A. (1993) Why should I learn this? Adolescents' achievement values for different activities. In P. Pintrich & M. Maehr (Eds.), *Advances in motivation and achievement* (Vol. 8, pp. 99–138). Greenwich, CT: JAI.

Wigfield, A. (1994). Expectancy-value theory of achievement motivation: A developmental perspective. *Educational Psychology Review, 6,* 49–78.

Wigfield, A., & Asher, S. (1984). Social and motivational influences on reading. In P. Pearson, R. Barr, Kamil, M., & Mosenthal, P. (Eds.), *Handbook of reading research* (pp. 423–452). New York: Longman.

Wilkerson, R., & White, K. (1988). Effects of the 4MAT system of instruction on students' achievement, retention, and attitudes. *Elementary School Journal, 88,* 357–368.

Witkin, H., Moore, C., Goodenough, D., & Cox, P. (1977). Field-dependent and field-independent cognitive styles and their educational implications. *Review of Educational Research, 47,* 1–64.

CHAPTER 10

Looking Back and Ahead: Integrating Motivational Goals into Your Planning and Teaching

If you have read through the rest of the book before turning to this chapter, you may be feeling that the whole topic of motivation is much more complicated than you thought. You also may be daunted at the prospect of trying to integrate so many principles into your teaching. This is understandable. After all, in the very first chapter I described factors built into schooling that limit your motivational options (i.e., the high student/teacher ratios, the public nature of much teacher–student interaction, the need to work through an established curriculum and assign grades to students instead of just acting as a mentor and resource person).

Then, in subsequent chapters, I developed a lengthy list of motivational principles for you to keep in mind, frequently attaching qualifications on when or how they should be used: If used as incentives, rewards should be delivered in ways that communicate verification of accomplishment rather than exercise of your power as an authority figure; praise should be communicated mostly in private rather than in public; feedback should emphasize advances in knowledge or skill rather than normative comparisons; value-oriented strategies should focus on developing students' motivation to learn rather than just on connecting with their existing intrinsic motivation; and so on. Implementation of many principles requires not just using a strategy but doing so in just the right way (i.e., delivering the right kinds of praise in the right situations, attributing successes to one set of causes but failures to another). In addition, you may need to make adjustments in response to developments in students (continuing to provide just the right levels of challenge as students gain confidence, doing less structuring and scaffolding of their learning efforts, and transferring more responsibility for self-regulation of learning to them as they develop expertise, etc.).

Clearly, motivation *is* complicated in several respects. Furthermore, it is important for you to face up to this fact and learn to address the complexities involved. You won't be a very effective motivator if you over-rely on a few techniques or try to reduce the detailed knowledge base synthesized in this book to just a few rules of thumb.

However, certain factors make these complexities more manageable than they might be otherwise. For one thing, you can become your own most powerful motivational tool by establishing productive relationships with each of your students. This alone will carry you a long way and minimize the likelihood that any mishandling of particular situations will have lasting demotivating effects on students. Also, the motivational principles emphasized in this book complement the emerging consensus concerning principles of good curriculum and instruction, so that the complete set of principles can be learned and implemented as an internally consistent and pedagogically powerful package. Another simplifier is that your efforts to incorporate motivational elements into your teaching can focus on establishing your classroom as a learning community and on planning curriculum and instruction for the class as a whole. You will need to supplement this with adaptations or motivational extras designed to meet special needs, but you will not have to develop unique motivational prescriptions for each student in your class.

Finally, it is worth repeating that this book has synthesized the motivational literature specifically for teachers. Although it may not seem like it at this point, its content has been streamlined and focused in two important ways. First, I have culled from a much larger scholarly literature the material that I think you ought to know because it will help you to motivate your students. A great many topics and details were omitted because they didn't seem to have such implications for teachers. Second, I have organized and presented the content primarily in terms of principles and strategies that you might use in your classroom, rather than just presenting a general coverage of the motivational literature and leaving it to you to try to figure out whether and how it might apply to your teaching.

Even so, I recognize that this content is lengthy and complex. Other scholars interested in motivation in education also have recognized these complexities and have developed organizing schemes to simplify the content for teachers and help them with their planning. I will briefly summarize three of these before proceeding to my own scheme based on the organization of this book.

THE TARGET CATEGORIES

The TARGET categories (task, authority, reward, grouping, evaluation, and time) have been discussed at two points in the book. The original version developed by Joyce Epstein (1989) was discussed in Chapter 9. This version described structures in the home through which families help prepare their children for school and support their progress as students. The elaborated version developed by Carole Ames (1992) was discussed in Chapter 2. This version summarized ways that teachers can work through these same six structures to motivate the students in their classrooms.

One way for you to systematically incorporate motivational principles into your planning is to check your curricular and instructional plans against the guidelines incorporated within the elaborated TARGET model. These are summarized in Table 2.1.

KELLER'S MODEL

John Keller (1983) synthesized many motivational principles within a model that features four major dimensions: interest, relevance, expectancy, and outcomes. Some of the major principles associated with these dimensions are summarized below.

- *Interest:* Interest refers to the extent to which the student's curiosity is aroused and sustained over time. Keller suggested five strategies for stimulating and maintaining students' interest and curiosity in lessons: (1) use novel, incongruous, conflictual, or paradoxical events, or arouse attention through an abrupt change in the status quo; (2) use anecdotes and other devices to inject a personal, emotional element into otherwise purely intellectual or procedural material; (3) give students opportunities to learn more about things they already know about and are interested in, but also give them moderate doses of the unfamiliar; (4) use analogies to make the strange familiar and the familiar strange; (5) guide students into a process of question generation and inquiry.
- *Relevance:* Relevance refers to the student's perception that the instruction is related to personal needs or goals. Keller argued that motivation increases when students perceive that a learning activity will satisfy basic motives such as needs for achievement, power, or affiliation. His strategies for increasing personal relevance call for (1) enhancing achievement striving by providing opportunities to achieve standards of excellence under conditions of moderate risk; (2) making instruction responsive to the power motive by providing opportunities for choice, responsibility, and interpersonal influence; and (3) satisfying the need for affiliation by establishing trust and providing opportunities for no-risk, cooperative interaction.
- *Expectancy:* Expectancy refers to the student's perceived likelihood of achieving success through personal control. Keller suggested four strategies for increasing success expectancies: (1) provide consistent success experiences (on meaningful tasks, not trivial or easy ones), (2) be clear about requirements for success, (3) use techniques that offer personal control over success, and (4) provide attributional feedback to help students relate success to personal effort and ability.
- *Outcomes:* Outcomes include the satisfaction of goal accomplishment and its effects on motivation for engaging in similar activities in the

future. To promote desirable outcomes, Keller suggested emphasizing the rewards that come naturally from successful completion of the activity rather than using artificial extrinsic rewards, as well as emphasizing praise and informative feedback over threats, surveillance, or external performance evaluations.

As with the six categories in the TARGET model, you can use the four categories in Keller's model as planning tools. To do so, treat the principles incorporated within the model as a checklist against which to evaluate your instructional plans.

WLODKOWSKI'S MODEL

Raymond Wlodkowski (1984) suggested a time continuum model for building motivational strategies into instructional planning. The model suggests that there are three critical periods in a learning sequence in which particular motivational strategies will have the most impact: attitude and needs strategies are most relevant at the beginning of the activity, stimulation and affect strategies during the activity, and competence and reinforcement strategies when ending the activity.

Attitude strategies address the question, What can I do to establish positive student attitudes toward the learning situation, as well as to establish the expectation that students will be able to meet task demands successfully? Potentially relevant strategies here include sharing something of value with students (e.g., task-related anecdotes, humor, or personal experiences), listening to them with empathy, treating them with warmth and acceptance, modeling enthusiasm for the subject, communicating positive expectations and encouragement, and helping students to set realistic goals.

Needs strategies address the question, How can I best meet the needs of the students? Potential strategies here include making sure that students are physically comfortable and free from fear or anxiety, establishing a collaborative rather than a competitive learning environment and being encouraging rather than critical in responding to students, structuring learning experiences and arranging for creation of products that support students' sense of identity and self-esteem, and including divergent thinking and exploration elements that appeal to students' needs for self-actualization.

Stimulation strategies address the question, What about this learning activity will continuously stimulate students' attention and sustain their engagement in the activity? These include using voice, body language, props, and other communication skills; relating material to students' interests; using humor, examples, analogies, or stories to personalize the content; asking questions, especially questions that call for higher-order thinking; and using spontaneity, unpredictability, or dissonance induction to periodically restimulate students' alertness and thoughtfulness.

Affective strategies address the question, How can I make the affective experience and emotional climate for this activity positive for students? These strategies include maintaining a positive group atmosphere throughout the activity, presenting content and asking questions that will engage students' emotions, and connecting the learning with things that are important to students in their lives outside of school.

Competence strategies address the question, How will this learning activity increase or affirm students' feelings of competence? These strategies help students to emerge from the activity feeling that they have made progress in developing their knowledge and skills. They involve first making sure that students appreciate their advances in progress and mastery by providing informative feedback and facilitating successful task completion, then encouraging students to take credit for these accomplishments by attributing them to sufficient ability plus reasonable effort.

Reinforcement strategies address the question, What reinforcement will this learning activity provide for students? These include calling students' attention to positive natural consequences of successful task completion, as well as providing them with praise or rewards (in ways consistent with the guidelines given in Chapter 5).

Wlodkowski's three-stage time continuum is worth keeping in mind as a way to make sure that you address motivational issues when planning how you will introduce an activity, what will occur as the activity unfolds, and how you will bring it to closure. In addition, the six categories in his model can be used as a checklist when developing instructional plans.

INCORPORATING PRINCIPLES PRESENTED IN THIS BOOK

To help you take into account all of the principles discussed in this book, I have provided the list of motivational strategies presented in Box 10.1 and the following set of motivational questions to consider when you are planning curriculum and instruction. You may want to simplify, elaborate, or otherwise adapt these tools to your personal needs.

If you are a new teacher or an experienced teacher who is planning a new course from scratch, you can incorporate motivational strategies by building them directly into the planning process. If you are already working with adopted curriculum guidelines and instructional materials, you can incorporate the strategies by adjusting existing plans as needed. One way to do so is to use Box 10.1 as a menu of potential strategies from which to choose or as a checklist against which to assess your instructional plans. Another way is to ask yourself the following sets of questions to stimulate your thinking as you develop your plans.

Questions to Consider for All Activities

The following questions should be considered in planning for any academic activity. First, what are its goals? Why will the students be learning this content or skill? When and how might they use it after they learn it? Answers to

Box 10.1.   Summary of Motivational Principles and Strategies

A. GENERAL PRINCIPLES

1. Focus on developing motivation to learn as your primary goal.
2. Think in terms of shaping students' motivational development, not just connecting with their current motivational systems.
3. Make yourself and your classroom attractive to students.
4. Use authoritative management and socialization strategies.
5. Establish your classroom as a learning community whose members engage in learning activities collaboratively.
6. Focus on learning goals rather than performance goals.
7. Teach things that are worth learning, in ways that help students to appreciate their value.
8. Teach for understanding, appreciation, and application of the learning.
9. Attend to both the expectancy- and the value-related aspects of students' motivation.

B. STRATEGIES FOR SUPPORTING STUDENTS' CONFIDENCE AS LEARNERS

1. Program for success (continuous progress achieved with reasonable effort).
2. Help students to set goals, evaluate their progress, and recognize effort-outcome linkages.
3. Emphasize informative feedback rather than grades or student comparisons.
4. Provide extra support to struggling low achievers.
5. Resocialize students with failure syndrome problems.

6. Help self-worth protective students shift emphasis from performance goals to learning goals.
7. Resocialize the attitudes of underachievers and encourage their commitment to appropriately challenging goals.

C. STRATEGIES FOR MOTIVATING THROUGH EXTRINSIC INCENTIVES

1. Praise and reward students for meeting performance/improvement standards.
2. Deliver praise and rewards in ways that encourage students to appreciate their learning.
3. Call attention to the instrumental value of the learning.
4. Perhaps use competition occasionally but depersonalize it and focus attention on learning goals.

D. STRATEGIES FOR CONNECTING WITH STUDENTS' INTRINSIC MOTIVATION

1. Respond to students' autonomy needs by encouraging them to function as autonomous learners and allowing them to make choices.
2. Respond to students' competence needs by emphasizing activities that offer opportunities to make active responses and get immediate feedback, incorporating gamelike features into learning activities, and assigning tasks that feature skill variety, task identity, and task significance.
3. Respond to students' relatedness needs by providing them with frequent opportunities to collaborate

(Continued)

Box 10.1.   Summary of Motivational Principles and Strategies—*Concluded*

with peers, especially within purely cooperative learning formats.

4. Adapt learning activities to students' interests.

5. Embellish traditional learning activities with simulation or fantasy elements.

6. Combine hands-on activities with minds-on learning.

E. STRATEGIES FOR STIMULATING STUDENTS' MOTIVATION TO LEARN

1. Socialize motivation to learn as a general disposition by modeling your own motivation to learn, communicating desirable expectations and attributions, and minimizing students' performance anxiety.

2. Shape students' expectations about learning by being enthusiastic (regularly) and by being intense (when material is especially important and requires close attention).

3. Stimulate situational motivation to learn by inducing curiosity or suspense; inducing dissonance or cognitive conflict; making abstract content more personal, concrete, or familiar; inducing task interest or appreciation; or inducing students to generate their own motivation to learn.

4. Scaffold students' learning efforts by stating learning goals and providing advance organizers, planning questions and activities to help students develop and apply powerful ideas, modeling task-related thinking and problem solving, inducing metacognitive awareness and control of learning strategies, teaching skills for self-regulated learning and studying, and teaching volitional control strategies.

5. Resocialize the attitudes and behaviors of apathetic students by developing and working within close relationships with them, using contracting and incentive systems, discovering and building on their existing interests, helping them to develop and sustain more positive attitudes towards schoolwork, and socializing their motivation to learn.

F. ADAPTATIONS TO THE NEEDS OF INDIVIDUAL STUDENTS

1. Where feasible, accommodate students' preferences based on differences in cognitive or learning styles, age-related abilities and needs, age- and gender-related interests, or family and cultural backgrounds that may be associated with social class, race, or ethnicity.

2. In making any such accommodations, however, emphasize the students' long-run best interests over their current preferences (if these conflict).

G. YOUR DEVELOPMENT AS A MOTIVATOR

1. Work on your own self-efficacy perceptions, performance attributions, etc. with respect to your development of knowledge and skills in the domain of student motivation.

2. Finally, work on metacognitive monitoring and self-regulation of your emotional reactions and the strategy adjustments that you make in working to motivate difficult students (i.e., stay goal-focused and resist temptations to give in to frustration or provocation).

these questions suggest information that should be conveyed when introducing the activity to the students.

Before getting into the activity itself, is there a way to characterize it using familiar, general terms that indicate its nature and provide students with organizing concepts? If so, communicate such advance organizers to the students.

What elements of the activity could you focus on to create interest, identify practical applications, or induce curiosity, suspense, or dissonance? Does the activity include information that the students are likely to find interesting or build skills that they are eager to develop? Does it contain unusual or surprising information? Can the content be related to events in the news or in students' lives? Are there aspects that they are likely to find surprising or difficult to believe? Are there ways to stimulate curiosity or create suspense by posing interesting questions?

Questions to Consider for Listening and Reading Activities

You might consider the following questions when planning activities that require students to attend to an oral presentation, watch a visual presentation, or learn by reading. First, what aspects of the content are interesting, noteworthy, or important, and why? Answers to these questions will help you to identify reasons for enthusiasm about the topic, and these reasons should be communicated to students.

Can you tell about personal experiences or display artifacts that are related to the content? Do you know content-related anecdotes about the experiences of others or about how the knowledge was discovered that could add spice to the presentation? Will the lesson contain sufficient variety in the cognitive levels of information communicated and the types of responses demanded? If it appears that there will be too much uninterrupted lecture or reading, when and how might you break it up by asking questions, initiating discussion, or allowing time for students to take notes or do a brief assignment?

How should students respond to the presentation or text? Should they take notes or summarize key ideas? Keep particular issues or questions in mind as they listen or read? Outline the material or respond to a study guide? Identify organizational structures embedded in the material? If you want them to do something more specific than just pay attention, then tell them what they should do, and if necessary, help by supplying questions, outlines, study guides, or information about how the material is organized.

Is there some key point that students might easily miss if not forewarned? Are there abstractions that will not be meaningful without additional explanation or concrete examples? Are there concepts that may be troublesome because they are subtle or difficult, because they are not well explained in the text, or because they conflict with the students' experiences? If so, you may want to call attention to these trouble spots to prepare students for viewing or reading.

Questions to Consider for Activities That Require Active Response

You might consider the following questions when planning activities that require students to do something more than just listen or read (answer questions, prepare a report, work on a project, etc.). Is the activity presented as an opportunity to apply knowledge or develop skills rather than as a test (unless it *is* a test)? When and how might students be encouraged to ask questions or seek help?

Does the activity demand new or complex responses that ought to be modeled? If so, what steps should be modeled at what level of detail? Will you need to model important hypothesis-testing strategies (e.g., considering alternatives at a choice point and then selecting the correct one after reasoning or brief experimentation) or troubleshooting or repair strategies (e.g., responding to confusion or errors with diagnosis of the problem or generation of alternative strategies)?

When, how, and from whom will students get feedback? What should they do if they do not understand a question or are not sure about how to get started on an assignment? What should they do when they think they are finished? How might they be encouraged to check their work, to generate and respond to their own questions about it, or to engage in follow-up discourse with peers?

The notion of planning and implementing motivational principles or strategies strikes some teachers as manipulative or grimly methodical. This image might be reinforced by the notion of using Box 10.1 as a checklist against which to evaluate your teaching plans. However, the suggestions given here are not intended to be implemented as a set of procedural mechanics. Instead, they are meant to be brought to life in the same way that you bring the curriculum to life: by bringing your personality and past experiences to the teaching role and implementing instructional units in ways that combine professional creativity with applied science. You may have to consciously prepare and practice using certain strategies at first, but eventually they will become second nature to you and get implemented in ways marked by your own personal touches.

MAINTAINING YOUR OWN MOTIVATION AS A TEACHER

This book has focused on applications of motivational principles to students' engagement in learning activities. However, these principles also apply to teachers' engagement in teaching activities. Keeping this in mind may help you to analyze and deal with any difficulties you may encounter in seeking to motivate your students to learn.

For example, motivational researchers have shown that students are likely to use more desirable learning strategies and produce more desirable outcomes when they engage in learning activities with learning goals rather than performance goals and when they are seeking primarily to understand what they are learning rather than responding to extrinsic pressures. The same is true of you as you engage in your teaching responsibilities.

Ideally, your planning and teaching would reflect your beliefs about the nature of your students' needs and about what constitutes a good professional effort to meet them. You would feel well prepared to meet those needs and would confidently set about doing so by establishing realistic goals, employing suitable strategies for accomplishing the goals, monitoring the effectiveness of these strategies, adjusting accordingly, and then taking satisfaction in seeing the goals accomplished. While engaged in these activities you would be in a flow-like state, focusing on the goals and processes involved rather than evaluating yourself in terms of success or failure. Subsequently you might engage in attributional thinking, by enjoying your successes (which you would attribute to the combination of sufficient ability and reasonable effort) and analyzing any failures with an eye toward developing plans for overcoming them. You would attribute these failures to reliance on incorrect information or inappropriate strategies, or perhaps to failure to persist long enough or put forth sufficient effort, but not to inherent limitations on your potential as a motivator or your students' potential for becoming motivated to learn.

Unfortunately, this ideal is difficult to attain routinely and impossible to sustain continuously. For one thing, you won't be operating under ideal conditions of intrinsic motivation. You will enjoy only limited opportunity to decide what goals to establish and how to pursue them. You will be expected to comply with state and district curriculum standards and guidelines, your time schedule may be regimented, your instructional resources will be limited and may include textbooks or other materials that you would not have selected on your own, and your students may be tested using standardized instruments that you may not view as valid. Your attempts to deemphasize extrinsic incentives or competitions may be resisted by students, parents, or administrators.

These and other externally imposed constraints and pressures can get you down. Experiments have shown that when two groups of teachers are asked to teach the same content or skills to comparable classes of students, the group instructed simply to help their students understand the content or master the skills tends to teach more efficiently and elicit better student achievement than the group instructed to prepare students to pass an achievement test. The former teachers place more emphasis on conceptual learning, are more responsive to their students' questions, and are generally more relaxed and supportive. The latter teachers are more controlling, pressuring their students to master what the test is going to cover but doing so in counterproductive ways (Flink et al., 1992).

To prevent such external pressures from having similar effects on you, you will need to develop sufficient confidence in your efficacy as a teaching professional to enable you to exercise some autonomy in setting goals for your students. The importance of this was shown in studies conducted by Fred Newmann (1990, 1992) on thoughtfulness in high school social studies classes. In classrooms high in thoughtfulness, interaction focused on sustained examination of a few topics rather than superficial coverage of many; the discourse was characterized by substantive coherence and continuity; students were given sufficient time to think before being required to answer questions; the teachers pressed the students to clarify or justify their assertions; the teachers modeled the characteristics of a thoughtful person; and the students generated many original and unconventional ideas. In contrast, other classrooms featured lecture, recitation, and seatwork. If the teachers did attempt to emphasize discussion, they did not foster much thoughtfulness because they skipped from topic to topic too quickly or accepted students' contributions uncritically.

Interviews with the two groups of teachers indicated that those whose classrooms were high in thoughtfulness emphasized long-range and far-reaching dispositional goals in addition to more immediate knowledge and skill objectives. Furthermore, although both groups felt pressure to cover more content, the teachers whose classes featured thoughtfulness experienced this pressure primarily as external and resisted it by emphasizing depth of topic development. In contrast, the other teachers experienced it primarily as internal pressure and succumbed to it by emphasizing breadth of coverage.

In the current climate of emphasis on achievement standards backed by high-stakes testing programs, there is increased pressure on teachers to elicit high test scores from their students. Many teachers respond to this pressure by narrowing the curriculum and teaching to the test (often at the urging of their school administrators). This is a bad idea, not only because it demotivates students but because it has counterproductive effects on their learning. Several studies (reviewed in Good & Brophy, 1997) have shown that an emphasis on teaching for understanding not only leads to better achievement of higher-order outcomes but also produces comparable or better achievement of the kinds of lower-order outcomes that are emphasized on standardized tests. Therefore, take courage. If you find yourself confronted by counterproductive emphases on high-stakes testing programs, don't allow these pressures to dislodge you from teaching your subjects for understanding and thus enjoying the learning and motivational benefits that this emphasis brings.

Typically, you will be trying to pursue several agendas simultaneously. Consequently, you often will have to accept partial solutions to motivational problems or suspend your motivational goals temporarily while you deal with time constraints or classroom management problems. You will need to develop concepts and language for describing types and levels of motivational success in these situations, so that you can recognize and take satisfaction in your accomplishments and learn to set realistic goals, assess progress, and reinforce yourself accordingly.

You also may need to work on your efficacy perceptions and failure attributions. That is, as you acquire motivational skills, you should recognize that you are doing so and appreciate these developments within an incremental view of your motivational ability. Positive perceptions of your motivational efficacy will help you to develop confidence and persistence in supporting your students' self-regulated learning, whereas low self-efficacy perceptions may leave you with a tendency to give up easily when you encounter difficulties, a controlling orientation toward students, and the belief that extrinsic rewards are necessary to motivate them (Reeve, 1996; Woolfolk, Rosoff, & Hoy, 1990).

In working with difficult students, you will need to support positive self-efficacy perceptions with productive management of your strategies and emotions. Just as students learning mathematics have to learn to cope with difficult problems by staying task-focused and avoiding attributional thinking or emotional reactions that lead to frustration and learned helplessness, so do teachers who encounter motivational problems such as failure syndrome, apathy, or resistance. You may be tempted to give up attempts to solve these problems by attributing failures to uncontrollable causes (your own limitations as a motivator or undesirable student motivation patterns that are too well-established to be changed). Many teachers develop these helplessness-inducing attributions and end up shifting from persistent motivational attempts to tacit bargains in which they lower their standards in exchange for classroom cooperation (Sedlak et al., 1986). In order to continue to work productively with difficult students, you need to commit yourself to pursuing challenging but reachable motivational goals, stay positive and task-focused when you encounter setbacks, and sustain the belief that you will begin to succeed more consistently as you discover and perfect the right strategies.

Management of emotional reactions is even more important for teachers seeking to motivate students than for students seeking to solve problems. Even though they can be frustrating, academic problems are impersonal—they just sit there, as it were, waiting for students to solve them. Unmotivated students, however, are human beings involved in personal relationships with their teachers. They can and often do frustrate their teachers by failing to respond positively to motivational strategies and by saying or doing things that express hostility or rejection, challenge the teachers' authority, or in other ways create additional problems. This can lead to vicious cycles of negative action and reaction that culminate in mutual avoidance or hostility (Brophy & Evertson, 1981; Skinner & Belmont, 1993).

When faced with consistent sullenness or resistance from certain students, teachers' natural tendencies are to attribute the students' behavior to internal, stable, and controllable causes; to perceive their provocations as intentional and become angry in response; and to treat the students in an authoritarian or punitive fashion. Such reactions are understandable, but they are not appropriate for teachers who have professional obligations toward their students, including students who are "undeserving." Acting on these natural response tendencies leads to counterproductive expectations and behavior, resulting in deterioration of teacher-student relationships and escalation of the behavior problems.

Thus, it will be important for you to recognize what is happening when these vicious cycles occur, to inhibit your natural but counterproductive reactions, and to replace them with more professional responses. In the process, you will need to "be the adult" by staying positive, focusing on goals, and pursuing strategies designed to resocialize the students' attitudes and behavior.

For more information about the behavioral causes and emotional dynamics that underlie such problems, see Brophy and Evertson (1981). For more information about types of problem students and strategies for working with them, see Brophy (1996). Finally, for information about ways to monitor and get feedback about your interactions with students and to work together with fellow teachers to improve your effectiveness, see Good and Brophy (1997).

SUMMARY

Given the many principles presented in this book and the qualifications attached to most of them, it is safe to say that motivation is a large and complicated topic. However, you can get off to a very good start by making yourself and your classroom attractive to students and establishing the kind of learning community described in Chapter 2. Also, you will find that the motivational principles presented here complement the curricular and instructional principles involved in teaching for understanding, so you can learn the larger set of principles as an integrated approach to teaching.

Many of the principles outlined in this book are included within the categories of the TARGET model, the Keller model, or the Wlodkowski model. All of the major principles are summarized in Box 10.1. To systematically build these motivational principles into your instructional planning, you can use these sources as checklists against which to assess your instructional plans. An alternative method is to answer the sets of questions included in the chapter (one set for all activities, a second for listening and reading activities, and a third for activities that require active response).

The book concludes with a section on maintaining your own motivation as a teacher. It points out that you need to develop confident self-efficacy perceptions, set challenging but reachable goals, adopt an incremental view of your developing motivational skills, attribute successes and failures accordingly, manage your emotions, self-regulate your selection and adjustment of strategies, and so on, in order to sustain optimal motivation to fulfill your potential in the domain of motivating students to learn. In short, you need to develop the same kinds of motivational characteristics in this domain as you want your students to develop in academic knowledge and skill domains.

In the process, you will need to learn to feel autonomously self-regulated and derive intrinsic satisfactions from your work despite curriculum mandates, testing programs, and other extrinsic constraints and pressures. In this regard, bear in mind the point made in Chapter 6 that intrinsic motivation is determined by the subjective experience of the person, not by the presence or absence of extrinsic pressures in the situation.

Prepare yourself to deal with students who are not merely unresponsive to your motivational efforts but sullen or hostile in their personal reactions to you. Read books or take courses in managing classrooms and dealing with problem students, so as to inoculate yourself against the natural but counterproductive tendency to slip into vicious cycles of negativity with them. If you stay professional, positive, and goal-oriented with these students, and especially if you communicate that you care about them despite their provocative behavior, you will gradually turn them around.

Finally, if you haven't done so already, go back and take a look at your answers to the questions posed to you in Chapter 1. To what extent are they congruent with the theory and research on motivation in education that was synthesized in this book? Are there any clear discrepancies? If so, develop a plan for following up on and eventually resolving the issues that underlie them.

REFERENCES

Ames, C. (1992). Classrooms: Goals, structures, and student motivation. *Journal of Educational Psychology, 84,* 261–271.

Brophy, J. (1996). *Teaching problem students.* New York: Guilford.

Brophy, J., & Evertson, C. (1981). *Student characteristics and teaching.* New York: Longman.

Epstein, J. (1989). Family structures and student motivation: A developmental perspective. In C. Ames & R. Ames (Eds.), *Research on motivation in education. Vol. 3: Goals and cognitions* (pp. 259–295). San Diego: Academic Press.

Flink, C., Boggiano, A., Main, D., Barrett, M., & Katz, P. (1992). Children's achievement-related behaviors: The role of extrinsic and intrinsic motivational orientations. In A. Boggiano & T. Pittman (Eds.), *Achievement and motivation: A social-developmental perspective* (pp. 189–214). Cambridge: Cambridge University Press.

Good, T., & Brophy, J. (1997). *Looking in classrooms* (7th ed.). New York: Longman.

Keller, J. (1983). Motivational design of instruction. In C. Reigeluth (Ed.), *Instructional-design theories and models: An overview of their current status* (pp. 383–434). Hillsdale, NJ: Erlbaum.

Newmann, F. (1990). Qualities of thoughtful social studies classes: An empirical profile. *Journal of Curriculum Studies, 22,* 253–275.

Newmann, F. (1992). *Student engagement and achievement in American secondary schools.* New York: Teachers College Press.

Reeve, J. (1996). *Motivating others: Nurturing inner motivational resources.* Boston: Allyn & Bacon.

Sedlak, M., Wheeler, C., Pullin, D., & Cusick, P. (1986). *Selling students short: Classroom bargains and academic reform in the American high school.* New York: Teachers College Press.

Skinner, E., & Belmont, M. (1993). Motivation in the classroom: Reciprocal effects of teacher behavior and student engagement across the school year. *Journal of Educational Psychology, 85,* 571–581.

Wlodkowski, R. (1984). *Motivation and teaching: A practical guide.* Washington, DC: National Education Association.

Woolfolk, A., Rosoff, B., & Hoy, W. (1990). Teachers' sense of efficacy and their beliefs about managing students. *Teaching and Teacher Education, 6,* 137–148.

Index